T0133977

INTELLIGENT SYSTEM ALGORITHMS AND APPLICATIONS IN SCIENCE AND TECHNOLOGY

Research Notes on Computing and Communication Sciences

INTELLIGENT SYSTEM ALGORITHMS AND APPLICATIONS IN SCIENCE AND TECHNOLOGY

Edited by

Sunil Pathak, PhD

Pramod Kumar Bhatt, PhD

Sanjay Kumar Singh, PhD

Ashutosh Tripathi, PhD

Pankaj Kumar Pandey, PhD

First edition published 2022

Apple Academic Press Inc.
1265 Goldenrod Circle, NE,
Palm Bay, FL 32905 USA
4164 Lakeshore Road, Burlington,
ON, L7L 1A4 Canada

CRC Press
6000 Broken Sound Parkway NW,
Suite 300, Boca Raton, FL 33487-2742 USA
2 Park Square, Milton Park,
Abingdon, Oxon, OX14 4RN UK

Library and Archives Canada Cataloguing in Publication

Title: Intelligent system algorithms and applications in science and technology / edited by Sunil Pathak, PhD, Pramod Kumar Bhatt, PhD, Sanjay Kumar Singh, PhD, Ashutosh Tripathi, PhD, Pankaj Kumar Pandey, PhD.
Names: Pathak, Sunil, editor. | Bhatt, Pramod Kumar, editor. | Singh, Sanjay Kumar (Research professional), editor. | Tripathi, Ashutosh, editor. | Pandey, Pankaj Kumar, editor.
Description: First edition. | Series statement: Research notes on computing and communication sciences | Includes bibliographical references and index.
Identifiers: Canadiana (print) 2021020379X | Canadiana (ebook) 20210203978 | ISBN 9781774630211 (hardcover) | ISBN 9781774639269 (softcover) | ISBN 9781003187059 (ebook)
Subjects: LCSH: Computational intelligence. | LCSH: Machine learning. | LCSH: Artificial intelligence. | LCSH: Internet of things. | LCSH: Big data. | LCSH: Computer networks. | LCSH: Process control.
Classification: LCC Q342 .I58 2022 | DDC 006.3—dc23

Library of Congress Cataloging-in-Publication Data

Names: Pathak, Sunil, editor.
Title: Intelligent system algorithms and applications in science and technology / edited by Sunil Pathak, PhD, Pramod Kumar Bhatt, PhD, Sanjay Kumar Singh, PhD, Ashutosh Tripathi, PhD, Pankaj Kumar Pandey, PhD.
Description: First edition. | Palm Bay, FL, USA : Apple Academic Press, 2022. | Series: Research notes on computing and communication sciences | Includes bibliographical references and index. | Summary: "Intelligent System Algorithms and Applications in Science and Technology explores the application of intelligent techniques in various fields of engineering and technology. The volume addresses a selection of diverse topics in such areas as machine learning based intelligent systems for healthcare, applications of artificial intelligence and the Internet of Things, intelligent data analytics techniques, intelligent network systems and applications, and inequalities and process control systems. The authors explore the full breadth of the field, which encompasses data analysis, image processing, speech processing and recognition, medical science and health care monitoring, smart irrigation systems, insurance and banking, robotics and process control, etc. The 21st century has witnessed massive changes around the world in intelligence systems in order to become smarter, energy efficient, reliable, and cheaper. This collection of peer-reviewed book chapters, contributed by renowned experts in the field, will help keep readers up to date; it sheds light on the culture of intelligent techniques in the field of engineering and technology"-- Provided by publisher.
Identifiers: LCCN 2021019214 (print) | LCCN 2021019215 (ebook) | ISBN 9781774630211 (hardcover) | ISBN 9781774639269 (paperback) | ISBN 9781003187059 (ebook)
Subjects: LCSH: Expert systems (Computer science) | Automation. | Artificial intelligence. | Algorithms.
Classification: LCC T56.24 .I69 2022 (print) | LCC T56.24 (ebook) | DDC 006.3/3--dc23
LC record available at https://lccn.loc.gov/2021019214
LC ebook record available at https://lccn.loc.gov/2021019215

ISBN: 978-1-77463-021-1 (hbk)
ISBN: 978-1-77463-926-9 (pbk)
ISBN: 978-1-00318-705-9 (ebk)

RESEARCH NOTES ON COMPUTING AND COMMUNICATION SCIENCES

EDITOR-IN-CHIEF

Dr. Samarjeet Borah
Department of Computer Applications,
Sikkim Manipal Institute of Technology,
Sikkim Manipal University (SMU),
Majhitar, East Sikkim-737136, India
Email: samarjeet.b@smit.smu.edu.in
samarjeetborah@gmail.com

Brief Description of the Series

Computing can be defined as the practice in which computer technology is used to do a goal-oriented assignment. It covers design and development of hardware and software systems for various purposes. Computing devices are becoming an integral part of life now-a-days, including desktops, laptops, hand-held devices, smartphones, smart home appliances, etc. The evolution of the Internet of Things (IoT) has further enriched the same. The domain is ever growing and opening up many new endeavors, including cloud computing, social computing, ubiquitous computing, parallel computing, grid computing, etc.

In parallel with computing, another field has emerged that deals with the interconnection of devices. It is communication, and without which, the modern world cannot be thought of. It works with a basic purpose of transferring information from one place or person to another. This technology has a great influence in modern day society. It influences business and society by making the interchange of ideas and facts more efficient. Communication technologies include the Internet, multimedia, e-mail, telephone, and other sound-based and video-based communication means.

This new book series consists of both edited volumes as well as selected papers from various conferences. Volumes of the series will contain the latest research findings in the field of communication engineering, computer science and engineering, and informatics. Therefore, the books cater to the needs of researchers and readers of a broader spectrum.

Coverage & Approach

The series

- Covers a broad spectrum of research domains
- Presents on market-demanded product-based research works
- Discusses the latest developments in the field

The book series broadly considers contributions from the following fields:

- Artificial Intelligence and Expert Systems
- Big Data Analytics
- Broadband Convergence System and Integration Technologies
- Cellular and Mobile Communication
- Cloud Computing Technologies
- Computational Biology and Bioinformatics
- Computer and Information Security
- Computer Architecture
- Computer Graphics and Video Processing
- Control Systems
- Database Management Systems
- Data Mining
- Design Automation
- Digital Signal Processing
- GSM Communication
- High Performance Computing
- Human-Computer Interaction
- IoT and Blockchains
- Machine Learning
- Natural Language Processing
- Next Generation Communication Technologies
- Operating Systems & Networking
- Pervasive Computing and Cyber-Physical Systems
- Robotics and Automation
- Signal Processing
- Smart Internet of Everything
- SOC and System Platform Design Technologies
- Social Network Analysis
- Soft Computing

Types of Volumes

This series presents recent developments in the domains of computing and communications. It will include mostly the current works and research findings, going on in various research labs, universities and institutions and may lead to development of market demanded products. It reports substantive results on a wide range of computational approaches applied to a wide range of problems. The series provides volumes having works with empirical studies, theoretical analysis or comparison to psychological phenomena. The series includes the following types of volumes:

- Conference Proceedings
- Authored Volumes
- Edited Volumes

Volumes from the series must be suitable as reference books for researchers, academicians, students, and industry professionals.

To propose suggestions for this book series, please contact the book series editor-in-chief. Book manuscripts should be minimum 250–500 pages per volume (11 point Times Roman in MS-Word with 1.5 line spacing).

Books and chapters in the series are included in Google Scholar and selectively in Scopus and possibly other related abstracting/indexing services.

BOOKS IN THE RESEARCH NOTES ON COMPUTING AND COMMUNICATION SCIENCES SERIES

- **Applied Soft Computing: Techniques and Applications**
  Editors: Samarjeet Borah and Ranjit Panigrahi
- **Intelligent System Algorithms and Applications in Science and Technology**
  Editors: Sunil Pathak, Pramod Kumar Bhatt, Sanjay Kumar Singh, Ashutosh Tripathi, and Pankaj Kumar Pandey
- **Intelligent IoT Systems for Big Data Analysis: Concepts, Applications, Challenges, and Future Scope**
  Editors: Subhendu Kumar Pani, Pani Abhay Kumar, Samal Puneet Mishra, Ruchi Doshi, and Tzung-Pei Hong
- **Computing and Communications Engineering in Real-Time Application Development**
  Editors: B. K. Mishra, Samarjeet Borah, and Hemant Kasturiwale

ABOUT THE EDITORS

Sunil Pathak, PhD

Sunil Pathak, PhD, is an Associate Professor and Head in the Department of Computer Science and Engineering, Amit School of Engineering and Technology at Amity University, Rajasthan, India. Before joining Amity University, he was an Associate Professor and Head in the Department of Computer Science and Engineering at Kautilya Institute of Engineering abd Technology. He was also formerly at Chanakya Technical Campus (Kauutilya Group of College) as Director of Academics and Poornima College of Engineering, Jaipur, India. He has published more than 40 papers in international and national journals and conference proceedings, 10 book and one edited volume. He received 3rd prize for his book *Web Programming (Hind Edition) 2010*, in the category of engineering diploma level by AICTE New Delhi. His areas of research include clustering in ad hoc networks, QoS supports in wireless networks, channel assignment in cognitive radio networks and WDM optical networks, machine learning, and deep learning. He is active as a reviewer for several journals, including *IEEE Transactions on Mobile Computing, IET Networks, EURASIP Journal on Wireless Communications and Networking, Recent Patents on Engineering, International Journal of Interactive Mobile Technologies (iJIM), IEEE Transactions on Network and Service Management, IEE Access*, etc. He is a professional member of IEEE, ACM, IACSE, and IAEN. He has received his bachelor's degree from Rajasthan University; MSc (Computer Science & Engineer); Master of Technology in Information Technology from Tezpur Central University, Assam, India; and PhD in Computer Science & Engineering from JK Lakshmipat University Jaipur, Rajasthan, India.

Pramod Kumar Bhatt, PhD

Pramod Kumar Bhatt, PhD, is Associate Professor and Coordinator of PhD Programmes with the Amity School of Engineering and Technology (ASET), Jaipur, Rajasthan, India. He has published research papers in indexed journals and conferences. His research interests include artificial intelligence, machine learning, soft computing applications in smart grid power quality analysis and enhancement, renewable energy integration challenges, opportunities in smart distribution and transmission systems, smart microgrids, industrial microgrids, and condition monitoring of smart grid components. For over 10 years he was extensively involved in industrial assignments, in particular, R&D, system designing, modification, commissioning, maintenance, systems automation such as PLC, SCADA, and power drive installation and testing. He has worked in various capacities at universities of national repute. His degrees include a BE (EE), ME (Power Electronics), and PhD in Electrical Engineering.

Sanjay Kumar Singh, PhD

Sanjay Kumar Singh, PhD, is an experienced academician and a research professional with around eight years of industrial experience and almost 16 years of teaching experience at engineering colleges. His research interests are in the areas of intelligent control and automation, bio-inspired techniques, modern instrumentation and control engineering, and industrial electronics with real-time applications. He was awarded his BE with a specialization in Instrumentation from Poona University, India, and MTech in Instrumentation from the School of Instrumentation, Devi Ahilya Vishvidyalaya Indore (MP), India. He was awarded a PhD degree in Engineering from M.N.I.T., Jaipur, India. He has published around 24 research papers in national and international journals and international conferences. He is a reviewer and editorial board member of various national and international journals. He is currently a member of IET UK, ICSES Iran, and IAENG and a lifetime member of ISTE India.

Ashutosh Tripathi, PhD

Ashutosh Tripathi, PhD, is Assistant Professor at Amity University, Rajasthan, India. He has presented and organized several conferences and seminars and has published papers in international journals. He has many years of teaching experience engineering and is currently guiding a research associate for a PhD. His area of interest is wireless communication and embedded technology. He received a PhD in Engineering.

Pankaj Kumar Pandey, PhD

Pankaj Kumar Pandey, PhD, is Associate Professor and Head, Chemical Engineering Department at Amity University Rajasthan, India. He has presented and organized several conferences and seminars and has published papers in international journals. He has 19 years of teaching experience at at the BE, ME and PhD levels. He is currently guiding a research associate for a PhD. His area of interest is adsorption engineering and wastewater treatment. He holds a PhD in Engineering.

CONTENTS

CONTRIBUTORS

Yojna Arora
Department of Computer Science and Engineering, Amity University, Haryana, India,
E-mail: yojana183@gmail.com

Ishita Banerjee
Research Scholar, Dayananda Sagar Academy of Technology and Management, Bangalore, Karnataka, India, E-mail: sakthi999@gmail.com

Pallav Kumar Baruah
Associate Professor, Department of Mathematics and Computer Science,
Sri Sathya Sai Institute of Higher Learning, Puttaparthi, Andhra Pradesh, India

Nagaraju Dasari
Department of Mathematics and Statistics, Manipal University Jaipur, Rajasthan, India

Praffulla Kumar Dubey
Department of Computer Science and Engineering, SRM Institute of Science and Technology, Chennai, Tamil Nadu, India, E-mail: praffullakrdubey@gmail.com

Neha Gahlot
Department of Mathematics and Statistics, Manipal University Jaipur, Rajasthan, India,
E-mail: gahlotneha1995@gmail.com

Sapna Gahlot
Department of Mathematics and Statistics, Manipal University Jaipur, Jaipur, Rajasthan–303007, India

Adarsh Garg
Professor, School of Computing Science and Engineering Galgotias University, Greater Noida,
Uttar Pradesh, India

Pratiyush Guleria
National Institute of Electronics and Information Technology, Shimla, Himachal Pradesh, India,
E-mail: pratiyushguleria@gmail.com

Rohan Yashraj Gupta
Doctoral Research Scholar in Actuarial Science, Department of Mathematics and Computer Science,
Sri Sathya Sai Institute of Higher Learning, Puttaparthi, Andhra Pradesh, India,
E-mail: rohanyashrajgupta@sssihl.edu.in

T. Kanagaraj
Assistant Professor, Department of ECE, Kalaignarkarunanidhi Institute of Technology (KIT),
Coimbatore, Tamil Nadu, India, E-mail: kanagaraj27.t@gmail.com

Phani Krishna Kandala
Visiting Faculty in Actuarial Science, Department of Mathematics and Computer Science,
Sri Sathya Sai Institute of Higher Learning, Puttaparthi, Andhra Pradesh, India

Nitish Katal
School of Electronics, Indian Institute of Information Technology, Una, Himachal Pradesh, India,
E-mail: nitishkatal@iiitu.ac.in

Arvinder Kaur
University School of Information and Communication Technology (U.S.I.C.T),
Guru Gobind Singh Indraprastha University (G.G.S.I.P.U), New Delhi, India

Harguneet Kaur
University School of Information and Communication Technology (U.S.I.C.T), Guru Gobind Singh Indraprastha University (G.G.S.I.P.U), New Delhi, India, E-mail: Harguneetphd@gmail.com

Manju Kaushik
Associate Professor, Amity Institute of Information Technology (AIIT), Amity University Rajasthan, India

Kavita
Jayoti Vidyapeeth Women's University, Jaipur, Rajasthan, India, E-mail: kavita.yogen@gmail.com

Rashi Kohli
Senior Member, IEEE, Institute of Electrical and Electronics Engineers, New York, US,
E-mail: rashikohli.amity@gmail.com

B. Suresh Kumar
Amity University, Rajasthan, India

Gireesh Kumar
Department of Computer Science Engineering, JK Lakshmipat University, Jaipur, Rajasthan, India

P. Madhumathy
Professor, Dayananda Sagar Academy of Technology and Management, Bangalore, Karnataka, India

Medhavi Malik
Research Scholar, Jayoti Vidyapeeth Women's University, Jaipur, Rajasthan, India;
Department of Computer Science and Engineering, SRM Institute of Science and Technology, Chennai, Tamil Nadu, India, E-mail: medhavimalik28@gmail.com

Aakanksha Mudgal
Amity University, Rajasthan, India

Satya Sai Mudigonda
Honorary Professor in Actuarial Science, Department of Mathematics and Computer Science,
Sri Sathya Sai Institute of Higher Learning, Puttaparthi, Andhra Pradesh, India

Udbhav Naryani
Department of Computer Science and Engineering, SRM Institute of Science and Technology, Chennai, Tamil Nadu, India, E-mail: udbhav.naryani@gmail.com

Sunil Pathak
Associate Professor, Department of CSE, Amity School of Engineering and Technology, Jaipur, Rajasthan, India

Laxmi Poonia
Department of Mathematics and Statistics, Manipal University Jaipur, Jaipur, Rajasthan–303007, India,
E-mail: laxmi.poonia@jaipur.manipal.edu

R. Ramesh
Department of ECE, Kalaignarkarunanidhi Institute of Technology (KIT), Coimbatore, Tamil Nadu, India, E-mail: vmramesh1993@gmail.com

Mohd. Rizwanullah
Associate Professor, Department of Mathematics and Statistics, Manipal University Jaipur, Jaipur, Rajasthan, India, E-mail: rizwansal@yahoo.co.in

S. R. Pranav Sai
Doctoral Research Scholar in Actuarial Science, Department of Mathematics and Computer Science, Sri Sathya Sai Institute of Higher Learning, Puttaparthi, Andhra Pradesh, India, E-mail: srpranavsai@sssihl.edu.in

Ram Naresh Saraswat
Department of Mathematics and Statistics, Manipal University Jaipur, Jaipur, Rajasthan–303007, India, E-mail: saraswatramn@gmail.com

Anulika Sharma
Department of Mathematics and Statistics, Manipal University Jaipur, Jaipur, Rajasthan–303007, India, E-mail: anulikasharma022@gmail.com

Madhuri Sharma
SRM IST Delhi NCR Campus, Modinagar, Ghaziabad, Uttar Pradesh, India, E-mail: madhurisharma44@gmail.com

Richa Sharma
Department of Mathematics, JK Lakshmipat University, Jaipur, Rajasthan, India, E-mails: richasharma@jklu.edu.in; aligarh.richa@gmail.com

Sanjay Sharma
Department of Mathematics and Statistics, Manipal University Jaipur, Jaipur, Rajasthan–303007, India

Priyanka Shukla
Research Scholar, School of Computing Science and Engineering Galgotias University, Greater Noida, Uttar Pradesh, India, E-mail: priyanka.Shukla@galgotiasuniversity.edu.in

Sanjay Kumar Singh
Department of EEE, Amity University Jaipur, Jaipur, Rajasthan, India

Soniya Soni
Department of Computer Science Engineering, JK Lakshmipat University, Jaipur, Rajasthan, India

Akula Padma Sri
Amity University, Rajasthan, India

K. Srihari
Associate Professor, Department of CSE, SNS College of Technology, Coimbatore, Tamil Nadu, India

Ashutosh Tripathi
Department of ECE, Amity School of Engineering and Technology, Noida, Uttar Pradesh, India

E. Udayakumar
Assistant Professor, Department of ECE, Kalaignarkarunanidhi Institute of Technology (KIT), Coimbatore, Tamil Nadu, India

Adeeba Umar
Department of Mathematics and Statistics, Manipal University Jaipur, Jaipur, Rajasthan–303007, India, E-mail: adeeba1506@gmail.com

Dileep Kumar Yadav
Galgotias University, Greater Noida, Uttar Pradesh, India, E-mail: dileep252000@gmail.com

Ranjeet Yadav
Amity University Rajasthan, India, E-mail: ranjeet480@gmail.com

ABBREVIATIONS

ACC	actuarial control cycle
AD	average difference
AHE	adaptive histogram equalization
AI	artificial intelligence
AMU	Aligarh Muslim University
API	application interface
ARB	aging-related bugs
AUC	area under the curve
BPM	beats per minute
CAM	cooperative mindfulness message
CEC	consumer electronics control
CNN	convolutional neural networks
CRM	customer relationship management
CSF	cerebrospinal fluid
CSI	camera serial interface
CSTR	continuous stirred tank reactor
CUL	channel utilization list
CW	contention window
DCF	dispersed coordination function
DoS	Daniel of service
DVI	digital visual interface
EDCA	enhanced disseminated channel
EGC	electrocardiogram
EHR	electronic health record
FP	false positive
FPR	false positive rate
GLCM	gray level co-occurrence matrix
GSM	Global system for mobile
HITECH	Health Information Technology for Economic and Clinical Health
I2V	infrastructure-to-vehicle
ID3	dichotomiser 3
IoT	internet of things
IRC	interest rate change
IRL	interest rate level

ISE	integral square of error
IT	insurer type
ITF	intuitionistic trapezoidal fuzzy
IVITFWG	interval-valued intuitionistic trapezoidal fuzzy weighted geometric
IVTrIFN	interval-valued trapezoidal IFN
JSON	JavaScript object notation
KNN	K-nearest neighbor
KPIs	key performance indicators
LDA	latent Dirichlet allocation
LOC	Lines of code
LSR	link-state routing convention
LT	launch time
LTI	linear time-invariant
MANETs	mobile uncommonly selected frameworks
MD	maximum difference
ML	machine learning
MOEA/D	multi-objective evolutionary algorithm based on decomposition
MOOCs	massive open online course
MOP	multi-objective optimization problem
MPR	multipoint relay
MSE	mean square error
NLP	natural language processing
OBUs	on board units
OCR	optical character recognition
OFDM	orthogonal frequency division multiplexing
ONF	open networking foundation
PCA	principal component analysis
PF	page fault
PNC	physical-layer network coding
POC	proof of concept
POS	pareto optimal solutions
PSNR	peak signal to noise ratio
QoS	Quality of service
QR	quick response
RBF	radial basis function
RMSE	root mean square error
ROC	receiver operating characteristics
RPA	robotic process automation
RQs	research questions

RRP	route request packets
RSU	roadside units
RW	Robertson-Walker
SMAC	social, mobile, analytic, cloud
SMO	sequential minimal optimization
SMS	short message service
SNA	social network analysis
SNIP	source normalized impact per paper
SPP	shortest path problems
SVM	support vector machine
TN	true negative
TP	true positive
TPR	true positive rate
TrIFN	trapezoidal IFN
TrIFWA	intuitionistic trapezoidal fuzzy weighted average
TSP	traveling salesperson problem
UI	unexpected inflation
UP	underwriting profits
URL	uniform resource locator
V2V	vehicle-to-vehicle
VANET	vehicular ad-hoc network
VoIP	voice over IP
WAGO	weighted arithmetic averaging operator
WAVE	wireless access in vehicular environment
WHO	World Health Organization
ZN	Ziegler Nichols

PREFACE

In the past few decades, intelligence in the field of engineering and technology has become a fundamental objective for developing and developed countries. The twenty-first century has witnessed massive changes around the world in intelligence systems in order to become smarter, energy efficient, reliable, and cheaper. Therefore, it is high time for the whole world to envisage and ponder devising an apt mechanism for the adoption of an intelligent system in the process of modernization.

The application of intelligence in engineering and technology is a vast field; however, we have tried to explore the full breadth of the field, which encompasses data analysis, image processing, speech processing, and recognition medical science and healthcare monitoring, smart irrigation systems, insurance, and banking, robotics, and process control, etc.

This book is an assortment of precious gem book chapters contributed by renowned experts that focus on various aspects of fostering and imbibing the culture of intelligent techniques in the field of engineering and technology. Furthermore, this book puts a spotlight on various aspects of the application of intelligent techniques in various fields of engineering and technology.

This book is separated into 24 chapters. Chapter 1 presents the patient-centric healthcare frameworks in the context of big data and discusses the Naïve Bayes, decision tree data mining techniques, and their solutions in the healthcare sector. Chapter 2 discusses "Cancer Cell Growth Discovery Utilizing Computerized Image Processing Strategies." Chapter 3 describes the different symptoms of asthma and implements different types of machine learning algorithms, like the random forest, decision tree, and Naïve Bayes algorithms in order to predict whether a person has asthma or not. Chapter 4 discusses the proposal to predict myocardial infraction disease by implementing various algorithms of machine learning like Naïve Bayes algorithm, decision tree, logistic regression, and random forest. Chapter 5 proposes a novel divergence measure under the refined neutrosophic environment with its proof of validity. The application of the proposed divergence measure is given in decision making such as in medical diagnosis and in project selection.

Chapter 6 focuses on the implementation of QR codes for the major purpose of effective and effortless laboratory report exchange and in healthcare monitoring. Chapter 7, for discussion, reflects on the latest progress of the study on an innovative approach to healthcare using machine learning. Chapter 8 in-depthly discusses artificial intelligence (AI), its importance, and its application in various fields. Chapter 9 is related to machine learning theory and the points to comprehend the basic standards of learning as a computational procedure and joins devices from computer science and statistics. Chapter 10 presents the sentiment analysis of online learners in higher education and seeks to explore the unstructured data in terms of sentiments of online learners on their perceived learning. Chapter 11 describes speech recognition with static and dynamic approaches in artificial neural networks and shows the relative benefits of both static and dynamic approaches with speech features for an improved visual speech recognition system. Chapter 12 focuses on the presence of aging-related bugs (ARB) using source code metrics. Six different machine learning algorithms are applied to predict the non-frequent occurring bugs from Zookeeper software. The experiment highlighted the Naïve Bayes classifier with the best results.

Chapter 13 presents an automated system that has been developed to irrigate plants. The normal growth of plants, yield, and the quantity of agricultural products are seriously affected by the water provided to them. This automated system waters the plant automatically as and when required without human interaction. Chapter 14 presents the main theories and key application of CART-based modeling in motor insurance fraud detection. Chapter 15 deals with big data analysis and artificial intelligence applications to help the students predict their performance and teachers to scrutinize the students' performance. Chapter 16 discusses the theories and key applications of neural networks for assessing the performance of the insurance business. Chapter 17 presents the derivation and model for the physical inflationary universe under the effect of the scalar field, which is purely massless and with a flat potential.

Chapter 18 proposes MADM problems for evaluating computer network security with TrIFN (intuitionistic trapezoidal fuzzy weighted average). Chapter 19 presents an optimization of a network problem using LINGO software to solve a campus-wide optical fiber network problem based on a spanning tree. Chapter 20 establishes some new coding bounds using well-known inequalities, and the results are proved through numerical illustrations, which will be of interest in information and coding theory. A major toolchain is formed by these inequalities for proving many outcomes in information theory. Chapter 21 presents robotic process automation (RPA), an automation technology based on software tools that could imitate human behavior for repetitive and on-value-added tasks such as tipping, copying, pasting, extracting, merging, and moving data from one system to another system. Chapter 22 introduced fuzzy ideals in Γ-near ring, for example, and verifys few properties. Chapter 23 presents a novel approach on sensors and examines the effects of a MAC layer, PHY layer remote channel situations, and versatility of vehicles on group structure. Chapter 24 investigates a metaheuristics-based multi-objective optimal design of robust controllers for a parametrically uncertain pH neutralization process. The controller design problem has been formulated as a multi-objective optimization problem (MOP) using various time domain and frequency domain performance indices.

The research contributions made by the academics of high pursuits not only show their deep sense of agony but also suggests numerous plausible solutions to conquer problems. Although this attempt is a tiny step intended towards the massive change, we hope it will be a valuable contribution to society at large.

—Editors

PART I

Machine Learning-Based Intelligent Systems for Healthcare

CHAPTER 1

BIG DATA ANALYTICS AND MACHINE LEARNING PARADIGM: PREDICTIVE ANALYTICS IN THE HEALTHCARE SECTOR

PRATIYUSH GULERIA

National Institute of Electronics and Information Technology, Shimla, Himachal Pradesh, India, E-mail: pratiyushguleria@gmail.com

ABSTRACT

Big data analytics is the emerging field of data mining where the major challenge is to discover meaningful information from raw data. Big data comprises of unstructured, semi-structured, and structured forms. The supervised and unsupervised learning techniques, i.e., classification and clustering algorithms of data mining helps to retrieve meaningful information. The big data managed using mining techniques have increased computational intelligence and effective decision-making. In this chapter, the author has proposed the patient-centric healthcare frameworks in the context of big data and has discussed the Naïve Bayes, Decision tree data mining techniques, and their solutions to the healthcare sector. The supervised and unsupervised machine learning (ML) algorithms are implemented on the dataset for data analysis and information retrieval.

1.1 INTRODUCTION

Big data analytics has received attention from different fields of computer science which involves data mining, artificial intelligence (AI), machine learning (ML), and mathematical analytics. The big data term is based on the characteristics, which are (a) volume, (b) velocity, and (c) variety. The first characteristics focus on the volume of data which may be in terabytes, petabytes, or more. The second characteristics are the velocity of data where the data emerges in every second, and the third is a variety of data. The data can be in any format, i.e., images, pdf files, office automation, or it can be data from internet resources, software, and database application files. The Big data analytics field utilization in medical and healthcare sectors is the demand of present research. The ML and data mining techniques have been working in close interrelation with big data analytics to provide solutions in (a) computer-aided medical diagnosis, (b) intelligent healthcare informatics system, (c) predictive analytics in healthcare, (d) electronic record maintenance of patients, (e) smart systems for identifying diseases and diagnosis, (f) IoT enabled devices for medical diagnostics, (g) intelligent web semantics for healthcare sector, (h) knowledge data discovery for healthcare sector. ML algorithms help in handling healthcare challenges and can discover the ethical implications of healthcare data, patient health optimization, etc.

Authors Liang and Kelemen [1] have discussed the healthcare functionalities, i.e., (a) clinical decision support, (b) diseases surveillance, (c) healthcare management, etc., concerning big data.

1.1.1 CHALLENGES OF BIG DATA IN HEALTHCARE SECTOR

The challenges in handling big data related to the healthcare sector involves:

1. Data generation from multiple sources;
2. Diversified data formats;
3. Huge voluminous data;
4. Symptoms vary from patient to patient;
5. Patients pertain to different geographical areas;
6. Non-availability of data in electronic form;
7. Hidden and missing values in the datasets;
8. Non-availability of diagnostic data;
9. Missing historical record of patients;
10. Diversified healthcare areas;
11. Challenges in the collection of clinical reports and drug prescribed information;
12. Drug prescriptions to patients are in unstructured and non-electronic form.

The vital role of Big data analytics in convergence with ML is to give useful insight into these challenges. The tasks of transforming the raw data into meaningful form, preprocess the data to detect outliers, and prediction of fruitful results can be done using big data analytics, ML. The healthcare data available in digital format enables the patients to communicate with the patients having similar problems and gain information like (a) disease symptoms, (b) side-effects of medicines, (c) clinical reports, etc. [2, 3]. The predictive analytics can be done using data mining techniques. With the help of mining and statistical techniques, future events can be predicted [4].

The big data consists of the MapReduce programming model which uses the Hadoop distributed file system for analyzing the big data. In this framework, the data is divided into <key, value> pair to filter the meaningful information. Authors in Ref. [5] have proposed the architectural framework for healthcare systems. The framework consists of layers where data extraction and transformation take place in Transformation Layer and then the data goes through staging processes. In the Big data platform layer, the Hadoop ecosystem works using MapReduce Programming models. After the Big data platform layer, the analytical layer work through data mining techniques, reporting, etc.

1.1.2 ELECTRONIC HEALTH CARE FRAMEWORK

In the traditional approach, the patient approaches the doctor with some symptoms, and in response, after the check-up of the patient, the doctor recommends him to take some tests and diagnose the patients with some medicines. The major challenge in this approach is that the data related to the symptoms and diagnosis is not maintained electronically. In such a scenario, big data analytics could help the patient, if the data is maintained electronically. The electronically maintained data of the patient can be analyzed using big data analytics and ML algorithms. It helps those patients who are having similar diagnostics and unable to visit the hospital to take telemedicine for their healthcare needs. The analytical results generated using the electronic healthcare record-keeping system can further trigger regular alerts to patients in the future.

The semantic compatibility in clinical records results in inefficiency in healthcare systems. The electronic health records (EHR) of patients need to be converted into Web ontology language. The semantic analytics of healthcare data helps in the classification and visualization of data [6].

A framework based on the doctor-patient-centric is proposed in Figure 1.1. The framework depicts the approach where the traditional approach needs to be converted into electronic healthcare, which becomes the first step for getting meaningful information from huge unstructured data collected per-second basis.

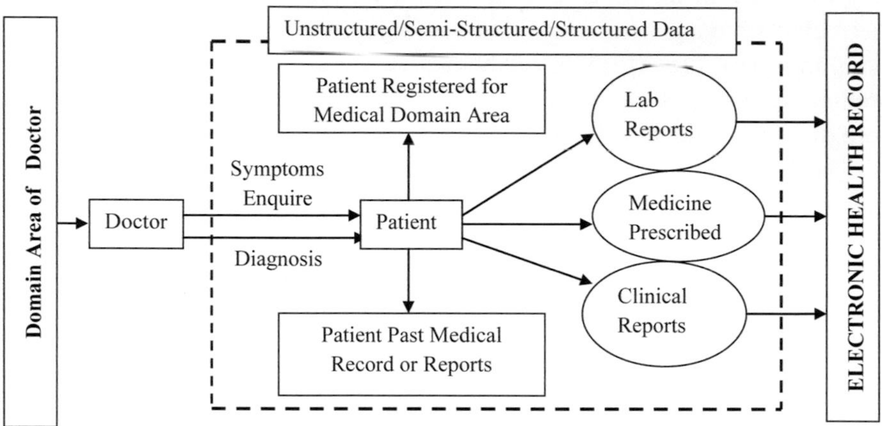

FIGURE 1.1 Healthcare framework in the context of big data analytics.

1.2 BIG DATA AND MACHINE LEARNING (ML) PARADIGM

Big data is related to storage, ingestion, and extraction tolls commonly Hadoop. In Big data, data analysis is done, the hidden patterns are discovered, and useful information is extracted from it. The ML techniques, i.e., supervised, semi-supervised, and unsupervised learning techniques are implemented on big data to find the hidden patterns and disseminate useful information. The supervised learning helps in developing predictive models based on both input and output data. The classification techniques in supervised learning are support vector machines (SVM), discriminant analysis, naïve Bayes and nearest neighbor, whereas linear regression and neural network are regression techniques.

In unsupervised learning, it helps in discovering an internal representation from the input data only. The unsupervised learning techniques involve clustering techniques like: k-means, hierarchical, and neural networks.

1.2.1 CHARACTERISTICS OF BIG DATA

Big data has four characteristics which are as follows:

1. The volume which means a quantity of data;
2. Velocity means processing speed of data;
3. Variety means data which can be structured, semi-structured or completely unstructured; and
4. Veracity means inconsistent and uncertain data, i.e., data having outliers.

The characteristics of big data are shown in Figure 1.2.

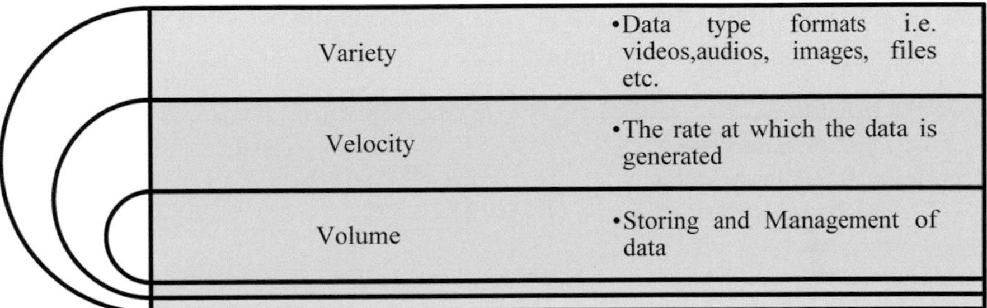

FIGURE 1.2 Characteristics of big data.

1.2.2 BIG DATA ANALYTICS TOOLS

There are Big data analytical tools for storing and analyzing data for effective decision-making and faster information retrieval. Some of the tools are shown in Table 1.1.

TABLE 1.1 Big Data Analytical Tools

Hadoop	Data storage and processing platform. The Hadoop ecosystem consists of Hadoop distributed file system, MapReduce, etc.
Hive	Performs SQL query and is used in data warehousing.
Splunk	Log analysis platform.
Apache Spark	Real-time processing of large amount of data. The data is analyzed using machine learning and perform faster execution. The programming development environments used are R, Python, and Scala.
Kafka	Messaging system.
Pig	Data analysis platform. It uses scripting language.
Apache HBASE	No SQL database.
Talend	Software integration platform.
MapReduce	Based upon parallel computing to handle big data.

1.3 BIG DATA AND MACHINE LEARNING (ML) RELATIONSHIP

Big data comprises of data like images, spreadsheets, tabular data files, custom files. Big data techniques use the file systems like HDFS/Hadoop and databases like SQL and NoSQL for convenient data access. The data is explored, processed, and analyzed using statistical techniques, ML techniques for storage of data into memory and to find the data which do not fit into memory.

The unsupervised and supervised ML techniques are implemented on big data to develop predictive models. The relationship between big data and ML techniques are shown in Figure 1.3.

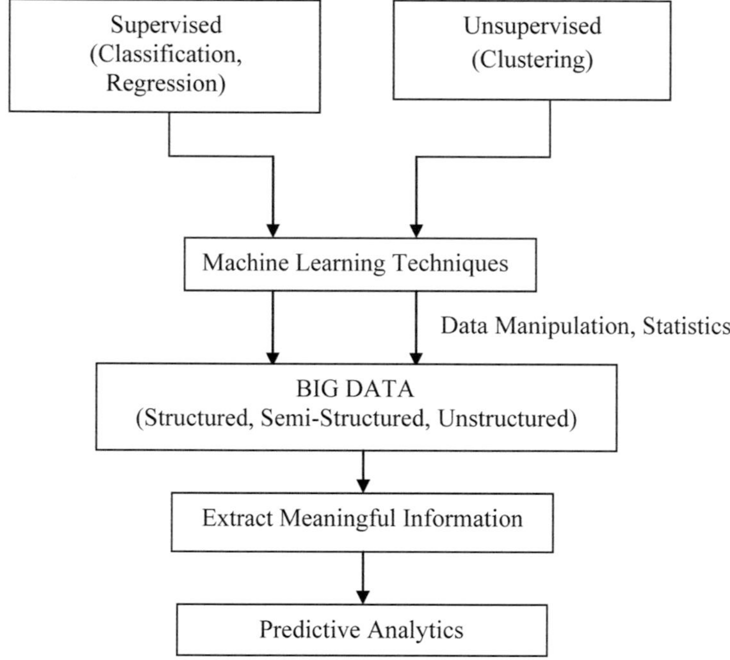

FIGURE 1.3 Big data and machine learning relationship.

1.3.1 MACHINE LEARNING (ML) PHASES

In ML, in the first phase, the data is accessed and explored. The data consists of files, databases, information from sensors, etc. In the second phase, the data is preprocessed which involves the following:

- Removal of outliers;

- Extraction of meaningful information from unstructured data;
- Data reduction, transformation;
- Feature extraction.

In the third phase, the predictive models are developed on big data. The predictive model involves:

- Model creation, i.e., ML;
- Parameter optimization;
- Model validation using techniques like neural network.

1.3.2 IMPORTANCE OF MACHINE LEARNING (ML) IN BIG DATA ANALYTICS

- Predicting future trends of market.
- Better solutions to complex market problems in a stipulated time frame.
- Healthcare solutions by identifying diseases at early stages.
- The effective decision-making process of businesses.
- ML is advantageous in pattern recognition like speech, images, etc.
- In developing financial algorithms, biological problems like tumor detection, drug discovery.

1.4 DATA ANALYTICS WITH MACHINE LEARNING (ML)

The big data, which may be structured, unstructured or semi-structured is analyzed through ML techniques for effective decision-making. ML uses data mining techniques to extract meaningful information from data and to develop ML models. In Figure 1.4, the steps for data analytics with ML are shown. The data which may be in the form of files like: .csv .arff .xlsx, images, word or pdf files, etc., are imported.

The data is then preprocessed, which includes removing missing and outliers. The learning techniques are then implemented to select and train the model, validate it for predictive analytics. Effective ML systems can be developed based on the following requirements:

- Effective data preparation capabilities;
- Algorithm development;
- Automotive and iterative processes;

- Scalable;
- Ensemble modeling.

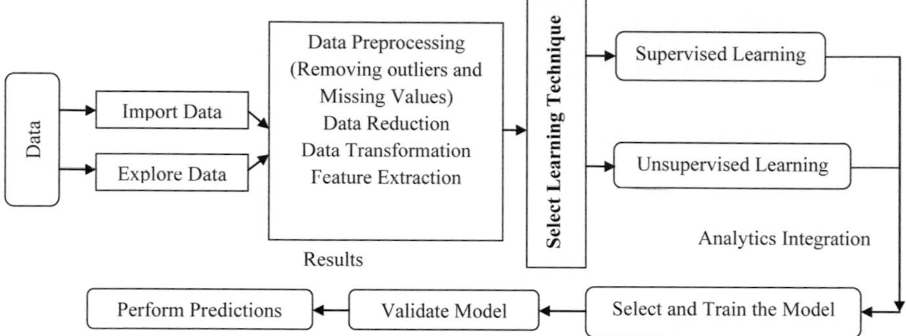

FIGURE 1.4 A framework for data analytics with machine learning.

1.4.1 MACHINE LEARNING (ML) APPROACHES

The Naïve Bayes and Decision tree classifiers are implemented for predictive modeling. The blood pressure values are predicted and validated for the dataset shown in Table 1.2. The semi-synthesized dataset is used for experimentation purposes. The attributes of the dataset are: {gender, age, wgt, smoke, systolic blood pressure, diastolic blood pressure}. The predictor names in the models implemented are: {sex, age, wgt, and smoke}.

The decision tree and naïve Bayes techniques are implemented as supervised ML techniques here because they require target variable to find the probability for a specific value of feature in Naïve Bayes and decision trees.

1.4.2 NAÏVE-BAYES

Here, one of the supervised learning approaches are implemented, i.e., Naïve-Bayes in WEKA tool. WEKA means Waikato Environment for Knowledge Analysis. It is a ML tool for data analysis and predictive modeling.

Bayesian theorem-based Naïve-Bayes algorithm is preferred when the dimensionality of the input is high and requires a small amount of training data. Naive-Bayes assumes that all the features are conditionally independent for a given class label [7, 8]. Bayes theorem states that if the probability of any event i conditional on event j is to be obtained, then calculate the probability of both i and j together and divide it by the probability of j. This is stated as follows: Pr (j | i) = Pr (i and j)/Pr (i) where P (j|i) is the Conditional probability denoting the probability of j given that i has already occurred [9].

$$P (i|j) = P (j|i) \times P (i)/P (j) \quad (1)$$

Eqn. (1) states that the probability of i given j equals the probability of j given i times the probability of i, divided by the probability of j. In Eqn. (1), i is the hypothesis to be tested and j is the evidence associated with i.

- **Objective:** The objective is to predict the Blood Pressure values using Bayes classifier. To model the systolic pressure as a function of patients, the attributes classified are mentioned as below:
  - Age;
  - Smoker;
  - Gender;
  - Weight.
- **Preprocess Data:** During the preprocessing of data, the outliers are detected and removed. The attributes, i.e., gender and smoke values are converted into categorical form, i.e., Gender = {'M,' 'F'}, Smoke = {1, 0}.

TABLE 1.2 Semi-Synthesized Dataset for Blood Pressure

Gender	Age	Weight	Smoking	Sys Blood Pressure	Dia Blood Pressure	Remarks
Independent Variable	**Independent Variable**	**Independent Variable**	**Independent Variable**			**The attribute "sex" and "smoke" values are defined as follows:**
f	43	174	1	125	92	**Sex** = { Male-'m,' Female-'f'
f	38	162	1	108	76	
m	37	134	0	124	81	
m	41	132	1	115	76	**Smoke** = {
f	48	120	0	121	81	1- 'yes'
f	45	141	0	122	71	0- 'no'
f	34	143	1	129	87	}
f	41	179	0	116	83	
f	39	174	0	125	94	
m	42	162	1	110	76	
----	----	----	----	----	----	
F	46	174	1	113	87	

The results are shown in the form of confusion matrix shown in Table 1.3. Table 1.3 shows the target class, i.e., blood pressure value for the predictor variables, i.e., age, smoke, gender, and weight.

TABLE 1.3 Naïve Bayes Classifier Model

Scheme: Naive Bayes classifier		
Instances: 100 Attributes: 7	sex, age, wgt, smoke, sys, dia, class	
Test mode: 10-fold cross-validation		
=== Classifier model (full training set) ===		
Class		
Attribute	**High**	**Normal**
	(0.33)	(0.67)
sex		
f	15.0	41.0
m	20.0	28.0
[total]	35.0	69.0
Time taken to build model: 0.01 seconds		
=== Stratified cross-validation === === Summary ===		
Correctly Classified Instances – 89% Incorrectly Classified Instances – 11%		
=== Confusion Matrix ===		
a...........b < Classified as		
28...........5 | a = High		
6...........61 | b = Normal		

1.4.3 DECISION TREE

A decision tree is a data mining technique that generates trees after testing the training set and defines predictions [10]. It is a supervised ML technique for classification of data using training dataset. A decision tree is a tree-like structure which uses if-then statements to generate decisions.

1.4.3.1 CALCULATION OF INFORMATION GAIN

Information gain, as the name specifies, it is the information that is obtained by knowing the attribute values. The parameter which best classifies the data is Entropy (H). Entropy is a good measure of the information carried by a group of events. There are two states, i.e., Positive and Negative examples from set S. Entropy of set S is denoted by H(S).

The entropy is shown by Eqn. (2), where; S=sample of n training events and Pi is the probability of occurrence of event.

$$H(S) = \sum_{i=1}^{n} -P_i \log_2 P_i \tag{2}$$

Such that: $\sum_{i=1}^{n} P_i = 1$

Information gain is a statistical quantity measuring how well an attribute classifies the data. The decision tree calculates the information gain for each attribute.

The information gain (Gain(S, Ai)) for each attribute is calculated using Eqn. (3). The attribute with the highest information gain has been chosen for decision-making. In Eqn. (3), Ai is the attribute selected for classification.

$$Gain(S, A_i) = H(S) - \sum_{v \in Values(A_i)} P(A_i = v) H(S_v) \tag{3}$$

The classifier model obtained using decision tree is shown in Table 1.4.

The decision tree is visualized in Figure 1.5. The figure shows that systolic blood pressure attribute, i.e., "sys" is the root node.

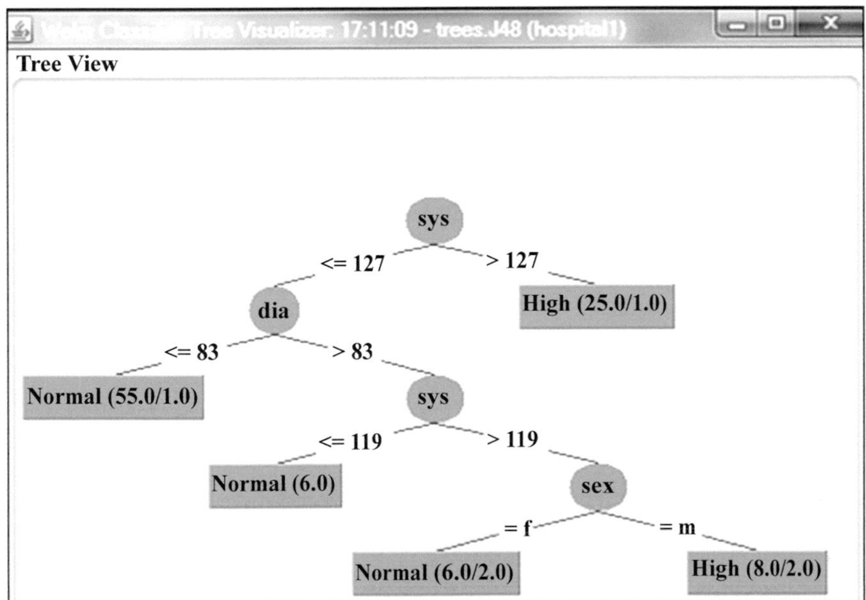

FIGURE 1.5 Decision tree.

TABLE 1.4 Decision Tree Classifier Model

=== **Run information** ===

Scheme: J48 classifier

Instances: 100

Attributes: 7 sex, age, wgt, smoke, sys, dia, class

Test mode: evaluate on training data

J48 pruned tree

sys <= 127

| dia <= 83: Normal (55.0/1.0)

| dia > 83

| | sys <= 119: Normal (6.0)

| | sys > 119

| | | sex = f: Normal (6.0/2.0)

| | | sex = m: High (8.0/2.0)

sys > 127: High (25.0/1.0)

Number of Leaves: 5

Size of the tree: 9

Time taken to build model: 0.01 seconds

=== Evaluation on training set ===

Time taken to build model: 0.01 seconds

=== Evaluation on training set ===

Time taken to test model on training data: 0 seconds

=== Summary ===

Correctly Classified Instances 94 94%

Incorrectly Classified Instances 6 6%

=== Confusion Matrix ===

a b <-- classified as

30 3 | a = High

3 64 | b = Normal

1.5 UNSUPERVISED LEARNING APPLICATIONS IN HEALTHCARE

The unsupervised learning approach deals with unlabeled data and there is no predefined training of input dataset is performed. In this approach, the information is extracted on the basis of patterns and similarity.

The clustering is performed in the WEKA tool on the dataset shown in Table 1.2. The K-Means clustering is applied on the dataset. K-Means is a distance-based algorithm and uses the Euclidean distance for distance calculation in clusters. The Clustering model obtained from the training dataset is shown in Table 1.5.

TABLE 1.5 K-Means Clustering Model

=== **Run information** ===

Scheme: Clustering

Instances: 100

Attributes: 7 sex, age, wgt, smoke, sys, dia, class

Test mode: evaluate on training data
Number of clusters selected by cross-validation: 2
Number of iterations performed: 1

	Cluster	
Attribute	0	1
	(0.67)	(0.33)
sex		
m	26.814	622.1854
f	41.7138	13.2862
[total]	68.5284	35.4716
age		
mean	37.8347	39.165
std. dev.	7.26	6.9315
wgt		
mean	149.5788	162.7876
std. dev.	25.5211	26.0312
smoke		
mean	0.0128	0.9904
std. dev.	0.1124	0.0978
sys		
mean	119.4177	129.4628
std. dev.	4.6113	4.8875
dia		
mean	79.3311	90.1729
std. dev.	4.5693	4.7376
class		
High	6.6772	28.3228
Normal	61.8512	7.1488
[total]	68.5284	35.4716

Time taken to build model (full training data): 0.14 seconds

=== Model and evaluation on training set ===
Clustered Instances

0	66 (66%)
1	34 (34%)

The clustering plot of two attributes, i.e., sys blood pressures with respect to age are shown in Figure 1.6. The sys is shown on Y-Axis and age is shown on X-Axis. The classes are categorized as High and Normal.

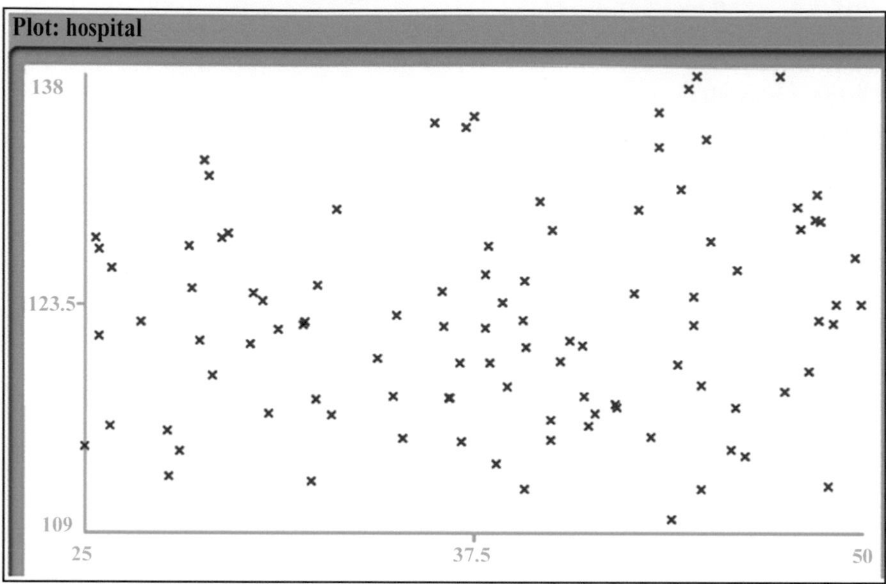

FIGURE 1.6 Clustering of sys (y-axis) and age (x-axis) attributes.

1.6 CONCLUSION

The confluence of big data technology and ML in the healthcare sector is a boon to society. The results obtained using these technologies can make accurate decisions, generate EHRs, save cost and improve livelihood. In this chapter, the role of big data technology and its challenges in the healthcare sector are discussed. The electronic healthcare and ML framework for data analytics are also proposed, which shows that the traditional approach of the healthcare sector which needs to be converted into Electronic healthcare. ML techniques are implemented on the healthcare data to develop a model and generate meaningful results. The ML techniques implemented on healthcare data help in better analysis of patient data and predictions. The ML techniques process the existing patient's data and provide personalized healthcare through improved, accurate diagnostics.

KEYWORDS

- **algorithms**
- **analytics**
- **artificial intelligence**
- **data analytics**
- **data mining**
- **healthcare management**
- **machine learning**
- **mathematical analytics**

REFERENCES

1. Liang, Y., & Kelemen, A. (2016). Big Data science and its applications in health and medical research: Challenges and opportunities. *J Biom Biostat, 7*(307), 2.
2. Bouhriz, M., & Chaoui, H., (2015). Big data privacy in healthcare Moroccan context. *Procedia Computer Science, 63*. 575–580. https://doi.org/10.1016/j.procs.2015.08.387.
3. Patil, H. K., & Seshadri, R., (2014). Big data security and privacy issues in healthcare. *IEEE Int. Congr. Big Data*, 762–765. doi: 10.1109/BigData.Congress.2014.112.
4. Mishra, N., & Silakari, S., (2012). Predictive analytics: A survey, trends, applications, opportunities and challenges. *International Journal of Computer Science and Information Technologies, 3*(3), 4434–4438.
5. Raghupathi, W., & Raghupathi, V., (2014). Big data analytics in healthcare: Promise and potential. *Heal. Inf. Sci. Syst., 2*(3). https://doi.org/10.1186/2047-2501-2-3.
6. Legaz-Garca, M. D. C., Martinez-Costa, C., Menarguez-Tortosa, M., & Fernandez-Breis, J. T., (2016). A semantic web-based framework for the interoperability and exploitation of clinical models and EHR data. *Knowledge-Based Syst., 105*, 175–189. https://doi.org/10.1016/j.knosys.2016.05.016.
7. Murphy, K. P., (2006). *Naive Bayes Classifiers*. University of British Columbia.
8. Parthiban, G., Rajesh, A., & Srivatsa, S. K., (2011). Diagnosis of heart disease for diabetic patients using naive Bayes method. *International Journal of Computer Applications, 24*(3), 0975–8887.
9. Khan, S. S., & Peer, M. A., (2013). Evaluation of knowledge extraction using various classification data mining techniques. *International Journal of Advanced Research in Computer Science and Software Engineering, 3*(6). ISSN: 2277128X.
10. Brefelean, V. P., (2007). Analysis and predictions on students' behavior using decision trees in Weka environment. *Proceedings of the ITI 2007 29th International Conference on Information Technology Interfaces*. Cavtat, Croatia.

CHAPTER 2

CANCER CELL GROWTH DISCOVERY UTILIZING COMPUTERIZED IMAGE PROCESSING STRATEGIES

MEDHAVI MALIK,[1] MADHURI SHARMA,[2] DILEEP KUMAR YADAV,[3] and KAVITA[1]

[1]*Jayoti Vidyapeeth Women's University, Jaipur, Rajasthan, India, E-mails: medhavimalik28@gmail.com (M. Malik), kavita.yogen@gmail.com (Kavita)*

[2]*SRM IST Delhi NCR Campus, Modinagar, Ghaziabad, Uttar Pradesh, India, E-mail: madhurisharma44@gmail.com*

[3]*Galgotias University, Greater Noida, Uttar Pradesh, India, E-mail: dileep252000@gmail.com*

ABSTRACT

Starting late, the image getting ready segments are used for the most part in a couple of correction areas to improve the earlier stages of dissemination and medication, where the time factor is essential to discover the patient's disease as much as possible, exclusively in various cancerous tumors like lung cancer. In recent years in lung cancer, the idea of treatment and sciatica systems has been associated with uncomfortable medication. The 2008 findings suggest that lung cancer attacks most people worldwide. Early revelation of lung cancer is critical for productive medication. There are very few systems open to perceive cancerous cells.

2.1 INTRODUCTION

Cancer is the growth of abnormal cells that are not controlled in the body. There are billions of cells of different abilities in the body. These cells grow and divide to work properly. As they age or become damaged, the cells pass and the new cells suppress them.

Cancer has a complex pathophysiology. This incorporates reason for the illness, analysis, how the malady creates (pathogenesis), system, and normal course of the sickness. They likewise manage biochemical highlights, movement, and anticipation or result of the ailment. Cancer is under the control of normal body control. The old cells make no noise and become wild, creating strange new cells. These extra phones can frame a mass of tissue called a tumor. Some tumors, such as leukemia, do not affect the tumor. Some types of cancers are:

- Colon cancer;
- Gynecologic cancer;
- Prostate cancer;
- Breast cancer;
- Brain cancer.

Cancer depicts a general gathering of maladies, all including unregulated cell development brought about by hereditary changes. Cancers contain the dangerous (tending to turn out to be more terrible) subset of neoplasms—a cell or gathering of cells that experience unregulated development and structure a mass of tissue—regularly alluded to as a tumor. A noteworthy sign of cancer is metastasis, the capacity of the cancer to spread among tissues and organs inside the body.

Non-harmful tumors are alluded to as kind; they are regularly slower developing and are frequently encompassed by a layer of connective tissue that counteracts metastasis. A typical case of a favorable tumor is a skin mole.

While ordinarily asymptomatic, favorable tumors can affect wellbeing, more often than not by debilitating organ work through the pressure of veins or nerve filaments.

2.1.1 SIGNS OF CANCER

Because of the variety of cancers, six characteristics make it possible to group and define cancers:

1. Unregulated growth and cell division;
2. Continuous growth and cleavage even with opposite signals;
3. Prevention of programmed cell death;

4. Unlimited cellular division; and
5. Promotion of vascularization.

2.1.2 SIGNS AND SYMPTOMS

Cancer is usually asymptomatic at first the symptoms occur when the tumor develops and invades other tissues. First symptoms are usually associated with a loss of organ function at the site of the tumor. For example, lung cancer patients often have symptoms such as shortness of breath and chronic cough, which can vary considerably from patient to patient. Because of this variation and the association of symptoms with other disorders, the early detection of cancer is often difficult. As the disease progresses, systemic symptoms such as weight loss, fever, and fatigue may occur. In addition, symptoms associated with metastases such as enlarged lymph nodes, enlarged liver, or hypertrophic spleen may develop.

2.1.3 TYPECASTING OF CANCER

Cancers are classified according to the cell type that the tumor cells look like, assuming that indicates the origin of the tumor. These include:

1. **Carcinoma:** Cancer derived from epithelial cells. This group includes most of the most common cancers, especially in the elderly, and almost all cancers that develop in the breast, prostate, lung, pancreas, and colon.
2. **Sarcoma:** Tumors of the connective tissue (bone, cartilage, fat, nerves) and which develop from mesenchymal cell located outside the bone marrow.
3. **Lymphoma and Leukemia:** Both tumors are formed by hematopoietic cells that leave the spinal cord and mature in the lymph nodes or blood.
4. **Germ Cell Tumor:** Tumors derived from pluripotent cells and more common in the testes or ovaries (seminomas or dysgerminomas).
5. **Blastoma:** Tumor of immature progenitor cells or fetal tissue. They are also more common in children.

KREBS is a company of the world. You can find more information on the salaries of people with disabilities in our online catalog. Lung cancer is one of the best on the market with a general overview, with the best of time for treatment and treatment of health. Learn more about the behavior of the person responsible for angling I am the first person in charge of the human rights management policy in the world. Estimated 85% in the market for children and women and 75% in manufacturing companies of this type. Learn more about the 1,660,290 years in the diagnostic database and immediate, starting at 580,350 working days, plus 1,600 months earlier. Cancer hover the second most typical purpose behind death in the US, representing about 1 of each 4 passing. The general endurance rate for a wide range of cancer is 63%.

2.2 BASIC SYSTEM

2.2.1 *IMAGE ACQUISITION*

The main phase will begin to obtain a wide variety of images from the CT scan database. The image is saved in MATLAB and shown as a duplicate image. CT imaging is a significantly lower imaging technique than CT imaging and MRI. So, we can do a CT scan to find the lungs. For the initial conditions of PC tomography images with better viscosity, smaller distortions, and curvature of the experimental images, the men acquired CT images and 10 images for the database and JPEG/PNG standard (Figure 2.1).

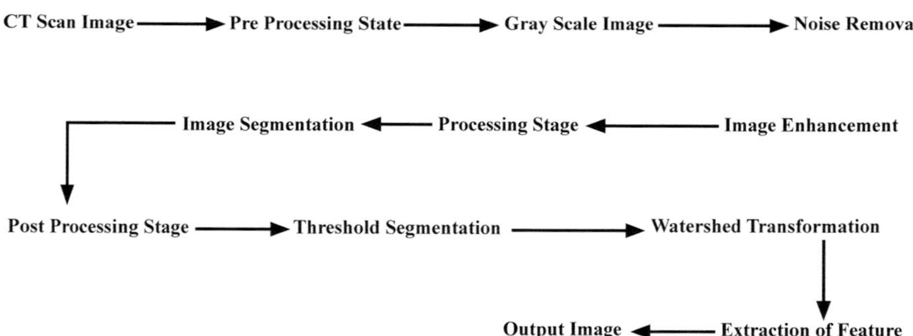

FIGURE 2.1 Stages of lung cancer detection.

2.2.2 *IMAGE PROPRIOCEPTIVE*

1. **Clamor Removal Image:** denoising calculations might be the for the most part utilized in picture preparing. The information picture

is a typical RGB picture. The RGB picture is changed over into dim scale picture in light of the fact that the RGB design is not bolstered in MATLAB. At that point the dim scale picture contains clamors, for example, repetitive sound, and pepper commotion and so on White clamor is one of the most widely recognized issues in picture preparing. This can be expelled by utilizing channel from the removed lung picture.

2. **Picture Enhancement Image:** upgrade characterized as an approach to improve the nature of picture, with the goal that the resultant picture is superior to the first one, the way toward improving the nature of a carefully put away picture by controlling the picture. For example, Interact to make the image lighter or darker or to add or remove. Tragically, there is no broad hypothesis for figuring out what "great" picture upgrade is with regards to human discernment. The point of picture upgrade is to improve the visual appearance of a picture, or to give a superior change portrayal for future robotized picture preparing. Many images, such as medical images, satellite images, animal pictures, and real photos, have high blood pressure and negative effects. In order to maximize image quality, contrast is important, and removal is important. The debugging process starts with a component and then adjusts the line according to its purpose. In this image editing program, we used the features of the Gibber Art feature.

2.2.3 PROCESSING

This stage includes, for the most part segmentation which is clarified as underneath.

2.2.3.1 IMAGE SEGMENTATION

In artificial vision, segmentation causes the possibility of dividing an extended image into many fragments. Image segmentation is often used to search for elements and boundaries in images. Even more clearly, image segmentation is the means by which a name is assigned to each pixel of an image so that pixels having a similar mark share certain visual qualities. The consequence of image segmentation is that a large number of parts overlap the entire image or many shapes extracted from it. All pixels of a neighborhood are comparable in terms of particular brands or pictorial properties, e.g., Shading, resistance, surface. All image preparation activities are usually aimed at a higher recognition of plot objects, that is, they can be recognized by different objects and foundations. The upcoming step is to check every single pixel to see if it has a location with an interesting object or not. This activity is considered segmentation and generates a binary image. A pixel has the value of one, which is at risk of having a place with the element, otherwise it is zero. After the segmentation, we recognize which pixel has a place with which object.

2.2.4 POSTPROCESSING

Posthandling division is finished utilizing some methods which are discussed in the following subsections.

2.2.4.1 THRESHOLDING APPROACH

Thresholds are important to ensure a more accurate vision of the foundation. By selecting an appropriate end view T, the opaque image can be switched to a dual image. The double image must contain all the essential information on the position and the status of the objects of interest (frontal zone). The advantage of having a parallel image is that it reduces data latency and examines the recognition and demand technique. The most common way to handle the transformation of an image from a fuzzy plane into a double image is to choose an estimate of the isolation limit (T). At this point, all the values of the level of darkness below this T are called blacks (0) and those above T are whites (1).

2.2.4.2 MARKER-CONTROLLED

Use the size columns in the section to separate the columns. Markers are multifunctional images where they are positioned. Marks are internal characters compared to external characters associated with the object and base of the plot. The isolation of contact objects in an image is one of the most difficult tasks in designing tasks. The change in the catchment area is often applied to this problem. The segmentation of the river basin by markers can segment one of the typical boundaries of an image. The quality of watershed segmentation is that a new response is created for a given image. The problem of excessive segmentation is further eliminated by the segmentation of river basins. For the most part, the change of the watershed is treated by the slope of the first image. It has a set of points of interest: it is a simple and instinctive strategy, it is fast and can be set in parallel, providing a complete division of the image into isolated areas, despite the fact that the differentiation is negative.

2.2.4.3 FEATURES EXTRACTION

Image highlighting Extract sorting is remarkable in image planning strategies that matter to distinguish and differentiate the different parts or essential shapes (highlights) of an image. After segmentation of the lung zone, it is possible to derive the features and the search rule can be understood to accurately identify the nodes of lung cancer. This analysis can eliminate the false discovery of cancerous masses caused by the split of the rules and give better conclusions.

2.2.4.4 BINARIZATION

Binarization approach depends upon the manner in which that the amount of dim pixels is significantly more critical than white pixels in regular lung pictures, with the objective that the checking starts the dull pixels for customary and surprising pictures to get a typical that can be used later as an edge, if the amount of the dim pixels of another image is increasingly vital that the edge, by then it shows that the image is standard, for the most part, if the amount of the dim pixels isn't actually the edge, it exhibits that the image is abnormal.

2.2.4.5 MASKING APPROACH

The masking approach depends on how most individuals appear as white junctures in the ROI (lung) as they increase the percentage of proximity to cancer. The presence of an RGB mass indicates the presence of solid blue lizards during collusion, indicating the proximity of cancer.

2.3 CONCLUSION

Lung cancer is the most hazardous and wide on earth, as showed by organizing the divulgence of the cancer cells in the lungs. This offers us the hint that the technique of area this contamination plays a huge and fundamental activity to avoid certifiable stages and to diminish its rate assignment on the planet. To acquire progressively exact outcomes, three phases were utilized: picture improvement organize, picture division stage, and highlights extraction arrange.

KEYWORDS

- **artificial vision**
- **cancer**
- **cancer identification**
- **feature extraction**
- **segmentation**
- **stages of cancer**
- **tumor**

REFERENCES

1. Bhagyashri, G. P., & Sanjeev, N. J., (2014). Cancer cells detection using digital image processing methods. *International Journal of Latest Trends in Engineering and Technology (IJLTET), 3*(4). ISSN: 2278-621X.
2. *Singapore Cancer Society*. (2021). http://www.singaporecancersociety.org.sg (accessed on 22 February 2021).
3. Al-Tarawneh, A. S., (2012). Lung cancer detection using image processing techniques. *Leonardo Electronic Journal of Practices and Technologies, 20*, 147–158. ISSN: 1583-1078.
4. Matthais, R., (2001). *Cancer, Cellular Health Series*.
5. Gonzalez, & Woods. (2002). *Digital Image Processing* (2nd edn).
6. Anita, C., (2012). Lung cancer detection on CT images by using image processing. *International Conference on Computing Sciences*.
7. Bedi, S. S., & Rati, K., (2013). *Various Image Enhancement Techniques: A Critical Review*.
8. Krishna, K. S., (2010). *Study of Image Segmentation Algorithms for Different Types of Images*.
9. Al-amri, S. S., Kalyankar, N. V., & Khamitkar, S. D., (2010). *Image Segmentation by Using Thresholding Technique*.

10. Sudha, V. J., (2012). *Lung Nodule Detection in CT Images Using Thresholding and Morphological Operations*.
11. Shubhpreet, K., & Gagandeep, J., (2011). Watershed segmentation of lung CT scan images. *International Journal of Computer and Electrical Engineering*.
12. Shanti, L. K., & Pinal, J. P., (2013). *Cancer Detection Using Modified Watershed*.
13. Disha, S., & Gangadeep, J., (2011). Identifying lung cancer using image processing technique. *International Conference of Computational Techniques and Artificial Intelligence*.
14. Ada, Ranjeet, K., (2013). *Feature Extraction and Principal Component Analysis for Lung Cancer Detection in Ct Images*.
15. https://pdfs.semanticscholar.org/2b24/efb5c9d853e9d32c37937be67f00bae25d7b.pdf (accessed on 22 February 2021).
16. https://courses.lumenlearning.com/boundless-ap/chapter/overview-of-cancer/ (accessed on 22 February 2021).

CHAPTER 3

ANALYSIS AND PREDICTION OF ASTHMA FROM COMMON SYMPTOMS USING DIFFERENT MACHINE LEARNING ALGORITHMS

UDBHAV NARYANI, PRAFFULLA KUMAR DUBEY, and MEDHAVI MALIK

Department of Computer Science and Engineering, SRM Institute of Science and Technology, Chennai, Tamil Nadu, India,
E-mails: udbhav.naryani@gmail.com (U. Naryani), praffullakrdubey@gmail.com (P. K. Dubey), medhavimalik28@gmail.com (M. Malik)

ABSTRACT

Asthma is a pulmonary disease which is spreading day-by-day because of the huge rise in Air Pollution in cities like New Delhi. With the use of air purifiers and pollution masks, it can be prevented to some extent. In this chapter, we have analyzed different symptoms and implemented different types of machine learning (ML) algorithm like Random Forest, Decision Tree and Naïve Bayes algorithms in order to predict whether a person is having asthma or not. In this chapter, we propose to find the most significant symptoms of asthma and determine which ML model is most accurate in prediction. We produce a prediction model with 96% accuracy for the prediction of asthma using the Random Forest Algorithm.

3.1 INTRODUCTION

Asthma is a long-term pulmonary disease which can never be cured. Each victim of asthma has a different type of treatment and a unique disease management plan that is organized to decrease everyday symptoms, maintain proper lung function, and at the same time allowing participation in everyday activities; it should also decrease the amount of minute Asthma problems [1]. It is impossible to predict the exact time when an asthma attack would take place, but if people know that they are suffering from asthma, they can take precautions they can be prepared for the attack whenever it comes.

3.1.1 ASTHMA AFFECTS DAILY ACTIVITIES OF PATIENTS

Asthma interferes with the daily life activity of the patients. Asthma patients suffer from breath shortness, constant wheezing, cough, and tightening of chest [1]. To predict whether a person is having asthma or not, patients have to keep a track of their health over a period of a month. They have to keep track of how often they have the above-mentioned problems, how often they wake up at night because of those problems and how these problems affect their lives. Asthma classification is also dependent on the age of the patient.

3.1.2 RISK OF ASTHMA ATTACK

Asthma victims are always at a very high risk of having minute asthma problems. People who have more serious attack and have soaring rates of asthma attacks generally have more serious disease. People with minute asthma problems can also have serious Asthma attacks [1]. People suffering from asthma should be well aware of the symptoms of asthma, so that they can be prepared for an attack.

3.1.3 SYMPTOMS OF ASTHMA

Symptoms of Asthma are breath shortness, constant wheezing, cough, and tightening of chest [1]. Wheezing can be caused by swelling and narrowing of the throat or the pathway to the lungs. These problems can also lead to breath shortness, because swelled-up lungs can only hold a small amount of air [2]. Most of the time, wheezing is felt by a person suffering from asthma but not always. When a person is having an attack, the pathway to lung becomes become narrower. In the beginning, the person having an attack wheezes while breathing air out, but when the attack becomes serious, wheezing occurs when the patient is breathing in. While an Asthma attack is underway, wheezing might be less because there is less air in the pathway to the lungs [2].

In this chapter, we will first analyze the symptoms and find out which symptoms are positively correlated to asthma. After we have found the symptoms we will design different prediction models.

3.2 ALGORITHMS

Machine learning (ML) involves different kinds of Supervised and Unsupervised Algorithms that can be used depending on the type of work that machine has to perform. In Supervised Learning, we use input as well as the output in order to train a ML algorithm. In Unsupervised Learning, we train the model with unlabeled data. The various types of Algorithms used in this research are explained below.

3.2.1 NAÏVE BAYES ALGORITHM

It is basically a classifier algorithm which is based on the Bayes theorem. It makes an assumption that there is a feature present in a class and that feature is not related to any other feature present in the same class. This algorithm is based on conditional probability of events. Every instance of the data D is associated to the class of highest probability (Figure 3.1) [6].

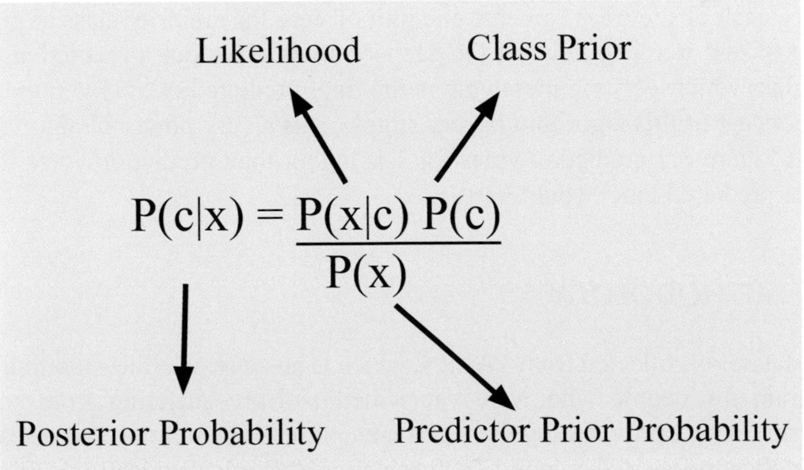

FIGURE 3.1 Naive Bayes formula.

3.2.2 DECISION TREE ALGORITHM

The Decision Tree ML algorithm is a kind of Supervised Learning algorithm that is used for predicting class labels. The shape of Decision Tree is just a tree-structured shape where every node is either a decision node or leaf node [7]. This algorithm is a simple algorithm which is easy to apply. The nodes of the decision tree are linked with each other. In this algorithm, we compare the root's attribute with the record's attribute, using this comparison, we match the branch which is similar to this attribute and move to the next node. The leaf nodes are called leaf nodes as they are the nodes that do not have any child or successor nodes, and these are just associated with a label [8]. Decision tree algorithm works efficiently with data in which class labels are in the form of categories. This algorithm works by breaking down the dataset into a smaller subset at each level or at each iteration a related decision tree is generated. The result at the end of all the iterations is a tree which has only decision nodes and leaf nodes. Each of the leaf nodes represents the predicted class labels and we reach on these predicted labels by making choices or decisions on the decision node.

3.2.3 RANDOM FOREST ALGORITHM

Random forests are basically a collection of decision trees. It is a type of classifier algorithms which consists a collection of tree shaped structures which are independently and identically distributed randomized vectors where each of the trees can cast one unit of vote for majority class at given input of that tree [9]. Each of the decision trees gives out a prediction and the class which gets the most vote is the final predicted class. Even though the concept of this algorithm is very simple, it is a very powerful algorithm. As in Figure 3.2 prediction votes for 1 is higher than prediction votes for 0 hence predicted label would be 1.

3.3 METHODOLOGY

The dataset is collected from VAERS, which is an adverse effects monitoring program for people who were vaccinated and are suffering from some illness; Dataset provided by them contains patient's symptoms and diseases in a very unorganized manner. The problem is lack of organization, and that huge amount of data is in textual form, this makes it very difficult to predict whether a person is having asthma or not from this dataset. For analysis and prediction, the dataset was first cleaned. After cleaning of the data filtration and restructuring of data was also performed. Repetitions present in the data are removed. There are many columns in the dataset which are not useful for us hence have been dropped from the dataset. After performing all the algorithms, the Random Forest algorithm gave us the high accuracy in prediction in comparison to other algorithms (Figure 3.3).

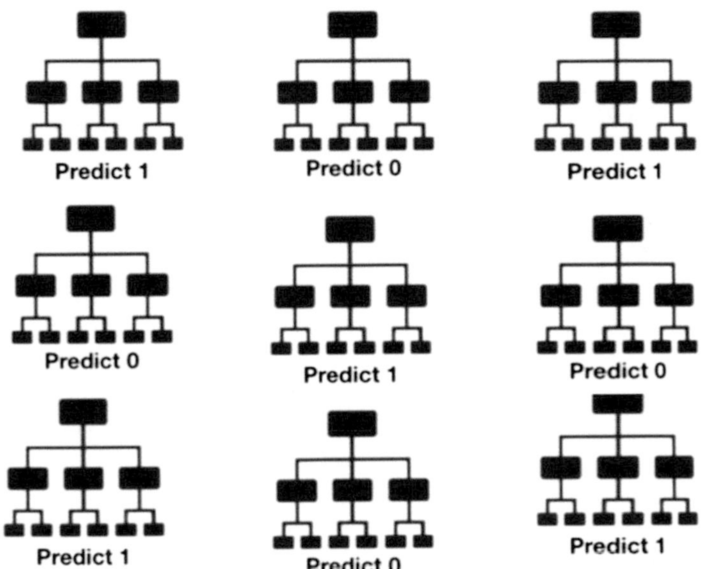

FIGURE 3.2 Random forest working.

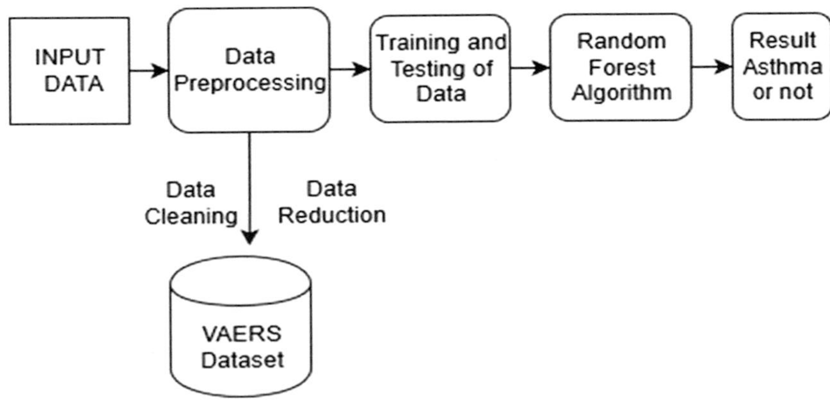

FIGURE 3.3 System architecture.

3.3.1 DATA PRE-PROCESSING

Pre-processing of data is a very crucial step in Knowledge Discovery from Data process. As the data has been collected from the users of VAERS, it has a lot of missing values. Cleaning of data is the process of identification and correction (or removal) of corrupted or inaccurate data records from a record dataset, table data and means differentiating inaccurate, incorrect or incomplete parts of the knowledge. It also includes substituting, modification, or deletion of the dirty or coarse data [3]. To make the dataset more relevant and specific, we have taken all the common symptoms throughout the dataset and matched them if their combination leads to asthma or not. In the dataset, there were many symptoms and other information that is not related to asthma, and hence we have removed that information.

3.3.2 DATA ANALYSIS

The dataset after pre-processing has the attributes as given in Table 3.1.

TABLE 3.1 Attributes Present in Dataset

Attribute Name	Meaning
AGE_YRS	Age of person in years
SLEEPING_PROB	Person has sleeping problem or not
CHEST_TIGHTNESS	Person feels chest tightness or not
BREATH	Person has breathing problem or not
COUGH	Person has cough or not
ALLERGY	Person has any allergy or not
WHEEZING	Person has wheezing or not
ASTHMA	Person has asthma or not

All of these attributes have true or false values except age. Age has numeric values. Then we plotted a Heat Map for the data to find attributes that are positively related to asthma.

3.4 PROPOSED ALGORITHM

Random forest algorithm is a supervised learning algorithm [4], steps we followed are:

- **Step 1:** We used the bootstrap method on the original data with the goal to be able to select J number of unique samples of the dataset, every bootstrapped sample will act as an individual decision tree.
- **Step 2:** We select m attributes from total M attributes as the candidate set of features. Now, construction of decision trees takes place. They are created by selection of random attributes from the candidate set of features (having m attributes). Finally, we get J results in the form of J classifications. We finally get J classification results by classifying every tree of the decision trees in the form of a completed tree.
- **Step 3:** In the end, the variable which gets the most votes gets selected as the output. The flowchart for the prediction model of the above algorithm is shown in Figure 3.4.

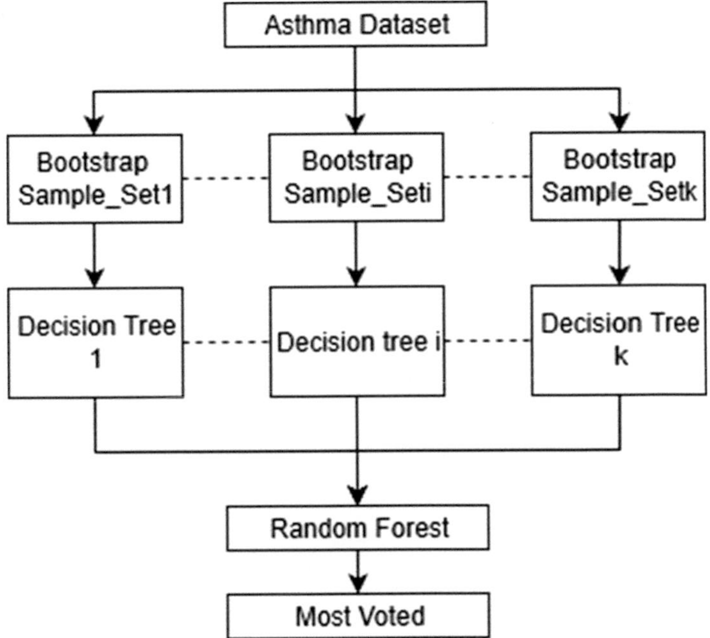

FIGURE 3.4 Random forest prediction model.

3.5 RESULT

In this research work, we implemented various ML algorithm including the Random Forest algorithm, Decision Tree Algorithm and Naïve Bayes Algorithm. After testing the trained model, we found out that Naïve Bayes

Algorithm provides 70% accuracy which is the worst among all three. Decision tree provides an accuracy of 84%. Random Forest Algorithm provides the most accurate predictions with an accuracy of 96%. The graph given below represents the performance of the various classifiers (Figures 3.5 and 3.6).

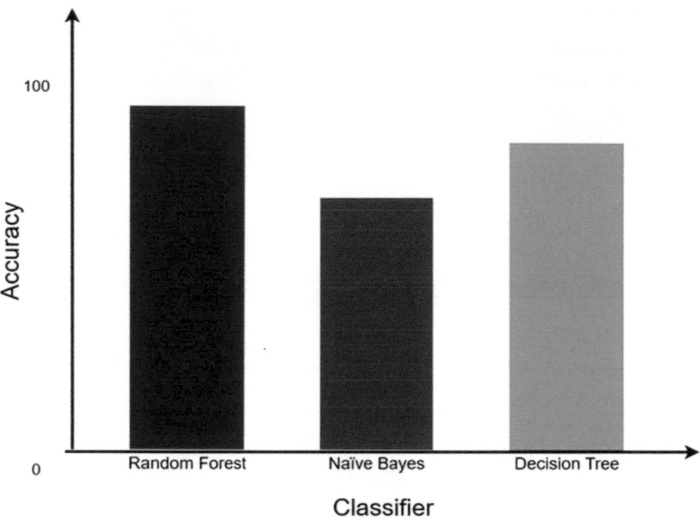

FIGURE 3.5 Classifiers vs. accuracy graph.

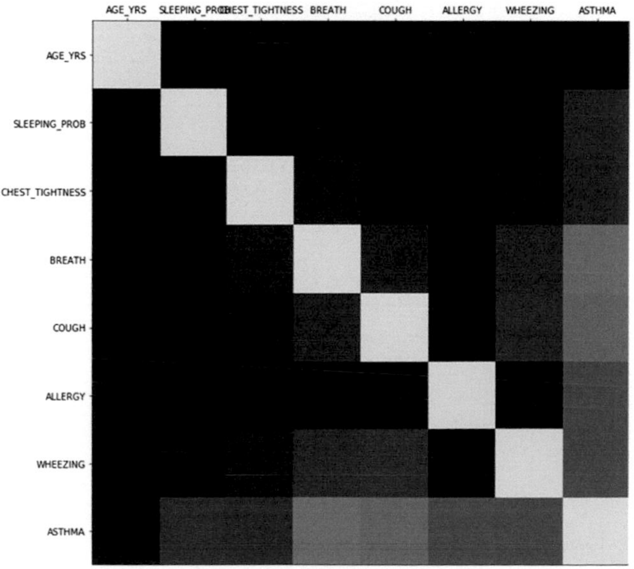

FIGURE 3.6 Heat map for the processed dataset.

As we can see from the Heat map, asthma is least dependent on age. This means that asthma can affect a person of any age group. A younger person is as probable of getting asthma as an old person. There is a slightly positive relation between sleeping problems and asthma; this means that a person who is having difficulty in sleeping might have asthma. Chest tightness is equally probable symptom for asthma as sleeping problems. Having allergies is a very high symptom for asthma. Wheezing is an equally probable symptom for asthma as allergies. The most common symptoms of asthma, according to the above Heat Map, is cough and breathing problems.

3.6 CONCLUSION AND FUTURE SCOPE

The dataset was extracted from VAERS, which is an adverse effects monitoring program for people who were vaccinated and are suffering from some illness. All the subjects in the dataset were vaccinated. This was an important limitation of this research. In the future, the next step would be to work on a dataset of subjects which were not vaccinated and then compare the results. We can also implement other ML algorithms to see if we can get better results and knowledge from this data. These models can also be implemented to predict pulmonary disease in animals by using a relevant dataset.

KEYWORDS

- **asthma analysis**
- **asthma prediction**
- **decision tree algorithm**
- **machine learning**
- **naïve bayes classifier**
- **prediction model**
- **pulmonary disease**
- **random-forest**

REFERENCES

1. National Heart, Lung, and Blood Institute, (2012). *Expert Panel Report 3 (EPR-3): Guidelines for the Diagnosis and Management of Asthma-Full Report 2007*. Accessed at: https://www.nhlbi.nih.gov/health-topics/guidelines-for-diagnosis-management-of-asthma (accessed on 22 February 2021).
2. *American College of Allergy, Asthma and Immunology*., (2014). *Signs of Asthma*. Accessed at: https://acaai.org/allergies/allergy-symptoms/wheezing-shortness-breath (accessed on 22 February 2021).
3. Menon, D., Schwab, K., Wright, D. W., & Maas, A. I., (2010). The demographics and clinical assessment working group of the international and interagency initiative toward common data elements for research on traumatic brain injury and psychological health. Position statement: Definition of traumatic brain injury. *Arch. Phys. Med. Rehabil., 91*, 1637–1640.
4. Consistency of Random Forests, by Erwan Scornet Sorbonne University, UPMC Paris 06, F-75005, Paris, France, by Gerard Biaú Sorbonne Universities, UPMC Univ Paris 06, F-75005, Paris, France.
5. Jehad, A., Rehanullah, K., Nasir, A., & Imran, M., (2012). *Random Forest and Decision Trees*. Computer Engineer UUET Peshwa, Pakistan.
6. Senthil, K. M., Chandrasegar, T., & Gautam, S., (2019). Effective heart disease prediction using hybrid machine learning techniques. *IEEE Access*.
7. Amin, U. H., Jian, P. L., Muhammad, H. M., Shah, N., & Ruinan, S., (2018). A hybrid intelligent system framework for the prediction of heart disease using machine learning algorithms. *Hindawi Mobile Information Systems, 2018*, 21. Article ID: 3860146. https://doi.org/10.1155/2018/3860146.
8. Hanen, B., Jalel, A., et al., (2014). Comparative study of different classification techniques, heart diseases use case. In: *13th International Conference on Machine Learning and Applications*.
9. Arnu, P., Surette, B., & Sarel, J. S., (2016). *A Meta-Analysis of Research in Random Forests for Classification*. Department of Statistics and Actuarial Science Stellenbosch University South Africa.

CHAPTER 4

LOGISTIC REGRESSION BASED MYOCARDIAL INFARCTION DISEASE PREDICTION

PRAFFULLA KUMAR DUBEY, UDBHAV NARYANI, and MEDHAVI MALIK

Department of Computer Science and Engineering, SRM Institute of Science and Technology, Chennai, Tamil Nadu, India, E-mail: praffullakrdubey@gmail.com (P. K. Dubey)

ABSTRACT

In today's world, due to the busy and fast lifestyle, people tend to be affected by various diseases like hypertension, migraine, diabetes, blood pressure, asthma, various heart diseases, etc. Myocardial Infraction Disease, also known as heart disease, is one of the common diseases that a person has these days. It can be termed as one of the most significantly occurring disease and cause of mortality these days. Deaths due to Myocardial Infraction disease in today's era is one of the major issues and approximately one person per one minute in the world dies due to myocardial disease. The problem of myocardial disease can occur at the very starting age, but mostly people of ages 26–75 have been diagnosed with heart disease and these include both males and females, and the ratio can vary. In the area of clinical health care data analysis, prediction of Myocardial Infraction disease is very tough. In the healthcare industry, machine learning (ML) is effective in predicting and making effective decisions on large data produced by various healthcare industries like hospitals and clinical labs. In this chapter, we propose to predict the Myocardial Infraction disease by implementing various algorithms of ML-like Naïve Bayes Algorithm, Decision Tree, Logistic Regression and Random Forest. An efficient performance model with 88.0% accuracy for prediction of Myocardial Infraction disease using Logistic Regression is proposed by us.

4.1 INTRODUCTION

Myocardial infraction disease is tremendously increasing on a daily basis in these modern lifestyles of the world. According to WHO, an estimated death of 17 million people each year is because of myocardial infraction disease, in particular strokes of heart and heart attacks [11]. This leads to the recording of symptoms and habits to be noted and recorded that lead to the contribution to myocardial infraction disease. The various tests like cholesterol, ECG, blood sugar, blood pressure are needed to be performed as these test records are necessary to diagnose the myocardial infarction disease. Various risk factors, which include diabetes and high blood pressure, make the identification of myocardial infarction disease difficult.

Numerous techniques in neural networking and data mining have been employed to find out the severity of heart disease among the humans [1]. The severity level of the myocardial disease could be classified on the basis of Decision Tree, Naïve Bayes Algorithm, Random Forest, and Logistic Regression. The type of heart disease is extremely complex and therefore, utmost care must be used to handle the disease [1]. If the disease is not analyzed and treated carefully, then it leads to loss of life, or it may cause premature death of the patient. Wrong treatment not always leads to death, but it can also affect the condition or health of heart.

Machine learning (ML) is widely being used for the prediction of myocardial infraction disease and the data related to it is being investigated and analyzed daily. It has been seen that decision trees used in predicting the accuracy of myocardial disease [1].

Medical organizations, throughout the world, collect various data on many health-related issues [2]. Using the ML algorithms on these collected data, we can get useful outputs. But as the data is gathered from various sources in extreme amounts leading the collection of data to be big enough, therefore, the data obtained is noisy data. These datasets collected are too attractive for the human brain to comprehend, can be easily examined using various techniques of ML [2]. Hence in recent times, all the algorithms are becoming necessary and important in accurately predicting the absence or presence of myocardial infarction disease or any other heart-related disease of a patient.

Various algorithms used gives various results on the same dataset, but our primary interest is to predict the disease accurately, and for this, we need to use the algorithm which gives the most accurate results of prediction. Speed of execution is also an important factor. The algorithm that predicts the disease faster and accurately is preferred over other algorithms. In this chapter, we have used Logistic Regression, Naïve Bayes Algorithm, Decision Tree, and Random Forest for the prediction of disease.

4.2 DIMENSIONALITY REDUCTION

Dimensionality reduction involves the reduction of the dimensions of the given data so that the given data mostly includes the task-relevant data. It also revolves around selecting a mathematical representation such that only the useful information is majorly included [2]. The dataset has a vast number of attributes, but it is always not necessary that all the attributes present in the dataset contribute to the prediction or influence the result. There is an increase in computational complexity due to attributes of larger numbers in the dataset, which might even lead to overfitting as a result of poor outputs. Thus, these factors make Dimensionality reduction one of the important steps for building a model. The two methods used for Dimensionality reduction are feature extraction and feature selection.

4.2.1 FEATURE EXTRACTION

In Feature Extraction, we can derive a contemporary set of features from the native feature set. It involves a remolding of the features [2]. There can also be a loss of a few important and useful information or data in this process; therefore, this transformation is not reversible. We can do feature extraction by various methods. Principal component analysis (PCA) is at most used for feature extraction. PCA is mostly used as a linear transformation algorithm. PCA finds the commands that maximize variance and finds the commands which are orthogonal mutually. It gives the best result; therefore, it can be considered as a global algorithm for Feature Extraction purposes.

4.2.2 FEATURE SELECTION

In Feature Selection, a subset from the original feature set are to be selected. We can select a key feature from Correlation-Based Feature Selection which is merged with the BFS method to lessen dimensionality. The Chi-Square test for statistics is mostly used to identify the most features significantly from the original features.

4.3 RELATED WORK

There have been a lot of experiments conduction on the datasets having medical data by using various algorithms and selection techniques of attributes. There is a small research on the classification of myocardial infarction disease data set. Most of them show a better classification accuracy [3]. ANN introduced the highest prediction model in the field of medicine. The backpropagation MLP of ANN predicts myocardial disease [1]. The secured results were compared and found more efficient and accurate than the other models that already existed in the same domain of heart disease prediction. The data collected from various sources are used for the discovery of various patterns by using algorithms like Random Forest, Naïve Bayes Algorithm, Decision Tree, and Logistic Regression. The proposed method gives the results of 88.0% for Logistic Regression which is considered as the maximum among all the classifiers used. Convolutional neural networks (CNN) can also be used. This mechanism examines the heart cycle with numerous start postures from the electrocardiogram (EGC) signals in the phase of training. It is able to spawn features with diverse positions in the phase of the patient testing [4, 5]. CCN classification without segmentation is used. In earlier works, the large data produced by vast medical industries was not effectively used. The new approaches presented in the chapter gives the accurate result, and these approaches are fast, easy, and more effective in the prediction of myocardial infarction disease. Many works have also included techniques like Deep Learning for the prediction of myocardial disease, which also gives high accuracy.

4.4 ALGORITHMS

ML includes supervised and unsupervised learning. In terms of the task of a machine, we can define supervised learning. We can define Supervised Learning as the task of ML to teach a computer's function that maps input to an output based on input-output examples is known as supervised learning. It contains various training example sets that are used to derive a function from the marked training data. The technique that is observed analyzes the training data and creates a deduced function that can be used to map new instances. Whereas, Unsupervised Learning can be defined as a technique of ML where we do not have to oversee the model. In this technique, we must only allow the model process on its own to predict the required results.

It is called unsupervised learning because the main focus of this learning is unlabeled data. This technique allows us to execute the more sophisticated task in comparison with supervised learning, but unsupervised learning can be highly unpredictable. The various algorithms used in this research are discussed below.

4.4.1 NAÏVE BAYES ALGORITHM

This algorithm applies the Bayes theorem rule through independent features. The Naive Bayes Algorithm is based on the conditional probability of events. Various illustration of the data D is associated with the classes of highest probability [1]. The features should not be correlated with one another in any possible way. This algorithm is called Naïve because if there is a dependency, then also all the attributes will be contributing independently to the probability.

$$P(S|G) = P(G|S) \times P(S)/P(G) \tag{1}$$

where; P(S|G) is the posterior probability, P(G|S) is the like hood, P(S) is the class prior probability, P(G) is the predictor prior probability and $P(S|A) = P(a_1|S) \times P(a_2|S) \times .... \times P(a_n|S) \times P(S)$.

4.4.2 DECISION TREE

Decision tree algorithm falls in the category of supervised ML. A decision tree figure is a tree where all nodes are decision node or leaf node [6]. The expertise of decision tree are easily understandable and very simple to implement. The various internal and external nodes of a decision tree are interlinked with one another. The decisions are made by the internal nodes of the tree, and the exterior nodes are associated with each other. The leaf nodes are called leaf nodes as they are the nodes that do not have any child or successor nodes, and these are just associated with a label [12]. Decision tree works well with the categorical data. Decision tree algorithm, firstly calculates the entropy value for each and every attribute of the data present. Then the data is categorized with the aid of the variables or predictors with supreme information gain or minimal entropy [2]. For the remaining attributes, these steps are performed recursively (Figure 4.1).

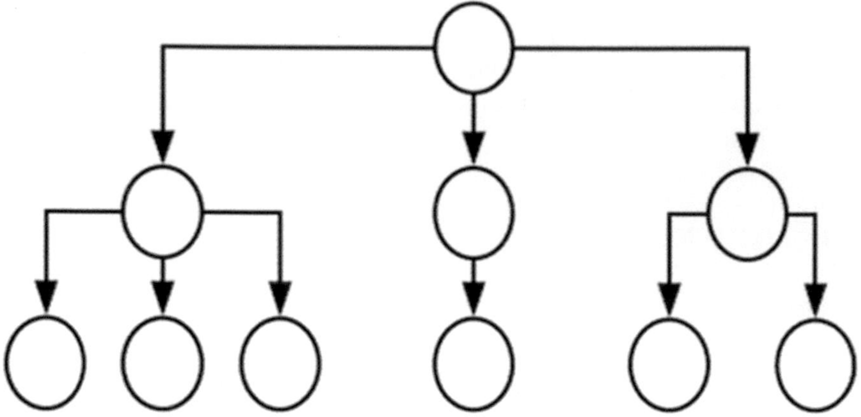

FIGURE 4.1 Decision tree.

4.4.3 RANDOM FOREST

Random forest can be termed as one the popular unsupervised learning algorithm among the various ML algorithms. Random Forest techniques are used for various tasks like regression and classification, but as observed, Random Forest mostly performs skillfully in classification tasks. Random Forest takes multi-decision trees into consideration prior to generating an output for the data present in the dataset. It is believed that the greater number of decision trees Random Forest considers, more accurate decision are made. A system called voting system is used for classification techniques whereas for the regression technique, mean the outputs generated by all decision tree. It can handle big dimensionality of data and data with a large number of attributes (Figure 4.2).

$$Entropy(S) = \sum_{i=1}^{c} -p_i \log_2 p_i$$

$$Gain(S, A) = Entropy(S) - \sum_{v \in Values(A)} \frac{|S_v|}{|S|} Entropy(S_v)$$

4.4.4 LOGISTIC REGRESSION

A logistic regression can be termed as classification algorithm [7–9]. Problem of Binary classification uses a predictive variable whose value belongs to either zero or one where we consider zero as a negative class and one as a positive class. It can also use multiple classifications to foresee the utility of the predictor variable where the value of the predictor variable can lie from 0 to n. To arrange the two classes of binary classification, i.e., 0 and 1, a hypothesis h (Θ) = Θ^T U is created. When the predictor variable predicts the value as 1, this interprets that the patient has myocardial disease, whereas when the predictor variable predicts the value as 0, then it signifies that there are no symptoms of myocardial disease. The sigmoid function of logistic regression can be represented as follows:

$$h\Theta\ (u) = q\ (\Theta^T U) \tag{2}$$

where; $q(r) = 1/(1 + x^{-p})$ and $h\Theta(u) = 1/(1+x^{-z})$.

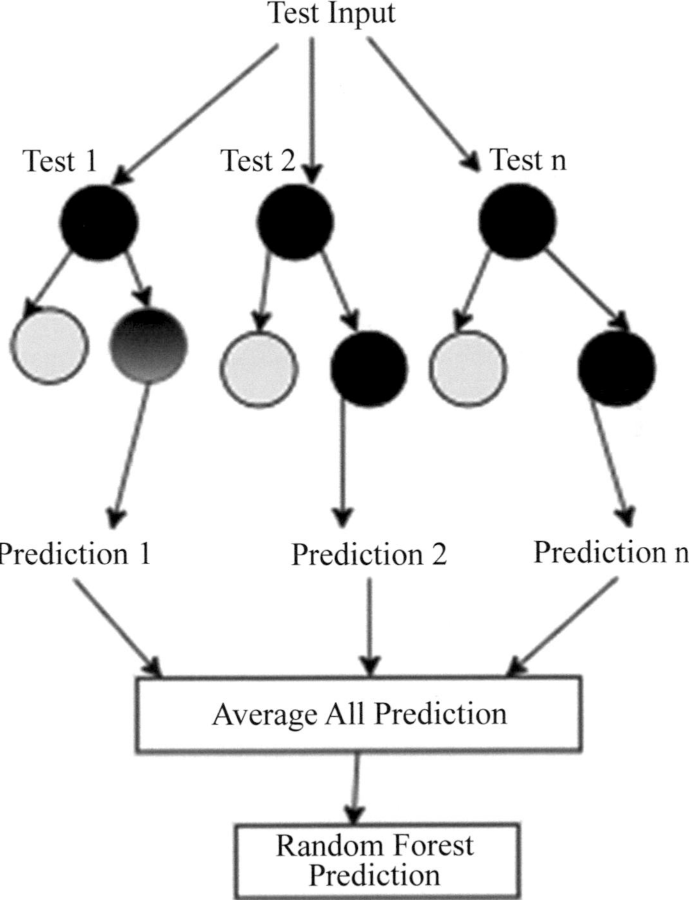

FIGURE 4.2 Random forest.

4.5 METHODOLOGY

Data science can be defined as a technique that processes and analyzes data, i.e., applied for a precise intention. This technique is also beneficial and can be implemented in different project performance predictions. There are six steps in this technique:

1. **Data Import:** We have obtained the relevant dataset for our project, i.e., 'patient.csv.' It is a csv file, and it contains 303 rows and 14 columns. This data set has been imported and used for analysis as well as prediction purposes.
2. **Data Cleaning:** It is one of the most time-consuming processes yet the most important step. Most of the data come with missing or null parameters or duplicate values or attributes, so it becomes important to clean our data so that our dataset consists of the only required data.
3. **Data Munging/Wrangling:** It is the process in which transformation and mapping of data are done from raw data into various new forms of data that can be termed as more appropriate for the analysis as well as prediction task.
4. **Data Visualization:** In this step, we visualize the data with the help of various patterns or graphs.
5. **Data Modeling:** This step shows the relationship among the various descriptive diagrams containing various types of information. These diagrams include scatter-plot, joint plot, bar-plot, histogram, etc.
6. **Cross-Validation:** The process of training the model on one set of the dataset and testing the model by using another dataset is called cross-validation [10]. We have used Logistic Regression to train our model and test our model to do prediction (Table 4.1 and Figure 4.3).

4.6 PROPOSED ALGORITHM (FIGURE 4.4)

4.7 RESULT

In the project, we have applied various ML algorithms like Naïve Bayes Algorithm, Decision Tree, Random Forest and Logistic Regression and after training our model on the dataset we found that Naïve Bayes Algorithm provides the worst result as the accuracy of our model trained using Naïve Bayes Algorithm is 65.1% whereas for Decision Tree the accuracy of the model is 85%, for Random Forest the accuracy is 86.1% and Logistic Regression performs the best and give the most accurate results and the accuracy of the trained model is 88% which is the highest amongst the all the applied algorithms. It can be observed from Figures 4.5–4.7 that the processing time in (seconds) is least for logistic regression, and the processing time is highest for the Naïve Bayes algorithm.

TABLE 4.1 Attributes of the Dataset

Attribute Value	Data Type	Representation	Summary
Age	Integer	age	Age of the patient in years
Sex	Integer	sex	Gender (1 = Male, O = Female)
Slop	Integer	slope	Slop of exercise
Blood pressure	Integer	trestbps	Blood pressure (mm Hg)
Cholesterol	Integer	chol	Cholesterol in mg/dl
ECG	Integer	restecg	ECG results
Oldpeak	Real	oldpeak	Depression level
Heart rate	Integer	thalach	Max. heart rate
Exercise level	Integer	exang	Exercise-induced
Chest pain type	Integer	cp	Type of chest pain suffered
Blood sugar	Integer	fbs	Fasting blood sugar level >120 mg/dl (0 = False, 1 = True)
Thal	Integer	thal	Defect type (normal, fixed, or irreversible)
Major vessels	Integer	ca	No. of various vessels colored by fluoroscopy
Class	Integer	class	0: healthy, 1: unhealthy

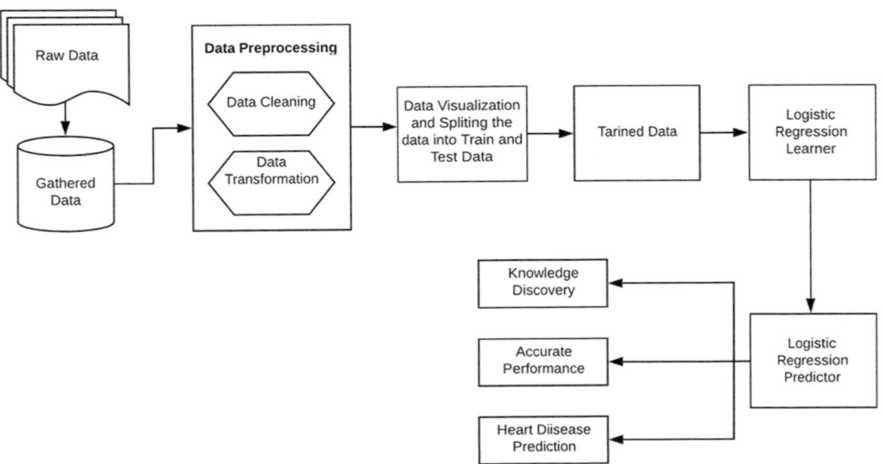

FIGURE 4.3 Methodology.

Step 1: Collect the patient data (RD_1, RD_2,……, RD_n) where RD = Resource Data
Step 2: Apply Data Preprocessing
  1) Cleaning of data i.e. cleaning of data
  2) Normalization i.e. normalize the values
  3) Transformation
  4) Integration of the data
Step 3: Splitting the data into Training Data and Test Data and train the model
Step 4: Create model using Logistic Regression
  LRModel=LogisticRegression()
Step 5: Apply Test data on model
    LRModel. Fit (X_train, y_train)
  predictions_heart=LRModel.predict(X_test)
Step 6: Predictive outcome
  1) Knowledge Discovery in terms of various graphs like Line Graph, Histogram, Scatter Plot, etc.
  2) Performance Accuracy of model
  3) Heart Disease Prediction of the patient

FIGURE 4.4 Proposed algorithm.

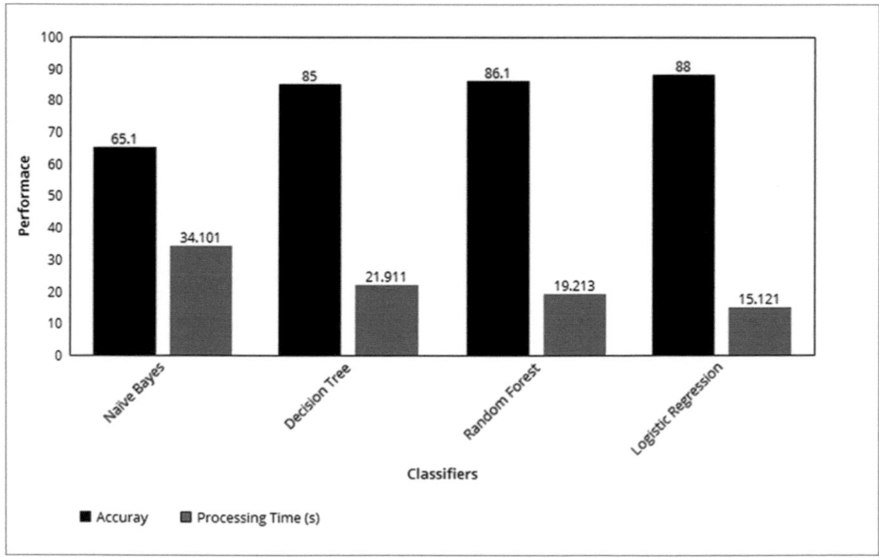

FIGURE 4.5 Classifiers vs. performance graph.

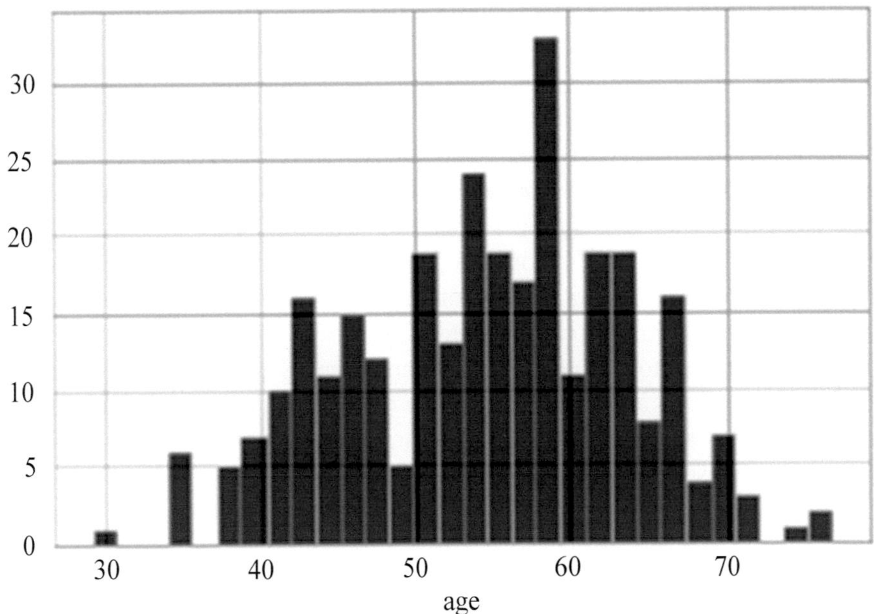

FIGURE 4.6 Graph for attribute 'age' distribution.

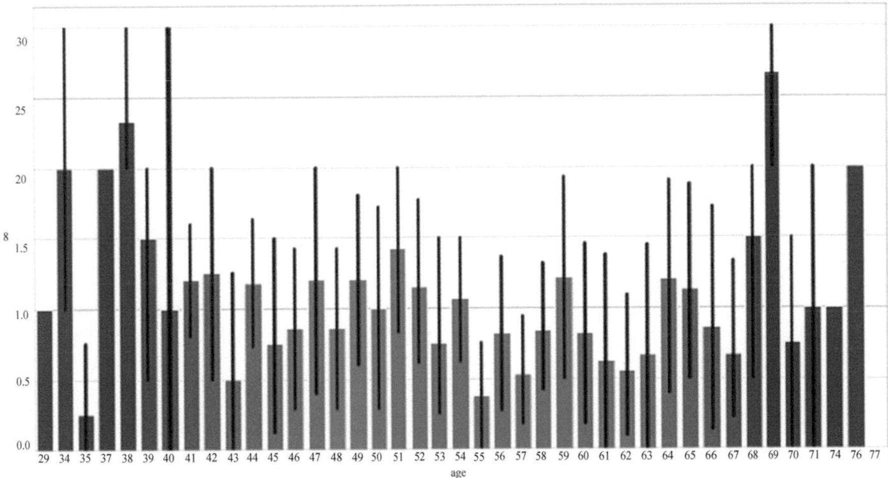

FIGURE 4.7 'Age' vs. 'cp' graph.

4.8 CONCLUSION AND FUTURE SCOPE

The limited dataset provided was an important limitation in working and carrying out this project. The next step required to increment the accuracy of prediction of myocardial infarction disease would be to test the various approaches proposed in this chapter using a dataset with increased size and more attributes. With the implementation of new techniques like deep neural networks like Keras and TensorFlow we can also archive higher accuracy. We can also develop similar models for the prediction of various other human diseases like lung failure, cancer prediction, and kidney failure prediction, and so on. These models can also be implemented to predict the diseases occurring in various animals and birds by training the model on the relevant dataset. Further accuracy of the implemented model can be increased by using unsupervised learning or reinforcement learning.

KEYWORDS

- **decision tree**
- **logistic regression**
- **machine learning**
- **myocardial infarction disease**
- **naïve bayes algorithm**
- **random-forest**

REFERENCES

1. Senthil, K. M., Chandrasegar, T., & Gautam, S. (2019). Effective heart disease prediction using hybrid machine learning techniques. *IEEE Access*.
2. Ramalingam, V. V., Ayantan, D., & Karthick, R. M., (2018). Heart disease prediction using machine learning techniques: A survey. *International Journal of Engineering and Technology, 7*(2.8), 684–687.
3. Fatima, M., & Pasha, M., (2017). Survey of machine learning algorithms for disease diagnostic. *Journal of Intelligent Learning Systems and Applications, 9*(1), 1.
4. Nahar, J., Imam, T., Tickle, K. S., & Chen, Y. P. P., (2013). Association rule mining to detect factors which contribute to heart disease in males and females. *Expert Syst. Appl., 40*(4), 1086–1093. doi: 10.1016/j.eswa.2012.08.028.

5. Zaman, S., & Toufiq, R., (2017). Codon based back propagation neural network approach to classify hypertension gene sequences. In: *Proc. Int. Conf. Elect. Comput. Commun. Eng. (ECCE)* (pp. 443–446).
6. Amin, U. H., Jian, P. L., Muhammad, H. M., Shah, N., & Ruinan, S., (2018). A hybrid intelligent system framework for the prediction of heart disease using machine learning algorithms. *Hindawi Mobile Information Systems,* 21. Article ID: 3860146, https://doi.org/10.1155/2018/3860146.
7. Harrell, F. E., (2015). Ordinal logistic regression. In: *Regression Modeling Strategies* (pp. 311–325). Springer, Berlin, Germany.
8. Larsen, K., Petersen, J. H., Budtz-Jørgensen, E., & Endahl, L., (2000). Interpreting parameters in the logistic regression model with random effects. *Biometrics, 56*(3), 909–914.
9. Vapnik, V., (2013). *The Nature of Statistical Learning Theory*. Springer Science & Business Media, Berlin, Germany.
10. Zhang, W., & Han, J., (2017). Towards heart sound classification without segmentation using convolutional neural network. In: *Proc. Comput. Cardiol. (CinC)* (Vol. 44, pp. 1–4).
11. Youness, K., & Mohamed, B., (2018). Heart disease prediction and classification using machine learning algorithms optimized by particle swarm optimization and ant colony optimization. *International Journal of Intelligent Engineering and Systems*.
12. Hanen, B., Jalel, A., et al., (2014). Comparative study of different classification techniques, heart diseases use case. In: *13th International Conference on Machine Learning and Applications*.

CHAPTER 5

NEW N-VALUED REFINED NEUTROSOPHIC DIVERGENCE MEASURE IN MEDICAL INVESTIGATION AND PROJECT SELECTION

ADEEBA UMAR and RAM NARESH SARASWAT

Department of Mathematics and Statistics, Manipal University Jaipur, Jaipur, Rajasthan, India, E-mail: adeeba1506@gmail.com (A. Umar)

ABSTRACT

Neutrosophic set which is a branch of neutrosophy, studies the scope, characterization and origin of the neutralities and their interconnection with various ideational expansion. Smarandache originally initiated the theory of neutrosophic sets, who combined non-standard analysis and a tri-component set to handle indeterminate and inconsistent information. Neutrosophic set is an influential framework which has been proposed recently. To deal with vagueness and uncertainty, the three functions which are truth membership function, indeterminacy membership function and falsity membership function play an important role and the sum of these three membership functions is less than three. This theory is used to depict the information more appropriately. In this chapter, a novel divergence measure for refined n-valued neutrosophic sets is introduced with the proof of its validity. An application of novel divergence measure is shown with illustrations for decision making in medical investigation and project selection in order to demonstrate its practicality, viability, and materialism.

5.1 INTRODUCTION

Florentin Smarandache proposed a neutrosophic set in 1995. After that, in Refs. [1] and [2], he gave the notion of a neutrosophic set that deals with imprecision, indeterminacy, inconsistency, and incompleteness of information. In 2005, Smarandache [3] studied the relation between intuitionistic fuzzy sets and neutrosophic sets and concluded that neutrosophic sets are the generalization of intuitionistic fuzzy sets. These consist of three membership functions which are truth-membership, indeterminacy-membership, and falsity-membership. Agboola [4] introduced refined neutrosophic algebraic structures and shown its elementary properties. Broumi [5] introduced the notion of n-valued neutrosophic sets with its basic operations and proposed some distances between n-valued INS. A new method for MCGDM for this approach and an application of this approach in medical diagnosis problem was also shown. Smarandache [6] introduced a brief history about the following: neutrosophic numbers, neutrosophic set, neutrosophic intervals, neutrosophic numerical components, neutrosophic literal components, neutrosophic dual number, neutrosophic special quasi dual number, neutrosophic special dual number, elementary neutrosophic algebraic structures, neutrosophic hypercomplex numbers of dimension n, neutrosophic linguistic interval-style number, neutrosophic linguistic number. Many authors introduced various similarity measures, such as: Broumi and Smarandache [7] gave cosine similarity measure for refined sets where cosine similarity measure for NS is the extension of improved cosine similarity measure for SVNS and an application of cosine similarity measure for RNS was given in medical diagnosis. Broumi and Smarandache [8] introduced a new distance measure between two neutrosophic refined sets based on extended Hausdorff distance of neutrosophic set and gave some of its basic properties and also applied this distance measure in medical diagnosis problem. Broumi and Deli [7] introduced correlation measures for neutrosophic refined sets, which is the extension of correlation measures for neutrosophic sets and intuitionistic fuzzy multi-sets and applied this measure in medical diagnosis and pattern recognition problems. Jun Ye [9] introduced two cotangent similarity measures of single-valued neutrosophic sets on the basis of cotangent function and then also proposed weighted cotangent similarity measures and gave a comparison study between cotangent similarity measures for SVNS and cosine similarity measures for SVNS. An application of cotangent similarity measure was also given in fault detection of steam turbine. Molodtsov [10] proposed a new concept of soft set theory as to deal with uncertainties. Maji et al. [11]

studied soft sets related operations. Maji [12] proposed neutrosophic soft sets as a combination of neutrosophic sets and soft sets and gave its applications in decision-making problems. Said and Smarandache [13] introduced the concept of intuitionistic neutrosophic soft set with operations and some of its properties. Shahin et al. [14] proposed the notion of neutrosophic soft expert set with its basic operations such as "union, complement, intersection, OR, and AND," and gave some of its properties and also applied it in decision-making problems. Karaaslan [15] proposed the notion of single-valued neutrosophic refined soft set, which is the extension of RSVNS and introduced the theoretical operations between SVNRSS and also studied elementary properties of these operations. Two methods for calculating correlation coefficient between two SVNRSS and a clustering analysis of the proposed one of the two methods were also introduced by him. Mukherjee and Sarkar [16] introduced a novel method for measuring similarity measure and weighted similarity measure between two NSS and compared it with the existing similarity measures for NSS. Many researchers introduced divergence measures, various notions on neutrosophic sets and applied them in different practical problems [17–32]. A method for solving decision-making problem was given with numerical illustration, and similarity measure was applied in pattern recognition problem.

5.2 EXPERIMENTAL METHODS AND MATERIALS

5.2.1 PRELIMINARIES

In this section, some basic concepts associated with neutrosophic sets are presented.

➢ **Definition 5.1:** [1] A neutrosophic set U defined on a universal set X is:

$$U = \left\{ d_j, \Upsilon(d_j), \Psi(d_j), \Theta(d_j) \mid d_j \in X \right\} \tag{1}$$

where; $\Upsilon(d_j)$ represents truth membership function, $\Psi(d_j)$ represents indeterminacy membership function and $\Theta(d_j)$ represents falsity membership function and are real standard or non-standard subsets of $\left]0^-, 1^+\right[$ that is $\Upsilon(d_j): X \to \left]0^-, 1^+\right[$, $\Psi(d_j): X \to \left]0^-, 1^+\right[$ and $\Theta(d_j): X \to \left]0^-, 1^+\right[$ and $0^- \leq \Upsilon(d_j) + \Psi(d_j) + \Theta(d_j) \leq 3^+$.

- **Definition 5.2:** [1, 6] A single-valued neutrosophic set U defined on a universal set X is:

$$U = \{d_j, \Upsilon(d_j), \Psi(d_j), \Theta(d_j) \mid d_j \in X\} \tag{2}$$

where; $\Upsilon(d_j)$, $\Psi(d_j)$, $\Theta(d_j) \in [0,1]$ such that $0 \le \Upsilon(d_j) + \Psi(d_j) + \Theta(d_j) \le 3$ for all $d_j \in X$.

- **Definition 5.3.** Let $U = \{d_j, \Upsilon_U(d_j), \Psi_U(d_j), \Theta_U(d_j) \mid d_j \in X\}$ and $W = \{d_j, \Upsilon_W(d_j), \Psi_W(d_j), \Theta_W(d_j) \mid d_j \in X\}$ be two SVNSs then the following operations are given as:

  i. $U = W$ if $\Upsilon_U(d_j) \le \Upsilon_W(d_j), \Psi_U(d_j) \ge \Psi_W(d_j)$ and $\Theta_U(d_j) \ge \Theta_W(d_j)$ for all $d_j \in X$.

  ii. $U = W$ if and only if $U \subseteq W$ and $U \supseteq W$.

  iii. $U^c = \{d_j, \Theta_U(d_j), \Psi_U(d_j), \Upsilon_U(d_j) \mid d_j \in X\}$

  iv. $U \cap W = \{d_j, \min(\Upsilon_U(d_j), \Upsilon_W(d_j)), \max(\Psi_U(d_j), \Psi_W(d_j)),$
  $\max(\Theta_U(d_j), \Theta_W(d_j)) \mid d_j \in X\}$

  v. $U \cup W = \{d_j, \max(\Upsilon_U(d_j), \Upsilon_W(d_j)), \min(\Psi_U(d_j), \Psi_W(d_j)),$
  $\min(\Theta_U(d_j), \Theta_W(d_j)) \mid d_j \in X$

- **Definition 5.4:** [18] Let $U = \{d_j, (\Upsilon^1{}_U(d_j), \Upsilon^2{}_U(d_j), ...\Upsilon^q{}_U(d_j)),$
$(\mid \Psi^1{}_U(d_j), \Psi^2{}_U(d_j), ...\Psi^q{}_U(d_j)), (\Theta^1{}_U(d_j), \Theta^2{}_U(d_j), ...\Theta^q{}_U(d_j)) \mid d_j \in X$
and
$W = \{d_j, (\Upsilon^1{}_W(d_j), \Upsilon^2{}_W(d_j), ...\Upsilon^q{}_W(d_j)), (\mid \Psi^1{}_W(d_j), \Psi^2{}_W(d_j),$
$.....\Psi^q{}_W(d_j)), (\Theta^1{}_W(d_j), \Theta^2{}_W(d_j), ...\Theta^q{}_W(d_j)) \mid d_j \in X$ be two n-valued refined neutrosophic sets then:
$U \subseteq W \Rightarrow \Upsilon_U(d_j) \le \Upsilon_W(d_j), \Psi_U(d_j) \ge \Psi_W(d_j)$ and
$\Theta_U(d_j) \ge \Theta_W(d_j)$ for all $d_j \in X$ (3)

5.2.2 NEW DIVERGENCE MEASURE

For two n-valued neutrosophic sets $U = \{d_j, \Upsilon_U(d_j), \Psi_U(d_j), \Theta_U(d_j) \mid d_j \in X\}$ and $W = \{d_j, \Upsilon_W(d_j), \Psi_W(d_j), \Theta_W(d_j) \mid d_j \in X\}$ defined on a universal set X, the divergence measure of A against U is the measure of discrimination between A and U and is defined as:

$$D_{UW}(U\|W)=\frac{1}{nq}\sum_{j=1}^{n}\sum_{k=1}^{q}\left[\left(\frac{\left(\Upsilon^k{}_U(d_j)-\Upsilon^k{}_W(d_j)\right)^2(\Upsilon^k{}_U(d_j)+\Upsilon^k{}_W(d_j))}{\left(3\Upsilon^k{}_U(d_j)+\Upsilon^k{}_W(d_j)\right)\left(\Upsilon^k{}_U(d_j)+3\Upsilon^k{}_W(d_j)\right)}+\frac{\left(\Psi^k{}_U(d_j)-\Psi^k{}_W(d_j)\right)^2(\Psi^k{}_U(d_j)+\Psi^k{}_W(d_j))}{\left(3\Psi^k{}_U(d_j)+\Psi^k{}_W(d_j)\right)\left(\Psi^k{}_U(d_j)+3\Psi^k{}_W(d_j)\right)}+\frac{\left(\Theta^k{}_U(d_j)-\Theta^k{}_W(d_j)\right)^2(\Theta^k{}_U(d_j)+\Theta^k{}_W(d_j))}{\left(3\Theta^k{}_U(d_j)+\Theta^k{}_W(d_j)\right)\left(\Theta^k{}_U(d_j)+3\Theta^k{}_W(d_j)\right)}\right)\right] \quad (4)$$

The divergence measure $D_{UW}(U\|W)$ satisfies the following postulates:

i. $D_{UW}(U\|W)\geq 0$;
ii. $D_{UW}(U\|W)=D_{UW}(W\|U)$;
iii. If $U\subseteq W\subseteq Y$, $D_{UW}(U\|Y)\geq D_{UW}(U\|W)$ and $D_{UW}(U\|Y)\leq D_{UW}(W\|Y)$.

➢ **Proof 5.1:**

i. As $0\leq\Upsilon_U(d_j),\Psi_U(d_j),\Theta_U(d_j)\leq 1$ and $0\leq\Upsilon_W(d_j),\Psi_W(d_j),\Theta_W(d_j)\leq 1$, then

$$\frac{\left(\Upsilon_U(d_j)-\Upsilon_W(d_j)\right)^2(\Upsilon_U(d_j)+\Upsilon_W(d_j))}{\left(3\Upsilon_U(d_j)+\Upsilon_W(d_j)\right)\left(\Upsilon_U(d_j)+3\Upsilon_W(d_j)\right)}\geq 0,$$

$$\frac{\left(\Psi_U(d_j)-\Psi_W(d_j)\right)^2(\Psi_U(d_j)+\Psi_W(d_j))}{\left(3\Psi_U(d_j)+\Psi_W(d_j)\right)\left(\Psi_U(d_j)+3\Psi_W(d_j)\right)}\geq 0 \text{ and}$$

$$\frac{\left(\Theta_U(d_j)-\Theta_W(d_j)\right)^2(\Theta_U(d_j)+\Theta_W(d_j))}{\left(3\Theta_U(d_j)+\Theta_W(d_j)\right)\left(\Theta_U(d_j)+3\Theta_W(d_j)\right)}\geq 0.$$

Hence, from Eqn. (4), $D_{UW}(U\|W)\geq 0$

ii. It is straightforward.

iii. If $U\subseteq W\subseteq Y$, from Eqn. (3):
$U\subseteq W\Rightarrow\Upsilon_U(d_j)\leq\Upsilon_W(d_j),\Psi_U(d_j)\geq\Psi_W(d_j)$
$\Upsilon_U(d_j)\leq\Upsilon_W(d_j),\Psi_U(d_j)\geq\Psi_W(d_j)$ and $\Theta_U(d_j)\geq\Theta_W(d_j)$ for all $d_j\in X$.
$W\subseteq Y\Rightarrow\Upsilon_W(d_j)\leq\Upsilon_Y(d_j),\Psi_W(d_j)\geq\Psi_Y(d_j)$ and $\Theta_W(d_j)\geq\Theta_Y(d_j)$ for all $d_j\in X$.
$U\subseteq Y\Rightarrow\Upsilon_U(d_j)\leq\Upsilon_Y(d_j),\Psi_U(d_j)\geq\Psi_Y(d_j)$ and $\Theta_U(d_j)\geq\Theta_W(d_j)$ for all $d_j\in X$.
Therefore, $\Upsilon_U(d_j)\leq\Upsilon_W(d_j)\leq\Upsilon_Y(d_j)$, $\Psi_U(d_j)\geq\Psi_W(d_j)\geq\Psi_Y(d_j)$ $\Theta_U(d_j)\geq\Theta_W(d_j)\geq\Theta_Y(d_j)$.

Also,

$$\frac{\left(\Upsilon_U(d_j)-\Upsilon_W(d_j)\right)^2(\Upsilon_U(d_j)+\Upsilon_W(d_j))}{\left(3\Upsilon_U(d_j)+\Upsilon_W(d_j)\right)\left(\Upsilon_U(d_j)+3\Upsilon_W(d_j)\right)}\leq\frac{\left(\Upsilon_U(d_j)-\Upsilon_Y(d_j)\right)^2(\Upsilon_U(d_j)+\Upsilon_Y(d_j))}{\left(3\Upsilon_U(d_j)+\Upsilon_Y(d_j)\right)\left(\Upsilon_U(d_j)+3\Upsilon_Y(d_j)\right)}$$

$$\frac{\left(\Upsilon_W(d_j)-\Upsilon_Y(d_j)\right)^2(\Upsilon_W(d_j)+\Upsilon_Y(d_j))}{\left(3\Upsilon_W(d_j)+\Upsilon_Y(d_j)\right)\left(\Upsilon_W(d_j)+3\Upsilon_Y(d_j)\right)}\leq\frac{\left(\Upsilon_U(d_j)-\Upsilon_Y(d_j)\right)^2(\Upsilon_U(d_j)+\Upsilon_Y(d_j))}{\left(3\Upsilon_U(d_j)+\Upsilon_Y(d_j)\right)\left(\Upsilon_U(d_j)+3\Upsilon_Y(d_j)\right)}$$

$$\frac{\left(\Psi_U(d_j)-\Psi_W(d_j)\right)^2(\Psi_U(d_j)+\Psi_W(d_j))}{\left(3\Psi_U(d_j)+\Psi_W(d_j)\right)\left(\Psi_U(d_j)+3\Psi_W(d_j)\right)}\leq\frac{\left(\Psi_U(d_j)-\Psi_Y(d_j)\right)^2(\Psi_U(d_j)+\Psi_Y(d_j))}{\left(3\Psi_U(d_j)+\Psi_Y(d_j)\right)\left(\Psi_U(d_j)+3\Psi_Y(d_j)\right)}$$

$$\frac{\left(\Psi_W(d_j)-\Psi_Y(d_j)\right)^2(\Psi_W(d_j)+\Psi_Y(d_j))}{\left(3\Psi_W(d_j)+\Psi_Y(d_j)\right)\left(\Psi_W(d_j)+3\Psi_Y(d_j)\right)}\leq\frac{\left(\Psi_U(d_j)-\Psi_Y(d_j)\right)^2(\Psi_U(d_j)+\Psi_Y(d_j))}{\left(3\Psi_U(d_j)+\Psi_Y(d_j)\right)\left(\Psi_U(d_j)+3\Psi_Y(d_j)\right)}$$

$$\frac{\left(\Theta_U(d_j)-\Theta_W(d_j)\right)^2(\Theta_U(d_j)+\Theta_W(d_j))}{\left(3\Theta_U(d_j)+\Theta_W(d_j)\right)\left(\Theta_U(d_j)+3\Theta_W(d_j)\right)}\leq\frac{\left(\Theta_U(d_j)-\Theta_Y(d_j)\right)^2(\Theta_U(d_j)+\Theta_Y(d_j))}{\left(3\Theta_U(d_j)+\Theta_Y(d_j)\right)\left(\Theta_U(d_j)+3\Theta_Y(d_j)\right)}$$

$$\frac{\Theta_W(d_j)-\Theta_Y(d_j)\big)^2(\Theta_W(d_j)+\Theta_Y(d_j))}{3\Theta_W(d_j)+\Theta_Y(d_j)\big)\left(\Theta_W(d_j)+3\Theta_Y(d_j)\right)}\leq\frac{\left(\Theta_U(d_j)-\Theta_Y(d_j)\right)^2(\Theta_U(d_j)+\Theta_Y(d_j))}{\left(3\Theta_U(d_j)+\Theta_Y(d_j)\right)\left(\Theta_U(d_j)+3\Theta_Y(d_j)\right)}$$

Hence, if $U\subseteq W\subseteq Y$, $D_{UW}(U\|Y)\leq D_{UW}(U\|W)$ and $D_{UW}(U\|Y)\leq D_{UW}(W\|Y)$.

Therefore, it can be noted that $D_{UW}(U\|W)$ is a valid measure of divergence.

5.3 RESULTS AND DISCUSSION

5.3.1 CASE STUDY IN MEDICAL ANALYSIS

In this section, a new method for medical analysis is proposed for neutrosophic refined sets followed by an illustration to demonstrate the practicality of the approach. Our aim is to find the correct diagnosis for each patient. The algorithm for finding the correct disease is as follows:

- To find the patients-symptom relation, the symptoms characteristics of the patients are given in Table 5.1.
- The symptom characteristics of diseases are given in Table 5.2.
- Using the proposed divergence measure Eqn. (4), the calculated distances are shown in Table 5.3.

- From Table 5.3, the least value in each row concludes that which patient is suffering from which disease.

5.3.1.1 ILLUSTRATIVE EXAMPLE [33]

Consider four patients P_1, P_2, P_3, and P_4. Symptoms for the patients are temperature, headache, stomach pain, cough, and chest pain. These four patients are suffering from one of these diseases, which are Viral Fever, Malaria, Typhoid, Stomach Problem, and Chest Problem. Now, to diagnose which patient is suffering from which disease. Characteristic symptoms of patients are given in Table 5.1, and characteristic symptoms of diagnosis are given in Table 5.2.

TABLE 5.1 Characteristic Symptoms of Patients

	Temperature	Headache	Stomach Pain	Cough	Chest Pain
P_1	(0.8, 0.1, 0.1)	(0.6, 0.1, 0.3)	(0.2, 0.8, 0.0)	(0.6, 0.1, 0.3)	(0.1, 0.6, 0.3)
	(0.6, 0.3, 0.3)	(0.5, 0.2, 0.4)	(0.3, 0.5, 0.2)	(0.4, 0.4, 0.4)	(0.3, 0.4, 0.5)
	(0.6, 0.3, 0.1)	(0.5, 0.1, 0.2)	(0.2, 0.3, 0.4)	(0.4, 0.3, 0.3)	(0.2, 0.5, 0.4)
P_2	(0.0, 0.8, 0.2)	(0.4, 0.4, 0.2)	(0.6, 0.1, 0.3)	(0.1, 0.7, 0.2)	(0.1, 0.8, 0.1)
	(0.2, 0.6, 0.4)	(0.5, 0.4, 0.1)	(0.4, 0.2, 0.5)	(0.2, 0.7, 0.5)	(0.3, 0.6, 0.4)
	(0.1, 0.6, 0.4)	(0.4, 0.6, 0.3)	(0.3, 0.2, 0.4)	(0.3, 0.5, 0.4)	(0.3, 0.6, 0.3)
P_3	(0.8, 0.1, 0.1)	(0.8, 0.1, 0.1)	(0.0, 0.6, 0.4)	(0.2, 0.7, 0.1)	(0.0, 0.5, 0.5)
	(0.6, 0.4, 0.1)	(0.6, 0.2, 0.4)	(0.2, 0.5, 0.5)	(0.2, 0.5, 0.5)	(0.2, 0.5, 0.3)
	(0.5, 0.3, 0.3)	(0.6, 0.1, 0.3)	(0.3, 0.4, 0.6)	(0.1, 0.6, 0.3)	(0.3, 0.3, 0.4)
P_4	(0.6, 0.1, 0.3)	(0.5, 0.4, 0.1)	(0.3, 0.4, 0.3)	(0.7, 0.2, 0.1)	(0.3, 0.4, 0.3)
	(0.4, 0.3, 0.2)	(0.4, 0.4, 0.4)	(0.2, 0.4, 0.5)	(0.5, 0.2, 0.4)	(0.4, 0.3, 0.4)
	(0.5, 0.2, 0.3)	(0.5, 0.2, 0.4)	(0.1, 0.5, 0.4)	(0.6, 0.4, 0.1)	(0.3, 0.5, 0.5)

TABLE 5.2 Characteristic Symptoms of Diagnosis

	Viral Fever	Malaria	Typhoid	Stomach Problem	Chest Problem
Temperature	(0.6, 0.3, 0.3)	(0.2, 0.5, 0.3)	(0.2, 0.6, 0.4)	(0.1, 0.6, 0.6)	(0.1, 0.6, 0.4)
Headache	(0.4, 0.5, 0.3)	(0.2, 0.6, 0.4)	(0.1, 0.5, 0.4)	(0.2, 0.4, 0.6)	(0.1, 0.6, 0.4)
Stomach Pain	(0.1, 0.6, 0.3)	(0.0, 0.6, 0.4)	(0.2, 0.5, 0.5)	(0.8, 0.2, 0.2)	(0.1, 0.7, 0.1)
Cough	(0.4, 0.4, 0.4)	(0.4, 0.1, 0.5)	(0.2, 0.5, 0.5)	(0.1, 0.7, 0.4)	(0.4, 0.5, 0.4)
Chest Pain	(0.1, 0.7, 0.4)	(0.1, 0.6, 0.3)	(0.1, 0.6, 0.4)	(0.1, 0.7, 0.4)	(0.8, 0.2, 0.2)

TABLE 5.3 Calculated Diagnosis Results of Proposed Divergence Measure

	Viral Fever	Malaria	Typhoid	Stomach Problem	Chest Problem
P_1	**0.0880**	0.1657	0.1972	0.3971	0.3489
P_2	0.2162	0.1343	**0.0836**	0.1520	0.3029
P_3	**0.1185**	0.1949	0.1638	0.4159	0.3917
P_4	**0.0832**	0.1119	0.1569	0.4259	0.2447

From Table 5.3, it is noted that P_1 is suffering from viral fever, P_2 is suffering from typhoid, P_3 is suffering from viral fever, and P_4 is also suffering from viral fever. Therefore, the proposed method is a reliable method to handle medical diagnosis problems.

5.3.2 CASE STUDY IN PROJECT SELECTION

Generally, in the problems of decision making, there is a set of alternatives and a set of attributes, but in this case, the attributes can have some sub-attributes. Consider:

$$R_k = \left\{T_j, \left(\Upsilon^1{}_{R_k}(T_j), \Upsilon^2{}_{R_k}(T_j)........\Upsilon^j{}_{R_k}(T_j)\right), \left(\Psi^1{}_{R_k}(T_j), \Psi^2{}_{R_k}(T_j)......\Psi^j{}_{R_k}(T_j)\right),\right.$$
$$\left.\left(\Theta^1{}_{R_k}(T_j), \Theta^2{}_{R_k}(T_j)........\Theta^j{}_{R_k}(T_j) \mid T_j \in T\right)\right\}$$

k = 1, 2,.... m j = 1, 2,....... n.

The divergence measure for decision making in project selection is given as:

$$D_{UW}(R_k \| S^*) = \frac{1}{n}\sum_{j=1}^{n}\sum_{k=1}^{q}\left[\left(\begin{array}{l} \dfrac{\left(\Upsilon^j{}_{R_k}(T_j) - \Upsilon^j{}_{S^*}(T_j)\right)^2 (\Upsilon^j{}_{R_k}(T_j) + \Upsilon^j{}_{S^*}(T_j))}{\left(3\Upsilon^j{}_{R_k}(T_j) + \Upsilon^j{}_{S^*}(T_j)\right)\left(\Upsilon^j{}_{R_k}(T_j) + 3\Upsilon^j{}_{S^*}(T_j)\right)} + \\ \dfrac{\left(\Psi^j{}_{R_k}(T_j) - \Psi^j{}_{S^*}(T_j)\right)^2 (\Psi^j{}_{R_k}(T_j) + \Psi^j{}_{S^*}(T_j))}{\left(3\Psi^j{}_{R_k}(T_j) + \Psi^j{}_{S^*}(T_j)\right)\left(\Psi^j{}_{R_k}(T_j) + 3\Psi^j{}_{S^*}(T_j)\right)} \\ + \dfrac{\left(\Theta^j{}_{R_k}(T_j) - \Theta^j{}_{S^*}(T_j)\right)^2 (\Theta^j{}_{R_k}(T_j) + \Theta^j{}_{S^*}(T_j))}{\left(3\Theta^j{}_{R_k}(T_j) + \Theta^j{}_{S^*}(T_j)\right)\left(\Theta^j{}_{R_k}(T_j) + 3\Theta^j{}_{S^*}(T_j)\right)} \end{array}\right) / q\right] \quad (5)$$

The single values of the functions $\Upsilon^j{}_{R_k}(T_j), \Psi^j{}_{R_k}(T_j)$ and $\Theta^j{}_{R_k}(T_j)$ can be defined by using refined neutrosophic sets. Steps for the procedure are as follows:

i. Construct refined neutrosophic decision matrix.
ii. From decision matrix, to find ideal solution which is denoted by S^*

$$S^* = \left\langle \left(\Upsilon^1{}_{S_m}{}^{\max}, \Upsilon^2{}_{S_m}{}^{\max}, \ldots\ldots \Upsilon^t{}_{S_m}{}^{\max} \right), \left(\Psi^1{}_{S_m}{}^{\min}, \Psi^2{}_{S_m}{}^{\min}, \ldots\ldots\ldots \Psi^t{}_{S_m}{}^{\min} \right), \left(\Theta^1{}_{S_m}{}^{\min}, \Theta^2{}_{S_m}{}^{\min}, \ldots\ldots \Theta^t{}_{S_m}{}^{\min} \right) \right\rangle$$

$$j = 1, 2, \ldots\ldots\ldots n \tag{6}$$

iii. According to the values of the divergence measures using Eqn. (5), rank can be given to the alternatives in descending order. The alternative with the minimum value will be the best alternative.

5.3.2.1 ILLUSTRATIVE EXAMPLE [34]

Consider, a construction company wants to select a construction project out of four projects. Hence, R_1, R_2, R_3, and R_4 are given as four alternatives. This project is to be selected on the basis of three attributes and these attributes have seven sub-attributes namely, financial state (T_1): budget control (T_{11}) and risk/return ratio (T_{12}); environmental protection (T_2): public relation (T_{21}), geographical location (T_{22}) and health and safety (T_{23}); technology (T_3): technical knowhow (T_{31}) and technological capability (T_{32}). Our aim is to select the best alternative out of these four alternatives under refined neutrosophic environment.

The refined neutrosophic decision matrix is given in Table 5.4. By using decision matrix in Table 5.4 and formula Eqn. (6), ideal solution can be calculated which is given as:

$$S^* = \left\{ \left\langle (0.8, 0.8), (0.1, 0.1), (0.2, 0.2) \right\rangle, \left\langle (0.9, 0.8, 0.8), (0.1, 0.1, 0.1), (0.1, 0.1, 0.1) \right\rangle, \left\langle (0.8, 0.8), (0.1, 0.2), (0.1, 0.1) \right\rangle \right\}$$

By using Eqn. (5) values of the divergence measures are as follows:

$D_{UW}(R_1 \| S^*) = 0.0360$, $D_{UW}(R_2 \| S^*) = 0.0181$, $D_{UW}(R_3 \| S^*) = 0.0361$ and $D_{UW}(R_4 \| S^*) = 0.0336$

It is noted that $D_{UW}(R_2 \| S^*) \prec D_{UW}(R_4 \| S^*) \prec D_{UW}(R_1 \| S^*) \prec D_{UW}(R_3 \| S^*)$. Therefore, the order of preference of the four alternatives is $R_2 \succ R_4 \succ R_1 \succ R_3$. Hence project R_2 is the optimum choice for the construction company.

TABLE 5.4 Neutrosophic Decision Matrix

	$T_1(T_{11}, T_{12})$	$T_2(T_{21}, T_{22}, T_{23})$	$T_3(T_{31}, T_{32}, T_{33})$
R_1	< (0.6, 0.7), (0.2, 0.1), (0.2, 0.3) >	< (0.9, 0.7, 0.8), (0.1, 0.3, 0.2), (0.2, 0.2, 0.1) >	< (0.6, 0.8), (0.3, 0.2), (0.3 0.4) >
R_2	< (0.8, 0.7), (0.1, 0.2), (0.3, 0.2) >	< (0.7, 0.8, 0.7), (0.2, 0.4, 0.3), (0.1, 0.2, 0.2) >	< (0.8, 0.8), (0.1, 0.2), (0.1, 0.2) >
R_3	< (0.6, 0.8), (0.1, 0.3), (0.3, 0.4) >	< (0.8, 0.6, 0.7), (0.3, 0.1, 0.1), (0.2, 0.1, 0.2) >	< (0.8, 0.7), (0.4, 0.3), (0.2, 0.1) >
R_4	< (0.7, 0.6), (0.1, 0.2), (0.2, 0.3) >	< (0.7, 0.8, 0.7), (0.2, 0.2, 0.1), (0.1, 0.2, 0.2) >	< (0.7, 0.7), (0.2, 0.3), (0.2, 0.3) >

5.4 CONCLUSION

In this chapter, a novel divergence measure under refined neutrosophic environment is proposed with its proof of validity. The application of the proposed divergence measure is given in decision making such as medical diagnosis and in project selection. It is noticed that when other existing divergence measures and decision-making methods are unable to find the solutions, the proposed method under refined neutrosophic environment works effectively to find better results.

KEYWORDS

- **decision making**
- **divergence measure**
- **fuzzy multi-sets**
- **medical diagnosis**
- **neutrosophic environment**
- **refined n-valued neutrosophic sets**

REFERENCES

1. Smarandache, F., (1995). *Neutrosophic Logic and Set, mss.* http://fs.gallup.unm.edu/neutrosophy.htm.

2. Smarandache, F., (1998). *Neutrosophy, Neutrosophic Probability, Set, and Logic.* American Research Press, Rehoboth, USA.
3. Smarandache, F., (2005). Neutrosophic set, a generalization of the intuitionistic fuzzy sets. *International Journal of Pure and Applied Mathematics, 24*, 287–297.
4. Agboola, A. A., (2015). On refined neutrosophic algebraic structures. *Neutrosophic Sets and Systems, 10*, 99–101.
5. Broumi, S., Deli, I., & Smarandache, F., (2015). *Critical Review* (Vol. X, pp. 45–69). Chapter 'n'-valued interval neutrosophic sets and their application in medical diagnosis. Center for Mathematics of Uncertainty, Creighton University, USA.
6. Smarandache, F., (1999). *A Unifying Field of Logics, Neutrosophy: Neutrosophic Probability, Set and Logic*. American Research Press, Rehoboth.
7. Broumi, S., & Deli, I., (2014). Correlation measure for neutrosophic refined sets and its application in medical diagnosis. *Palestine Journal of Mathematics, 3*(1), 11–19.
8. Broumi, S., & Smarandache, F., (2015). Extended Hausdorff distance and similarity measures for neutrosophic refined sets and their application in medical diagnosis. *Journal of New Theory, 7*, 64–78.
9. Ye, J., (2015). Single-valued neutrosophic similarity measures based on cotangent function and their application in the fault diagnosis of steam turbine. *Soft Computing*, 1–9.
10. Molodtsov, D., (1999). Soft set theory-first results. *Computers and Mathematics with Applications, 37*, 19–31.
11. Maji, P., Roy, A., & Biswas, R., (2003). Soft set theory. *Computers and Mathematics with Applications, 45*, 555–562.
12. Maji, P., (2013). Neutrosophic soft set. *Annals of Fuzzy Mathematics and Informatics, 5*(1), 157–168.
13. Broumi, S., & Smarandache, F., (2013). Intuitionistic neutrosophic soft set. *Journal of Information and Computing Science, 8*(2), 130–140.
14. Shahin, M., Alkhazaleh, S., & Ulucay, V., (2015). Neutrosophic soft expert sets. *Applied Mathematics, 6*, 116–127.
15. Karaaslan, F., (2016). Correlation coefficients of single- valued neutrosophic refined soft sets and their applications in clustering analysis, *Neural Computing and Applications*, 1–13.
16. Mukherjee, A., & Sarkar, S., (2015). A new method of measuring similarity between two neutrosophic soft sets and its application in pattern recognition problems. *Neutrosophic Sets and Systems, 8,* 63–68.
17. Broumi, S., & Smarandache, F., (2014). Neutrosophic refined similarity measure based on cosine function. *Neutrosophic Sets and Systems, 6*, 42–48.
18. Deli, I., Broumi, S., & Smarandache, F., (2015). On neutrosophic refined sets and their applications in medical diagnosis. *Journal of New Theory, 6*, 88–98.
19. Khatod, N., & Saraswat, R. N., (2019). Symmetric fuzzy divergence measure, decision making and medical diagnosis problems. *Journal of Intelligent and Fuzzy Systems, 36*(6), 5721–5729.
20. Mondal, K., & Pramanik, S., (2015). Neutrosophic refined similarity measure based on cotangent function and its application to multi-attribute decision making. *Global Journal of Advanced Research, 2*(2), 486–496.
21. Mondal, K., & Pramanik, S., (2015). Neutrosophic refined similarity measure based on tangent function and its application to multi-attribute decision making. *Journal of New Theory, 8*, 41–50.

22. Saraswat, R. N., & Umar, A., (2020). New fuzzy divergence measure and its applications in multi-criteria decision making using new tool. *Mathematical Analysis II: Optimization Differential Equations and Graph Theory, Springer Proceedings in Mathematics and Statistics*. Springer, Singapore, 307191-205.
23. Saraswat, R. N., & Khatod, N., (2020). New fuzzy divergence measures, series, its bounds and applications in strategic decision making. *Intelligent Computing Techniques for Smart Energy Systems, Lecture Notes in Electrical Engineering (Springer), 607*, 641–653.
24. Smarandache, F., (1998). *Neutrosophy, Neutrosophic Probability, Set, and Logic*. American Research Press, Rehoboth, USA.
25. Smarandache, F., (2005). Neutrosophic set, a generalization of the intuitionistic fuzzy sets. *International Journal of Pure and Applied Mathematics, 24*, 287–297.
26. Umar, A., & Saraswat, R. N., (2020). Novel divergence measure under neutrosophic environment and its utility in various problems of decision making. *International Journal of Fuzzy System Applications, 9*(4).
27. Umar, A., & Saraswat, R. N., (2020). New generalized intuitionistic fuzzy divergence measure with applications to multi-attribute decision making and pattern recognition. *Recent Advances in Computer Science and Communications (Recent Patents on Computer Science)*, 13.
28. Wang, W. J., (1997). New similarity measures on fuzzy sets and elements. *Fuzzy Sets and Systems, 85*(3), 305–309.
29. Ye, J., & Du, S., (2019). Some distances, similarity and entropy measures for interval-valued neutrosophic sets and their relationship. *International Journal of Machine Learning and Cybernetics, 10*(2), 347–355.
30. Ye, J., (2019). Hesitant interval neutrosophic linguistic set and its application in multiple attribute decision making. *International Journal of Machine Learning and Cybernetics, 10*(4), 667–678.
31. Yong, R., Zhu, A., & Ye, J., (2019). Multiple attribute decision method using similarity measure of cubic hesitant fuzzy sets. *Journal of Intelligent and Fuzzy Systems, 37*(1), 1075–1083.
32. Zhang, X., Wang, X., Smarandache, F., Jaiycola, T. G., & Lian, T., (2019). Singular neutrosophic extended triplet groups and generalized groups. *Cognitive Systems Research, 57*, 32–40.
33. Samuel, A. E., & Narmadhagnanam, R., (2017). Neutrosophic refined sets in medical diagnosis. *International Journal of Fuzzy Mathematical Archive, 14*(1), 117–123.
34. Ye, J., & Smarandache, F., (2016). Similarity measure of refined single-valued neutrosophic sets and its multi-criteria decision-making method. *Neutrosophic Sets and Systems, 12*, 41–44.

CHAPTER 6

IMPLEMENTATION OF QUICK RESPONSE CODE IN ELECTRONIC RECORDS FOR HEALTHCARE MONITORING

ISHITA BANERJEE[1] and P. MADHUMATHY[2]

[1]*Research Scholar, Dayananda Sagar Academy of Technology and Management, Bangalore, Karnataka, India,*
E-mail: sakthi999@gmail.com

[2]*Professor, Dayananda Sagar Academy of Technology and Management, Bangalore, Karnataka, India*

ABSTRACT

With the growing population and increasing demand of medical supervision for maintaining a healthy society, the need for digitalization of medical data has a supreme importance. The traditional way to detail the health-related reports in chapter format has many drawbacks for long-term health monitoring or critical health-related issues. Here comes the importance of electronic health records (EHR) that can provide an uninterrupted flow of health-related information when and where required. To monitor chronically ill people, this EHR can be a very significant tool in the hands of medical practitioners. For example, patients with heart disease need a constant monitoring of the heart functionalities even if they are at a remote location. Even patients who need frequent laboratory checkups also face difficulty in maintaining the gradual reports. This remote EHR can reduce the cost of health care as well as more reliable, robust, and time-sensitive tools. With the ever-increasing rise in mobile technology and wireless communication, this electronic health monitoring can be proved to be the most promising platform for maintaining and sharing health records. In this chapter, we propose an effective method of quick response (QR) codes that can be implemented for health care monitoring. We propose to implement the QR code in various places of the hospital. The QR code reader application will be implemented on smartphones or other electronic devices such as tablets. These devices can scan the QR codes which are generated by the hospitals in several copies along with the specific identity of each patient. Here we also recommend using the QR identity tag that will help the users of this application to carry their own health-related information. This QR code-based EHR maintenance tool can be proved to be cost-effective if implemented on a large scale, taking a whole nation into consideration. The use of this tool can eliminate the security hazards such as lack of integrity, confidentiality, and authenticity. Advanced encryption standard is one of the encryption schemes that is used for improving the security of the data stored in the QR code. In this chapter, the implementation of the QR code is done for the major purpose of laboratory report exchange effectively and effortlessly.

6.1 INTRODUCTION

To maintain a country's health profile, it is important to adapt the digitalization of medical sector in terms of keeping the patient's laboratory records. The most traditional way of keeping a laboratory report is in chapter format which could be lost/damaged easily. Even to compare several consecutive results or analyze long-term recovery reports, it is a tedious task to compare, read, and work with the chapter documents. To maintain the continuity of the health reports, past, present, and future health reports can be integrated effectively using electronic health records (EHR) [1, 2]. It is a personal repository of health-related data and laboratory reports that are to be kept for treatment or further reference. The accuracy, robustness, and availability of data save many lives in critical situations [3]. EHR could be highly accepted by medical professionals, nurses, and medical technicians due to its various advantages [4, 5]. Implementation of EHR might ask for some extensive planning and a good amount of investment but could lead to the betterment of the health of the people of the country. Professionals from the corners of the world have accepted the introduction of digital data gathering techniques, which could lead to the success of EHR due to its user-friendly application.

The increased number of chronically ill people and their long-term monitoring has become a new challenge to the health care field. Irrespective of whether they need hospital accommodation or not, they need an assistive service for them even in the remote location. Day-by-day, remote health care monitoring is being well accepted by the patients and medical professionals both. To facilitate this different mobile and wireless technologies come into picture [6]. With the advancement of medical science, telemedicine extended its application though the movement is restricted for the patient. Remote health care monitoring with mobile technologies are more convenient since they support mobility of the patient [7]. The usage of mobile phones, tablets, and other supporting electronic devices are working hand in hand as an interface to connect the medical world to the patient remotely [8]. In the case of health care monitoring at a remote place, the health-related parametric data is to be collected, and according to the necessity, it is transferred to the medical center for any action to be taken if required. Initially, the data collected by the respective sensor is stored in the mobile server, and then it is processed/transferred to the caregiver. On receiving the health-related data, the patient gets instructions from the medical team for further actions to be taken. To make this more user-friendly and accessible, we propose to keep the patient data in the form of a QR code. We have worked on the laboratory reports that can be stored and made available via the QR codes, but this can also be implemented to provide remote health care monitoring where the data collected by the sensor network can also be stored in the QR codes to increase the security and robustness of the system [9–11].

QR codes or 2D barcodes are incorporated with mobile devices to implement the EHR as proposed. This supports an authentic and personalized mobile learning environment. The QR code is implemented on white background with black bars. Generally, it may contain subject data or URL or text encapsulated in a black and white square pattern. Mobile phones or other supporting electronic devices can scan the QR code with its camera and replicate the information encapsulated in the code. For this purpose, the QR code reader application is to be implemented in the mobile device. This approach minimizes the chapter-based record-keeping system and also enhances the authenticity and security of user data making it user-friendly [12–14].

6.2 MOTIVATION

To access the patient medical records or medical test related data digitally, it is very important to take some degrees of security measurements. Information stored in the electronic format may be tampered with by the patient unintentionally or by a third party which may cause a huge impact on the patient's treatment. If the patient record is in chapter format, this may lead to mishandling and any unauthorized body can maliciously use and affect the patient information. To maintain the integrity, authenticity, and confidentiality of the patient medical information, we propose a system of storing the patient laboratory reports in the form of QR codes. Implementation of such QR code promises secure transfer of data from the laboratory to patient and then to the physicians or healthcare adviser with greater confidentiality [14, 15].

6.3 LITERATURE SURVEY

Patient medical records have been one of the active and challenging research areas in the field of medicine day-by-day, different techniques and methodology are proposed for making patient medical details simpler to carry anywhere, anytime. In this proposed work, we have referred to the following chapters as discussed.

The authors state in "The psychology behind QR codes" that QR-codes or quick response codes are widely used in the medical field to give support to the medical team as well as to the patient [16]. In this chapter, authors have made use of QR code to communicate laboratory results of the patients. This is done to transmit data between the laboratory and a patient and then between the patient and the EHR. AES was implemented for increasing the security of data stored in the QR-code segment. To conduct the experiment LabSeq is used. The mobile application used here enables a decoding technique. The enciphered data is also stored. This work is proposed to be applied on the electronic glass devices which can read graphical patterns and process the data accordingly. The electronic glass can be simulated using a mobile phone as discussed in this chapter. Health Level 7 standards or JavaScript object notation (JSON) is used to transfer the data between the patient and the EHR. To integrate the data faster for information exchange between patient and healthcare professional this scheme was proposed.

1. As stated in "Identity Document Authentication Based on VSS and QR Codes," that the proposed system in the above-mentioned chapter consists of QR-codes that can be installed at convenient places in the hospital and the mobile devices with QR code readers can scan the code to gather the required information about the stored data of the patient [17]. Many copies of the patient records are produced for each patient. The QR code also provides identification of the patients. QR identity tag helps in performing the identification-related issues. Using this, the patient can monitor the health-related data on their

own. The proposed method in this chapter claims to be cost-effective if implemented in developing countries.

2. We can see that researchers proposed a bar code technology in "Understanding 2D-barcode technology and applications in m-commerce-design and implementation of a 2D barcode processing solution" [18]. Bar-code and QR codes are used to provide information about the product. For accessing the information hidden in the code, the users need to read and decipher the code. Here the authors have proposed an encryption and decryption-based QR coding system to keep the Personal Health Record. The use of Asynchronous Encryption Standard strengthens the security aspect of the data stored in the bar code. The proposed chapter contains three modules LabSeq-P, LabSeq-L, LabSeq-D, where P dictates for Patient and L dictate for Laboratory and D dictates for Doctor. Patient must access the required information in JSON. Here also the data exchange is done with the help of mobile devices and EHRs.
3. As discussed in "A Novel Secret Sharing Technique Using QR Code." the impact of several risk factors related to healthcare [19]. In Malaysia, following the medication schedule is a prior factor to be taken care of. The issues related to the failure of following the medication guidelines are discussed in the chapter. The reasons for not consuming the medicines can be financial or due to lack of understanding of the prescribed regime or due to outcome of some side effects of the medicines. The above-stated issues can be taken care of sensitively so that the patient medicine intake can be continued as required for their health. The authors have proposed an application to track the medicine intake of the patients again using smartphones and QR codes. For each medicine intake, a proof work is done to signify maintaining the correct medicine intake regime. The QR code is printed on the medicine labels, which can be scanned and kept stored in the QR code. The prime contribution of this work is to maintain a regular routine for the patients about the medications they are taking. The data such as URL links or document files or texts can be stored in the form of a bar code. In this chapter, the bar code used is known as QR code. The QR code looks like a small square box. Each box is a combination of small white and black color arrangements. QR code generator is software that converts data into a QR code. If a camera is available in a mobile device with a QR code reader application, then it can easily scan and retrieve the data stored in the QR code. QR codes have widespread applications in the

business, retail, industry, and healthcare field. In this chapter referred the authors describe different techniques of implementing QR codes in the education field. QR codes provide a collaborative and interactive teaching and learning environment.

4. In "authentication system using QR code." reports an automated data entry for health notification mobile application [20]. The proposed work can automate the data entry technology and integrate it with mobile health or m-health. This also makes use of encoded data in the form of QR code and eliminates the scope of chapter-based data storage system. This m-health application has android based OS and devices. The application is associated with an automated data entry system regarding medication time, doctor appointment, etc. The proposed application makes use of the traditional android features such as the Broadcast and Broadcast Receiver, and Alarm Manager.
5. As discussed in "Poultry Contractual Farming Decision Support System" that QR codes are two dimensional barcodes that can effectively store data and can be scanned to decode it using something like smartphones that support QR code reader software [21]. The major issues related to QR codes are related to the security and authenticity. Some malicious programs might run programs to hack the sensitive information hidden in the code, which can be harmful for the users. There comes the most important aspect of implementing encoding and decoding or encryption and decryption of QR codes using reliable techniques. This proposed work may run in android based system, which could prove to be little overhead for the system nut keeping in mind the security aspect, it must be highly appreciated. The authors have also taken care about the validity of information stored in the QR code as well the authentication of the user is taken care of.
6. Here the authors noted the appearance of occurrence of QR codes in day-to-day life and approach to learn the work as proposed in "service learning meets mobile computing" [22]. The author proposed a methodology in which the text is entered onto the web browser, and that can generate the corresponding QR code. Drupal module and libqrencode C library develops the user level interface on the web browser. This also encapsulated data to create QR Code symbol. To conduct this experiment, two different languages were taken into account, such as English and Thai. With these languages, multiple and single lines of texts were considered. This resulted in

the success of the experiment where the required QR codes were correctly formed. The URL shortening services can generate QR codes which may direct a user to open the desired link by scanning the QR code with a QR code reader.

7. As authors state in their chapter "Contextual QR codes," that in the times of digitization and technological involvement in most of the fields, data security became a prime concern for the researchers [23]. The information stored in the QR codes is easily accessible and thus are open to security threats. There are several methods such as cryptography, watermarking, etc., that can provide security to some extend, but a greater work needs to be done to protect the information stored in the QR codes. In order to regularize the vehicle tracking, a Toyota subsidiary named Denso Wave invented QR code in 1994. This was initially invented to track and scan vehicle components. This QR code is a license free technique as Dense Wave did not impose any licensing on using it. The smartphone image reader can sense the bar code and interpret it into readable form by the system interpreter. With the advancement in technology, QR codes are widely in use in the healthcare sector [24, 25]. These techniques are highly reliable in log management for patient health records [26].

6.4 PROPOSED METHODOLOGY

In the era of digitization, it is very easy to transfer data, but the major challenge lies in maintaining the privacy of the job. To make the data reach to the desired destination is very important to maintain a higher level of confidentiality to avoid any kind of malicious attacks on the data traveling. It is also important to keep in mind that only the authorized person must access the information and no one else. Let us discuss our approach to meet such challenges and propose a system to overcome them. The block diagram of the proposed system is discussed below:

6.4.1 TRAINING PHASE

- Here we propose to create one easy and accessible technique of data exchange maintaining standard formats and focusing on the system architecture. The laboratory results will be interpreted into QR codes for the ease of interaction and maintenance of information.

- QR codes are implemented in many fields of real-life including healthcare sector. Here we propose a system that will help the doctor a speedy and reliable access to the patient information (Figure 6.1).

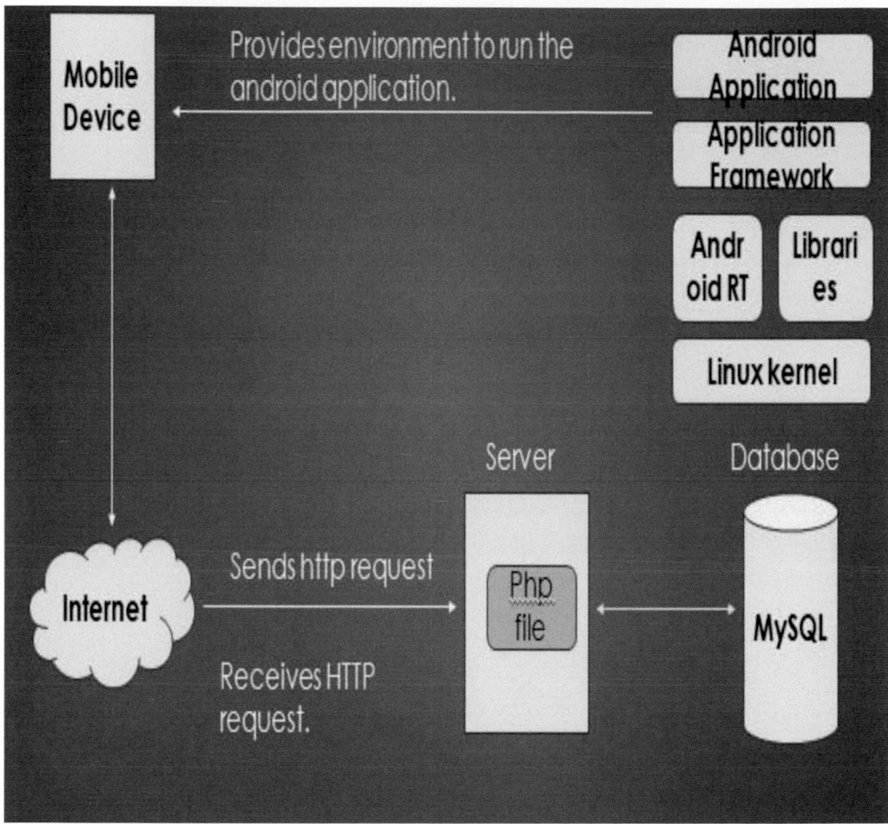

FIGURE 6.1 Training phase.

- In our proposed work, we though implement a system that helps exchange of medical reports between doctor and the patient but focusing more towards the patient so that the patient can conveniently access the laboratory reports which are encapsulated and stored in the QR code as a form of encrypted medical information.
- Along with the above factors, we also propose to provide mobile application support to implement the proposed work. This application will transfer data from chapter format to EHRs. The data must be securely handled (Figure 6.2).

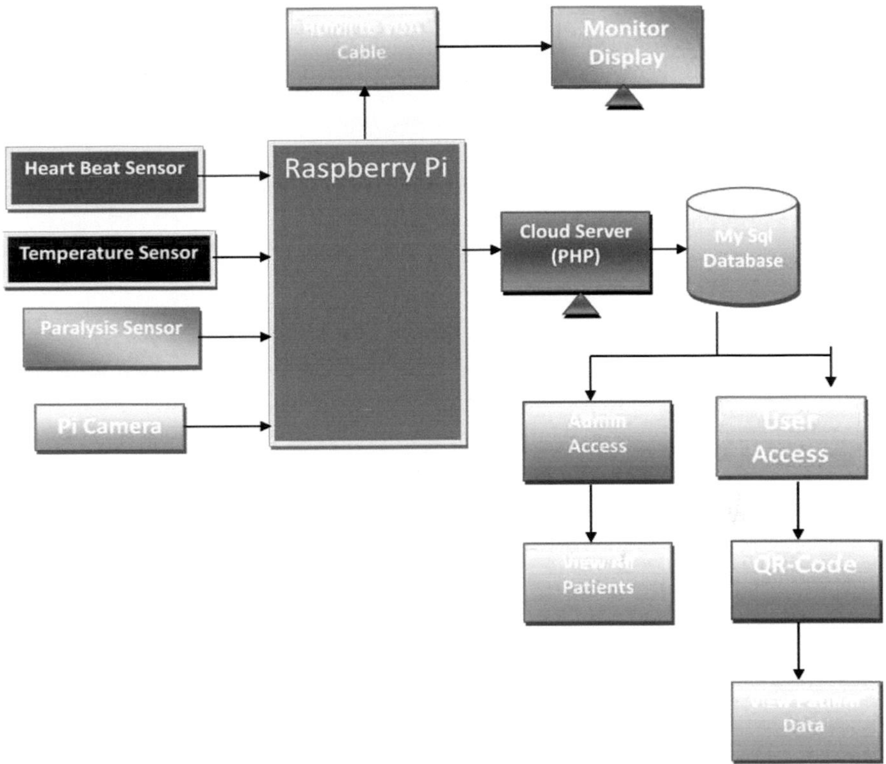

FIGURE 6.2 Testing phase.

6.4.2 TESTING PHASE

QR codes are generally implemented in terms of bar codes. Here we propose a system to be implemented for exchange of laboratory results. This work helps the patients to get information from the laboratory and also gives access to the EHRs. To provide security to the data encapsulated in the bar code, the AES scheme is used for data encryption. LabSeq is used to implement the proposed scheme. To simulate the electronic glasses, a smartphone is considered. The laboratory results of the patients are stored in the patient's personal database by LabSeq setup. The mobile application of our proposed project helps to keep the order and integrity of the patient records in the system database. The upcoming scopes in the form of eGlasses can open more and more possibilities to this field. The support physicians and patients are getting in this process is commendable as accessing the test results of the patients are very reliable and easy using this technique which can improve the accuracy and promptness of the healthcare process.

The hardware we used are interfaces with raspberry pi. Temperature sensor LM35 or LM34 could be used. We used LM34. These are types of precision integrated-circuit temperature sensors. The output voltage of LM34 is linearly proportional to the temperature (in Fahrenheit). The temperature range supported by LM34 is rated to –50° to +300°F whereas LM35 can give the temperature in terms of centigrade. According to application specific needs, any of the of precision integrated-circuit temperature sensors such as LM34 or LM35 can be used. The temperature range supported by LM35 from –55°C to +150°C. The users are open to use any of these two temperature sensors according to their requirements. Similarly, we can now discuss about the heart rate sensor. We make use of flash LED where each LED flash indicates a single heartbeat. The microcontroller installed can measure the beats per minute (BPM) rate. It takes account of the heart rate measurement by measuring the blood flow finger per heartbeat.

The measurement of our circuit board is 25 mm × 20 mm × 9 mm. This can interconnect the Raspberry Pi camera serial interface (CSI) bus connector to a flexible ribbon cable. The camera in use must follow few critical specifications, such as the native resolution of five megapixels. It must contain a lens which is having a fixed focus. For still images the camera resolution is up to 2592 × 1944 and for video resolutions the figure is 1080p30, 720p60 and 640 × 480p60/90. To measure the acceleration, we made use of accelerometers in the digital devices such as tablets or smartphones to display the images on screen upright. Accelerometers basically consist tilt sensors. As we know, force (= mass * acceleration), when the system faces linear acceleration, a force acts on the mass. The result is a deflection that can be sensed by suitable arrangements. This measured deflection is then converted to an electrical signal.

HDMI supports EIA/CEA-861 standards, to implement video and waveforms. It also supports compressed, uncompressed, LPCM audio and auxiliary data. It can implement VESA EDID. HDMI carries CEA-861 signals which are electrically compatible with the digital visual interface (DVI). The use of DVI-to-HDMI adapter does not account for any loss of signal quality of the video format. There is no need to convert the signal separately. The CEC (consumer electronics control) capability supports the interactive property of HDMI devices so that they can interact with each other when multiple devices are in use. For a user it is very convenient to handle many devices with a single handheld remote:

- The camera is ON and sensing for the arrival of the QR code.
- The input image is captured from the Pi camera. The image is taken to processing if not, the step is followed back from Pi camera.
- After taking the appropriate parameters from the sensors, they check for the relevant QR code.
- Then the sensor thresholds are taken care of, i.e., it compares the values of the patient to the threshold.
- Once this process is done then the prescription information is attained.
- The result is been viewed by the patient. The hardware circuit is shown in Figure 6.3.
- Phase-locked loop is been used in the hardware circuit.
- One the image information is been collected, then it has been processed to the amplifier block for amplification.
- A 10-bit analog to digital converter is to convertor the image to perfect digital form.
- First-in first-out principle is worked out here.
- The amplifier block is controlled through appropriate gain.

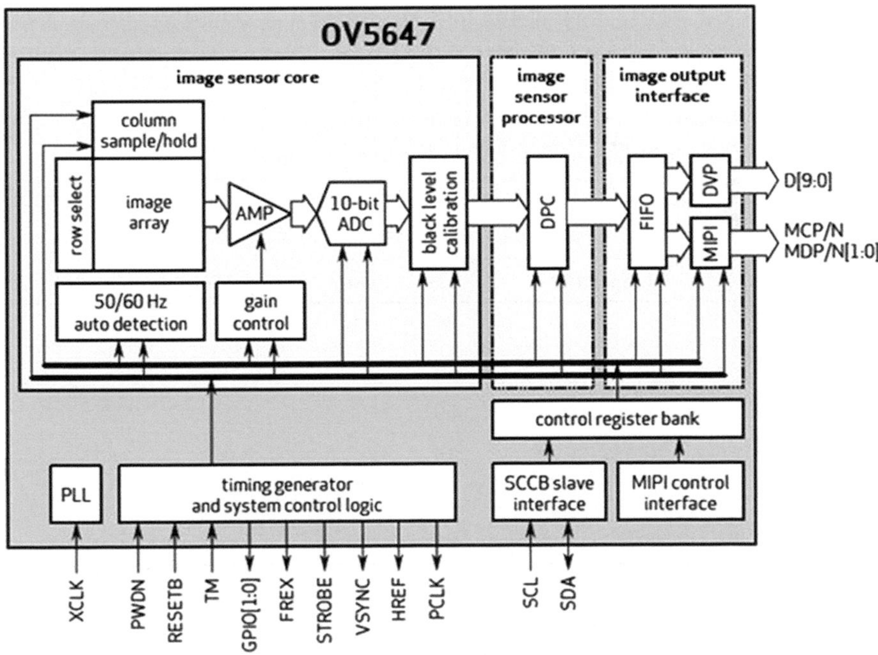

FIGURE 6.3 Hardware circuit.

6.5 RESULTS

To make the data reach to the desired destination is very important to maintain a higher level of confidentiality to avoid any kind of malicious attacks on the data traveling. It is also important to keep in mind that only the authorized person must access the information and no one else. To achieve this greater security, integrity, and confidentiality, we have implemented and evaluated the proposed work as discussed in subsections.

QR codes are specifically bar codes that are used in many live applications, including the healthcare sector. We have approached the use of QR codes to store and access the laboratory results of the patients. The data exchange between a laboratory and a patient first. This data is then stored in EHRs. The data encryption and encapsulation to store it in the form of QR codes are done by Advanced Encryption Standard. The experimental setup uses LabSeq. The electronic glass simulator is a smartphone in this proposed system. Once the patient's data is received from the laboratory, LabSeq is stored and managed as a patient's personal database.

We make use of a LabSeq mobile application to monitor, store, and make the access of the EHRs easy to the patients as well as doctors. This process promises to ease the data access for the doctor for timely response and prompt treatment. This process also eliminates the drawbacks of storing information in a chapter format. The test results of how the data is accessed by scanning the QR codes are tabulated (Table 6.1; Figures 6.4 and 6.5).

TABLE 6.1 Data Accessed for a Patient After Scanning the Code

Patient Name	Temperature	Heart Beat	Mobility
David	28	85	65
Naveen	28	85	0
Naveen	127	60	1
Naveen	28	85	0
Naveen	28	85	0
Naveen	28	85	0

The usefulness of HER can be considered very attractive to maintain the digital health profile for population health management. Public health care in local/state/national level has been a prime concern in developing

```
Putty
$ type screen
screen is a function
screen ()
{
    sessionname=$(echo $@ | sed 's/.*-S \([^ ]\+\).*/\1/');
    echo -ne "\033]0;$sessionname\007";
    command screen $@;
    echo -ne "\033]0;Putty\007"
}
$ screen -T screen -U -S session-1
```

FIGURE 6.4 Data access by putty.

```
Putty
$ type screen
screen is a function
screen ()
{
    sessionname=$(echo $@ | sed 's/.*-S \([^ ]\+\).*/\1/');
    echo -ne "\033]0;$sessionname\007";
    command screen $@;
    echo -ne "\033]0;Putty\007"
}
$ screen -T screen -U -S session-1
```

FIGURE 6.5 Screenshot of server and putty.

countries and requires a quality healthcare system that can involve routine health reports of each patient. The labor behind collecting the chapter-based data, analyzing them is a time-consuming and error-prone process which even may have security concerns. The manual process of data collection and extraction may lead to major errors, thus leading o health hazards to the patients. The data formats supported by the EHRs are standardized so that it can be accessed from any sector. This technology might reduce the burden of data collection and storage problems and can maintain authenticity, integrity, and availability of data in a better way. The accuracy and ease of analyzing the data digitally also reduce the effort of the medical professionals. Certifies EHRs can help to provide financial benefits offered by Medicare and Medicaid by the government or government-aided companies. If the medical professionals access information from EHRs and also provide their inputs to the EHRs, they might also receive financial support from the government. Using EHRs, it is ensured that the medical staff can get accurate information before/during the appointment with the patient. The medical team can create EHR profiles related to each patient that can reduce the chapter work and typing job for the medical assistant team. With the advent of mobile computing and technical awareness of the major population, PHR can be expected to be widely accepted by patients and medical practitioners. We can comment that PHRs are an extension of EHRs that helps patients to manage their own test records for healthcare monitoring. These records show HER that can provide information about laboratory results and report summary. It also includes patient-generated data such as information about symptoms and other difficulties/information that the patient wants to convey to the medical support team. Whether the implementation is tethered or interconnected or stand-alone, accordingly EHR or PHR functionalities can be chosen. The PHR is though more patient-centric, i.e., it gives patients more flexibility of using this application such as appointment fixing/rescheduling, prescription refill, etc. The recent development of PHR can integrate all the patient's available data individually that can be detected to measure and predict the health condition of the patient. It can also provide ratings for each medical practitioner and provide social support as and when the patient requires this. The United States currently is leading successfully in the field of PHR data analytics. The major reason for this success could be an approach of incentive-driven research work. The Partnership for the Future of Medicare states that it is easy to implement PHRs when the patients self-monitor to acquire effective care. This approach will make the data readily available and accessible. Making use of PHR to its full potential definitely needs more understanding of PHR data formats, contents, and sources.

In recent days one successful and convenient way of patient data storage is known as PHR systems. By authentic sources and patient authorization, PHR data can be accessed for further research. These EHRs and PHRs are highly reliable and helpful disease prediction, risk assessment of any affected patient and also for prediction of health condition according to the symptoms given by the patients. This can lead to improvement of the quality of the healthcare system also proves to be cost-effective for the patients. Though there still lies many changes to be addressed to make this process a success.

In the research field, PHR data is still very important for analytical purposes to improve the functionalities of the PHRs further. There are several issues such functionalities, aim, security, and privacy concerns and legal issues for global implementation which need to be addressed and fixed for the wide acceptance of this method. Considering a literature review of the US survey, we can also propose to find the issues related to we increase the opportunities and control the challenges that is faced currently. Though our study or literature review is more of US-based, there are many research aspect that is going on in this field globally.

6.6 CONCLUSION

QR codes are one of the emerging techniques which is widely used in many of the real-life fields including medical and healthcare department. We have proposed a system that can help to exchange the laboratory results in terms of QR codes. The data transfer security is maintained using AES to exchange data between laboratory and patient and also data access from EHRs. The information to be stored must be encapsulated using Advanced Encryption Standard and then it can be stored as a QR code. The main transformations are done by LabSeq which can store and maintain the patient database for future reference. A mobile phone or smartphone with a QR code reader can simulate the electronic glasses. The mobile application supports LabSeq to store data and provide information from EHRs. This makes the information exchange between the patient and the medical team an ease. The medical team can easily obtain the entire history of the patient in a hassle-free manner and also provide their suggestion immediately or as required. The newer extension of EHR is known as PHR, which is a patient-centric platform that can support the health care industry to a large extend. The patient can share information in collaboration with the medical team with higher accuracy and lower costs. In recent days this has been a booming research area in developed and developing countries. The United States of the Health Information Technology for Economic and Clinical Health (HITECH) Act was passed in 2009, which makes usage of PHR data more common. The initial work is to integrate technology and the medical field to store a huge amount of patient reports available in the medical industry. Later the patients can online access the data or store their data according to the requirement.

KEYWORDS

- **beats per minute**
- **camera serial interface**
- **consumer electronics control**
- **digital visual interface**
- **electronic health record**
- **health information technology**
- **JavaScript object notation**

REFERENCES

1. Alipour, J., Erfannia, L., Karimi, A., & Aliabadi, A., (2013). Electronic health record acceptance: A descriptive study in Zahedan, Southeast Iran. *J. Health Med Inform, 4*, 120. doi: 10.4172/2157-7420.1000120.
2. Agarwal, S., & Lau, C. T., (2010). Remote health monitoring using mobile phones and web services. *Telemedicine and E-Health, 16*(5), 603–607.
3. Kulkarni, P., & Ozturk, Y., (2011). mPHASiS: Mobile patient healthcare and sensor information system. *Network and Computer Applications, 34*(1), 402–417.
4. Dăgtas, S., Pekhteryev, G., Sahinŏglu, Z., Am, H. C., & Challa, N., (2008). Real-time and secure wireless health monitoring. *International Journal of Telemedicine and Applications*, 1–10.
5. Pawar, P., Van, B. B. J., Hermens, H., Wac, K., & Konstantas, D., (2009). Context-aware computing support for network-assisted seamless vertical handover in remote patient monitoring. *The International Conference on Advanced Information Networking and Applications Workshops (WAINA 2009),* 351–358S.
6. Oleshchuk, V., & Fensli, R., (2011). Remote patient monitoring within a future 5G infrastructure. *Wireless Personal Communications, 57*, 431–439.
7. Carayon, P., Cartmill, R., Blosky, M. A., Brown, R., Hackenberg, M., et al., (2011). ICU nurses' acceptance of electronic health records. *J. Am. Med. Inform Assoc., 18*, 812–819.
8. Holden, R. J., (2010). Physicians' beliefs about using EMR and CPOE: In pursuit of a contextualized understanding of health IT use behavior. *Int. J. Med. Inform., 79*, 71–80.
9. Deutsch, E., Duftschmid, G., & Dorda, W., (2010). Critical areas of national electronic health record programs-is our focus correct? *Int. J. Med. Inform., 79*, 211–222.
10. Emran, N. A., & Leza, F. N. M., (2014). Data accessibility model using QR code for lifetime healthcare records. *World Appl. Sci. J., 30*, 395–402.
11. Dube, S., Ndlovu, S., Nyathi, T., & Sibanda, K., (2015). QR code based patient medical health records transmission: Zimbabwean case. *Proceedings of Informing Science and IT Education Conference (InSITE)*, 521–530.

12. Bellot, J., Shaffer, K., & Wang, M., (2015). Use of quick response coding to create interactive patient and provider resources. *J. Nurs. Educ., 54*(4), 224–227.
13. Bui, T. V., Vu, N. K., Nguyen, T. T. P., Echizen, I., & Nguyen, T. D., (2014). Robust message hiding for QR code. *Intelligent Information Hiding and Multimedia Signal Processing (IIH-MSP)* (pp. 520–523). IEEE.
14. Ho, A. T. P., Hoang, B. A. M., Sawaya, W., & Bas, P., (2014). Document authentication using graphical codes: Reliable performance analysis and channel optimization. *EURASIP Journal on Information Security, 9*(1), 2014.
15. Lin, P. Y., Chen, Y. H., Lu, E. J. L., & Chen, P. J., (2013). Secret hiding mechanism using QR barcode. *Proc. IEEE Int. Conf. Signal-Image Technol. Internet-Based Syst. (SITIS),* 22–25.
16. Dong-Hee, S., Jaemin, J., & Byeng-Hee, C., (2012). The psychology behind QR codes: User experience perspective. *Computers in Human Behavior, 28*, 1417–1426.
17. Espejel-Trujillo, A., Castillo-Camacho, I., Nakano-Miyatake, M., & Perez-Meana, H., (2012). Identity document authentication based on VSS and QR codes. *Procedia Technology, 3*, 241–250.
18. Gao, J., & Prakash, L. J., (2007). Understanding 2D-barcode technology and applications in m-commerce-design and implementation of a 2D barcode processing solution. *Proceedings of the Computer Software and Applications Conference*. Beijing.
19. Jun-Chou, C., Yu-Chen, H., & Hsien-Ju, K., (2013). A novel secret sharing technique using QR code. *International Journal of Image Processing (IJIP), 4*(5).
20. Kheder, L. S., & Alvi, A., (2013). Authentication system using quick response code. *International Journal of Management, IT and Engineering, 3*(2), 373–386.
21. Nyathi, T., Dube, S., Sibanda, K., & Mutunhu, B., (2013). Poultry contractual farming decision support system. *IST Africa 2013 Proceedings* (pp. 1–8). Kenya: IST Africa.
22. Reiser, S., & Bruce, R., (2008). Service-learning meets mobile computing. *Proceedings of the Annual Southeast Regional Conference.* Auburn, Alabama.
23. Rouillard, J., (2008). Contextual QR codes. *Proceedings of the 3rd International Multi-Conference on Computing in the Global Information Technology.* Athens, Greece.
24. Charoensiriwath, C., Surasvadi, N., Pongnumkul, S., & Pholprasit, T., (2015). Applying QR code and mobile application to improve service process in Thai hospital. In: *IEEE 12th International Joint Conference on Computer Science and Software Engineering (JCSSE)* (pp. 114–119).
25. Rahman, M. N. A., Rahman, A. A., Seyal, A. H., & Timbang, I., (2015). QR code for health notification mobile application. *International Conference on Network Security and Computer Science (ICNSCS-15)*. Kuala Lumpur, Malaysia.
26. Avidan, A., Weissman, C., & Levin, P. D., (2015). Integration of QR codes into an anesthesia information management system for resident case log management. *Int. J. Med. Inform., 84*(4), 271–276.

CHAPTER 7

AN INNOVATIVE APPROACH TO HEALTHCARE USING MACHINE LEARNING

T. KANAGARAJ,[1] E. UDAYAKUMAR,[1] K. SRIHARI,[2] and SUNIL PATHAK[3]

[1]*Assistant Professor, Department of ECE, Kalaignarkarunanidhi Institute of Technology (KIT), Coimbatore, Tamil Nadu, India, E-mail: kanagaraj27.t@gmail.com (T. Kanagaraj)*

[2]*Associate Professor, Department of CSE, SNS College of Technology, Coimbatore, Tamil Nadu, India*

[3]*Associate Professor, Department of CSE, Amity School of Engineering and Technology, Jaipur, Rajasthan, India*

ABSTRACT

The cerebrum is a greatly significant part of the central sensory system. The principle errand for the specialists is to distinguish the tumor, which is a tedious for which they feel trouble. Mind tumor is an intracranial strong neoplasm. In proposed, subjective examination like morphological activity and quantitative investigation like component extraction and picture quality appraisal is utilized to fragment the malignant growth recognized part. To fragment the part, first need to sift through the gained picture dependent on the veiling procedure. The morphological capacity including widening and disintegration technique, will be applied removed all through the separated picture. By the strategy for morphological jumping box will be drawn over the influenced partition. At that point, the locale encased by jumping box will be splitted out independently. Subsequent to separating and complexity improvement, picture quality appraisal MSE, PSNR is determined to look at different methods. In the wake of dividing tumor district, the patient's guardian can get the subtleties through E-mail as report and short message service (SMS) utilizing global system for mobile (GSM) module. At long last precision estimation will be accomplished for calculation productive level.

7.1 INTRODUCTION

A brain tumor is a weird improvement of cells inside the cerebrum or skull; some are mindful, others hazardous. Tumors can make from the cerebrum tissue itself (fundamental), or infection from elsewhere in the body can spread to the psyche (metastasis). Treatment decisions separate subordinate upon the tumor type, size, and territory. Treatment goals may be helpful or focus on lessening signs. A monstrous number of the 120 sorts of psyche tumors can be viably treated. New medications are improving the future and individual fulfillment for explicit people. Standard cells make in a controlled manner as new cells revoke old or hurt ones. For reasons not totally grasped, tumor cells copy uncontrollably. A focal cerebrum tumor is a difficult to miss improvement that begins in the psyche and generally does not spread to various bits of the body. Focal cerebrum tumors may be kind or risky [1].

A positive cerebrum tumor creates a little bit at a time, has clear cutoff centers, and once in a while spreads. Notwithstanding how its cells are not hazardous, obliging tumors can be perilous at whatever point sorted out in a fundamental locale. An unsafe cerebrum tumor grows quickly, has inconsistent cutoff centers, and spreads to way to deal with mind zones. In spite of how they are routinely called cerebrum malady, subverting mind tumors do not fit the significance of trading off progress since they do not spread to organs outside the cerebrum and spine. Metastatic (discretionary) cerebrum tumors start as hazard elsewhere in the body and spread to the brain [2]. They structure when harmed cells are passed on in the circulatory framework. The most thoroughly observed malignancies that spread to the psyche are lung and chest.

Whether or not a cerebrum tumor is careful, risky, or metastatic, all are possibly hazardous. Encased inside the hard skull, the cerebrum cannot relax up to course of action for a creation mass. In like manner, the tumor packs and discharges typical cerebrum tissue. Some psyche tumors cause a blockage of cerebrospinal fluid (CSF) that streams around and through the cerebrum. This blockage increases intracranial weight and can develop the ventricles (hydrocephalus). Some cerebrum tumors cause creating (edema). Size, weight, and building up all make "mass effect," which cause an incredible heap of the symptoms.

It is arranged as a fundamental and helper tumor. Different sorts of the computations were made for mind tumor disclosure. Helping radiologists in examining restorative pictures is the key idea from PC helped end structure by strategy for using submitted PC decisive limits reliant on natural effects among the PC and the radiologist and with AI procedures and restorative picture examination [8]. There are in excess of 100 classes of rule mind tumors, different them conflicting. Of course, not all cerebrum tumors, or even all hazardous psyche tumors, are for each situation savage.

7.1.1 K-MEANS SEGMENTATION

K-suggests is one of the clearest independent learning estimations that deal with the exceptional gathering issue. The technique seeks after a fundamental and straightforward way to deal with bunch a given educational file through a particular number of packs fixed a need. The standard thought is to depict k centroids, one for each social event. These centroids ought to be set in a craftiness way considering a diverse area causes grouped district causes various outcomes. Along these lines, the better decision is to put them at any rate much as could be ordinary far away from one another. The following stage is to each organize having a spot toward a given instructive variety and accessory it to the closest centroid [11].

Right when no point is pending, the basic development is done and an early groupage is finished. By and by, we expected to re-find k new centroids as Bary's central purposes of the groups coming to fruition because of the past turn of events. After we have these k new centroids, other ties must be done between practically identical edifying record places and the closest new centroid. A circle has been conveyed. Because of this circle, we may see that the k centroids change their territory a tiny bit at a time until no more changes are done. Finally, this estimation targets restricting an objective work, for this circumstance a squared.

7.1.2 MORPHOLOGICAL OPERATION

Morphological activity depends just on the general requesting of pixel esteems, not on their numerical qualities, and in this manner are especially fit to the preparing of twofold pictures. Disintegration is one of the principal tasks in morphological picture preparing from which all other morphological activities are based. It was initially characterized for parallel pictures, later being stretched out to dark scale pictures, and along these lines to finish grids. Expansion activity ordinarily utilizes an organizing component for examining and extending the shape containing in the information picture. Dark scale organizing components are likewise elements of a similar configuration [13], called organizing components.

7.1.3 WATERSHED ALGORITHM

There are additionally various calculations to register watersheds. Watershed calculation is utilized in picture handling essentially for picture division reasons. A hierarchal watershed change changes over the outcome into chart show that is the neighbor relationship of the sectioned districts are resolved and applies further watershed change recursively.

7.2 RELATED WORK

Watershed segmentation algorithm evacuates the salt and pepper commotion without upsetting edges. It is exceptionally simple for a programmed and exact count of tumor territory. Sobel edge identification-based improved edge recognition calculation gives better execution over regular division calculation. The Otsu division strategy for mind tumor makes the finding and treatment arranging all the simpler and more precise. Morphological administrators can be utilized in the discovery of tissues in the sweep picture of tumor [7]. The utilization of PCA in streamlining the highlights acquired from portioned locale can give awesome outcomes when contrasted with different techniques. The force-based and wavelet-based highlights are exceptionally valuable for the characterization of amiable and threatening tumors. From this chapter, he clarified the idea of Artificial Neural Network for grouping the tumors.

PC-supported identification application has figured out how to make significant commitments to the clinical world in the present innovation. Right now, it says that the location of mind tumors in attractive reverberation pictures was performed. This investigation proposes a PC helped identification framework that depends on morphological remaking and rule-based location of tumors that utilizing the morphological highlights of the locales of premium. The means engaged with this examination are: the pre-preparing stage, the division organize, the phase of identification of the locale of intrigue and the phase of recognition of tumors. With these techniques applied on 497 attractive reverberation picture cuts of 10 patients, the presentation of the PC-supported identification framework is accomplished 84.26% precision.

Clinical picture handling and its division is a functioning and intriguing region for specialists. It has come to at the huge spot in diagnosing tumors after the disclosure of CT and MRI. X-ray is a helpful instrument to distinguish the mind tumor and division is performed to complete the valuable bit from a picture. The motivation behind this chapter is to give a diagram of various picture division techniques like watershed calculation, morphological activities, neutrosophic [9] sets, thresholding, K-implies grouping, fluffy C-implies and so forth utilizing MR pictures. Right now, clarified about the comparison of various strategies referenced right now. K-suggests is one of the quickest autonomous [20] learning watches that deal with the dumbfounding social event issue. The procedure searches for after an essential and key way to deal with oversee pack a given enlightening once-over through a particular number of gatherings fixed a need. The standard thought is to delineate k centroids, one for each social gathering. These centroids should be set in an astuteness way considering an assorted territory causes masterminded zone causes different results. Henceforth, the better choice is to placed them regardless much as could be ordinary far away from each other. The resulting stage is to each arrange having a spot toward a given informative assortment and partner it to the nearest centroid [11].

Accurately when no point is pending, the central improvement is done and an early groupage is done. Before long we expected to re-choose k new centroids as Bary focal reasons for the packs working out as intended due to the past headway. After we have these k new centroids, other ties must be done between proportionate lighting up overview networks and the nearest new centroid. A circle has been passed on. In view of this circle, we may see that the k centroids change their territory a smidgen without a moment's delay until no more changes are done. Finally, this estimation targets restricting an objective work, for this circumstance, a squared bumble work.

X-bar, a PC-based picture, is getting the ready framework for seeing and diagnosing mind tumors. Division of pictures in MRI urges us to see Ref. [17]—tumor size, a zone, and shape. There are various frameworks for division in picture managing. Division structures are locale-based, the limit based and edge-based. Edge framework combines an entropy-based algorithmic strategies that are on a very basic level noteworthy for early revelation of cerebrum tumor. At this moment, we are taking a gander at and looking at specific edge entropy set up division systems regarding the clarification of joy results. Entropy strategies like Shannon, Renvi, Vajda,

Havrda-Charvat, and Kapur are applied to the MRI pictures of cerebrum tumor or any internal structure of our body, are destitution blasted down and reviewed a method of edge selection of pictures subject to entropy methodology are found astoundingly amazing in assessment of brain tumor [12]. In the wake of isolating and taking a gander at through distraction results, we saw that Havrda-Charvat entropy performs better than some other entropy estimations.

Magnetic resonance Imaging mind tumor pictures Classification is a maddening undertaking because of the change and multifaceted plan of cancers. This chapter's future methodology to engineer the MR hominid cerebrum pictures [16]. The projected strategy system contains three phases, to be express, pre-arranging, join extraction and confirmation, and social affair. Highlights are confined by utilizing the diminished level co-event structures [18].

The essential objective of clinical imaging is to detach basic and precise data from these photographs with the least bungle conceivable. Out of the different sorts of clinical imaging structures open to us, MRI is the most solid and safe. It excludes acquainting the body with any sort of poisonous radiation. This MRI would then have the choice to be prepared, and the tumor can be divided. Tumor Segmentation intertwines the utilization of a few specific systems [15]. The entire arrangement of perceiving cerebrum tumor from an MRI can be assembled into specific classes: processing, Optimization, and Feature Extraction. He shows that the layout consolidates looking into the evaluation by different masters and assembling it one chapter.

7.3 SYSTEM DESIGN

In the proposed technique, subjective examination like morphological activity and quantitative investigation like element extraction and picture quality evaluation is utilized to fragment the malignant growth distinguished part. To fragment the bit, first need to sift through the procured picture dependent on the covering strategy. The morphological capacity including expansion and disintegration strategy will be applied separated all through the sifted picture. By the strategy for morphological jumping box will be drawn over the influenced segment [6]. At that point, the locale encased by jumping box will be splitted out independently. Subsequent to separating and complexity improvement, picture quality appraisal is determined to think about different methods. In the wake of portioning tumor locale, the patient's overseer can get the subtleties through E-mail as report and short message service (SMS) utilizing global system for mobile (GSM) module. At long last precision estimation will be accomplished for calculation proficient level. The block diagram of the software unit is shown in Figure 7.1.

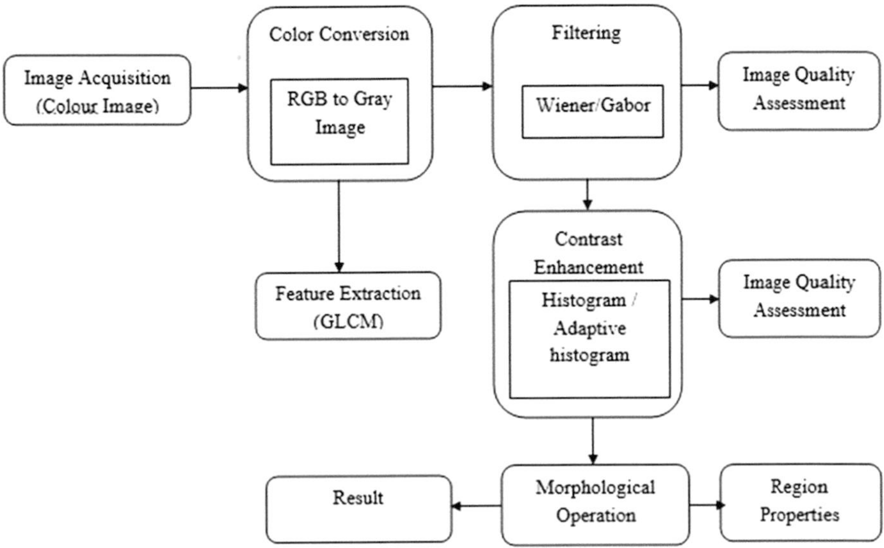

FIGURE 7.1 Block diagram for software unit.

7.3.1 IMAGE ACQUISITION

Propelled imaging or modernized picture getting is the development of a deliberately encoded depiction of the visual characteristics of an article, for instance, a physical scene or within structure of a thing. The term is routinely expected to surmise or fuse the taking care of, pressure, storing, printing, and show of such pictures [21]. A key favored situation of a propelled picture, versus a straightforward picture, for instance, a film photograph, is the limit make copies and copies of copies cautiously uncertainly with no loss of picture quality. Propelled imaging can be described by the kind of electromagnetic radiation or various waves whose variable narrowing, as they experience or reflect off things, passes on the information that involves the image. In all classes of cutting-edge imaging, the information is changed over by picture sensors into mechanized signs that are taken care of by a PC and made yield as a conspicuous light picture.

7.3.2 ADAPTIVE HISTOGRAM EQUALIZATION (AHE)

Adaptive histogram equalization (AHE) is a PC picture preparing structure used to improve separate in pictures. It contrasts from standard histogram evening out in the regard that the adaptable system shapes several histograms, each appearing differently in relation to a particular bit of the picture, and uses them to redistribute the refinement estimations of the picture. It is in this manner reasonable for improving the territory discrete and upgrading the ramifications of edges in every area of an image. Delineates and shows the consequence of differentiation improvement for the Gabor disengaging picture. Regardless, AHE tends to over elevate change in all things considered homogeneous regions of a picture. An assortment of adaptable histogram evening out called CLAHE forestalls this by obliging the expansion.

7.3.3 IMAGE QUALITY ASSESSMENT

Estimation of picture quality is examination is solidly related to picture closeness relies upon the differentiation (or comparability) between a debased picture. It is hard to execute them into modified steady structures. Target appraisals are modified and numerical described computations. Enthusiastic estimations can be used to affirm the accommodation of target estimations. Likewise, target systems have pulled in more contemplations of late. Eminent objective appraisal computations for assessing picture quality consolidate MSE and PSNR are incredibly clear and easy to use. Estimation of picture quality is vital to many pictures getting ready systems. In light of regular physical controls and money-related reasons, the nature of pictures and chronicles could indisputably degenerate right from the minute that they are gotten to the minute that they are seen by a human onlooker. Perceiving the image quality gauges that have the most important affectability to these mutilations would help effective arrangement of coding, correspondence, and imaging systems and of improving or upgrading the image quality for a perfect nature of the organization in any event cost.

7.3.4 GRAY LEVEL CO-OCCURRENCE MATRIX (GLCM)

Feature incorporates improving the proportion of benefits required to depict a tremendous course of action of data correctly. Examination with innumerable factors all-around requires a ton of memory and count [7] control or a gathering estimation which over fits the arrangement test and summarizes insufficiently to new models. Surface material or visual trait of a surface. Surface examination points in finding one of a kind [23] method for speaking to the basic attributes of surfaces and speak to them in some more straightforward yet one-of-a-kind structure, with the goal that they can be utilized for hearty, precise arrangement and division of articles. Despite the fact that surface assumes a noteworthy job in picture investigation and example acknowledgment, just a couple of designs execute locally available textural include extraction. In this chapter, Gray level co-occurrence grid is planned to get factual surface highlights. Various surface highlights might be extricated from the GLCM. Just four-second request includes in the particular rakish second minute, relationship, opposite contrast minute, and entropy are processed. These four measures give the high segregation precision required to film estimation.

7.3.5 SVM CLASSIFIER

The support vector machine (SVM) is a hypothetically prevalent strategy with extraordinary outcomes in design acknowledgment. Particularly for regulated characterization of high-dimensional datasets and has been discovered aggressive with the best AI calculations. Previously, SVMs were tried and assessed distinctly as pixel-based picture classifiers. During ongoing years, propels in Remote Sensing happened in the field of Object-Based Image Analysis with a blend of low level and significant level PC vision procedures [9]. Moving from pixel-based systems towards object-based portrayal, the elements of remote detecting symbolism include space increments fundamentally. This outcome to expanded multifaceted nature of the order procedure, and makes issues customary arrangement plans. The goal of this investigation was to assess SVMs for their viability and possibilities for object-based picture examination as an advanced computational knowledge strategy. Here, a SVM approach for multi-class grouping was pursued, in light of crude picture objects gave by a multi-goal's division calculation. At that point, a component choice advance occurred so as to give the highlights to characterization which included unearthly, surface, and shape data. By utilizing SVM classifier, we can arrange the encephalon tumor as favorable and dangerous.

7.3.6 GABOR FILTER

In picture setting up, a Gabor channel, named after Dennis Gabor, is a straight channel used for surface appraisal, which interprets that it on an incredibly basic level secludes whether there are a specific repetitive substance in the image in unequivocal heading in a restricted area around the point or space of assessment. Repeat and course depictions of Gabor channels are ensured by various contemporary vision analysts to resemble those of the human visual structure, regardless there is no observational confirmation and no significant method for derivation to support the idea. They have been viewed as particularly reasonable for surface depiction and bundle. In the spatial space, a 2D Gabor channel is a Gaussian part work composed by a sinusoidal plane wave. A couple of makers ensure that key cells in the visual cortex of mammalian characters can be showed up by Gabor limits. In like way, picture assessment with Gabor channels is thought by some to take after assertion in the human visual structure.

7.3.7 WIENER FILTER

A perfect or target discretionary system by linear time-invariant (LTI) isolating of a viewed uproarious method, expecting known stationary sign and upheaval spectra, and included substance commotion. The Wiener channel confines the mean square mix-up between the assessed subjective system and the perfect method. The goal of the Wiener channel is to process a quantifiable check of a dark sign using a related sign as a data and filtering that alluded to movement toward produce the measure as a yield. For example, the acknowledged sign may involve a dark indication of interest that has been demolished by included substance noise. The Wiener channel can be used to filter through the fuss from the spoiled sign to offer a check of the principal hint of interest. The Wiener channel relies upon a quantifiable system, and an undeniably authentic record of the theory is given in the base mean square slip-up (MMSE) estimator article. Ordinary deterministic channels are planned for a perfect repeat response. Regardless, the arrangement of the Wiener channel [22] receives a substitute methodology. One is acknowledged to think about the ghost properties of the primary sign and the disturbance, and one searches for the straight time-invariant channel whose yield would come as close to the main sign as could be permitted.

7.4 HARDWARE DESCRIPTION

7.4.1 POWER SUPPLY

Power supply is a reference to a wellspring of electrical force. A device or system that arrangements electrical or various sorts of imperativeness to a yield weight or assembling of weights is known as a force supply unit or PSU. The term is most commonly applied to electrical imperativeness supplies, less routinely to mechanical ones, and inconsistently to others. The block diagram of the hardware unit is shown in Figure 7.2.

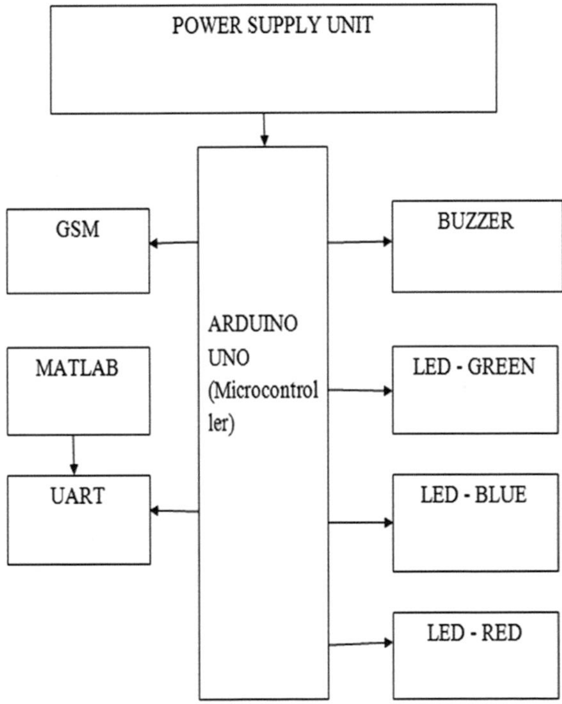

FIGURE 7.2 Block diagram for hardware unit.

7.4.2 ARDUINO UNO

An Arduino is really a microcontroller-based unit which can be either utilized truly by procuring from the merchant or can be made at home utilizing the parts, inferable from its open-source gear fuse.

7.4.3 GLOBAL SYSTEM FOR MOBILE (GSM)

Global system for mobile (GSM) is the Mobile trades is a standard made by the European Telecommunications measures foundation (ETSI) to depict the shows for second-age (2G) moved cell structures utilized by PDAs, for example, telephones and tablets. 2G systems were made as a substitution for extraordinary fundamental cell structures, and the GSM standard basically outlined a pushed, circuit-exchanged system refreshed for full-duplex voice communication. GSM is a trademark ensured by the GSM affiliation. It might, in like way, recommend the most eminent voice codec utilized, full-rate [19].

7.5 RESULTS AND DISCUSSION

Encephalon tumor division reenacted in MATLAB 2015b form with 10 pictures as database. From the outcomes that show SVM classifier which sections the mind tumor from the unaffected bit and GLCM include extraction strategies are utilized.

The example input pictures are taken from the database, which is expected to recognize the mind tumor and sectioning the distinguished part of encephalon tumor and characterizing them as generous and threatening. Figure 7.3 shows the example input pictures for dissecting the tumor.

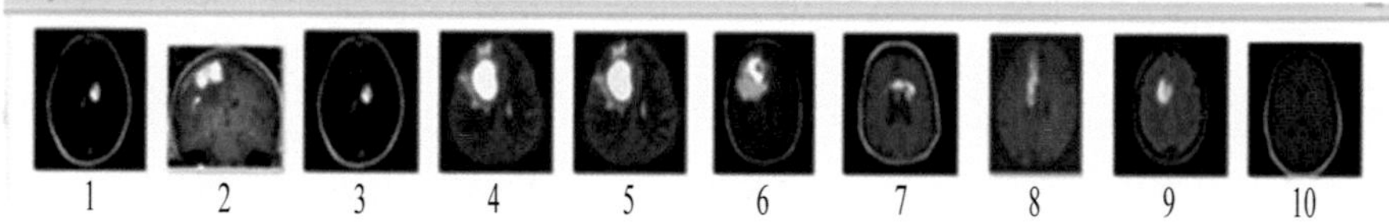

FIGURE 7.3 Sample input images.

Gabor filtering graph shows the average difference (AD), high difference, MSE, and peak signal to noise ratio (PSNR) between the estimated value and original value of given input image as shown in Figure 7.4.

Figure 7.5 shows the relationship between the original value and estimated value of the image about the AD, maximum difference (MD, PSNR), mean square error (MSE) and also root mean square error (RMSE).

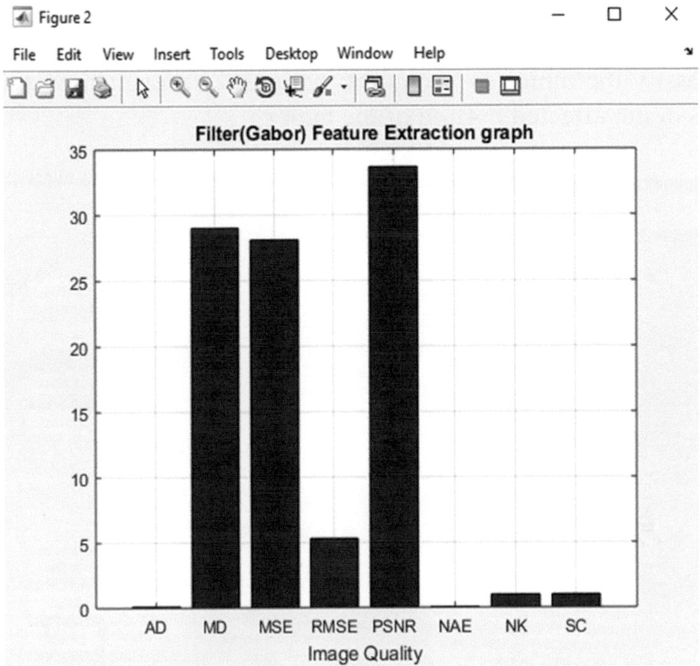

FIGURE 7.4 Gabor filtering graph.

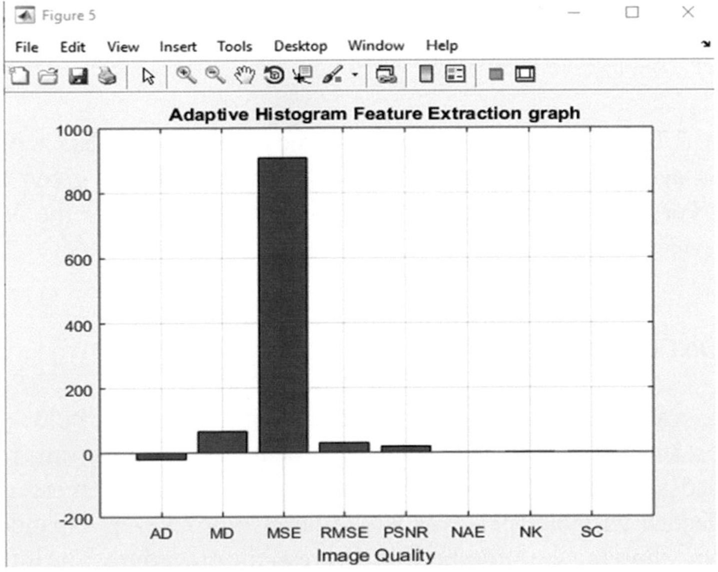

FIGURE 7.5 Adaptive histogram equalization graph.

Figure 7.6 describes the output of encephalon tumor by segmenting the brain image as tumors portion that is affected area and non-affected area. It also classify the tumor as benign or malignant. It also shows the region properties of the affected portion of the tumor.

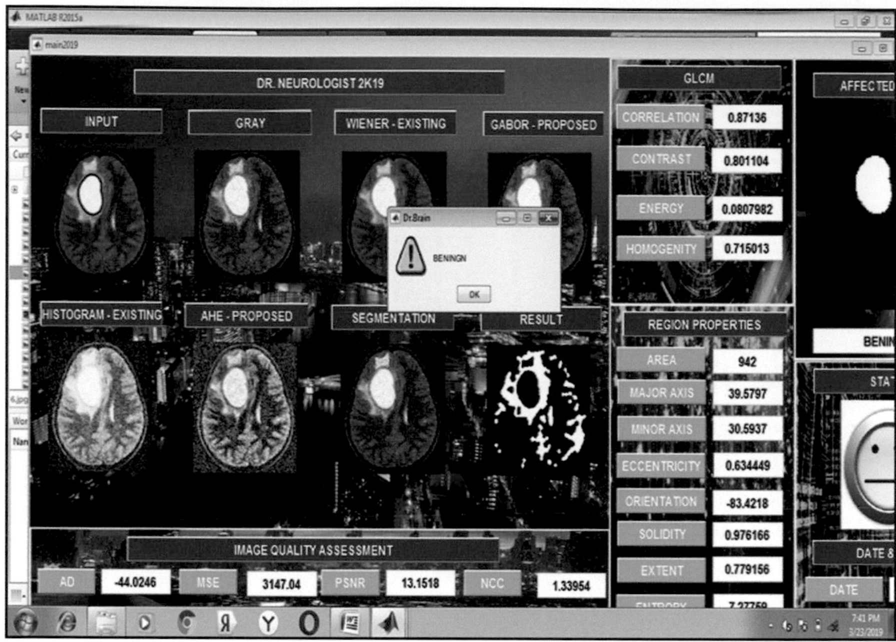

FIGURE 7.6 Result of the encephalon tumor.

Figure 7.7 shows, if the brain image is the benign, blue LED is blowing, or if it is malignant, then red LED is blowing, otherwise green LED is blowing. For all this case, the alert message will be given for the doctor to treat the patient.

7.6 CONCLUSION

Bentonite was changed and used to expel Congo red from color-gushing water. It is demonstrated to be a viable adsorbent. The harmony time required is resolved as 4 hrs. Univariate parametric investigations were directed and ineffectual variable (pH) was wiped out. Color take-up expanded with temperature showing the endothermic nature of the procedure. The impacts of different parameters and their communications were contemplated utilizing the response surface procedure. Profluent fixation and Dosage were recognized as the most persuasive parameters, and the subsequent request impacts of the equivalent are likewise affecting the procedure. A factual quadratic model was created, and its strength was tried according to the principles given in the writing. 3D Response surface charts and Contour plots were created and investigated.

FIGURE 7.7 Hardware output.

KEYWORDS

- **adaptive histogram equalization**
- **dilation**
- **gray-level co-occurrence matrix**
- **machine learning**
- **mean square error**
- **segmentation**
- **tumor**

REFERENCES

1. Krishnammal, P. M., (2015). Automated brain image classify using NN approach and abnormality analysis. *Int. Jrnl. of Engg. and Tech., 7*(3).
2. Chen, X., Nguyen, B. P., Chui, C. K., & Ong, S. H., (2017). Reworking multilabel brain tumor segmentation. *Proc. IEEE Conf. Systems, Man, and Cybernetics.* Budapest, Hungary.
3. Chen, X., et al., (2016). Automated brain tumor segmentation using kernel dictionary learning and super pixel-level features. *Proc. IEEE Conf. Systems, Man, and Cybernetics, Budapest, Hungary*, 2547–2552.
4. Madhcswaran, M., & Anto, D., (2015). Classification of brain MRI images using SVM with various kernels. *Biomedical Research, 26*(3).
5. Said, C., Redouan, L., & Lalitha, (2014). A novel approach for brain tumor detection using neural network. *Int. Jrnl. of Research in Engg. and Tech., 2*(7), 93–104.
6. Thiagarajan, A. J. J., et al., (2014). Kernel sparse models for automated tumor segmentation. *Int. J. Artif. Intell. Tools, 23*(3).
7. Gordillo, N., Montseny, E., & Sobrevilla, P., (2013). State of the art survey on MRI brain tumor segmentation. *Magn. Reson. Imaging, 31*(8), 1426–1438.
8. Bauer, S., Wiest, R., Nolte, L. P., & Reyes, M., (2013). A survey of MRI-based medical image analysis for brain tumor studies. *Phys. Med. Biol., 58*(13), 97.
9. Mustaqeem, et al., (2012). An efficient brain tumor detection algorithm using watershed and thresholding based segmentation. *International Journal of Image, Graphics and Signal Processing, 4*(10), 34–39.
10. John, P., (2012). Brain tumor classification using wavelet and texture based neural network. *Int. J. Sci. Eng. Res., 3*(10), 1–7.
11. Geremia, E., Menze, B. H., & Ayache, N., (2012). Spatial decision forests for glioma segmentation in multi-channel MR images. *Workshop Proceedings of the Medical Image Computing and Computer-Assisted Intervention Challenges* (pp. 14–17). France.
12. Evangelia, I. Z., (2009). Classification of brain tumor type and grade using MRI texture and shape in a machine learning scheme. *Magn. Reson. Med., 62*(6), 1609–1618.
13. Georgiadis, P., Cavouras, D., et al., (2008). Improving brain tumor characterization on MRI by probabilistic neural networks and non-linear transformation of textural features. *Computer Methods and Programs in Biomedicine, 89*, 24–32.
14. Santhi, S., et al., (2017). An unified Reeb analysis for cortical surface reconstruction of MRI images. *Biomedical and Pharmacology Journal, 10*, 939–994.
15. Vetrivelan, P., et al., (2017). TB screen based SVM and CBC technique. *Current Pediatric Research, 21*, 338–342.
16. Vetrivelan, P., et al., (2017). An Investigation of Bayes algorithm and neural networks for identifying the breast cancer. *Indian Journal of Medical and Pediatric Oncology, 38*(3), 340–344. Medknow Publications.
17. Santhi, S., et al., (2017). Automatic detection of diabetic retinopathy through optic disc using morphological methods. *Asian Journal of Pharmaceutical and Clinical Research, 10*, 28–31.
18. Vetrivelan, P., et al., (2017). An Identify of efficient vessel feature of endoscopic analysis. *Research Journal of Pharmacy and Technology, 10*, 2633–2636.
19. Sindhumathy, S., et al., (2018). Analysis of magnetic resonance image segmentation using spatial fuzzy clustering algorithm. *Journal of Global Pharma Technology, 10*(12), 88–94.

20. Ramesh, C., et al., (2018). Detection and segmentation of optic disc in fundus images. *International Journal of Current Pharmaceutical Research, 10*(5), 20–24.
21. Sivaganesan, S., et al., (2017). Design and development of smart glucose monitoring system. *International Journal of Pharma and Biosciences, 8*(3), 631–638.
22. Yogeshwaran, K., et al., (2019). An efficient tissue segmentation of neonatal brain magnetic resonance imaging. *Research Journal of Pharmacy and Technology, 12*(6), 2963–2966.
23. Ramesh, C., et al., (2018). A review on diagnosis of malignant melanoma from benign lesion by using BPNN and ABCD rule parameters. *International Research Journal of Pharmacy, 9*(10), 1–7.

CHAPTER 8

MACHINE LEARNING THEORY AND METHODS

RANJEET YADAV[1] and ASHUTOSH TRIPATHI[2]

[1]*Amity University Rajasthan, India, E-mail: ranjeet480@gmail.com*

[2]*Department of ECE, Amity School of Engineering and Technology, Noida, Uttar Pradesh, India*

ABSTRACT

Machine learning alludes to the changes in frameworks that perform correlate functions connected with computing. This chapter presents introduction varieties and the application of machine learning. This chapter additionally presents the essential structures of Machine learning, the process and basic ideas associated with the varied machine learning techniques like Naive Thomas Bayes classifier, support vector machine, k-nearest-neighbor, decision trees and regression analysis algorithms. At the top a number of the necessary applications square measure bestowed.

8.1 INTRODUCTION

Machine learning (ML) theory points to comprehend the basic standards of learning as a computational procedure and joins devices from Computer Science and Statistics. The current SMAC (social, mobile, analytic, cloud) innovation pattern prepares for a future where wise machines, arranged procedures, and large information are brought together. This virtual world has created a tremendous measure of information which is quickening the selection of ML arrangements and practices. AI empowers PCs to emulate and adjust human-like conduct. Utilizing ML, every communication, and each activity performed, becomes something the framework can learn and use as an understanding for whenever. This work is a diagram of this information examination strategy which empowers PCs to learn and do what easily falls into place for people, for example, gain as a matter of fact. It incorporates the fundamentals of AI, the definition, classification, and applications' depicting it as what, how, and why. The innovation guide of AI is talked about to comprehend and check its potential as a market and industry practice. The essential purpose of this work is to give knowledge into why ML is what is to come.

ML empowers PCs to emulate and adjust human-like conduct. Utilizing ML, every collaboration, and each activity performed, becomes something the framework can learn and use as an understanding for whenever. This work is an outline of this information examination technique which empowers PCs to learn and do what comes normally to people, for example, ML as a matter of fact. It incorporates the starters of ML, the definition, classification, and applications' portraying it is what, how, and why. The innovation guide of ML is talked about to comprehend and check its potential as a showcase and industry practice. The essential purpose of this work is to give knowledge into why ML is what is to come.

Learning as a nonexclusive procedure is tied in with gaining new, or adjusting existing, practices, values, information, aptitudes, or inclinations. Behaviorism, Cognitivism, Constructivism, Experientialism furthermore, Social Learning characterize the hypothesis of individual learning, for example how people learn. Machines depend on information in spite of what falls into place without a hitch for people: gaining for a fact. At the basic level AI (ML) is a classification of manmade consciousness that empowers PCs to think and learn without anyone else. It is tied in with causing PCs to alter their activities so as to improve the activities to accomplish more exactness, where precision is estimated as far as the occasions times the picked activities results into right ones.

Analysts have officially characterized ML across appropriate writing. The term was authored by Arthur Samuel in 1959 [1], who characterized ML as a field of concentrate that gives learning capacity to PCs without being expressly modified [1]. More as of late, Tom Mitchell gave a "well-presented" definition that has demonstrated progressively helpful to designing set-up: "A PC program is said to gain for a fact E as for some undertaking T and some exhibition measure P, if its presentation on T, as estimated by P, improves with experience E [2]."

Composing a PC program is somewhat similar to recording directions for an amazingly exacting kid who simply happens to be a huge number of times quicker than you. However, a significant number of the issues we currently need PCs to tackle are never again errands we realize how to unequivocally advise a PC how to do. These incorporate recognizing faces in pictures, self-sufficient driving in the desert, finding applicable reports in a database (or tossing out superfluous ones, such as spam e-mail), discovering designs in huge volumes of logical information, and altering inward parameters of frameworks to enhance execution. That is, we may ourselves be acceptable at recognizing individuals in photos, however we do not have a clue how to straightforwardly tell a PC how to do it. Rather, techniques that take marked preparing information (pictures named by who is in them, or on the other hand e-mail messages marked by whether they are spam) and afterward learn proper guidelines from the information, appear to be the best ways to deal with tackling these issues. Moreover, we need frameworks that can adjust to evolving conditions, that can be easy to understand by adjusting to necessities of their individual clients, and that can improve execution after some time.

8.2 IMPORTANCE OF MACHINE LEARNING (ML) THEORY

ML Theory, otherwise called Computational Learning Theory, expects to understand the central standards of learning as a computational procedure. This field looks for to comprehend at an exact scientific level what abilities and data are intellectually expected to learn various types of assignments effectively and to comprehend the essential algorithmic standards engaged with getting PCs to gain from information and to improve performance with input. The objectives of this hypothesis are both to help in the plan of better robotized learning techniques and to comprehend principal issues in the learning procedure itself.

ML theory draws components from both the Theory of Computation and Measurements and includes undertakings, for example:

- Creating numerical models that catch key parts of ML, in which one can investigate the intrinsic simplicity or trouble of various kinds of learning issues.
- Proving ensures for calculations (under what conditions will they succeed, how much information and calculation time is required) and creating AI calculations that provably meet wanted criteria.
- Mathematically dissecting general issues, for example, "For what reason is Occam's Razor a decent thought?," "When would one be able to be sure about expectations produced using constrained information?," "How much force does dynamic interest include over

uninvolved perception for learning?" and "What sorts of strategies can learn even within the sight of enormous amounts of diverting data?

8.3 A FEW APOTHEOSIS

Probably the most punctual outcome in Computational Learning Theory is that there is to be sure a reason as a strategy to search out straightforward clarifications when planning forecast rules. In standard, for proportions of effortlessness remembering portrayal length for bits, Vapnik-Chervonenkis measurement which quantifies the successful number of parameters, and more up to date gauges being contemplated in flow investigate, one can change over the degree of effortlessness into a level of confidence in future execution. While a portion of these hypothetical outcomes are very mind boggling, at a significant level, the instinct is only the accompanying: there are a lot increasingly confounded clarifications conceivable than straightforward ones. Along these lines, if a straightforward clarification happens to accommodate your information, it is significantly less likely this is going on just by some coincidence. Then again, there are such huge numbers of entangled clarifications conceivable that even a lot of information is probably not going to administer all of them out, and even some that have nothing to do with the main job are probably going to in any case endure and fool your framework. This instinct would then be able to be transformed into numerical ensures that can control ML calculations.

ML theory additionally has various key associations with different orders. In cryptography, one of the key objectives is to empower clients to impart with the goal that a spy cannot gain any data about what is being said. ML can be seen right now creating calculations for the spy. Specifically, provably great cryptosystems can be changed over to issues one cannot would like to learn, and hard learning issues can be changed over into proposed cryptosystems. Also at the specialized level, there are solid associations between significant strategies in ML and procedures created in Cryptography. For instance, Boosting, ML technique intended to remove however much force as could reasonably be expected out of a given learning calculation, has close associations with strategies for intensifying cryptosystems created in cryptography.

ML theory additionally has close associations with issues in Economics. AI strategies can be utilized in the plan of sell-offs and other valuing components with ensures on their exhibition. Versatile AI calculations can be seen as a model for how people can or ought to conform to evolving situations.

Also, the improvement of particularly quick-adjusting calculations reveals insight into how surmised balance states may rapidly become to in a framework, in any event, when every individual has an enormous number of various potential options. The other way, financial issues emerge in ML when not exclusively is the PC calculation adjusting to its environment, but it additionally is influencing its condition and the conduct of others in it also. Associations between these two territories have gotten progressively solid as of late as the two networks intend to create instruments for demonstrating and encouraging electronic trade.

8.4 THE STRUCTURE SQUARES OF MACHINE LEARNING (ML)

The structure squares of ML can be condensed as in Figure 8.1.

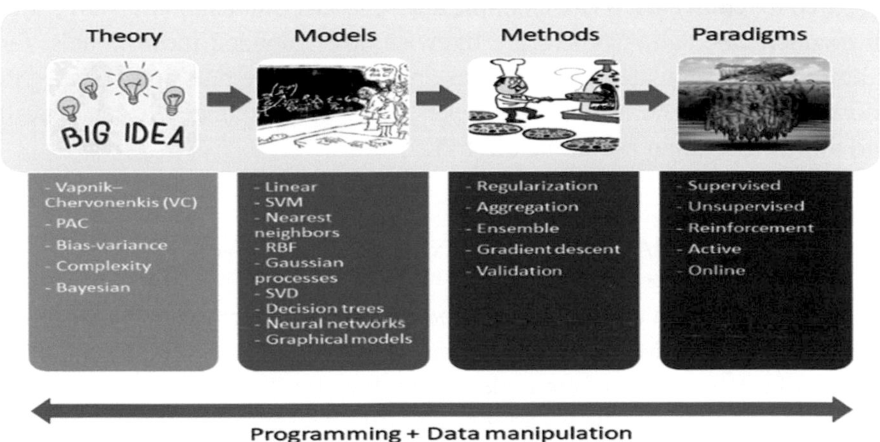

FIGURE 8.1 The building block of machine learning.

Source: https://towardsdatascience.com/learn-machine-learning-the-fun-way-554833891b73.

This is unquestionably not a comprehensive rundown; however you get the thought. All models and calculations you experience start with some general hypothesis behind. This is on the grounds that ML can be seen from numerous perspectives: factual perspective, computational intricacy perspective, and so forth. Try not to get confounded when you see some ML books that present generally numerical hypotheses and confirmations, while some others are increasingly useful with information and programming-language explicit. They are simply taking a gander at ML from various edges.

From these various hypotheses, we thought of various kinds of learning models (straight, Decision Trees, neural systems, and so forth.).

In any case, to cause a model that to can sum up well on genuine dataset, we have to utilize some additional methods (for example, regularization to maintain a strategic distance from over-fitting, gathering strategies to lessen predisposition/difference in the educated model). This is the placc a wide range of varieties of a similar model originate from. For instance, straight relapse including some regularization terms makes new sorts of models (for example, Rope, Ridge or Elastic nets). The equivalent goes for choice trees: utilizing distinctive troupe strategies we concoct Random Forest, AdaBoost, and so forth.

At long last, models fall into various standards relying upon how you apply them on the genuine datasets. For instance, neural systems are administered learning calculation when prepared on a named dataset. In any case, when it is prepared to remake itself (for example auto-encoder), at that point it turns into an unaided calculation. There are likewise other blended ideal models, for example, semi-regulated learning, yet once you get the nuts and bolts right, you will comprehend it in an eye flicker. In this way, realize the center well and things will begin becoming all-good.

8.5 THE ESSENTIALS OF MACHINE LEARNING (ML)

ML is the utilization of calculations and insights to information. In this way, In request for your ML activity to be fruitful, you will have to approach the right skills. A basic error is to under-assess the significance of the Math and Statistics information when working with ML. The accomplishment of your drive will rely upon picking the right calculation for your answer, realizing how to knead your information lastly accurately tuning the hyperparameters of your picked calculation. These errands all require a strong establishing in math and statistics (Figure 8.2).

8.6 PROCESS OF MACHINE LEARNING (ML)

The procedure is as follows (Figure 8.3):

1. **Problem Identification:** Any ML task should begin with a Question or Hypothesis. Would could it be that we are attempting to accomplish? Try not to fear being excessively explicit here. The Problem

can generally be identified in the event that we learn more as the task advances. A decent Data Scientist will guarantee that the Question or Hypothesis is one that ML can reply.

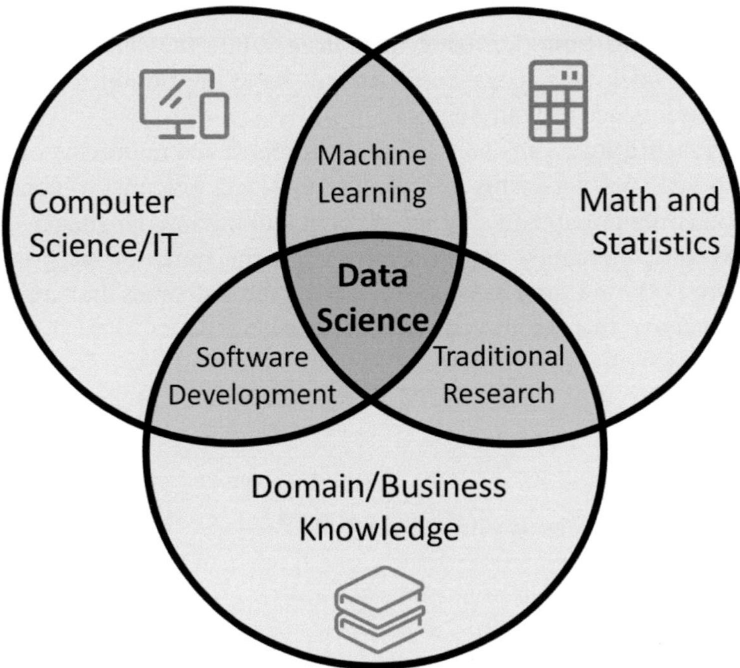

FIGURE 8.2 Machine learning fundamentals.

Source: https://www.bouvet.no/bouvet-deler/6-tips-for-getting-started-with-machine-learning.

2. **Data Collection:** The subsequent stage is to assemble our information. This can require some investment, as we may need to total information from various sources. Or then again, maybe we have to verify authorization from framework proprietors. Now, we may not know precisely what sort of information we have, or how great the information quality is.
3. **Preliminary Data Analysis:** When we have our information, we have to get it. By applying measurable strategies and perceptions to the information, your Data Scientist will begin to see how the information fits together. Would we be able to answer our theory with the given information? Do we have to address absent or opposing information?

4. **Formal Analysis:** At last, your Data Scientist is prepared to make a last ML model! By this point, they ought to have a smart thought of which calculations they wish to give it a shot.
5. **Evaluation:** Subsequent to making your ML model you will have to comprehend what it gives you. It might be that the outcome is not true to form. Utilizing their insight into the calculation hidden the model, your Data Scientist will have the option to clarify the consequence of your venture.
6. **Presentation:** The data scientist will report and impart the outcomes to your partners. This will require the Data Scientist to convey the outcome in Layman's terms, without sinking into language!
7. **Result:** Congrats, you have arrived at the finish of the procedure. Presently the time has come to assess the outcomes and apply what you have realized in your next undertaking!

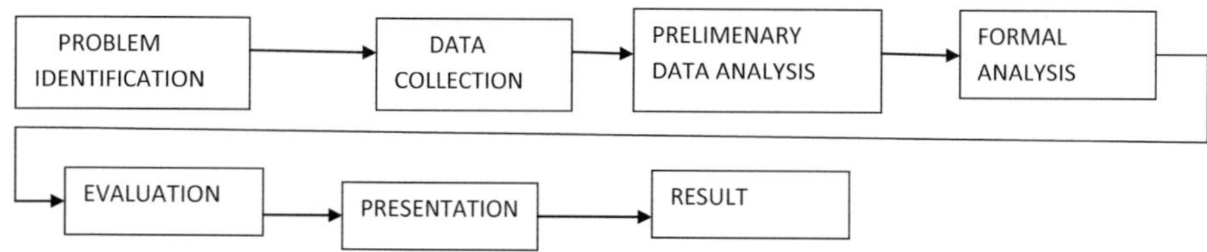

FIGURE 8.3 The process of machine learning.

8.7 TYPES OF MACHINE LEARNING (ML)

The subsequent stage is to comprehend what you can really accomplish with ML. To do this you should know the three fundamental sorts of ML delineated beneath:

1. **Supervised Learning:** Supervised Learning is tied in with anticipating new results, in light of verifiable information. An administered learning model will endeavor to discover the connection between your verifiable information sources of info and yields. Use cases may incorporate anticipating house costs, discovering objects in pictures and interpretation of archives.
2. **Unsupervised Learning:** Unsupervised Learning is tied in with depicting your information. The model uses measurable examination to discover designs in your information, as per the information's own properties. Use cases may be finding new client sections in your business information or record grouping.

3. **Reinforcement Learning:** Reinforcement Learning gives a unique model that is continually attempting to improve its own presentation through experimentation. After some time, the model improves its system and shows signs of improvement and better-simply like somebody playing a game. Use cases incorporate stock exchanging and stock administration (Figure 8.4).

Supervised Learning
Model trained on historical data. Resulting model can be used to make predictions on new data.
Use Case: Predicting a value based on patterns discovered in previous data.
Unsupervised Learning
Algorithm finds trends and patterns in data, without prior training on historical data.
Use Case: Describing your data based on statistical analysis.
Reinforcement Learning
Model uses a feedback loop to iteratively improve it's performance.
Use Case: Learning how to best solve a problem based on trial and error.

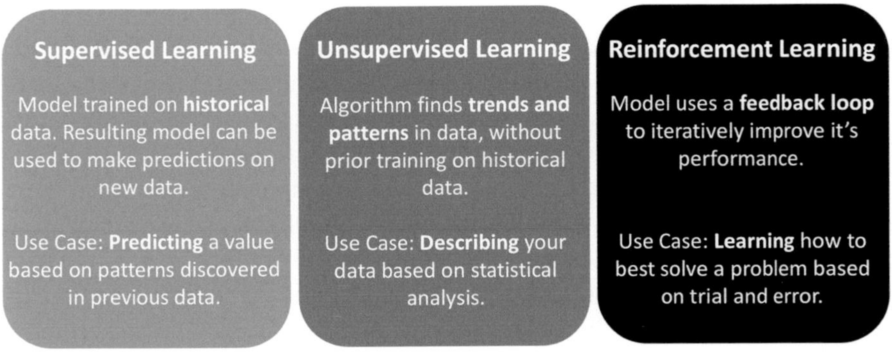

FIGURE 8.4 Three types of machine learning.

Source: https://www.bouvet.no/bouvet-deler/6-tips-for-getting-started-with-machine-learning.

8.8 MACHINE LEARNING (ML) ALGORITHMS

8.8.1 DECISION TREE ALGORITHM

Decision Tree Analysis is a general, prescient demonstrating apparatus that has applications spreading over various zones. As a rule, Decision Trees are developed by means of an algorithmic methodology that recognizes approaches to part an informational index dependent on various conditions. It is one of the most broadly utilized and useful techniques for administered learning. Decision Trees are a non-parametric directed learning strategy utilized for both grouping and relapse errands. The objective is to make a model that predicts the estimation of an objective variable by taking in straightforward choice standards deduced from the information highlights.

A Decision tree is a tree-like chart with hubs speaking to where we pick a property and pose an inquiry; edges speak to the appropriate responses to the inquiry; and the leaves speak to the genuine yield or class mark. They are utilized in non-straight dynamic with straightforward direct choice surface.

Decision trees characterize the models by arranging them down the tree from the root to some leaf hub, with the leaf hub giving the order to the model. Every hub in the tree goes about as an experiment for some property, and each edge plummeting from that hub relates to one of the potential responses to the experiment. This procedure is recursive in nature and is rehashed for each sub tree established at the new hubs.

Decision Tree is a method for approximating discrete esteemed objective capacity which speaks to the required capacity as a Decision tree [11]. Decision tree orders occurrences by arranging them from root to a few leaf hubs based on include esteems. Each hub speaks to some choice (test condition) on quality of the occasion while each branch speaks to a potential incentive for that include. Characterization of a case begins at the root hub called the choice hub. Based on the estimation of the hub, the tree cross down along the edge, which relates to the worth of the yield of highlight test. This procedure proceeds in the sub-tree headed by the new hub toward the finish of the past edge. At last, the leaf hub means the order classes or an ultimate conclusion. While utilizing a choice tree, center is around how to choose which characteristic is the best classifier at every hub level. Factual measure like data gain, Gini list, Chi-square, and entropy are determined for every hub to figure the value of that hub [11]. A few calculations are utilized to actualize choice trees. The most well-known ones are: classification and regression tree (Truck), iterative Dichotomiser 3 (ID3), programmed interaction detection (CHAID), Chi-squared C4.5 and C5.0 and M5.

8.8.2 NAÏVE BAYES ALGORITHM

Guileless Bayes groups utilizing Bayes' theorem of likelihood. Bayes' hypothesis computes the back likelihood of an occasion guaranteed some earlier likelihood of occasion B spoke to by P(A/B) as follows:

$$P(A / B) = \frac{P(B / A)P(A)}{P(B)}$$

where;

A and B are occasions.

P(A) and P(B) are the probabilities of watching An and B free of each other.

P(A/B) is the restrictive likelihood, for example Likelihood of watching A, given B is valid.

P(B/An) is the likelihood of watching B, given An is True.

Gullible Bayes' classifiers fall under the classification of basic probabilistic classifiers dependent on the idea of Bayes' theorem having solid freedom suppositions among the highlights. It is especially fit when the dimensionality of the sources of info is high [4, 5].

8.8.3 SUPPORT VECTOR MACHINE (SVM)

"Support vector machine" (SVM) is a regulated ML calculation which can be utilized for both order or relapse difficulties. In any case, it is for the most part utilized in order issues. In the SVM calculation, we plot every datum thing as a point in n-dimensional space (where n is a number of highlights you have) with the estimation of each component being the estimation of a specific facilitate. At that point, we perform arrangement by finding the hyper-plane that separates the two classes. Support Vectors are basically the co-ordinates of individual perception. The SVM classifier is a wilderness which best isolates the two classes.

SVMs can be utilized for order just as relapse issues. It is an administered learning calculation. It chips away at the idea of edge figuring. Right now, information thing is plotted as a point in n-dimensional space (where n is the quantity of highlights we have in our dataset). The estimation of each element is the estimation of the comparing coordinate. It groups the information into various classes by finding a line (hyperplane) which isolates the preparation datasets into classes. It works by augmenting the separations between the closest information point (in the two classes) and the hyperplane that we can call as edge.

8.8.4 REGRESSION ANALYSIS ALGORITHM

Regression is a strategy for demonstrating an objective worth dependent on free indicators. This technique is, for the most part utilized for determining and discovering circumstances and logical results connection between factors. Regression methods, for the most part, contrast dependent on the quantity of autonomous factors and the sort of connection between the free and ward factors.

Basic direct regression is a sort of relapse investigation where the quantity of free factors is one and there is a straight connection between the independent(x) and dependent(y) variable. The red line in the above diagram is alluded to as the best fit straight line. In view of the given information focuses, we attempt to plot a line that models the focuses the best.

Regression examination is a prescient displaying strategy which researches the relationship between a reliant (target) and free variable(s) (indicator). It is a significant instrument for breaking down and displaying of information. Right now strategy, we attempt to fit the line/bend to the information focuses to limit the distinctions between separations of information focuses from the bend or then again line. There are different sorts of regression investigation like straight, strategic, and polynomial.

8.8.5 K-MEANS CLUSTERING

K-implies is a well-known solo AI calculation for group investigation. It will probably parcel 'n' perceptions into 'k' groups in which every perception has a place with the bunch having the closest mean, filling in as a model of the group. The mean of the perceptions in a specific bunch characterizes the focal point of the group.

Bunching examination should be possible based on highlights where we attempt to discover subgroups of tests dependent on highlights or based on tests where we attempt to discover subgroups of highlights dependent on tests. We will cover here grouping dependent on highlights. Bunching is utilized in advertise division; where we attempt to find clients that are like each other whether as far as practices or characteristics, picture division/pressure; where we attempt to amass comparable districts, record grouping dependent on points, and so forth.

In contrast to regulated picking up, bunching is viewed as an unaided learning strategy since we do not have the ground truth to look at the yield of the grouping calculation to the genuine names to assess its presentation. We just need to attempt to explore the structure of the information by gathering the information focuses into unmistakable subgroups.

8.9 APPLICATIONS OF MACHINE LEARNING (ML)

There are several applications of ML in day to day life few of the applications are listed in Table 8.1.

8.10 CHALLENGES OF MACHINE LEARNING (ML)

Given the wide scope of relevance of ML, it faces various difficulties. Some of them are as follows:

TABLE 8.1 Application of Machine Learning

Application	Description
Virtual personal assistants	ML is a significant piece of these individual colleagues as they gather and refine the data based on your past association with them. Afterward, this arrangement of information is used to render results that are customized to your inclinations. Siri, Alexa, Google Now are a portion of the well-known instances of virtual individual collaborators. As the name proposes, they help with discovering data, when asked over voice.
Videos surveillance	The video reconnaissance framework these days are controlled by AI that causes it conceivable to identify wrongdoing before they occur. They track bizarre conduct of individuals like standing unmoving for quite a while, lurching, or snoozing on seats and so forth. The framework would thus be able to give a caution to human orderlies, which can at last assistance to keep away from incidents. What is more, when such exercises are accounted for and checked to be valid, they help to improve the reconnaissance administrations. This occurs with AI carrying out its responsibility at the backend.
E-mail spam and malware filtering	There are various spam sifting approaches that e-mail customers use. To find out that these spam channels are ceaselessly refreshed, they are fueled by ML. At the point when rule-based spam sifting is done, it neglects to follow the most recent stunts embraced by spammers. Multilayer perceptron, C 4.5 Decision Tree Induction are a portion of the spam separating systems that are controlled by ML. More than 325, 000 malwares are distinguished ordinary and each bit of code is 90–98% like its past renditions. The framework security programs that are fueled by AI comprehend the coding design. In this way, they recognize new malware with 2–10% variety effectively and offer insurance against them.
Search engine result refining	Google and other web crawlers use AI to improve the list items for you. Each time you execute a pursuit, the calculations at the backend keep a watch at how you react to the outcomes. On the off chance that you open the top outcomes and remain on the website page for long, the internet searcher expects that the outcomes it showed were in understanding to the inquiry. Additionally, on the off chance that you arrive at the second or third page of the indexed lists yet do not open any of the outcomes, the web search tool assesses that the outcomes served did not coordinate prerequisite. Along these lines, the calculations working at the backend improve the indexed lists.
Online fraud detection	ML is demonstrating its capability to make the internet a protected spot and following money related fakes online is one of its models. For instance: Paypal is utilizing ML for insurance against illegal tax avoidance. The organization utilizes a lot of apparatuses that encourages them to look at a large number of exchanges occurring and recognize authentic or ill-conceived exchanges occurring between the purchasers and vendors.

- The ML calculations require enormous volumes of information to be exact and productive, which is as yet not accessible to scientists. Tech mammoths like Facebook and Google have approached such huge information, which is the reason they are driving in the field of artificial intelligence (AI). It turns out to be much progressively hard to get this information in the fields like banking and medicinal services where scanty computerized information is accessible, making it intense to make precise forecasts.
- Spam Detection: Given e-mail in an inbox, the savvy frameworks grew so far are as yet not ready to effectively distinguish the spam mail. It winds up in sending spam in the inbox and non-spam sends to spam registry.
- ML calculations have not yet been effective in recognizing the articles and pictures. This field is as yet an open research field for AI. In spite of the fact that we have referenced a couple of difficulties in AI, there are a lot more fields which despite everything trying for profound learning calculations for example discourse understanding, Visa extortion discovery, face location, digit acknowledgment given a postal district, and item suggestion and so on.

8.11 CONCLUSION

Right now, the wide outline of ML containing both hypothetical and handy viewpoints is introduced. AI is commonly made out of demonstrating and advancement, and the essential part to perform ML is a reasonable dataset for information learning. For the hypothetical angle, we present the fundamental thought, order, structure, and criteria of ML. What is more, for the down to earth perspective, a few standards and systems of both unaided and directed learning are talked about.

Digitalization and the Internet upheaval have prompted a mounting volume of organized and unstructured information which should be used for examination. ML as a key innovation driver includes the wise capacity to saddle the information from the accessible information. In addition, the appropriation of ML answers for complex genuine issues by the two scientists and specialists has made this field a powerful zone of research with a functioning cooperation across businesses and nations.

KEYWORDS

- **constructivism**
- **dichotomiser 3**
- **key innovation driver**
- **machine learning**
- **social, mobile, analytic, cloud**
- **support vector machine**

REFERENCES

1. Samuel, A. L., (1959). Some studies in machine learning using the game of checkers. *IBM Journal of Research and Development, 3*(3), 210–29.
2. Mitchell, T., (1997). *Machine Learning* (p. 2). McGraw Hill. ISBN: 978-0-07-042807-2.
3. Avrim, B. (2014). *Machine Learning Theory*. Department of Computer Science, Carnegie Mellon University.
4. Jafar, A., Anand, N., & Akshi, K., (2019). Machine learning from theory to algorithms: An overview. *Second National Conference on Computational Intelligence (NCCI 2018), IOP Conf. Series: Journal of Physics: Conf. Series 1142: 01201*. doi: 10.1088/1742-6596/1142/1/012012.
5. Sandhya, N. D., & Charanjeet, K. R., (2016). A review on machine learning techniques. *International Journal on Recent and Innovation Trends in Computing and Communication (IJRITCC), 4*(3). 395–399. ISSN: 2321-8169.
6. Ayon Dey, (2016). Machine Learning Algorithms: A Review, *International Journal of Computer Science (IJCSIT), 7*(3), 1174–1179. ISSN: 0975-9646.
7. A report by Royal Society, (2017). Machine learning: the power and promise of computers that learn by example. *Information Technologies, 7*(3), 1174–1179. ISBN: 978-1-78252-259-1.
8. Minton, S., & Zweben, M., (1993). Learning, planning, and scheduling: An overview. In: *Machine Learning Methods for Planning* (pp. 1–29).
9. Han, J., Cai, Y., & Cercone, N., (1993). Data-driven discovery of quantitative rules in relational databases. *IEEE Transactions on Knowledge and Data Engineering, 1*(1), 29–40.
10. Shokri, R., Stronati, M., Song, C., & Shmatikov, V., (2017). Membership inference attacks against machine learning models. In: *Security and Privacy (SP), 2017 IEEE Symposium* (pp. 3–18). IEEE.
11. Li, M., Andersen, D. G., Park, J. W., Smola, A. J., Ahmed, A., Josifovski, V., Long, J., et al., (2014). Scaling distributed machine learning with the parameter server. In: *OSDI* (Vol. 14, pp. 583–598).

12. Chen, J. X., (2016). The evolution of computing: AlphaGo. *Computing in Science and Engineering, 18*(4), 4–7.
13. Al-Jarrah, O. Y., Yoo, P. D., Muhaidat, S., Karagiannidis, G. K., & Taha, K., (2015). Efficient machine learning for big data: A review. *Big Data Res., 2*(3), 87–93.
14. Khan, A., Baharudin, B., & Lan, H. L., (2010). A review of machine learning algorithms for text documents classification. *Journal of Advances in Information Technology, 1*(1).
15. Zhou, Z. H., (2009). Ensemble Learning. In: Li, S. Z., & Jain, A., (eds.), *Encyclopedia of Biometrics.* Springer, Boston, MA.
16. Alzubi, Jafar & Nayyar, Anand & Kumar, Akshi (2018). Machine Learning from Theory to Algorithms: An Overview. Journal of Physics: Conference Series. 1142. 012012. 10.1088/1742-6596/1142/1/012012.
17. Kumar, A., & Abraham, A., (2017). Opinion mining to assist user acceptance testing for open-beta versions. *Journal of Information Assurance and Security, 12*(4), 146–153. ISSN: 1554-1010.
18. Pazzani, M. J., & Billsus, D., (2007). Content-based recommendation systems. In: *The Adaptive Web* (pp. 325–341). Springer, Berlin, Heidelberg.

PART II

Applications of Artificial Intelligence and the Internet of Things

CHAPTER 9

ARTIFICIAL INTELLIGENCE (AI)

MANJU KAUSHIK

Associate Professor, Amity Institute of Information Technology (AIIT), Amity University Rajasthan, India

ABSTRACT

Artificial intelligence (AI) refers to machines that are programmed to think like humans that simulate human intelligence and to mimic their actions. This solves the problem of word learning that can be applied to any machine such displays symptoms associated with the human mind.

AI is a branch of computer science that places special importance on the development of humans and machines. For example, to resolve voice recognition, problems, learning, and planning.

The four types of AI are:

1. reactive machines;
2. limited memory;
3. theory of mind; and
4. self-awareness.

In the same way, Siri was developed by SRI International Center for AI at the start. The name speaks for itself. All stated above some short, yes, Siri is undoubtedly an example of AI. Amazon Alexa, which is only known as Alexa, developed by Amazon, is an AI virtual assistant technology, which was first developed by Amazon Echo to use a smart speaker.

Psychologists are often not only a characteristic representation of the human intellect, but also including a variety of capabilities. AI investigation mainly focuses on the following components: language learning, reasoning, problem solving, perception, and use [1, 2].

9.1 COMPONENTS OF AI

9.1.1 LEARNING

There are many different ways to learn about artificial intelligence (AI). Learning by trial and error is the easiest thing to do. For examplc, a simplc computer program to solve chess problems in a partner may try random movements until finding a mate. Programs can store solutions with this situation so remember the solution to meet the same status the next time the computer. It is known individual elements and processes as roto Learning is relatively easy to implement simple nostalgia, computer. Implementing is called more challenging generalization to the problem. Normalization involves applying past experience to include new circumstances. For example, a program that learns from the past tense of regular English verbs by heart, he will not be able to produce the past tense of a word, as long as it has not been presented with the first violation, while is a program which is common to learn it. Rules. Add "Ed" and build such past tense jump based on experience with similar actions.

9.1.2 REASONING

To conclude what is appropriate for the situation, injection is classified as either cut or inductive. An example of the former: "Fred must be in one of the museums or cafes. He is not in the cafeteria; so he is in the museum and later," such were caused by previous accidents failures on the computer. Therefore, the accident occurred due to an equipment failure. Among these forms of reasoning is the most important difference is that the complex reality in terms of cuts guarantees the veracity of the findings. While the truth of the premise in the inductive case supports the conclusion without total assurance, inductive reasoning is general in science where data are composed and temporal models are developed to describe future behavior until heterogeneous data forces. Do not cut the appearance of modifying the model. General in Mathematics and Logic and predict future behavior unless that does not modify the heterogeneous data forces the appearance of models. Deductive logic in mathematics and logic are built from a small group of common, where wide irrefutable theorems structures axiom and rules [3, 4]. The drawing information had considerable success in computer programming, especially deductive infarction. However, the exact reasoning only closing; Including relevant to the solution of a particular task or situation. It is one of the most difficult problems faced by AI.

9.1.3 PROBLEM SOLVING

To solve the trouble, particularly in AI, can be portrayed as a search systematically through a series of possible actions to achieve the goal or solution. A technique of trouble solving has been separated into a precise reason and a common goal. A special-purpose method is tailor-made for a specific problem and is often exploited very specific characteristics of the situation in which the underlying problem. In contrast, a general-purpose method is applied to problems of many kinds. A general-purpose means end-to-end analysis of technology-current status and gradual or gradual reduction of the difference between the final target to be used in AI. The program selects the actions of the media list, in case of a simple robot, which pick up the target completion may include: putdown, move forward, move back, move left as well as move right. By AI programs have been resolved to a variety of problems. Examples of a board to prepare the way to win the game (or order), mathematical tests moves and built computer world is to manipulate the "virtual goods."

9.1.4 PERCEPTION

The perception, the environment is decomposed into different objects in different sensory organs, different spatial relationships are scanned through real or artificial, and visualization. Analyze how much contrast with the surrounding area different than can be seen where it looked towards the light in the scene and intensity and object to an object that is complicated by the fact that depending on the angle. Optical sensors allow people to recognize self-directed vehicles to drive at modest speeds on the open road, as well as artificial perception is enough for robots to visit buildings carrying empty soda cans. One of the first systems to integrate perception as well as action was FREDDY, a stationary robot with a moving television eye plus pinner arm, built at the University of Edinburgh, Scotland, during the period 1966–1973 under the direction of Donald Mixie. FREDDY was able to identify a wide variety of objects.

Since a random stack of mechanism, one can be instructed to gather easy artifacts, like toy cars.

9.1.5 LANGUAGE

A system of a language signals meaning conference. In this sense, language should not be limited to the spoken word. For example, traffic signal make a minor language, because this convention means in some countries is a matter of "Forward danger." This is exactly the meaning of convergence of linguistic units which are different from those languages, and linguistic meaning is much different is called natural means, "means those clouds rain" means the pressure of "falling" valve malfunction.

Unlike the cry of birds and road signs, it is an important feature of the productivity of the entire human languages. Manufacturer language can produce different types of sentences.

9.2 METHODS AND GOALS IN ARTIFICIAL INTELLIGENCE (AI)

9.2.1 SYMBOLIC VS. CONNECTIONIST APPROACHES

AI investigate is that two separate, and somewhat competing, methods, symbolic (or "top-down") approach, and connectionist (or "bottom-up") following approaches. Top-down approaches symbol processing-symbol by analyzing independent sensation of biological structure of the brain in terms of label tries to replicate intelligence. On the other hand, is a down-up approach to artificial neural networks to mimic the structure of the brain-where the connection is labeled.

9.2.2 PROS OF ARTIFICIAL INTELLIGENCE (AI)

The probability of error is almost Nil and greater precision and accuracy are achieved. Robots can do some laborious tasks. Fraud can be detected in smart card-based systems using AI. The machines require no rest or rest, and can run non-stop.

AI will have a lower error rate than humans if coded properly. They have incredible accuracy, precision, and speed. They are not affected by threatening environment. So they are able to carry out hazardous tasks, discover space and tolerate problems, which will damage or destroy us.

9.2.3 INTELLIGENT ROBOTS

AI Advantages	AI Disadvantages
Error reduction	High cost
Difficult exploration	No replicating humans
Daily application	No improvement with experience
Digital assistants	No original creativity

AI machines that simulate the human process (computer systems). These processes include learning, reasoning, and self-improvement. We require AI for the reason that we who work for it is growing day-by-day. Therefore, it is an excellent idea to computerize habitual work.

AI is a computing issue that aims to build machines and computers that can improve logical operations. AI systems have the talent to perform daily jobs linked with human being intellect, such as voice recognition, decision making, visual perception, and language translation. One of the main disadvantages is that it will cause job loss. AI will change millions of jobs that are presently engaged with humans. One of the jobs to begin emotion the warmth of work defeat as a consequence of AI is motivating jobs.

The outlook of AI involves superior cognitive systems able of liability what machine learning (ML) systems cannot. They will interact fluently and intelligently with human experts, providing articulated explanations and responses, even on the edge of the web or on robotic devices. AI streamlines our lives every day. AI powers a lot of programs and services that help us do daily things with friends, by email program or ride-sharing service. Until AI has developed to the point of developing machines that can interact, participate, think, adapt, and react in exactly the same way as humans, it is not possible for such intelligent machines to completely transform human resources.

De facto, the BLS AI: accountants, forensic scientists, geological technicians, technical writers, MRI operators, diet experts, financial experts, web developers, loans, medical secretaries, and customer service is faster than average job growth in many businesses that affect. The majority of us are trying to be better general public furthermore better citizens. AI can also take part in a role in serving us in daily life. AI can also assist us to interact with people in our network who advise us on the proper way to behave or react in context [5, 6].

- Eight jobs artificial intelligence be able to substitute:
  - Telemarketing;
  - Bookkeeping clerks;
  - Compensation and benefits managers;
  - Receptionists;
  - Couriers;
  - Proofreaders;
  - Computer support specialists; and
  - Market research analysts;
- Eight jobs artificial intelligence be not able to substitute:
  - Human resource managers;
  - Sales managers;
  - Marketing managers;
  - Public relations managers;
  - Chief executives;
  - Event planners;
  - Writers; and
  - Software developers.

Can a machine have feelings? If "emotions" are defined in terms of their effect on behavior or how they function within an organism, then emotions can be seen as a mechanism that an intelligent agent maximizes the usefulness of their actions uses for. As researchers hypothesize, the "human" profession will be related to emotional intelligence in the future. Today, everyone agrees that AI was created not to change people but to help, improve, improve, and accelerate.

Here are the eight best jobs of the next decade or so:

1. Registered nurses; Reuters/mike wood;
2. Applications software developers;
3. General and operations managers;
4. Financial managers;
5. Accountants and auditors;
6. Management analysts;
7. Physicians, surgeons, etc.;
8. Market research analysts and marketing specialists.

9.2.4 JOHN MCCARTHY

John McCarthy, Alan Turing, Allen Newell, Herbert A. Simon, and Marvin Minsky are considered as the founding fathers of the technology that has revolutionized countless industries. In addition to net job idea, there are supplementary reasons to be expectant concerning the impact of AI and mechanization. Fundamentally, jobs that can bring robots back to the primary position are not high-quality jobs, and at a senior level, AI, and computerization will also help relieve disease and worldwide shortages. Some of the AI features are:

- Data ingestion;
- Eliminate dull and boring tasks;
- Chatbots;
- Quantum computing;
- Natural language processing (NLP).
- Artificial neural network: Research in AI has focused primarily on the subsequent mechanism of intelligence: learning, reasoning, problem solving, perception, plus language understanding.
- Learning: It varies in different ways.
- Reasoning.
- Problem-solving.
- Perception.
- Language-understanding.

AI refers to the simulation of a person intellect on technology that is programmed to believe similar to humans along with imitate their proceedings. The perfect feature of AI is its capability to create the best chance of achieving a particular goal.

There are four kinds of AI: reactive machines, limited memory, theory of mind, and self-awareness.

- Reactive machines;
- Limited memory;
- Theory of mind; and
- Self-awareness.

The main objective of AI is to develop intelligent machines that can learn on their own. There is no more person obstruction to nurture data to machines. With AI, machines can be developed that can read and understand human languages, known as natural learning processing (Figure 9.1) [7–9].

5 Benefits Advantages Of Artificial Intelligence AI
REASONING
This slide is 100% editable. Adapt it to your needs and capture your audience's attention.
BIG DATA
This slide is 100% editable. Adapt it to your needs and capture your audience's attention.
TEXT HERE
This slide is 100% editable. Adapt it to your needs and capture your audience's attention.
TEXT HERE
This slide is 100% editable. Adapt it to your needs and capture your audience's attention.
PROBLEM SOLVING
This slide is 100% editable. Adapt it to your needs and capture your audience's attention.
LEARNING
This slide is 100% editable. Adapt it to your needs and capture your audience's attention.
TEXT HERE
This slide is 100% editable. Adapt it to your needs and capture your audience's attention.

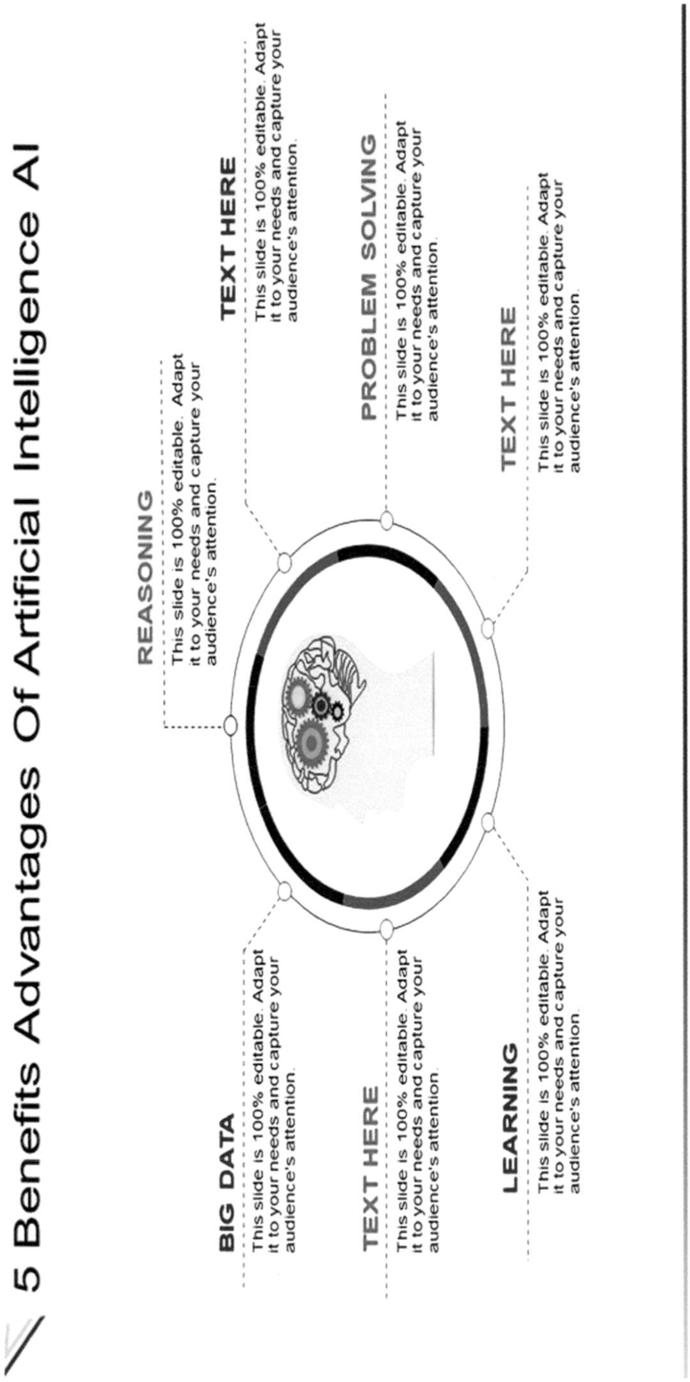

FIGURE 9.1 Benefits advantages of artificial intelligence AI.

9.2.5 *LIMIT OF ARTIFICIAL INTELLIGENCE (AI)*

Theoretically speaking, there is no long-term limit because smart machines will eventually design and manufacture the next generation of smart machines. This is an AI edition of natural development.

Strong AI has a complex algorithm that helps it function in various situations, while in weak AI, all actions are preprogrammed by humans. Powerful AI machines have their own brains. They can process independent decision making, while weak AI-based machines can only simulate human behavior.

Since 90% of organizations implement AI projects, companies understand AI's imperatives for valuable industry processes. Cash burn in AI projects ongoing ultimately long can cut manual tasks that people must. This is not just a budgetary expense, but tasks like data analysis and tracking have expired before human hands.

AI provides ease of use and convenience for data processes for past efforts. That is why 96% of organizations said that they hope to keep moving ML project in the subsequently 2-years. AI opens novel doors to some surprising approaches in various fields, many usage challenges arise. In advance, problems with AI execution are routinely attributed to require of employee engagement amid novelty, raising expectations by business experts to learn and adapt. Organizations must often pursue exterior ability to assist them make the majority of their resources. Anyway, community has not completely to blame for the limitations of AI.

9.2.6 *DATA*

Using records is one of the key constraints of AI. There is any need for the data to start the program. It does not matter what it is or execution phase of the program training phase, your desire for data is never complete. If we anticipate being relevant AI in a program, the process first, smart robots with the time required to gain some skills. There are also robots with sophisticated cognitive skills using techniques such as ML, optical character recognition (OCR), NLP, and robotic process automation (RPA). To be removed from the document the importance of restricted data. Since then, various roles have become possibly the most important factors, such as automation of tasks including critical thinking or decision making.

9.2.7 CULTURAL LIMITATIONS

Originally placed; It is about a change in resistance. Generally, there will be a creature of individuals, normally, instinct; when we do is important to take care of the business are searching for a strategy to accomplish a task and effectively manifested, we prefer to stick. This often puts some impact before we see the disruption and cost that certainly changed the methodology or bring about the adoption of new procedures; they will deserve all the benefits that they bring. It is human employees who manage technology infrastructure, who can be as simple as a reluctance to be seen as a control "control" is, whether it is precise to the machines, otherwise give the AI.

9.2.8 BIAS

Hidden bias persons and data are available in both, and the bias is to move data in light of individuals from time to time. We cannot fulfill these responsibilities without receiving data. At that point, you go off in search of data, and maybe a bias in the data about which you do not think. Do you just ignore it? One mock-up is from the earth of autonomous cars. We will find the information in the neighborhood because it will be the first autonomous vehicle where is the place.

AI is deciding the most excellent thing to hold that organizations must consider that it is why they need it. Try to AI not AI. Do not start with a business case based on customer insights from behavior analysis and market surveys. Businesspeople waste a lot of moment in time as well as wealth to run AI exclusive of some appropriate cause. Make sure your group has the data as well as philosophy initial, and after that executes it.

9.2.9 EMOTIONAL INTELLIGENCE

While AI has become more amazing step-by-step, we do not prevent have achieved a point where computational power or speed again. This is a great opportunity to work on the emotional intelligence of the AI so that it can rapidly communicate like humans. NLP must be sufficiently efficient to understand what someone is bothering to do along with the approach behind it. In basic terms, AI must understand the perspective of interaction.

The point is that AI lacks emotional intelligence because it cannot classify a person's emotions and mindset into different types of record points otherwise profile. Anyway, the stuff will start to be modified in a few years.

9.2.10 SHORTAGE OF STRATEGIC APPROACH

Here and there, it is an amalgamation of diverse restrictions: lack of talent, lack of management, acquisition, and digital conversion in point's insufficient culture and interest and practical aspects of AI. It is often not consistent with the results of AI activities that are not planned at a strategic level, strategic business objectives Failure to complete, and the business growth and the company's overall operations for development.

Regular here is because the organizations are considering the importance of embracing widely AI innovations and can offer favorable benefits, they do not see it from a strategic perspective; This means data applied from aggregation workforce and have a full understanding of the points of AI all aspects of operations to be working and objectives.

The answer is fairly straightforward, companies will always be set in advance a silly process that should ensure and pilots are spending expensive and resource-intensive AI initiative to create and misunderstood right to those benefits.

They emulate human intelligence processes by what AI or AI brings machines, mainly computer systems. These processes comprise learning, reasoning, and self-improvement. Several AI applications comprise expert systems, speech recognition, and machine vision.

The following have applications of AI:

1. AI in astronomy. The complex universe to solve the problems in AI can be very useful;
2. AI in healthcare;
3. AI in gaming;
4. AI in finance;
5. AI in data security;
6. AI in social media;
7. AI in travel and transport;
8. AI in automotive industry.

9.2.11 USE OF ARTIFICIAL INTELLIGENCE (AI)

In today's society there are many applications of AI. It is becoming necessary for today because it can efficiently solve complex troubles in many industries such as healthcare, entertainment, finance, education, and more. AI has made our life more at ease and faster [10, 11].

The following have applications of AI (Figure 9.2).

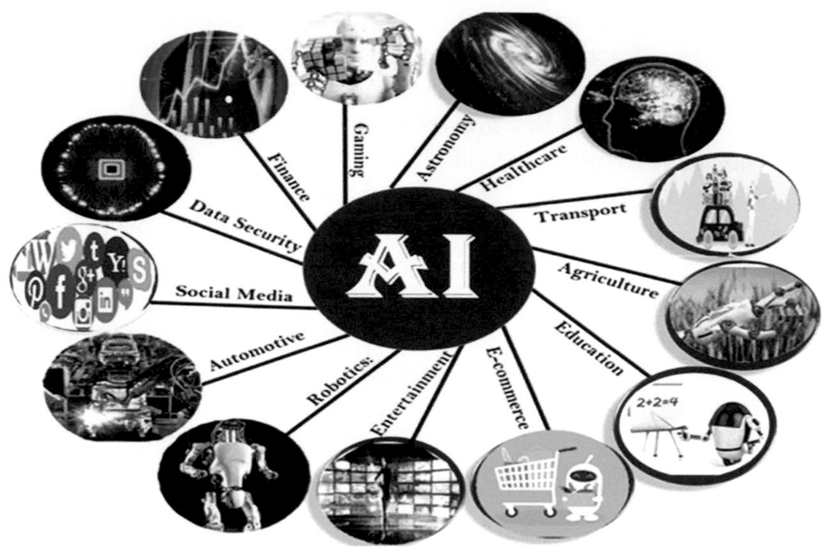

FIGURE 9.2 Application of artificial intelligence.

1. **AI in Astronomy:**
    - AI to solve the multiple problems in the universe can be very helpful. AI to understand the universe techniques may be useful, such as its operation, source, and so on.
2. **Artificial Intelligence (AI) in Healthcare:**
    - In the previous 5 to 10 years, AI has become additional beneficial to the healthcare industry plus has made an important impact on the business.
    - Better than the healthcare industry people and implementing the AI for rapid diagnosis. AI can doctors to determine whether the patient when you are wrong to have access to first-aid patient hospitalization.
3. **Artificial Intelligence (AI) in Gaming:**
    - For gaming purposes may be used in AI. AI machines can participate in a game of chess, where the machine has to know a large number of possible locations.
4. **Artificial Intelligence (AI) in Finance:**
    - AI and the financial industry's best combination with each other. Financial Industry Automation, Chatbot, adaptive intelligence, has been applied to algorithmic trading and ML in financial processes.

5. **Artificial Intelligence (AI) in Data Security:**
    - Cyber-attacks are growing very rapidly in the digital world, so data security is important for every business. Financial intelligence can be used to create data secure. Such as Egg-Bot, the AI2 platform is better determined software bugs and cyber-attacks.
6. **Artificial Intelligence (AI) in Social Media:**
    - Social networking sites for instance Facebook, Twitter, and Snapchat have billions of client profiles, which should be managed as well as stored very efficiently. AI can organize and manage data on a large scale. AI can analyze a lot of data to identify the latest trends, hashtags, and needs from different users.
7. **Artificial Intelligence (AI) in Travel and Transport:**
    - AI is in high demand from travel industry. AI travel-related is capable of various tasks, such as organizing trips for hotels, flights, and suggesting the best options for clients. Industries are using A-I technology chatbots, which can interact humanely with customers for better and appropriate responses.
8. **Artificial Intelligence (AI) in Automotive Industry:**
    - Some automotive industry is using AI to provide virtual assistant for improved performance to its users. As Tesla has introduced a smart virtual assistant, Teslabot.
    - Currently, a wide variety of industries have been worked on to develop autonomous cars that can make your trip safer.
9. **Artificial Intelligence (AI) in Robotics:**
    - The significant role of AI in robotics. General robots are usually programmed so that they can work something repeated, but with the help of AI, we can move on their own experiences of pre-programming, without which you can create a great robot.
    - Humanoid robot AI in robotics are the most exemplary, Erica, and intelligent Humanoid robot named Sophia lately developed that can speak similar to humans and behavior.
10. **Artificial Intelligence (AI) in Entertainment:**
    - Presently, we are using AI-based applications in their everyday life with a variety of services like Amazon and Netflix. In the midst of the assist of ML/AI algorithms, these are services programs or display recommendations for programs.
11. **Artificial Intelligence (AI) in Agriculture:**
    - Agriculture is one area where the best results are diverse resources, labor, need money and time to achieve. Agriculture today is digital,

and AI is emerging in this area. Applying the AI as Agricultural robotics, concrete, and crop monitoring, predictive analysis. It can be very useful for AI farmers in agriculture.

12. **Artificial Intelligence (AI) in E-Commerce:**
    - AI e-commerce industry is becoming more in providing a competitive advantage, and e-commerce demand business. AI shoppers are the recommended size, help to search for products associated with the color or brand.
13. **Artificial Intelligence (AI) in Education:**
    - Can automate AI grading so much time teaching to the tutors. AI would chatbot can correspond with students as teaching assistants.
    - From this time forth, AI can serve as a personal virtual tutor for students, easily available anytime, anywhere [12–14].

9.3 CONCLUSION

It is a new venture to create computational models of AI. These intelligence structures (symbolic or other) can be represented in expressions of symbol structures as well as symbolic operations that are programmed into digital computers. The idea that machines can think and act as machines are thousands of years old. The cognitive truths articulated in AI and ML systems are also not new. The theory and development of computer systems are capable of performing tasks requiring human intelligence, like visual perception, speech recognition, decision making, and translation with languages.

KEYWORDS

- **artificial intelligence**
- **cognitive skills**
- **machine learning**
- **natural language processing**
- **optical character recognition**
- **robotic process automation**
- **sensory organs**

REFERENCES

1. Aamodt, A., & Plaza, E., (1994). Case-based reasoning: Foundational issues, methodological variations, and system approaches. *AI Communications, 7*(1), 39–59.
2. Bobrow, D. G., (1993). Artificial intelligence in perspective: A retrospective on fifty volumes of artificial intelligence. *Artificial Intelligence, 59*, 5–20.
3. Boutilier, C., Brafman, R. I., Domshlak, C., Hoos, H. H., & Poole, D., (2004). Cp-nets: A tool for representing and reasoning with conditional ceteris paribus preference statements. *Journal of Artificial Intelligence Research, 21*, 135–191.
4. Bowling, M., & Veloso, M., (2002). Multiagent learning using a variable learning rate. *Artificial Intelligence, 136*(2), 215–250.
5. Brooks, R. A., (1991). Intelligence without representation. *Artificial Intelligence, 47*, 139–159.
6. Buchanan, B. G., (2005). A (very) brief history of artificial intelligence. *AI Magazine, 26*(4), 53–60.
7. Campbell, M., Hoane, Jr. A. J., & Hse, F. H., (2002). Deep blue. *Artificial Intelligence, 134*(1/2), 57–83.
8. Chapman, D., (1987). Planning for conjunctive goals. *Artificial Intelligence, 32*(3), 333–377.
9. Cheng, J., & Druzdzel, M., (2000). AIS-BN: An adaptive importance sampling algorithm for evidential reasoning in large Bayesian networks. *Journal of Artificial Intelligence Research, 13*, 155–188.
10. Dechter, R., (1996). Bucket elimination: A unifying framework for probabilistic inference. In: Horvitz, E., & Jensen, F., (eds.), *Proc. Twelfth Conf. on Uncertainty in Artificial Intelligence (UAI-96)* (pp. 211–219). Portland.
11. Dietterich, T. G., (2000). Hierarchical reinforcement learning with the MAXQ value function decomposition. *Journal of Artificial Intelligence Research, 13*, 227–303.
12. Felner, A., Korf, R. E., & Hanan, S., (2004). Additive pattern database heuristics. *Journal of Artificial Intelligence Research (JAIR), 22*, 279–318.
13. Kautz, H., & Selman, B., (1996). Pushing the envelope: Planning, propositional logic and stochastic search. In: *Proc. 13th National Conference on Artificial Intelligence* (pp. 1194–1201). Portland.
14. Kambhampati, S., Knoblock, C. A., & Yang, Q., (1995). Planning as refinement search: A unified framework for evaluating design tradeoffs in partial-order planning. *Artificial Intelligence, 76*, 167–238. Special issue on Planning and Scheduling.
15. https://www.google.com/url?sa=i&source=imgres&cd=&cad=rja&uact=8&ved=2ahUKEwj5trLrnr3pAhVS4HMBHeWuBsAQjRx6BAgBEAQ&url=https%3A%2F%2Fwww.slideteam.net%2F7-benefits-advantages-of-artificial-intelligence-ai-powerpoint-slide.html&psig=AOvVaw3pm8rf9g80Ys2u_JB3PcAh&ust=1589885411744587 (accessed on 22 February 2021).
16. https://www.google.com/url?sa=i&url=https%3A%2F%2Fwww.javatpoint.com%2Fapplication-of-ai&psig=AOvVaw3inlYXqqZe1BTjswg0K-86&ust=1589885258598000&source=images&cd=vfe&ved=0CAIQjRxqFwoTCICfr9GevekCFQAAAAAdAAAAABAD (accessed on 22 February 2021).

CHAPTER 10

SMART IRRIGATION USING IOT

AKULA PADMA SRI, AAKANKSHA MUDGAL, and
B. SURESH KUMAR

Amity University, Rajasthan, India

ABSTRACT

In this chapter, an automated system has been developed to irrigate the plants. The normal growth of plants, yield, and the quantity of agricultural products is seriously affected by the water provided to them. This chapter attempts to develop an automated system that waters the plant automatically as and when required without human interaction. Smart irrigation system is developed using sensors like soil sensor, moisture sensor, relay module, and Arduino Uno development board. The values based on moisture; humidity parameters are used to water the plant.

10.1 INTRODUCTION

Indian economy is mainly depending on the Agriculture Industry. It is the heart and soul of the Indian economy as 50% of the people are employed in agriculture, and it contributed 17–18% to country's GDP. Hence agriculture is indispensable part of India. Smart Irrigation System is a boon to farmers living in areas with water scarcity. In this world where automation is the future smart irrigation has been of great help for the farmers. Smart irrigation system is the solution to reduce the workload of farmers by automating the complete irrigation system.

With the help of the internet of things (IoT), we can connect the physical devices, home appliances, and other devices embedded with electronics, software, sensors, and networks which allow these things to connect and interchange data, generating opportunities for directing merging of the physical world into the computer-based system, resulting in the reduced intervention of humans. By the year 2050, the global population is set to reach 9.6 billion. So, to serve the needs of this population, the solution is to adopt IoT technology by the farming industry. To meet the demand for more food against the challenges such as intense weather conditions and exhaustive farming practices. Smart farming-based IoT technologies enhance crop production in the farming industry.

The key concept of smart irrigation is to monitor the moisture content of the soil during wet and dry conditions with the help of a soil moisture sensor. Water, the elixir of life, is also saved to a great extent by using the Smart irrigation method. The smart irrigation method uses the current moisture level of the soil and waters the plant accordingly.

Hence, the fields are watered according to their requirement, and therefore the extra water is saved from being wasted. It also helps us to save electricity as instead of using electricity as a power supply, and we can switch on to renewable sources of energy like Solar energy. With this Automation, the form can utilize the water resources as per the requirement without the involvement of farmer.

In order to replace the expensive controllers in current existing system, Arduino Uno development board is used in this system as it an affordable microcontroller. Arduino Uno is programmed in such a way that analyzes the signals from soil sensors and predicts the moisture level. Similarly using Smart irrigation, we can also provide pesticides and fertilizers to the plant. This will help us to use pesticides and fertilizers effectively. It will also reduce the workload of farmers. Moreover, as we are giving only the required amount of pesticides to the plants and excessive pesticides and fertilizers are being prevented from going into the soil. It also helps us to reduce soil erosion to a huge extend. The key concept behind about how to implement this is the use of sensors which will help us to know how much amount of pesticides and fertilizers should be supplied to the fields. Since we are automating this process, the supply of pesticides and fertilizers will be cut off automatically once the required amount of pesticides and fertilizers are supplied. Smart irrigation system will reduce the issue of lack of water, issue of lack of rainfall, issue of lack of underground water. Oman is a region which is having such kind of issues, and they can be solved by smart irrigation. The use of easily available components reduces the manufacturing and maintenance cost. This makes the proposed system to be economical and low maintenance solution for applications, especially in rural areas and for small-scale agriculturists. This will help in increasing the yield of crops within the budget of farmers.

10.2 EXPERIMENTAL METHODS AND MATERIALS

10.2.1 ARDUINO UNO

The microcontroller we used in this system is Arduino Uno which is based on AT mega328p. It has 6 analog inputs, 14 digital input/output pins, a USB connection, 16 MHz quartz crystal, a power jack, ICSP header and reset button. Arduino microcontrollers are of many types such as Arduino Uno, Arduino nano, Arduino mega. Arduino contains everything needed to support the microcontroller; simply connect it to a computer with a USB cable or power it with AC-to-DC adapter or battery to get started. Uno means one in Italian and was chosen to mark the release of Arduino Software (IDE) 1.0. The Uno board and version 1.0 of Arduino Software (IDE) were the reference versions of Arduino. The Uno board is the first in a series of USB board switch was used in this project (Figure 10.1).

FIGURE 10.1 Arduino development board.

10.2.2 SOIL SENSOR

Soil sensor is the type of sensor which is used to detect the content of water with in the soil. The straight gravimetric dimension of soil moisture needs eliminating, drying, as well as sample weighting. These sensors measure the volumetric water content not directly with the help of some other rules of soil like dielectric constant, electrical resistance, otherwise interaction with neutrons, and replacement of the moisture content.

The relation between the calculated property and moisture of soil should be adjusted and may change based on ecological factors like temperature, type of soil, otherwise electric conductivity. The microwave emission which is reflected can be influenced by the moisture of soil as well as mainly used in agriculture and remote sensing within hydrology. Generally, these sensors are named as soil water potential sensors which uses gypsum blocks and tensiometer (Figure 10.2).

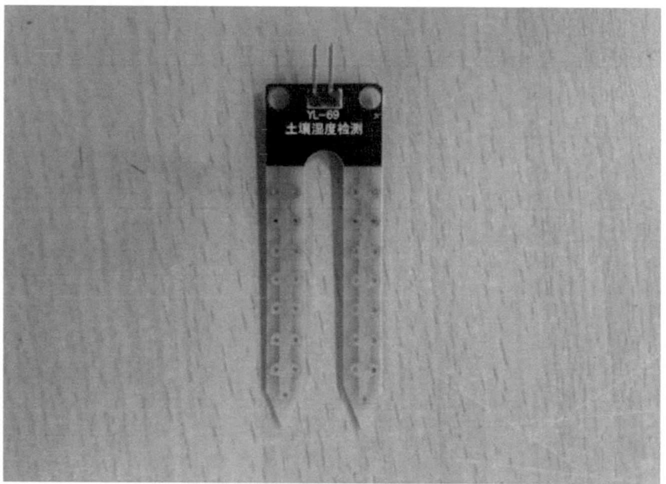

FIGURE 10.2 Pin diagram of soil sensor [1].

The soil moisture sensor contains four pins:

- VCC pin is used for power supply;
- A0 is for analog output;
- D0 is for digital output; and
- GND pin is ground.

10.2.3 METHODOLOGY

This sensor mainly utilizes capacitance to gauge the water content of the soil (dielectric permittivity). The working of this sensor can be done by inserting this sensor into the earth, and the status of the water content in the soil can be reported in the form of a percent.

In the field of sciences like environmental science, agricultural science, biology, soil science, botany, and horticulture, this sensor is suitable to execute the experiments.

10.2.4 SPECIFICATIONS

Input Voltage	3.3–5 V
Output Voltage	0–4.2 V
Input Current	35 mA
Output Signal	Both analog and digital

10.2.5 RELAY MODULE

The Capacity of Arduino is up to 5 V to control the devices. If the device required more than 5 V to controller AC devices, then we will use relay module through which we can control A. Caswell as DC devices (Figure 10.3).

FIGURE 10.3 Relay module.

A relay is a type of switch which was operated by electromagnet, which requires very less voltage to activate which gave from the Arduino. Once it is activated, it will help to make the contact to the high voltage circuit.

10.2.6 BLOCK DIAGRAM

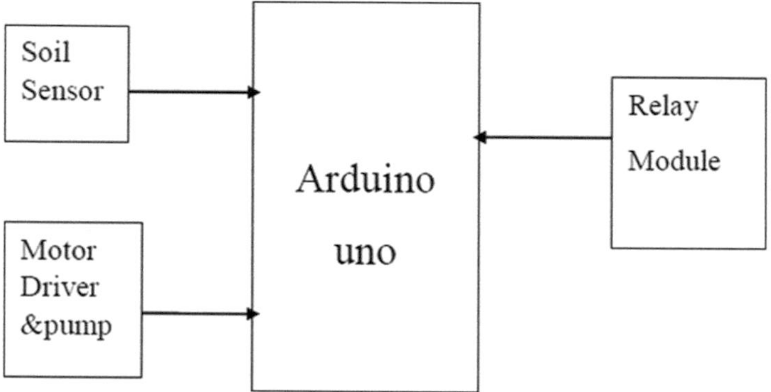

The block diagram shows the hardware implementation of the proposed system. The hardware components are connected according to the following block diagram. Steps followed for connecting the components:

- Connect VCC pin of soil moisture sensor to 3V pin of Arduino Uno;
- Connect ground pin of soil moisture sensor to ground pin of Arduino Uno;
- Connect D0 pin of soil moisture sensor to either digital or analog pin of Arduino Uno;
- Connect Ground pin of relay module to ground pin of Arduino;
- Connect VCC of relay module to 5V pin of Arduino Uno;
- Connect C1 pin of relay module to 13th pin of Arduino.

Once these components are connected, we will connect the motor driver with the relay module. This motor drives sucks the water when moisture in the soil is extremely low and starts watering automatically and stops watering when the moisture content is high. Software required for this system is Arduino IDE. We should write the code on Arduino IDE and then upload code to the Arduino Uno development board. Moisture content of the soil will be displayed on serial monitor.

10.2.7 FLOW CHART

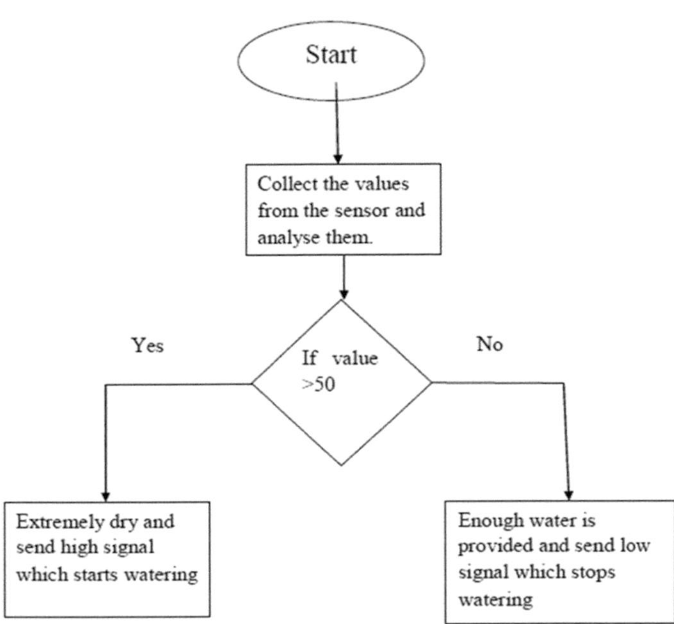

The above flowchart depicts the basic principle that is followed in smart irrigation system. In the very first step, the values of moisture present in the soil is collected.

These values are actually the output of the soil sensor, whereas the moisture content of the soil is the input for the sensor.

Now the values are checked against various conditions. If the moisture level in the soil is good enough, then the low signal is generated, and no action is taken.

If the moisture level is low and the soil is dry or contains very little water, than high signal is sent to the relay, and the system starts watering the plants. When the water level is increased sufficiently, then the water is stopped automatically without human intervention.

10.3 RESULTS AND DISCUSSIONS

The following pictures depict the result of Smart Irrigation System that we have received from sensors that we used in our system (Figure 10.4).

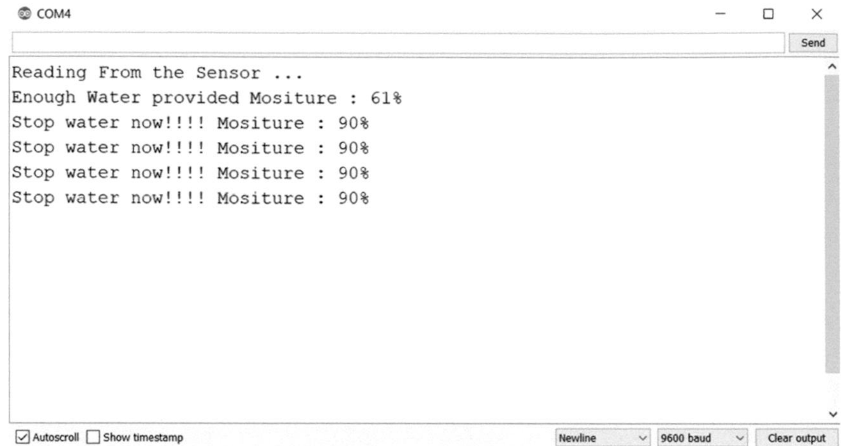

FIGURE 10.4 Snapshot of the result of irrigation system.

Figure 10.4 shows the values that are given by the soil sensor. These are the values that are checked against conditions, and according to these values given by the soil sensor (which depicts the level of moisture in soil), our system decides whether to water the plants or not (Figure 10.5).

COM4

Send

```
Stop water now!!!! Mositure : 90%
Stop water now!!!! Mositure : 90%
Stop water now!!!! Mositure : 90%
Stop water now!!!! Mositure : 90%
Stop water now!!!! Mositure : 89%
Stop water now!!!! Mositure : 89%
Stop water now!!!! Mositure : 90%
Stop water now!!!! Mositure : 90%
Stop water now!!!! Mositure : 90%
Extremely dryMositure : -23%
Extremely dryMositure : -22%
Extremely dryMositure : -23%
Extremely dryMositure : -24%
Extremely dryMositure : -25%
```

Autoscroll Show timestamp Newline 9600 baud Clear output

FIGURE 10.5 Snapshot of the Arduino console.

Figure 10.5 is another example of values given by soil sensor. In the above picture, the sensor is placed in two different soil with different moisture content. Hence there are two different values, and our system acts accordingly to both the values. When the sensor senses good moisture content in the soil, no action is taken.

On the other hand, when the sensor is placed in another soil which is dry, the sensor gives a negative value due to lack of moisture content in the soil. In this case, the high signal is generated and the system starts watering the plants. After watering is started, the moisture level starts improving and watering is continued till sufficient moisture content is established. Once the optimal value is reached, the water is stopped automatically.

10.3.1 COMPARATIVE ANALYSIS

In previously proposed model's energy consumption is very high, whereas in our model, we can even use renewable resources which makes it energy efficient. In our system, there are many other advantages also like less wastage of water, cost-efficient, energy-efficient, easy to use.

- **Advantages:**
  - This model optimizes water levels which is helpful in less consumption of resources and increase the productivity.
  - As this device is working with following the safety measures and no manpower is required.
  - It Controls Uneven water levels which reduces soil erosion and nutrient leaching.
  - As we stated, this model is optimizing water resources so less water consumption with this model.

10.4 CONCLUSION

The Project 'Smart Irrigation System' was designed by using soil moisture sensor which senses the moisture level and it can optimize the water usage level without involvement of farmer in agricultural field. The microcontroller controls the pump accordingly with the soil sensor, whenever the sensor senses the low moisture level, then the pump will ON as per instructions of the micro-controller. This model optimizes the usage of water for irrigation so that we can save water. This system was designed in consideration of Indian Agricultural lands as all you know India is mainly based on Agriculture Industry, so this device is available in affordable price and very easy to use. This model is also helpful where the water levels are not sufficient for the crop.

10.5 FUTURE SCOPE

There are many future scope for this system as it will help us in saving water. Water is prevented from being wasted through smart irrigation method.

Moreover, instead of using electricity as the source to drive this system we can implement this device with the help of renewable sources of energy like solar energy, wind energy, etc. Geothermal energy can also be used for the same.

Another future scope of this system is that, like water, we can supply pesticides and fertilizers to the soil. We can use sensors that will tell us the amount of pesticides or fertilizers to be given. Like water is supplied automatically as and when required, pesticides and fertilizers can also be supplied to the plants. Since only the required amount of pesticides is given to the plants, the chances of soil erosion are decreased to a huge extent.

Another problem that the farmers face is the devastation of fields by harmful birds. This problem can also be fixed by this system by connecting this system to drums which start beating as soon as the fields are attacked by harmful birds.

To make sure that the drums start beating only in the presence of harmful birds' object detection is used. Through this method, the birds are not harmed and are chased away easily.

KEYWORDS

- **agriculture industry**
- **Arduino Uno**
- **automation**
- **farming industry**
- **fertilizers**
- **interchange data**
- **internet of things**
- **microcontroller**
- **smart irrigation**

REFERENCE

1. https://soilsensor.com/ (accessed on 22 February 2021).

PART III

Intelligent Data Analytics Techniques

CHAPTER 11

A STUDY FOR MAKING UNIVERSITIES INTELLIGENT USING DATA ANALYTICS AND ARTIFICIAL INTELLIGENCE

YOJNA ARORA[1] and RASHI KOHLI[2]

[1]*Department of Computer Science and Engineering, Amity University, Haryana, India, E-mail: yojana183@gmail.com*

[2]*Senior Member, IEEE, Institute of Electrical and Electronics Engineers, New York, US, E-mail: rashikohli.amity@gmail.com*

ABSTRACT

Big Data refers to the huge amount of data that is getting generated. This data can provide various insights that can be utilized as a major support in generating prediction models. It is assumed that Big Data possess great significance and meaning but fetching the meaning out of it the real task. Big Data Analytics helps in achieving this goal. This chapter explains big data analytics in Education for making universities intelligent. The universities can utilize various techniques to implement effective and smart learning for students and also for recognizing strengths and weaknesses.

11.1 INTRODUCTION

In this era, where technology is flourishing, big data has a major influence on driving various networks, the internet, artificial intelligence (AI), and digital technology in several industries. Big data in alignment with AI is having an impact over all the spheres of life, and education is not an exclusion which perhaps turns into a productive tool in the education framework. In the most recent decade, learning has transformed the process from a passive to an active experience. Thereby, educational institutions no longer require to proceed with training fundamentally. New advancements permit schools, universities, and colleges to break down completely everything that happens. Big data analytics can help students predict their performance and teachers can scrutinize the student's performance, create instructional strategies, accommodate or create behavioral [1], plans, testing results, career development, etc. "Data has always been the "quintessence of AI."

Big data is supporting educational institutions and companies to understand things they could not have previously. The major application of big data in Higher education is to help the weaker students avoid the situations of dropping out (Figure 11.1) [3].

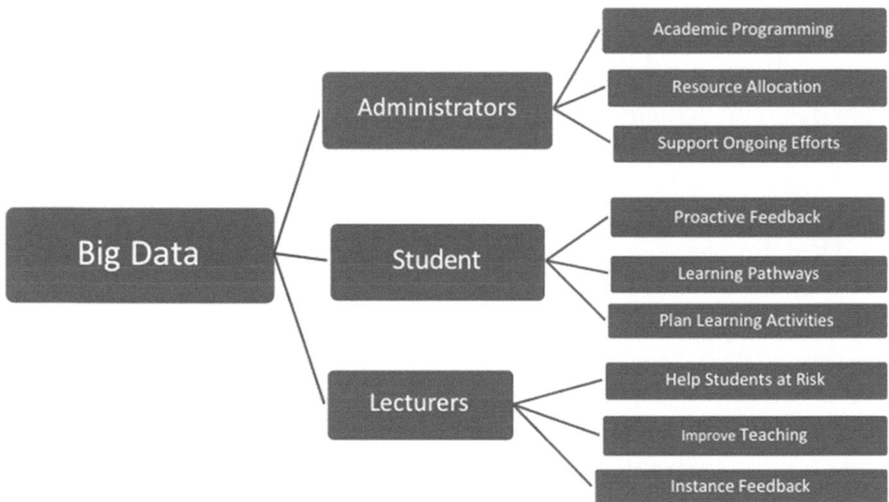

FIGURE 11.1 Framework: Three end-users in the higher education scenario.

The urge to market to students and families has only strengthened over the last several years as technology made it easier for schools to reach more students and demographic shifts upped the pressure on colleges to fill their classes. What is more, colleges now have more refined ways of collecting and responding to data about students, so they can target them in more specific ways than ever. Schools and colleges can utilize big data in adopting new methodologies to teach students other than the traditional methods. It can also help in optimum and relevant resource a location. The student data is analyzed by the teachers to adjust the learning needs of the students to meet the learning accommodations of the students [4, 5].

11.1.1 NEED OPPORTUNITIES AND CHALLENGES

The Framework has been created in Figure 11.2 to highlight the analytics of big data and how they are linked to the challenges, their needs, and the opportunities of the big data, which can help predict future outcomes using AI techniques and Big data analytics.

The biggest challenge here would be the security of big data, which can be achieved by using cryptographic algorithms by ensuring the overall cost and overheads are maintained. There are different algorithms available that can help secure the big data, for example, AES, XTEA, SHA [11, 13]. Strategies of Big data create opportunities for effective learning, cost reduction, risk reduction and thereby help the learners and the teachers in developing effective research-based curriculum and learning process.

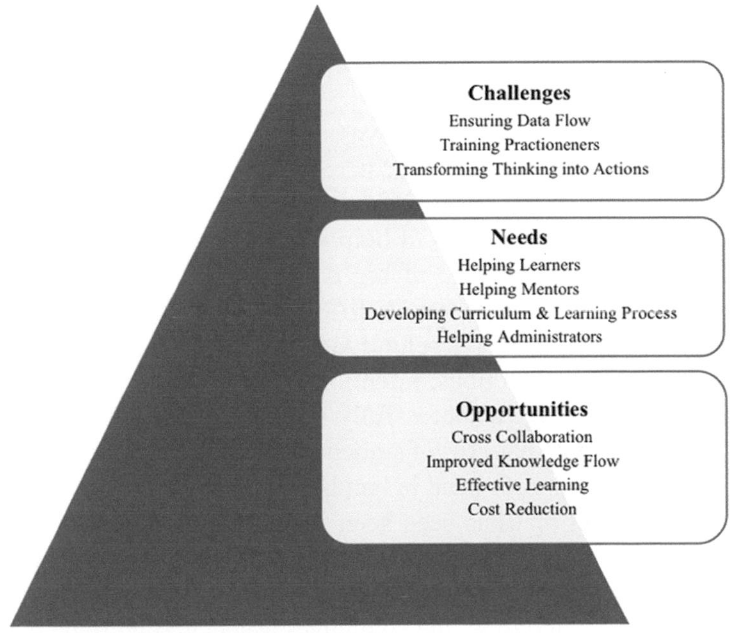

FIGURE 11.2 Role of big data analytics in education.

11.2 LITERATURE SURVEY

The application of big data relies heavily on the information system. They are also potentially and gradually transforming the management decision-making theory [7, 12]. The process of "big-data" integrates the growing research field of data mining, data encryption and learning analytics in the field of education. Big data analytics help in identifying opportunities and challenges in higher education.

The education system requirement of universities is to analyze the data of students in terms of their achievement level and ability level [5].

With the constant increase and growth of more and more virtual education and the development of MOOCs (massive open online course) all the secure information and the records get a whole new picture to the application. To motivate this trend, it was highlighted that Purdue University has developed a system called 'Course Signals,' which helps to predict academic and behavioral issues within students [2]. In the context of higher education, big data in alignment with AI helps to interpret the extensive series of data with operational information was gathered and procedures designed at evaluating official performance and progress in order to envisage future performance using AI applications as mentioned in Ref. [10] and then take necessary actions to identify prospective concerns related to academic programming, research, instruction, and learning [2, 9].

An OECD (2013) report which was examined had suggested that the higher level of learning and teaching can reinvent and have a major impact on the education sector. The evidence of the results in the education sector can be collected using AI techniques to help make decisions about educational outcomes, maybe with the help of big data analytics. It was investigated before that the student's network with different aspects of knowledge and its technologies, they tend to leave behind facts trails which thereby can reveal the thoughts, social connections, intentions, and goals [6, 8]. Some of the researchers in the past have successfully used such type of data which can carefully study multiple patterns of student performance over time. Thus the role of Big data and AI goes hand in hand.

The major impact that has been seen is because they continue to break all faces of higher education, the valuable evidence is being generated by students, computer applications, and their systems. The major application of big Data can also talk about the challenges associated with the discovery of the data at the right time when data is getting dispersed across several unlinked different data systems in institutions. This way by categorizing by incorporating different ways of gathering data across systems can help significantly to improve decision-making capability. Table 11.1 discusses various use cases developed by other researchers in the domain of big data in education sector.

TABLE 11.1 Use Case of Big Data in Education

Author's Name	Aim	Technique Applied	Key Features	Advantages	Results Attained
Yojna Arora, Abhishek Singhal, and Dr. Abhay Bansal [13]	To predict student's performance and generate warning accordingly	Radial basis function (RBF)	The interrelation of data sets	The supervised learning capability of data set	Depending on student's past performance, the prediction about the future is made and each student is counseled accordingly
Christos Vaitsis, Vasilis Hervatis and Nabil Zary [14]	To analyze educational big data	Learning analytics methods: Data-driven, need-driven	Specific analytics Descriptive analytics	Quality improvement in education is presented	Healthcare big data is analyzed using various learning analytics methods
Jacqueline A. Reyes [15]	To understand the role of big data in education	Learning analytics	Gathering analyzing reporting data	Involvement of all stakeholders	Various solutions that allows learning analytics to transform learning and teaching
Katrina Sin and Loganathan Muthu [16]	To study various applications of big data in education	Learning analytics Educational data mining	Regression Nearest neighbor Clustering Classification	Support for data prediction and visualization	A detailed literature about application of big data in education and learning analytics is presented
Yojna Arora [13]	To understand application of big data in education	Supervised learning methods	Linear regression Apriori Algorithm	Correlation in data set is identified	Student data is analyzed and a prediction model is implemented

11.3 ADVANTAGES OF BIG DATA IN EDUCATIONAL INSTITUTIONS

11.3.1 IMPROVING STUDENT RESULTS

Analyzing student data can help in the prediction of their future performance. The analyzed data can be used in taking corrective measures and thus help in improving performance and results. AI plays a great role in proposing such a prediction model. Since every student produces unique data patterns for a similar set of questions and queries, it can work as a differentiated instruction for the students.

11.3.2 CREATE MASS-CUSTOMIZED PROGRAMS

Big data analysis of the information can support to produce a customized program for every student. In the current scenario, the education system requires support for Blended Learning. The use of various tools and techniques can help students learn and understand better. Online Learning provides a benefit to students for learning any time, any place according to student's own pace. However, the traditional method of offline learning helps students in interacting with the teachers in person and clarifying doubts. These customization methods prove to be beneficial for the students. These techniques can be implemented in both Schools and Universities and can be extended to many different levels.

11.3.3 IMPROVE THE LEARNING EXPERIENCE IN REAL-TIME

A combination of big data and AI can better monitor a student's performance. Big data depicts how a student learns in a customized environment and the pace of learning can be identified using the AI technique. With the availability of course content online, the learning of students is increased and the monitoring capability of the teacher is also enhanced. Students can learn online by various online platforms provided by the educational institution.

11.3.4 REDUCE DROPOUTS, INCREASE RESULTS

Predictive analytics over big data of students will improve student's results and thus reduce the dropout rates. This is because due to the close monitoring of the students and the reception of timely feedback, they tend to take timely corrective measures. This monitoring can be extended and performed after they pass out. This data can be further used by future students in making better decisions (Figure 11.3).

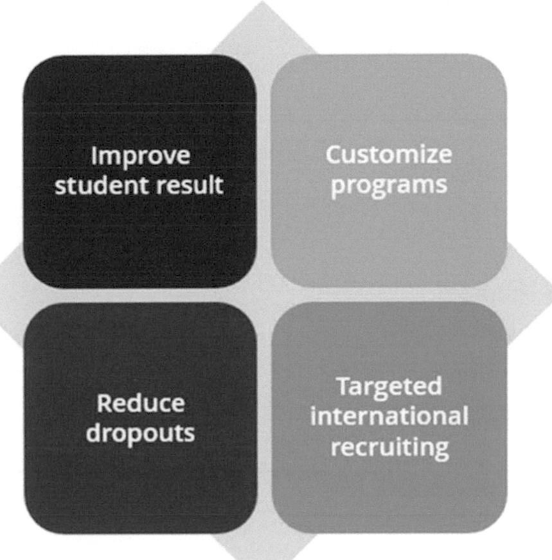

FIGURE 11.3 Big data application in education.

11.4 CONCLUSION

The objective of any innovation is to make the life of an individual simple and comfortable. The big data, with the help of AI strategies modify the method for learning by making it simple, easy, and interesting and helping the teachers or professors to analyze the data and predict future scope using AI algorithms. The customary classroom condition is not anymore required for learning.

Innovation will consistently make adoptions that are simple for the comfort of students. Through the best possible utilization of big data analytics, the progressive advancement in the educational sector could be accomplished. Rather than some natural difficulties, big data analytics can represent customized learning environments to the learners, can reduce potential dropouts and failure and can develop long term learning plans.

These are conceivable through the viable improvement and utilization of big data analytics in educational organizations. Therefore, it is time we embrace big data in the education sector. In the future, we can implement and design the algorithm to support the approach that interacts with Big data and AI strategies, also making it secure using cryptographic algorithms [12].

KEYWORDS

- **artificial intelligence**
- **big data**
- **data analysis**
- **digital technology**
- **intelligent universities**
- **massive open online course**
- **security/cryptography**

REFERENCES

1. Shikha, A., (2014). Big data analytics in the education sector. *International Journal of Research in Computer and Communication Technology, 3*(11).
2. Ben, D., (2014). Big data and analytics in higher education: Opportunities and challenges. *British Journal of Educational Technology*.
3. Naveen, J., (2017). *Ways Big Data is Transforming the Education Sector*. https://www.allerin.com/blog/4-ways-big-data-is-transforming-the-education-sector (accessed on 22 February 2021).
4. *Big Data and Analytics for Education*., (2016). http://www.insightssuccess.com/big-data-and-analytics-for-education/ (accessed on 22 February 2021).
5. *Four Ways Big Data Will Revolutionize Education*., (2006). https://datafloq.com/read/big-data-will-revolutionize-learning/206 (accessed on 22 February 2021).
6. Rowley, J., (1998). Creating a learning organization in higher education. *Industrial and Commercial Training, 30*(1), 16–19.
7. Boyd, D., & Crawford, K., (2012). Critical questions for big data. *Communication and Society, 15*(5), 662–679. doi: 10.1080/1369118X.2012.678878.
8. Nicola, J., & O'Malley, B., (2016). *Are Universities Making the Most of Their Big Data?* 398.
9. Mikhail, Z., (2016). *The Colleges are Watching*. https://www.theatlantic.com/education/archive/2016/11/the-colleges-are-watching/506129/ (accessed on 22 February 2021).

10. Kumar, N., Kharkwal, N., Kohli, R., & Choudhary, S., (2016). Ethical aspects and future of artificial intelligence. *Innovation and Challenges in Cyber Security (ICICCS-INBUSH) 2016 International Conference* (pp. 111–114).
11. Arora, Y., & Goyal, D., (2015). Big data technologies: Brief overview. *Int. J. Comput. Appl., 131*(9), 1–6.
12. Rashi, K., & Manoj, K., (2013). FPGA implementation of cryptographic algorithms using multi-encryption technique. *International Journal of Advanced Research in Computer Science and Software Engineering, 3*(5).
13. Yojna, A., Abhishek, S., & Abhay, B., (2014). Prediction and warning: A method to improve student's performance. *ACM Sig Soft Software Engineering Notes, 39*(1).
14. Christos, V., Vasilis, H., & Nabil, Z., (2016). Introduction to big data in education and its contribution to the quality improvement processes. In: Sebastian, V. S., José, M. L., & Alberto, C., (eds.), *Big Data on Real-World Applications*. IntechOpen. doi: 10.5772/63896.
15. Jacqueleen, A. R., (2015). *The Skinny on Big Data in Education: Learning Analytics Simplified.* Springer US. doi: https://doi.org/10.1007/s11528-015-0842-1.
16. Katrina, S., & Loganathan, M., (2015). Application of big data in education data mining and learning analytics: A literature review. *ICTACT Journal of Soft Computing, Special Issue on Soft Computing Models for Big Data, 5*(4).

CHAPTER 12

SENTIMENT ANALYSIS OF ONLINE LEARNERS IN HIGHER EDUCATION: A LEARNING PERSPECTIVE THROUGH UNSTRUCTURED DATA

PRIYANKA SHUKLA and ADARSH GARG

School of Computing Science and Engineering Galgotias University, Greater Noida, Uttar Pradesh, India,
E-mail: priyanka.Shukla@galgotiasuniversity.edu.in (P. Shukla)

ABSTRACT

Online learning platform provides asynchronous communication through the discussion forum. The learner is communicating and indulged in discussions with peers and instructors through this platform for their doubts and also give their views about the running course and the instructor. A huge amount of text and graphics is generated through this communication. Each learner have their sentiments or opinion, emotions or attitude towards a specific course and instructor as well. The sentiments shared are more in the form of incomplete and short sentences, jargons, images, emoticons, etc. This makes the analysis more difficult but more realistic without any formal process to evaluate the perceived learning. The present study seeks to explore the unstructured data in terms of sentiments of online learners on their perceived learning.

12.1 INTRODUCTION

In the current world of education, the traditional classroom learning is moving more towards to the online learning. Higher educational institutions are providing the online learning facility to the learners for some of the courses. A learner can learn from any geographical area at any time with this facility of online learning. A learner can be anyone who is employed or unemployed, professional, student. However, the motivation of learning can be to get a job or to improve personal profile. Educational institute are now willing to explore the different learning method for learner's vis-a-vis blended learning, flipped class learning and e-learning through varied learning sources like Learning Management System (Moodle), Massive open online course (MOOC) portal (Coursera, Udacity, Edx, Udemy, Swayam, NPTEL), social media (Facebook, Twitter). The learning process extends from offering a course to the evaluation of the performance of the learners, including the effectiveness of the offered course through feedback/open discussion forums.

While learning from online sources, huge data is produced about a learner/course/instructor/learning. The collection, analysis, measurement of online educational data to improve the education is called learning analytics. In the available research, learning analytics is considered as a study to analyze the learning behavior, cognitive behavior, improvement in learning, to analyze student satisfaction for particular course, give the feedback to the instructor and for the enhancement of curriculum. The learners have their sentiments or opinion, emotions or attitude towards a specific course and/or instructor. These sentiments now need to be analyzed to determine the usefulness of online learning. In recent years, sentiment analysis has moved from studying online product reviews to social media texts and graphics from social media sites like (Facebook/Twitter) and feedback on the online learning platform. There are numerous topics which are exterior from product reviews like stock markets, medicine, disaster, elections, software engineering, and cyberbullying extend the utilization of sentiment analysis.

Sentiment analysis, also known as opinion mining, is one of the fastest growing research areas since 2004. It has been explained as a "field of study that analyzes people's opinions, sentiments, evaluations, appraisals, attitudes, and emotions towards entities such as products, services, organizations, individuals, issues, events, topics, and their attributes" [7]. The use of sentiment analysis has flourished in various areas like review of customers on products, prediction of financial markets, reactions to political activities, public opinion, etc. Further, sentiment analysis and natural language processing (NLP) has also addressed the needs of the online learners. In higher education, understanding the positive and negative sentiments of online learners can help instructors understand the students better, enhance the course structure, improve the teaching pedagogy. The efforts have been made to study every aspect of sentiments, be it polarity or optimism and/or pessimism of the sentiments.

The sentiment analysis is the area which become so enormous that any single researcher would face a lot of issues when keeping track of all the happenings in the area and the information surplus. However, the sentiments analyzed so far include the structured data of a learner toward the course alignment, the instructor's performance, course outline, enhancement of the course outline in a structured manner. While the global online forums do not facilitate the structured data. The sentiments shared are more in the form of incomplete and short sentences, jargons, images, emoticons, etc. This makes the analysis more difficult but more realistic without any formal process to evaluate the perceived learning. The present study seeks to explore the unstructured data in terms of sentiments of online learners on their perceived learning. Specifically, we attempt to find the answer to the following question:

How sentiments of the online learner are available as unstructured data, can be analyzed to predict the perceived learning through the online platform?

12.2 OBJECTIVE

The objective of this study is to study the sentiments of online learners to evaluate the usefulness of sentiment analysis in perceived learning.

12.3 THEORETICAL PERSPECTIVE

The interest on other's opinion/sentiments is probably the most important and effective way to deliberate on the existing problems and finding the solution to those problems: (a) sentiment analysis is set of tools and technologies to extract the useful information from the subjective opinion in the form of language/gesture about some event, phenomenon, process, product or person. In general, the person giving opinion on something may be optimistic, pessimistic or neutral, i.e., opinion polarity; (b) with the burgeon growth of social media, such opinions/sentiments have been made public using social media. There has been a massive increase in the analysis of the sentiments during the recent years and since 2004 sentiment analysis is now the emergent research areas in the field of politics, finance, business, education, etc.; (c) the research area of sentiment analysis has outsized to an extent that the researcher finds it difficult to deal with information overload.

Now a day's sentiment analysis is a trend to analyze the behavior of a learner in higher education. In higher education, understanding the sentiments of students who are enrolled in course using online platforms like MOOCs, Coursera, Edx, Udemy, etc. Sentiment analysis not only helps to find the positive and negative sentiments it also used to find and analyze the mood, attitude of the learner which can be classify in some more different classes like anger, frustration, confusion, sadness, etc. Sentiment analysis can help the instructors to understand the requirements of online learners. It also helps in terms of curriculum improvement, course content improvement. There are different steps to be follow for sentiment analysis are data collection, pre-processing, cleaning, steaming, and lemmatization and tokenization. There are various techniques to analyze the sentiments of the online learners on their learning experience vis-a-vis course content, course timing, course instructor, etc. There are various techniques to analyze the sentiments to know the likelihood of a successful learning.

Sentiment analysis are coming under the NLP in which analysis of text, emoticons, and slangs, etc., can be processed. There are different levels of analysis are document level, sentence level and aspect level. In document level overall sentiment of the review is given. Sentence level analysis gives the sentiment of every sentiments. And the aspect level analysis give the sentiment of word-level analysis it is also called feature-based analysis. There are different techniques of sentiment analysis are lexicon-based approach, machine learning (ML) techniques cross-domain classification and cross-language classification [23]. In cross-domain classification the sentiment of is representing positive mean and same sentence may give negative sentiment will be handled in this classification [23]. In this book study given that an author suggested a POS-based ensemble model to assimilate features with different types of POS tags to progress the classification performance. Because in different domain the POS tagging are usually domain-independent but some are domain free. Cross-language classification means performing classification which is of different language [23]. Lexicon-based approach is again categorized into dictionary-based and corpus-based. In which there is a lexicons are available or can be added manually, if not existing in dictionary. Dictionary-based techniques are better than the corpus-based approach because in corpus-based it is difficult to make a large corpus to include all the words in English [18]. There are various dictionaries are available are SentiWordNet, LIWC, wordnet, MPQA, etc. ML techniques are those techniques in which ML algorithms are used. These techniques are further categorized into supervised, unsupervised learning techniques and semi supervised techniques [17]. Unsupervised learning approach in which labeled data is not require and in supervised learning approach data is already labeled. Topic modeling technique which is comes under the unsupervised learning. The major topic modeling technique is LDA, which is apply on unlabeled data. Clarizia et al. [3] proposed that the mood of the learner is to be detected using LDA (latent Dirichlet allocation) approach, the effectual and suitable results are drawn. In some of the chapter's hybrid approach is used to analyze the sentiments of online learners. Liu et al. [11] used a hybrid approach SVM and dictionary-based approach to develop a SentBuk. Nassirtoussi et al. [20] used BLSTM neural networks and SVM. Moreno-Marcos et al. [24] does the comparison of different ML algorithm to detect the polarity of massages. The different supervised (random forest, logistic regression, support vector machine (SVM), decision tree and unsupervised (dictionaries and SentiWordNet) learning algorithm used are. And found that the random forest and dictionaries based performed well. Rani and Parteek [12] proposed a e-learning system for automatics sentiment analysis using Bayesian classification in which naïve Bayes is used for creating classifiers. Harris and Vivekanandan [7] analyzed discussion forum massages to have individuality in different levels of Bloom's taxonomy to find out the cognitive learning. Moreno-Marcos et al. [24] explored the issue that occurred in MOOC systems and proposed a feedback management system in MOOC for an enrolled learner for interactive communication. Shatnawi, Mohamad, and Mihaela [26] analyzed the most active user on the discussion forum of MOOC. The analysis is done on the post, comment, and votes. Wöllmer et al. [18] talk about the learning inclination of learners based on big data on the MOOC platform. Cohen, Udi, and Rafi [5] tells that the learner is not interacting only for social purpose in discussion forum rather they may interact for their cognitive purpose too. Jian-Syuan et al. [25] have used naïve Bayes algorithm for sentiment analysis for Chinese Twitter. Table 12.1 is about some more discretion of parameters.

12.4 DATA COLLECTION AND METHODOLOGY

The dataset of online reviews of learners is collected from the Kaggle, and this data set consists of large reviews. That data is updated till 2018 for

TABLE 12.1 Some Categories of Parameter

Focus of the Research	Sentiments Polarity	Number of Categories of Sentiments	Author/Year
Digital learning	Confusion or frustration	2	Steven C. Harris and Vivekanandan Kumar, 2018
Sentiment analysis in MOOCs	Positive, negative, and neutral	3	Pedro Manuel Moreno-Marcos, 2018
Topic modeling approach	Positive, negative, and confusion	3	Zhi Liu, Tai Wang and Lingyun Kang, 2018
Sentimental and behavioral tendencies of learners	Positive and negative	2	Sannyuya Liu, Xian Peng, Hercy N. H. Cheng, Zhi Liu, Jianwen Sun and Chongyang Yang, 2018
E-learning and sentiment analysis	Mood of learner is found positive, negative, neutral	3	Clarizia, Fabio, 2018
Semantic analysis of learners' emotional tendencies	Happy, sad, angry, disappointed, surprised, proud, in love, scared	8	Ling Wang, Gongliang Hu and Tiehua Zhou, 2018
Measuring learner tone and sentiment	Positive, negative, and tone analysis.	2	Michael Schubert, Damian Durruty, and David A. Joyner, 2018
Characteristics of learner's discourse in discourse in forum	Social, cognitive, meta-cognitive, and disciplinary	4	Cohen, Anat, UdiShimony, and Rafi Nachmias, 2017
Sentiment analysis of students' comment	Strongly positive, moderately positive, weakly positive, strongly negative, moderately negative, weakly negative or neutral.	7	Khin Zezawar Aung and Nyein Myo, 2017
Sentiment analysis to track emotion and polarity in student fora	Positive, negative, and neutral	3	Andreas F. Gkontzis, Christoforos V. Karachristos and Chris T. Panagiotakopoulos, 2017
Sentiment analysis system to improve teaching and learning	Two categories (+ and –) include eight categories—anger, anticipation, disgust, fear, joy, sadness, surprise, and trust—from which it computes satisfaction or dissatisfaction	8	Sujata Rani, 2017

TABLE 12.1 *(Continued)*

Focus of the Research	Sentiments Polarity	Number of Categories of Sentiments	Author/Year
Sentiment analysis on self-evaluated comments	Positive, negative, and neutral	3	Yu, Lee, Pan, Chou, Chao, Chen, Tseng, Chan, Lai, 2017
Sentiment recognition	Positive, negative, and neutral	3	Zhi Liu, Sanya Liu n, Lin Liu, Jianwen Sun, Xian Peng, and Tai Wang, 2015
Identifying e-learner's opinion	Positive, negative, and neutral	3	Bharathisindhu and Brunda, 2014
Sentiment analysis in Facebook	Positive negative and neutral	3	Alvaro Ortigosa, José M. Martín and Rosa M. Carro, 2013
Emoticon-based sentiment analysis system	Angry, disgusting, sadness, and joyful	4	Jichang Zhao, Li Dong, Junjie Wu, and Ke Xu, 2012
Sentiment analysis of users' opinions	Positive and negative	2	Zied Kechaou, Mohamed Ben Ammar, Adel. M Alimi, 2011

different subjects of Coursera. The reviews of multiple courses are taken for analysis. For sentiment analysis, some basic steps to be followed in the text.

12.4.1 DATA PREPROCESSING AND CLEANING

This is the major step in every text analysis. In this different functions like lowercase, remove punctuations, remove stop words, remove white space, remove numbers multiple steps to be follow gives as we know there are words in upper and lower case both in the reviews. To remove confusion first we transform all the reviews in lower case, missing values like punctuations, stop words (e.g., are, a, an, the, etc.), are to be remove which has no impact on reviews that are just to use to combine the sentences. But some time punctuation may be used when the emoticons and hashtags are to be in consideration.

12.4.2 STEMMING AND LEMMATIZATION

Stemming is one the major step in sentiment analysis. In this the word is to chop from its affix, e.g., there are words like automates, automatic, automated all are to reduce in single word automat. There is a function SnowballC in R for stemming. Lemmatization is different from stemming it does not cut the word instead trying to give meaning full word.in R there is no direct package for lemmatization.

12.4.3 TOKENIZATION: AFTER CLEANING THE DOCUMENTS ARE TOKENIZED

A huge number of features is generated after tokenization. Some of these are listed below with there the count. Feature is the individual word in whole reviews and the frequency of word is the number of time that word appears in all reviews. The range of the frequency of words are from 1 to 25516. Sample of the frequency of words are in Table 12.1. In Table 12.1 the highest used feature is 'course,''great' and 'good.' The frequency of words are calculated in R tool. In this research R tool is used for preprocessing and analysis of the reviews of learners. For the visualization Word cloud is used. This representing the highest frequency of word having the largest size and then decreasing accordingly.

12.4.4 SEGMENTATION OF SENTIMENTS

sentiments are segmented in positive and negative sentiments. Bag of words are there for segmentation. There are bag of words for positive and negative words both. This is called lexicon-based approach. In this, the reviews are matched with positive sentiment bag of words. When word match with positive bag of word file will count to one like that the processes is going on. The same is with negative word count. Like that total number of positive word and a total number of negative words are calculated. After this process score is calculated by finding the difference between a number of positive words and number of negative words. Score tell us that the overall reviews are positive or negative. The total number of positive words are 243045 and the total number of negative words are 36219 approximately.

To find the number of positive words and number of negative words and then find the score:

Score = Number of positive words – Number of negative words

If Score > 0, positive sentiments in reviews;
If Score < 0, negative sentiments in reviews;
If Score = 0, neutral sentiments.

12.5 RESULTS (FIGURES 12.1–12.6)

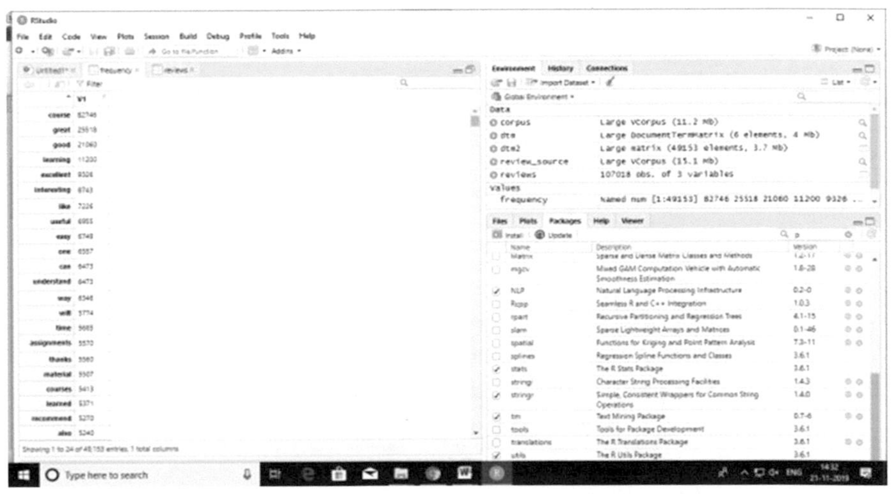

FIGURE 12.1 Frequency of all terms.

FIGURE 12.2 Word cloud of all terms.

FIGURE 12.3 Word cloud for positive term.

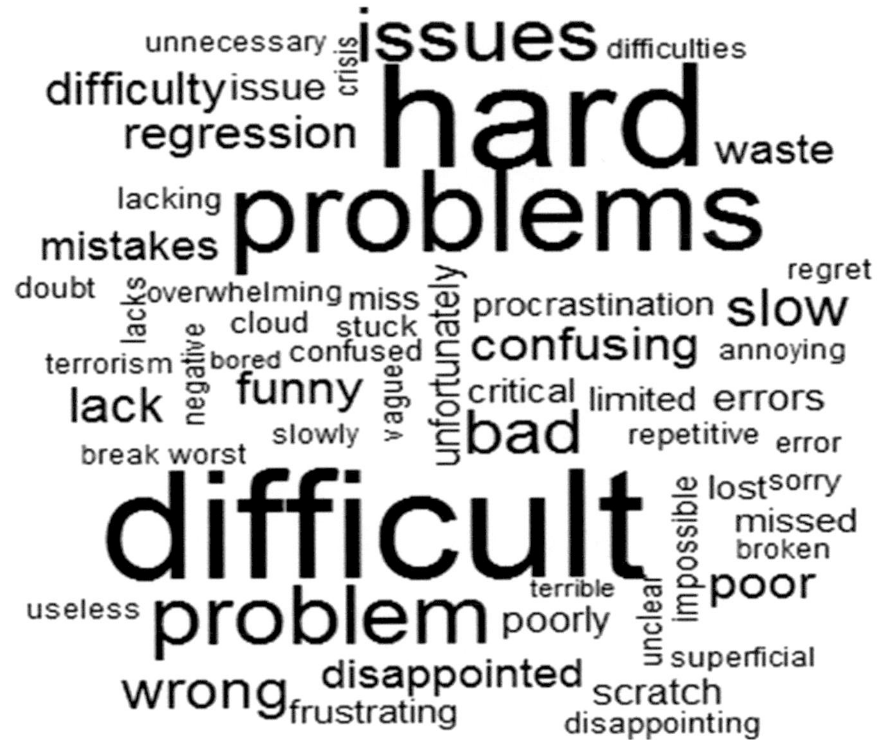

FIGURE 12.4 Word cloud for negative term.

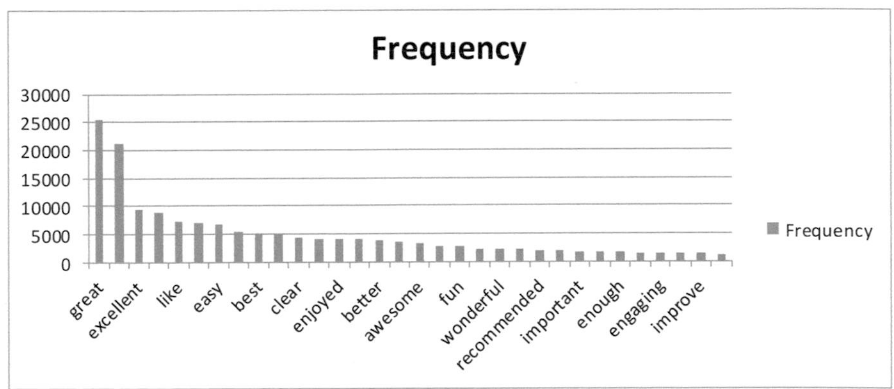

FIGURE 12.5 Frequency of positive terms.

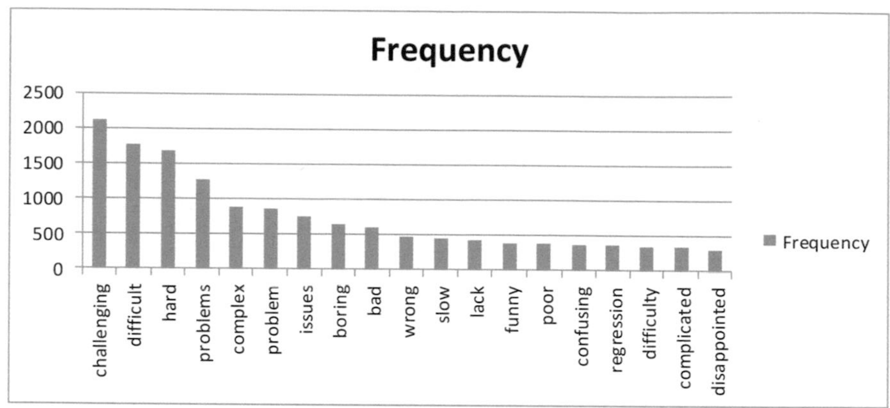

FIGURE 12.6 Frequency of negative terms.

12.6 DISCUSSION AND CONCLUSION

We have calculated the frequency of each word. In this the most frequently used words are "course," great" "good," "interesting," "excellent," etc. The frequency of positive and negative words are also calculated separately and found that the score of sentiments are greater than zero (Figure 12.1). So we can say that the overall positive reviews are present in the reviews. In this, we can now also say that the inclination of learner towards the online learning is there. Figure 12.2 represents the word cloud for all the terms in the review. Figure 12.3 shows the word cloud for positive words and Figure 12.4 shows the words cloud for the negative words. In this highest frequency of a word is in bold and accordingly the frequency of word is decreasing the size of the word in word cloud is also shown in small size. Figure 12.5 shows the frequency of positive terms and Figure 12.6 shows the frequency of negative terms. So this can tell us that sentiment analysis is useful for finding the positive and negative terms from the reviews which can helps learner to choose the particular course or this will also help instructor to improve their teaching or may also beneficial for the course improvement point of view. The terms that are other than negative and positive words are considered as neutral words. Neutral words are those which does not have any meaning. This study is in process for some more analysis on online learner.

KEYWORDS

- **geographical area**
- **latent Dirichlet allocation**
- **learning analytics**
- **learning management system**
- **machine learning**
- **online learning**
- **sentiment analysis**

REFERENCES

1. Rahate, R. S., & Emmanuel, M., (2013). Feature selection for sentiment analysis by using SVM. *International Journal of Computer Applications, 84*(5), 24–32.
2. Buenaño-Fernández, D., Villegas-Ch, W., & Luján-Mora, S., (2018). Using text mining to evaluate student interaction in virtual learning environments. In: *2018 IEEE World Engineering Education Conference (EDUNINE)* (pp. 1–6). IEEE.
3. Clarizia, F., Colace, F., De Santo, M., Lombardi, M., Pascale, F., & Pietrosanto, A., (2018). E-learning and sentiment analysis: A case study. In: *Proceedings of the 6th International Conference on Information and Education Technology* (pp. 111–118).
4. Bharathisindhu, P., & Brunda, S., (2014). Identifying e-learner's opinion using automated sentiment analysis in e-learning. *IJRET: International Journal of Research in Engineering and Technology, 3*(1).
5. Cohen, A., Udi, S., & Rafi, N., (2017). Content analysis of MOOC forums: The characteristics of the learners' discourse in forums. In: *2017 Intelligent Systems Conference (IntelliSys)* (pp. 893–897). IEEE.
6. Jian-Syuan, W., Bart, P., Anna, D., & Bernard, J. J., (2015). Analyzing MOOC discussion forum messages to identify cognitive learning information exchanges. *Proceedings of the Association for Information Science and Technology, 52*(1), 1–10.
7. Harris, S. C., & Vivekanandan, K., (2018). Identifying student difficulty in a digital learning environment. In: *2018 IEEE 18th International Conference on Advanced Learning Technologies (ICALT)* (pp. 199–201). IEEE.
8. Kechaou, Z., Mohamed, B. A., & Adel, M. A., (2011). Improving e-learning with sentiment analysis of users' opinions. In: *2011 IEEE Global Engineering Education Conference (EDUCON)* (pp. 1032–1038). IEEE.
9. Velioğlu, R., Tuğba, Y., & Savas, Y., (2018). Sentiment analysis using learning approaches over emojis for Turkish tweets. In: *2018 3rd International Conference on Computer Science and Engineering (UBMK)* (pp. 303–307). IEEE.
10. Ortigosa, A., José, M. M., & Rosa, M. C., (2014). Sentiment analysis in Facebook and its application to e-learning. *Computers in Human Behavior, 31*, 527–541.

11. Liu, Z., Sanya, L., Lin, L., Jianwen, S., Xian, P., & Tai, W., (2016). Sentiment recognition of online course reviews using multi-swarm optimization-based selected features. *Neurocomputing, 185*, 11–20.
12. Rani, S., & Parteek, K., (2017). A sentiment analysis system to improve teaching and learning. *Computer, 50*(5), 36–43.
13. Gkontzis, A. F., Christoforos, V. K., Chris, T. P., Elias, C. S., & Vassilios, S. V., (2017). Sentiment analysis to track emotion and polarity in student fora. In: *Proceedings of the 21st Pan-Hellenic Conference on Informatics* (pp. 1–6).
14. Aung, K. Z., & Nyein, N. M., (2017). Sentiment analysis of students' comment using lexicon-based approach. In: *2017 IEEE/ACIS 16th International Conference on Computer and Information Science (ICIS)* (pp. 149–154). IEEE.
15. Dolianiti, F. S., Dimitrios, I., Sofia, B. D., Sofia, H., José, A. D., & Leontios, H., (2018). Sentiment analysis techniques and applications in education: A survey. In: *International Conference on Technology and Innovation in Learning, Teaching and Education* (pp. 412–427). Springer, Cham.
16. Liang-Chih, Y., Lee, C. W., Pan, H. I., Chih-Yueh, C., Po-Yao, C., Chen, Z. H., Tseng, S. F., et al., (2018). Improving early prediction of academic failure using sentiment analysis on self-evaluated comments. *Journal of Computer Assisted Learning, 34*(4), 358–365.
17. Liu, B., (2009). Handbook chapter: Sentiment analysis and subjectivity. *Handbook of Natural Language Processing.* Marcel Dekker, Inc. New York, NY, USA.
18. Wöllmer, M., Felix, W., Tobias, K., Björn, S., Congkai, S., Kenji, S., & Louis-Philippe, M., (2013). YouTube movie reviews: Sentiment analysis in an audio-visual context. *IEEE Intelligent Systems, 28*(3), 46–53.
19. Yorozu, T., Hirano, M., Oka, K., & Tagawa, Y., (1987). Electron spectroscopy studies on magneto-optical media and plastic substrate interface. *IEEE Translation Journal on Magnetics in Japan, 2*(8), 740, 741.
20. Nassirtoussi, A. K., Saeed, A., Teh, Y. W., & David, C. L. N., (2014). Text mining for market prediction: A systematic review. *Expert Systems with Applications, 41*(16), 7653–7670.
21. Liu, B., (2012). Sentiment analysis and opinion mining. *Synthesis Lectures on Human Language Technologies, 5*(1), 1–167.
22. Zhao, J., Li, D., Junjie, W., & Ke, X., (2012). MoodLens: An emoticon-based sentiment analysis system for Chinese tweets. In: *Proceedings of the 18th ACM SIGKDD International Conference on Knowledge Discovery and Data Mining* (pp. 1528–1531).
23. Liu, B., Minqing, H., & Junsheng, C., (2005). Opinion observer: Analyzing and comparing opinions on the web. In: *Proceedings of the 14th International Conference on World Wide Web* (pp. 342–351).
24. Moreno-Marcos, P. M., Alario-Hoyos, C., Muñoz-Merino, J. P., Estévez-Ayres, I., & Carlos, D. K., (2018). Sentiment analysis in MOOCs: A case study. In: *2018 IEEE Global Engineering Education Conference (EDUCON)* (pp. 1489–1496). IEEE.
25. Jian-Syuan, W., Bart, P., Anna, D., & Bernard, J. J., (2015). An analysis of MOOC discussion forum interactions from the most active users. In: *International Conference on Social Computing, Behavioral-Cultural Modeling, and Prediction* (pp. 452–457). Springer, Cham.
26. Shatnawi, S., Mohamad, M. G., & Mihaela, C., (2014). Text stream mining for massive open online courses: Review and perspectives. *Systems Science and Control Engineering: An Open Access Journal, 2*(1), 664–676.

CHAPTER 13

PREDICTION OF AGING-RELATED BUGS USING SOFTWARE CODE METRICS

ARVINDER KAUR and HARGUNEET KAUR

University School of Information and Communication Technology (U.S.I.C.T), Guru Gobind Singh Indraprastha University (G.G.S.I.P.U), New Delhi, India, E-mail: Harguneetphd@gmail.com (H. Kaur)

ABSTRACT

The increasing complexity of software systems causes the occurrence of the number of software faults which can drastically affect industrial benefits and reputation. Ongoing software systems sometimes result in degrading the execution and ultimately fail because of the growth of errors in the system state. This phenomenon is known as softwarc aging, in which software bugs can be unreleased file descriptors, memory leaks, stale threads, data corruption, unreleased locks, round-off error accumulation, and divide by zero error. These software bugs are aging-related bugs (ARB). Predictive analysis is performed to locate the ARB in complex software. The approach is evaluated on the open-source dataset to gather data about ARBs. Then software code metrics are extracted from the project used as predictor variables, and feature selection techniques and machine learning (ML) algorithms are then applied to build fault prediction models which identify aging prone files. From the results, it is concluded that the Naïve Bayes algorithm outperforms the other five ML algorithms, achieving the value of 54.4 for the Balance performance measure.

13.1 INTRODUCTION

Software aging is the phenomenon in which software slowly degrade its performance in the long run and ultimately break down due to the collection of bugs in runtime. It also lead to progressive resource depletion, which results in software hanging or crashing state. Aging-related bugs (ARB) are software bugs that have a serious impact on the system availability due to the aggregation of errors after long term software execution. ARBs can be categorized as memory bugs [3], unterminated threads, unreleased files and lock and disk fragmentation [1]. Categorization and sub-categorization of ARBs are given in Table 13.1.

TABLE 13.1 Type of ARBs

Category	Sub Category
Memory bugs	Dangling pointer
	Leak in memory
	Overflow error
	Dereference of NULL pointer
	Uninitialized memory read
Unterminated threads	–
Unreleased files and lock	–
Disk fragmentation	–

It is very difficult to locate ARBs during testing. In recent works, the technique known as software rejuvenation is adapted where the ongoing software is stopped working occasionally, and then the system's internal state is cleaned and the system gets restarted. The best example of system rejuvenation is rebooting the system.

This chapter is focused on finding the location of non-frequent ARB in java classes instead of minimizing the influence of ARBs in complex software. It is an essential step while developing a complex software system that is made up of thousands of files and millions of codes. We have used source code metrics as predictors and applied machine learning (ML) algorithm with the aim of finding ARB prone files.

The hypothesis which is put forward in this chapter is that ARB are however related to static software features such as complexity and software size [1, 4]. There are a number of static software features, but only a few majorly relate to ARBs. Thus the underlying principle is that there is a need to apply feature selection techniques on all software metrics as to extract only those metrics which predict ARBs in software. In a complex software system there are thousands of files but only in very few files, we can predict ARBs which give rise to class imbalance problem [5], i.e., uneven fraction of ARB prone with ARB free modules. Three research questions (RQs) are formulated in the study depending upon the issues occur in predicting ARB:

- **RQ 1:** If the prediction of ARB is possible, what are the keywords for selecting the ARB from bug reports?
- **RQ 2:** Is the performance of ARB prediction improved by applying feature selection ranking methods?
- **RQ 3:** Is there an exceptional variation in the prediction of distinct ML algorithms?

To answer the above questions, we have followed a manual approach where we categorized the ARB based on keywords [1, 3] given in their bug reports. We have conducted an experimental analysis on a large software system, i.e., apache/Zookeeper, an open-source dataset. To be precise, we: (a) analyzed all the closed and resolved bug reports manually and categorized them according to the aging-related keywords which answered the research question 1; (b) All the java files which are affected by ARB are tabulated; (c) extracted software code metrics; (d) applied feature selection techniques to extract only those static software code metrics which majorly affect the prediction. This step answered Research question 2; (e) built fault prediction models using ML algorithms and identify which prediction model is predicting the best. Here research question 3 is answered.

According to the results, ARB prone modules can be best predicted by the Naïve Bayes algorithm. We have also concluded that after applying preprocessing methods and feature selection ranking techniques, few complexity code metrics commit good results for predicting ARB. The formation of the chapter is as follows: Section 13.2 describes the related work on *software aging*. The research background which explore the dataset used in the study and collection of software metrics with ARBs is described in Section 13.3. Section 13.4 provides the description of fault prediction models and feature selection techniques applied, followed by the results of the experimental analysis. Section 13.8 ends with the conclusions and future directions.

13.2 RELATED WORK

Cotroneo et al. [1] identified the areas of ARB in three complex real time software system using complexity metrics and then built fault prediction models and then prediction models are evaluated and compared. This chapter used all the complexity metrics but in our chapter, we have applied the ranking method of feature selection techniques on code metrics so as to use only those metrics which majorly affect the prediction of ARB.

Fangun et al. [4] proposed a new approach which experimented with the prediction of cross projects. It has taken training data from another project and testing data from different and then applied traditional ML algorithms. It has also identified the class imbalance problem where ARB prone files get less concentration than ARB free files.

Lov Kumar et al. [6] presented analysis on software metrics to place ARB. It also applied various feature selection methods to check out the influence of imbalanced data.

Shoyu et al. [7] applied ML algorithm to detect aging in OS of android with the help of indicators like launch time (LT), page fault (PF) and a combination of both. It concluded that PF is better than LT on the basis of accuracy.

Cotroneo et al. [2] performed empirical analysis of android devices to identify software aging. It observed software aging issues with the help of metrics like memory, storage and garbage collection.

13.3 RESEARCH BACKGROUND

Our study uses the large-scale software project namely Zookeeper of Apache. Apache Zookeeper is an open-source project under Apache Software Foundation. It is a service which provide distributed synchronization, maintain configuration information, and is a highly reliable centrally distributed server. Table 13.2 provides the main characteristics of software project taken in this study.

TABLE 13.2 Software Project Description

Project	Version	Language	#Files
Zookeeper	3.5.4	Java	547

We also present the method to identify and extract the ARB. Bug reports of Zookeeper are collected from open-source bug repository (https://issues.apache.org/jira/issues). Then we manually analyzed each bug report description and identified if it belong to aging. Categorization [1, 3] is done based on some keywords associated with memory bugs like leakage in memory, dereference of null pointer, overflow error, dangling pointer, memory read which is uninitialized and other bugs like unreleased files, disk fragmentation and Unterminated threads.

This chapter has taken the resolved and closed bug reports from the bug repository. Resolved bug reports are those whose verification is pending by the reporter but has been solved. closed bug reports are finished bugs which are no more bugs now and the solution is also validated. We have manually analyzed 1242 bug reports in total, out of which 124 bug reports are identified as ARBs. For each bug report we extracted its Bug id, summary, the type of ARB and the java files that are influenced because of ARB. They have been categorized as memory leak, deadlock, deallocating, dereference, overflow buffer, lock, improper synchronization, null pointer exception, race condition, socket leak, uninitialized variables.

The purpose of this study is to identify the relation between software metrics and ARBs for bug prediction. Object-oriented metrics are divided into four categories Project, Class, Package, and Method Metrics which are further subdivided given in Table 13.3 [16].

TABLE 13.3 Metrics

Project Metrics	Class Metrics
LOC (lines of code)	Lines of code
Size	Depth of inheritance tree
	Weighted method count
	CBO
	LCOM
	Number of methods
	Number of children
	RFC
	CAM
	Number of fields
	Number of static fields
	Number of overridden methods
	Specialization index
	Number of static methods
	Access to foreign data
	SRFC
	Lack of tight class cohesion
Package Metrics	**Method Metrics**
Afferent coupling	McCabe cyclomatic complexity
Lines of code	
Efferent coupling	

13.4 FAULT PREDICTION MODELS

Fault prediction is the intelligent way of automating the process of testing the ML techniques for better efficiency and cost-effectiveness. Fault prediction is developing a predictive pattern for defects found in dataset using metrics. The realization of the prediction model is the number of actual defects against the number of predicted defects for each of the module. We have implemented ML techniques to conclude this relationship whether software complexity metrics can be used to determine ARB. The dependent variable in our binary classification problem is if the file is ARB prone or ARB free. We have not taken the number of ARBs in each file as ARB give rise to class imbalance problem during prediction. The non-frequent class which is ARB prone class gains little priority than ARB free class, which will have a negative impact on prediction. Different ML algorithms are considered for bug prediction:

13.4.1 NAIVE BAYES

It is a simple binary (two-class) and multi-class stable algorithm for prediction based on mathematical Bayes theorem:

$$\text{Prob(hyp|da)} = (\text{Prob(da|hyp)} \times \text{Prob(hyp)})/\text{Prob(da)}$$

where; Prob(hyp|da) is the probability of hypothesis h when data instance d is given; Prob(da|hyp) is the probability of data instance d when the hypothesis h is already true; Prob(hyp) is the probability of hypothesis h; Prob(da) is the probability of the data.

13.4.2 K-NEAREST NEIGHBOR (KNN) ALGORITHM

This is a supervised classification as well regression ML algorithm based on distance calculation among parameters. The KNN algorithm assumes that like things exist in group. It is also known as instance-based learning with parameter k.

13.4.3 SIMPLE LOGISTIC

This one is the most popular ML algorithm for binary prediction, which works well for a wide range of problems. It predicts the probability of nominal variable (dependent) using the measurement variable (independent). The logistic regression based on the equation:

$$\text{logit}(v)=\log(v/(1-v)) = b_0 + b_1x_1 +\ldots+ b_kx_k$$

where; the coefficients refer to each b_i.

13.4.4 RANDOM FOREST

It is a combination of more than one algorithm of the same or different kind for classification. For example, SVM, Decision Tree, and Naïve Bayes works collectively and consider the final best result of the class. This classifier create a number of decision trees from training set at random. It then assemble the results from different decision trees to finalize the class of test data.

13.4.5 SEQUENTIAL MINIMAL OPTIMIZATION (SMO)

This algorithm works on quadratic problem that used for training the support vector machines. It is an iterative process that divides the problem into sub problems and then solve it analytically.

13.4.6 ITERATIVE OPTIMIZATION ALGORITHM

It is the Meta classifier which chooses the best iterations for an iterative classifier with the help of percentage split evaluation or by using cross-validation method.

13.5 FEATURE SELECTION TECHNIQUES

There are n number of attributes in the dataset which are not necessarily relevant to make predictions. Therefore, there is a process called Feature selection which selects the reduced number of features in data to model the problem. Feature Selection techniques are categorized into two: Attribute Evaluator and Search Method. Attribute evaluator measures how every attribute in data is connected in context of output variable whereas search method shortlist the features by trying different combinations. There are various feature selection techniques, but we have used few techniques with the ranker search method given in Table 13.4.

TABLE 13.4 Feature Selection Techniques

Feature Selection Technique	Description
InfoGainAttributeEval. Ranker	In this entropy is calculated for each varying from 0(none information) to 1(maximum information).
ClassifierAttributeEval. Ranker	It shows the improvement in merit extracted by building a classifier based on the selected predictor attribute when compared to not using any predictor attributes at all.
Correlation.ranker	It evaluates the relation of each attribute with the dependent variable.
GainRatioAttribute Eval.Ranker	Gain ratio of attribute is calculated with respect to the class: GR(C, A) = (H(C) – H(C|A))/H(A) where; GR = gain ratio; C = class; A = attribute.
OneRAttributeEval. Ranker	It consider minimum error attribute for prediction and calculates the ranking of attributes by using one R classifier.
ReliefFAttributeEval. Ranker	The worth of the attribute is calculated by continuously sampling the instance.

13.6 DATA ANALYSIS

We have followed an approach for predicting ARBs given in Figure 13.1. The ARB prediction is done by using the dataset Zookeeper Apache and then build a classification model with the help of training and testing data. 22 software metrics are extracted from the tool IntelliJ Idea. These metrics then undergo preprocessing step where the metrics whose values are constant or not effecting the data are removed. Thus 18 metrics are left after preprocessing step. 120 java files out of 547 java files which are manually selected as ARB prone from the bug reports are marked as Yes under the dependent variable (ARB prone/ARB free) and other java files (ARB free) are marked as No. Then these 18-software metrics and one ARB dependent metric undergo attribute selection techniques where further refinement of metrics is done. The feature selection procedure is adapted where ranking search method is used and all the metrics are ranked according to the weightage they are effecting the data. Then the average of ranks for different six feature selection techniques of a particular metric is calculated. The top 10 software metrics are selected along with one dependent variable. This is how our data is prepared for building fault prediction models.

13.7 PERFORMANCE MEASURES

The file which is correctly classified as ARB prone known as true positive (TP) and true negative (TN) if they are correctly classified as ARB free.

Similarly, the files which are not correctly identified as ARB prone are known as False Negative (FN), and files that are incorrectly classified as ARB prone are known as false positive (FP). In our study, measures calculated for validating the models are precision, recall, FPR, accuracy, F1 score, and balance.

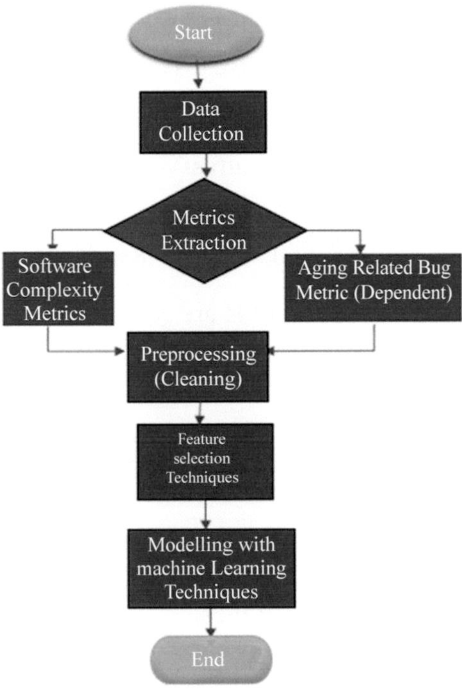

FIGURE 13.1 Data analysis.

1. **Precision:** It is the ratio of how many instances that are identified are correct.

$$\text{Precision} = \frac{\text{TP}}{\text{True Positive} + \text{False Positive}}$$

2. **Recall (Sensitivity):** It is the ratio of actual instances which are correctly classified.

$$\text{Recall} = \frac{\text{TP}}{\text{TP} + \text{FN}}$$

3. **Accuracy:** It measures the percentage of correct results that a classifier has achieved.

$$\text{Accuracy} = \frac{\text{True Positive} + \text{True Negative}}{\text{TP} + \text{FP} + \text{TN} + \text{FN}}$$

4. **FPR (False Positive Rate):** It measures the number of negative instances predicted as positive.

$$\text{FPR} = \frac{\text{False Positive}}{\text{True Negative} + \text{False Positive}}$$

5. **F1 Score:** It is the harmonic mean of recall and precision. It gives equal weight to both the measures.

$$\text{F1 Score} = \frac{2 \times \text{precision} \times \text{recall}}{\text{Precision} + \text{Recall}}$$

6. **Balance (Bal):** Recall and FPR are comparable measures, therefore, a tradeoff is needed. Balance is the Euclidian distance from Recall and FPR.

$$\text{Bal} = 100 - \frac{\sqrt{((0 - FPR)^2 + (100 - Recall)^2)}}{\sqrt{2}}$$

We have presented our results of multivariate analysis of the dataset for each classifier in Table 13.5. Classification algorithms that are performed using the Weka tool are Naïve Bayes, instance-based learning, simple logistic, random forest, sequential minimal optimization (SMO), and iterative classifier optimizer. Some of these classifiers are selected as previous studies [8] indicate that these provide better performance in bug prediction. We have calculated accuracy, precision, recall, F1 score, FPR, and balance as performance measures, but we do not consider precision and accuracy because they provide unreliable results for dataset where the percentage of target class, i.e., ARB prone is low. Therefore, we have used FPR, recall, and balance [1] for comparing different ML algorithms.

According to the results, Naïve Bayes shows the best value among other ML algorithms for Zookeeper dataset with respect to Balance (Euclidian distance from Recall = 100[%] and FPR = 0[%] [9]) value as 54.408. In all cases Recall<50%, which mean most of ARB prone files are not identified. This problem arises as it is difficult for a classifier to correctly identify ARB prone files, which is very less in number as compared to non-ARB prone files. The high balance value provides the best tradeoff between FPR and Recall. The poor performance of other classifiers is just because of a small proportion of ARB prone files in the dataset.

TABLE 13.5 Results of Performance Measures

Algorithm	Accuracy	Precision	Recall	F1 Score	FPR	Balance
Naïve Bayes	0.777	0.494	0.364	0.419	0.106	54.408
Ibk	0.739	0.402	0.372	0.386	0.157	54.227
Simple Logistic	0.801	0.65	0.215	0.323	0.033	44.443
Random Forest	0.806	0.941	0.132	0.231	0.002	38.623
SMO	0.806	0.703	0.215	0.329	0.026	44.462
Iterative Classifier Optimizer	0.808	0.648	0.289	0.399	0.045	49.624

13.8 CONCLUSION AND FUTURE WORK

In our research, we predicted the presence of ARB using source code metrics. Six different ML algorithms are applied to predict the non-frequent occurring bugs from Zookeeper software. The experiment highlighted the Naïve Bayes classifier with the best results in our chapter. In the future, we aim at n number of large projects enhancing cross project prediction to validate our approach regarding ARB.

KEYWORDS

- **aging-related bugs**
- **bug prediction**
- **false positive**
- **k-nearest neighbor**
- **launch time**
- **lines of code**
- **machine learning**
- **software code metrics**

REFERENCES

1. Cotroneo, D., Natella, R., & Pietrantuono, R., (2013). Predicting aging-related bugs using software complexity metrics. *Performance Evaluation, 70*(3), 163–178.

2. Cotroneo, D., Fucci, F., Iannillo, A. K., Natella, R., & Pietrantuono, R., (2016). Software aging analysis of the android mobile OS. In: *2016 IEEE 27th International Symposium on Software Reliability Engineering (ISSRE)* (pp. 478–489). IEEE.
3. Li, Z., Tan, L., Wang, X., Lu, S., Zhou, Y., & Zhai, C., (2006). Have things changed now? An empirical study of bug characteristics in modern open-source software. In: *Proceedings of the 1st Workshop on Architectural and System Support for Improving Software Dependability* (pp. 25–33).
4. Qin, F., Zheng, Z., Bai, C., Qiao, Y., Zhang, Z., & Chen, C., (2015). Cross-project aging related bug prediction. In: *2015 IEEE International Conference on Software Quality, Reliability and Security* (pp. 43–48). IEEE.
5. Kumar, L., & Sureka, A., (2017). Aging related bug prediction using extreme learning machines. In: *2017 14th IEEE India Council International Conference (INDICON)* (pp. 1–6). IEEE.
6. Kumar, L., & Sureka, A., (2018). Feature selection techniques to counter class imbalance problem for aging related bug prediction: Aging related bug prediction. In: *Proceedings of the 11th Innovations in Software Engineering Conference* (pp. 1–11).
7. Huo, S., Zhao, D., Liu, X., Xiang, J., Zhong, Y., & Yu, H., (2018). Using machine learning for software aging detection in android system. In: *2018 Tenth International Conference on Advanced Computational Intelligence (ICACI)* (pp. 741–746). IEEE.
8. Kaur, A., & Kaur, I., (2018). An empirical evaluation of classification algorithms for fault prediction in open-source projects. *Journal of King Saud University-Computer and Information Sciences, 30*(1), 2–17.
9. Menzies, T., Greenwald, J., & Frank, A., (2006). Data mining static code attributes to learn defect predictors. *IEEE Transactions on Software Engineering, 33*(1), 2–13.
10. Qin, F., Zheng, Z., Qiao, Y., & Trivedi, K. S., (2018). Studying aging-related bug prediction using cross-project models. *IEEE Transactions on Reliability, 68*(3), 1134–1153.
11. Alonso, J., Torres, J., Berral, J. L., & Gavalda, R., (2010). Adaptive on-line software aging prediction based on machine learning. In: *2010 IEEE/IFIP International Conference on Dependable Systems and Networks (DSN)* (pp. 507–516). IEEE.
12. Grottke, M., Matias, R., & Trivedi, K. S., (2008). The fundamentals of software aging. In: *2008 IEEE International Conference on Software Reliability Engineering Workshops (ISSRE Wksp)* (pp. 1–6). IEEE.
13. Tan, L., Liu, C., Li, Z., Wang, X., Zhou, Y., & Zhai, C., (2014). Bug characteristics in open-source software. *Empirical Software Engineering, 19*(6), 1665–1705.
14. Li, J., Qi, Y., & Cai, L., (2018). A hybrid approach for predicting aging-related failures of software systems. In: *2018 IEEE Symposium on Service-Oriented System Engineering (SOSE)* (pp. 96–105). IEEE.
15. Cotroneo, D., Natella, R., Pietrantuono, R., & Russo, S., (2014). A survey of software aging and rejuvenation studies. *ACM Journal on Emerging Technologies in Computing Systems (JETC), 10*(1), 1–34.
16. Kaur, A., Kaur, K., & Kaur, H., (2015). An investigation of the accuracy of code and process metrics for defect prediction of mobile applications. In: *2015 4th International Conference on Reliability, Infocom Technologies and Optimization (ICRITO) (Trends and Future Directions)* (pp. 1–6). IEEE.

CHAPTER 14

APPLICATION OF CART-BASED MODELING IN MOTOR INSURANCE FRAUD

ROHAN YASHRAJ GUPTA,[1] SATYA SAI MUDIGONDA,[2] PHANI KRISHNA KANDALA,[3] and PALLAV KUMAR BARUAH[4]

[1]*Doctoral Research Scholar in Actuarial Science, Department of Mathematics and Computer Science, Sri Sathya Sai Institute of Higher Learning, Puttaparthi, Andhra Pradesh, India,*
E-mail: rohanyashrajgupta@sssihl.edu.in

[2]*Honorary Professor in Actuarial Science, Department of Mathematics and Computer Science, Sri Sathya Sai Institute of Higher Learning, Puttaparthi, Andhra Pradesh, India*

[3]*Visiting Faculty in Actuarial Science, Department of Mathematics and Computer Science, Sri Sathya Sai Institute of Higher Learning, Puttaparthi, Andhra Pradesh, India*

[4]*Associate Professor, Department of Mathematics and Computer Science, Sri Sathya Sai Institute of Higher Learning, Puttaparthi, Andhra Pradesh, India*

ABSTRACT

Artificial intelligence (AI) provides computer systems with the ability to automatically improve and learn from the data provided without programming it explicitly. The process of "learning" starts from the observation of data to look for patterns in the data provided. Machine learning (ML) can be categorized into supervised, unsupervised and semi-supervised learning methods. A supervised learning method is where an algorithm is used to learn a function to map the input variable (X) to the output variable. The aim here is to find a function so good that when new data (X) is set as an input, the model should be able to predict the output (Y) for the given data. Here, the training dataset has input data (X) which has a known corresponding output (Y). The unsupervised learning method is where for a given data its associated properties are studied. However, there are cases wherein for a given input data the response or output is not known in its entirety. Such problems are addressed using semi-supervised learning methods.

Classification and regression trees (CART) based model falls under the category of supervised learning method. When the problem at hand has a discrete output variable, it is called a classification problem e.g. "fraud" or "not fraud" and when it has a continuous output variable, it is called a regression problem e.g. "temperature" or "volume". Gradient boosting method (GBM) is one of the various ML technique which is used for classification and regression problems. Boosting is an iterative method that aims at combining many weak predictions into one powerful one. The application of such machine learning models in the insurance industry is being explored by researchers all over the world. Some potential areas where machine learning can be used in the insurance industry include underwriting and claim analytics, product pricing, claims handling, fraud detection, sales and customer experience, etc.

Fraud detection in insurance using machine learning techniques is one area where a lot of research is being done. The list of some of the widely used approaches which were identified from 27 of 450 research articles and studies, by the research team in the Society of Actuaries include data mining, statistical analysis, regression, stratified sample, Monte Carlo simulation, random sampling. Most of the methods identified are machine learning methods. This indicates the fact that how extensively machine learning methods are being used in the area of fraud detection. The ability to detect fraud has various social relevance and benefits. Reduced fraud would decrease the losses faced by the insurer. This would directly or indirectly reduce the premiums charged to policyholders and increase confidence in the financial system.

14.1 INTRODUCTION

Fraud acts as a major deterrent towards the growth of an organization. It affects the financial status of the company. Both the insurers and policy-holders are affected by it. To compensate for this loss, insurers increase the premium rates. A higher rate of fraudulent cases may reduce the level of confidence of the customers and shareholders in the company. This also affects the reputation of the company and subsequently brings down the credit rating of the company.

The insurance industry consists of over 7,000 insurers, which collects a total of $1 trillion in premium each year. It is estimated that around $40 Billion is lost due to non-health fraud ("Insurance Fraud, FBI" n.d.). Efforts to detect, prevent, manage, and control industry-wide fraud are being made by various industries. In the year 2012, the Insurance Regulatory and Development Authority of India requested a proposal for analysis and reporting of industry-wide fraud trends. Industries are looking at incorporating the latest technology in building a fraud detection model ("Tenders," n.d.).

Technological advancements provide an opportunity to both fraudsters and those who try to stop them. As fraudsters are finding new ways to commit fraud, industries must build models that can stop them. However, the issues involved are many. Which technology is most effective to manage the risk due to fraud? Which tools and techniques would provide benefits that would outweigh the cost?

According to a report, the use of artificial intelligence (AI) and machine learning (ML) in building anti-fraud models is increasing at a rapid pace and is expected to triple in the next two years. In 2018, the Coalition Against Insurance Fraud and SAS surveyed insurers with an aim to study how insurers are using technology to detect and prevent fraud. In the study, 40% of the insurers increased their yearly budget towards anti-fraud technology in 2019 of 84 participating insurers. Many of the companies are embracing predictive modeling and 21% of the insurers said that they have plans to invest in AI technology for anti-fraud models ("The State of Insurance Fraud Technology, SAS" n.d.).

As of date, various innovative fraud detection methods are being used by organizations. Some of which are discussed below:

1. **Social Network Analysis (SNA):** It is possible that when fraud happens, many people are involved in carrying it out. Often, this aspect is missed out in traditional anti-fraud solutions. When looked at individually, such cases of fraud cannot be detected. Social network analysis (SNA) can help to identify such patterns in the data and helps to identify people who are associated with committing such fraud.

   The diagrammatic representation of the SNA is given in Figure 14.1.

   In the GE Consumer and Industrial Home Service Division, the claims generally come from technicians who repair products that are under warranty. One of the major problems they faced was that they could not identify patterns in claims. This inability did not allow them to identify any unusual behavior also given the fact that the amount of data generated was huge. They implemented the SNA solution provided by SAS to tackle this problem. The claims data was fed into this system and indicators were calculated. There were around 26 claims-level analyzes that were performed on the dataset. GE estimated that it saved nearly $5.1 million within the first year of implementing this solution.

2. **Predictive Analytics for Big Data:** Predictive analytics is used to build models that use historical data to predict future fraud cases. A good predictive model can help in predicting fraud much early in the claim process cycle. In using this method, it is important to understand which data is useful and what is available for building a fraud detection model. Building such a model can be challenging and has to go through several steps such as data pre-processing, identifying fraud indicator variables and the relationship between them, model building and validation. The schematic representation is depicted in Figure 14.2.

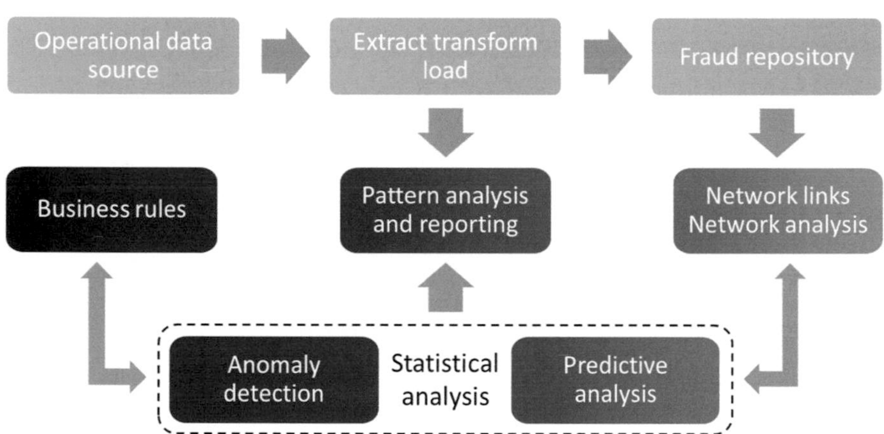

FIGURE 14.1 Insurance fraud detection using social network analysis (SNA).

Infinity, a P&C company, came up with the idea of using a scoring-based method to identify suspicious activities and identify fraud. Its customers are the main drivers with a higher risk than usual and pay higher rates compared to others. Infinity uses predictive analytics method to identify fraudulent claims. Using this method increased the success rate of pursuing fraudulent claims from 50–80% and reduced the time required to refer questionable claims for investigation by as much as 95% [17].

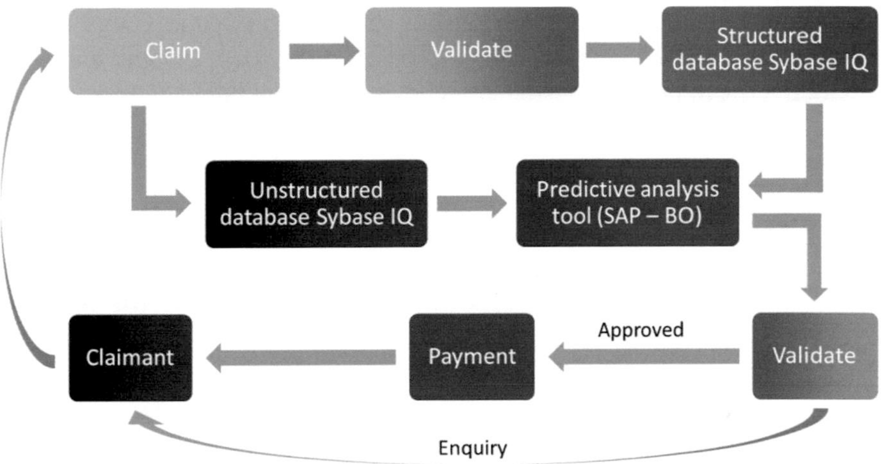

FIGURE 14.2 Steps in insurance fraud detection using big data analysis.

3. **Social Customer Relationship Management (CRM):** It is a process in which it is required for the insurer to link social media to their CRM. This allows the insurer to get additional data about its customers. The data extraction is done using 'listening' tools, this data acts as the reference for the existing CRM data. The combined data is sent into the anti-fraud model that analyzes the data based on a business rule. The decision made is sent as a response. Depending on whether the response indicates the case is fraudulent or not, the case is sent for further investigation. The schematic representation is depicted in Figure 14.3.

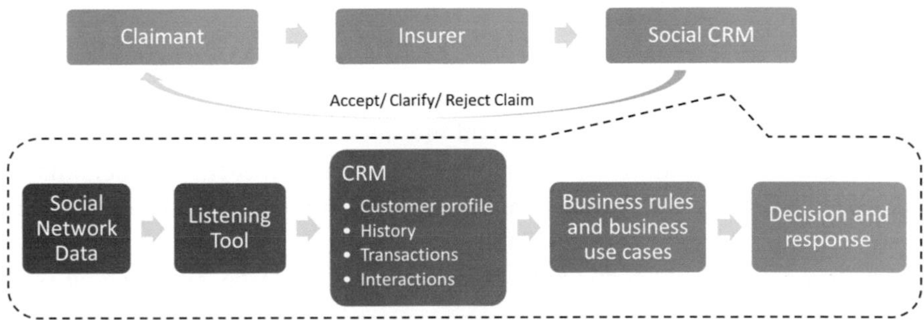

FIGURE 14.3 Insurance fraud detection using social CRM.

A Turkish insurance company, AXA OYAK, is using a Social CRM solution provided by SAS to prevent fraud. Here, all the customer-related information is integrated with a single and coordinated corporate vision. They were able to clean up the customer data and perform better analysis. This helped them find and correct inconsistencies in the data. Cleaner data also provided AXA to perform customer analysis more accurately and investigate fraudulent claims more efficiently. Recent trends in the area of insurance fraud detection are as follows:

1. **High-Performance Computing:** The conventional IT platform consumes a lot of time to analyze the data-sometimes we may have to wait for hours and days for the results. With the use of high-performance computing technology, the same work can be done in a much lesser period. This allows the insurers to run various models and identify which works the best. Lower run time also means the models can be deployed for use sooner, thereby giving them faster response time for new types of fraud.
2. **Hybrid Analytical Techniques:** These can help detect and prevent fraud with much higher accuracy. Hybrid models use the insurers' data as the core component, and in combination with some other external data; a better fraud model is created.
3. **Behavioral Analytics:** Fraudsters can trick rule-based anti-fraud models; thus it is required to have advanced analytical systems in place that can detect unknown risks.

A behavioral analytical approach captures a behavioral pattern in the claimants and evaluates that information in every transaction. This process builds up with every transaction. More information gives a better understanding of whether a given transaction is legitimate or not.

14.2 EXPLORING ACTUARIAL AND AI-TOOLS AND TECHNIQUES

Traditional methods of detecting fraud are not efficient to identify fraud as the fraudsters are finding new ways to deceive the anti-fraud mechanism. Advanced analytical techniques enable insurers to look at the data and identify suspicious patterns that lead to fraud.

Building a fraud detection model comprises of three broad steps (see Figure 14.4):

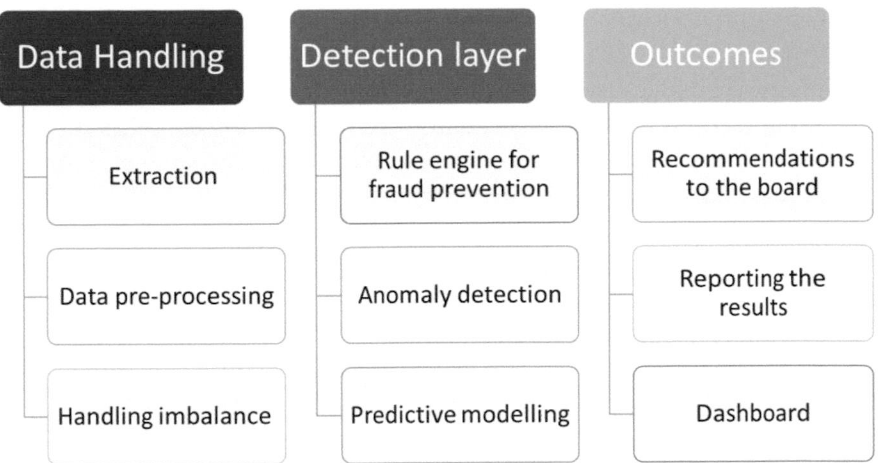

FIGURE 14.4 Steps in creating a fraud detection model.

1. **Data Handling:** Relates to dealing with data and related issues. This is the first phase and the most crucial phase for building any fraud detection model. The extraction, pre-processing, and handling imbalance nature of the data needs to be done. This is a very crucial step, as good data mean good results. There could be various issues that may come along like missing values, identifying the most influential fields, feature engineering, etc.
2. **Detection Layer:** This is the detection layer wherein fraud detection and prevention model is built. The three different types of analytics to fight fraud are rule-based analysis, anomaly detection and predictive modeling. Rule-based analysis is where the rule engine is built, which prevents fraud, based on a set of rules, e.g., size of the claims higher than expected, claiming mutually exclusive events together, etc. In the anomaly detection phase, the unusual behavior in the claims pattern is flagged based on the historical or industry data. Predictive modeling phase is where the expected actual versus expected behavior in the claim's patterns are observed to determine the suspicious claims. This phase is where advanced AI technology can be made used to develop a fraud detection model.
3. **Outcomes:** The final stage wherein the results obtained are analyzed and recommendations are made to the board based on the inferences made from the results. Dashboards for giving a snapshot of the current status can also be created.

Keeping the above steps into perspective, our approach for managing fraud would be an integration of actuarial techniques and computing technology. The detailed list of the identified actuarial techniques and computing technology that was found to be relevant for data-driven fraud detection and prevention are listed below. They can be broadly categorized into three parts:

14.2.1 INFRASTRUCTURE AND TOOLS

Various tools have been identified which could be used for building a fraud detection model. The tools to be used are divided into three categories:

1. **Language and Framework:** This contains the programming languages that can be used for large-scale model development, e.g., "R" and "Python" [12, 20, 28].
2. **Cloud-based Platforms:** Computing services that are offered by organizations like Amazon, Microsoft, Google, etc., that run on the same resources that the organizations use. This will enable us to run the model (depending on the requirement) on their infrastructure in a more cost-effective way [4, 9].
3. **Visualization Tools:** These tools are used for producing graphical images and interface to the model [15].

14.2.2 CONCEPTS AND METHODS

14.2.2.1 COMPUTING TECHNOLOGY

1. **Supervised Learning:** Gradient boosting method, classification trees, neural networks, generative adversarial network [6, 13, 18, 22, 27].
2. **Unsupervised Learning:** K-means cluster [25, 26].
3. **Computing:** Cloud computing, high-performance computing [4, 29].

14.2.2.2 ACTUARIAL TECHNIQUES

One very well-known framework in the actuarial domain is the ACC (actuarial control cycle) which gives a framework for solving any actuarial problems. The ACC, which comprises three main components viz. specifying the problem, developing the solution and monitoring the results, is a model that can be applied to many aspects of actuarial work to find a solution. With further analysis into the framework, the following actuarial techniques have been identified which can be used in fraud detection.

14.2.2.2.1 Applied Statistical Models and Statistical Tests

A lot of research underwent on applied statistical models such as GLM, GBM, GAM, and others to arrive at a direction or solution for the existing uncertainties. We study the features of the given data and apply the statistical and mathematical models such as exponential family for GLM to generalize the model structure for the existing problem of Fraud detection and study the impact of each feature on to the final output such as the probability of fraud or severity impact of fraud. For example, when age (feature) increased from 51 to 54, the premium increased by 20% (final output).

Statistical tests are used to determine the optimal set of features. This helps us to assess whether the addition of any new feature would have the desired improvement in output or would be neutral.

Predictive analytics, suspicious scoring, clustering, significance testing, linear regression, logistic regression, Box Plot, classification trees, peak analysis, and random sampling are the list of some of the various applied statistical methods.

14.2.2.2.2 Diagnostics and Analysis of Emerging Experience

Diagnostics are metrics that help us to interpret data or results and verify underlying methodologies and assumptions. For example: in a typical quota share arrangement, we need to have a reinsurance income to gross ratio to be consistent across all contracts, we can identify those contracts which do not exhibit this behavior and investigate further. Here, the diagnostic used by us is RI to gross ratio. Interpretation of diagnostics is one of the most important constituents where care needs to be taken.

A direct application of the ACC framework is seen in the analysis of emerging experience. Here we monitor the impact of deviation from the expected results both in the short term as well in the long term. This is a very useful tool to monitor the current methodology used for fraud detection and quantification of fraud amount. It would capture the following aspects:

- Change in methodology;
- Change in assumptions;
- Movement solely due to experience.

14.2.2.2.3 Economic Models Including Behavioral Finance

Behavioral finance as an economic model is generally an important constituent to understand the nature of an individual profile which includes both monetary and non-monetary transactions.

ML is used to understand, predict or anticipate behaviors at the most granular level for each transaction. Features for non-monetary transactions generally include a change of address, request for a duplicate identity card or a request for password reset are used to understand the behavior type. These features have more explanatory power about the existing mental bias or rational/irrational behavior that we use to detect fraudulent behavior.

Monetary transactions also help us to understand the behavioral aspects such as steady/sudden increase in wealth, spend velocity and number of days between transactions of similar type. These directly help us to understand the quantitative aspect of the fraud.

14.2.2.2.4 Extreme Value Theory

The idea is to consider the modeling of risks with low frequency but high severity. Low frequency/high severity events can have a devastating impact on companies and investment funds. However, their low frequency means that little data exists to model their effects accurately.

After performing trigger functionality on the given data, we would have obtained a subset of events that we would be interested to investigate. To perform this investigation, a suitable class of models would be those models that have low frequency and high severity impact. These are generally present in the tails of the distribution that is best described by generalized extreme value and generalized Pareto type of distributions. This helps us to obtain the quantum of loss due to a particular type of fraud/suspicion [3, 7, 16].

However, there is a class of fraud which are opposite in nature, i.e., low severity but high-frequency claims. A different approach needs to be adopted to model such claims.

14.2.3 DATA AND DATA HANDLING

- **Imbalance:** SMOTE, MWMOTE, GAN, ADASYN [1, 2, 5, 8, 11, 14].
- **Storage and Modeling:** MySQL, CSV.
- **Retrieval, NLP, and CV:** Selenium, beautiful soup, text processing.

One of the major challenges faced while building a fraud detection model is the imbalanced nature of the data. There are various approaches which are proposed to handle this problem. Some of them are described below:

14.2.3.1 SYNTHETIC MINORITY OVERSAMPLING TECHNIQUES (SMOTE)

Synthetic minority oversampling techniques is one of the most used methods to handle the data imbalance problem. The basic idea of this technique is that the minority instances (original values) are used to oversample the minority to obtain a balanced dataset [6, 18].

One of the major parameters in using this technique is to determine the number of k-nearest neighbors (KNNs). For example, if the number is one, then for each of the "original values" one nearest neighbor is found and a number is randomly generated as the weighted average of the two. If the number is two, then two such samples are created for each of the "original values" and so on. The number of samples to be generated depends on the number of KNNs to consider and the total number of the original samples.

14.2.3.2 BORDERLINE-SMOTE

This method is similar to SMOTE, with the main difference being in the minority samples taken to oversample. It is generally observed the samples present in the border are more difficult to classify compared to the other dataset [13]. Thus in this method, more emphasis is given to the borderline samples. The synthetic samples are generated using these borderline samples.

14.2.3.3 MAJORITY WEIGHTED MINORITY OVERSAMPLING TECHNIQUE (MWMOTE)

This is another method of oversampling. The idea of MWMOTE can be categorized into three phases. In the first phase, the most important hard-to-learn minority samples formed as one group. In the second phase, weights are given to the members of this set based on the importance in the set [1]. In the last phase, minority samples are created using the set of minority samples incorporating the weight distribution found in the second phase.

14.2.3.4 ADAPTIVE SYNTHETIC (ADASYN)

The idea of ADASYN is that density distribution of the dataset is used as a criterion to generate the samples from the minority set. This method gives a balanced representation of the data distribution. This method also forces the learning to happen in such a way that more focus is given to hard-to-learn samples [8, 21].

The target is rare, so we need to be careful about fraud representation in both databases (train and test). We can choose to divide the database randomly in various proportions viz. 70%–30%, 80%–20%, etc.

14.3 FRAUD DETECTION AND PREVENTION FRAMEWORK

Upon considering various works which are done to create an anti-fraud model, a framework has been developed. The core part of the framework has a cyclic component that signifies the fact that the fraud model should have a feedback loop that improves with the results obtained in each iteration. The first step is the prevention of prospective fraudulent cases that is done using the trigger-based mechanism. Triggers are parameters or a set of parameters, which can help identify and raise alerts for suspicious activities. This rule engine (which is a set of triggers) flags any claims that have suspicious claims pattern. Triggers are developed based on cases that were identified as fraudulent or those on which some kind of actions were taken like reduced claim payment, claims denial, etc. Some of the examples of triggers identified in the automobile insurance business are as follows (see *Appendix* for more):

- Claims just a few days before the end of the policy term;
- Losses include a large amount of cash.

Figure 14.5 depicts the framework for data-driven fraud detection and prevention.

However, this is not an automatic process. The feedback mechanism requires the actuary to exercise judgment. Many fraud detection tools available today focus only on a specific function of the insurance business. To build a robust fraud detection tools, all the functions in the insurance business need to be considered. One which examines all areas of insurance business-claims, underwriting, sales, reporting, etc.

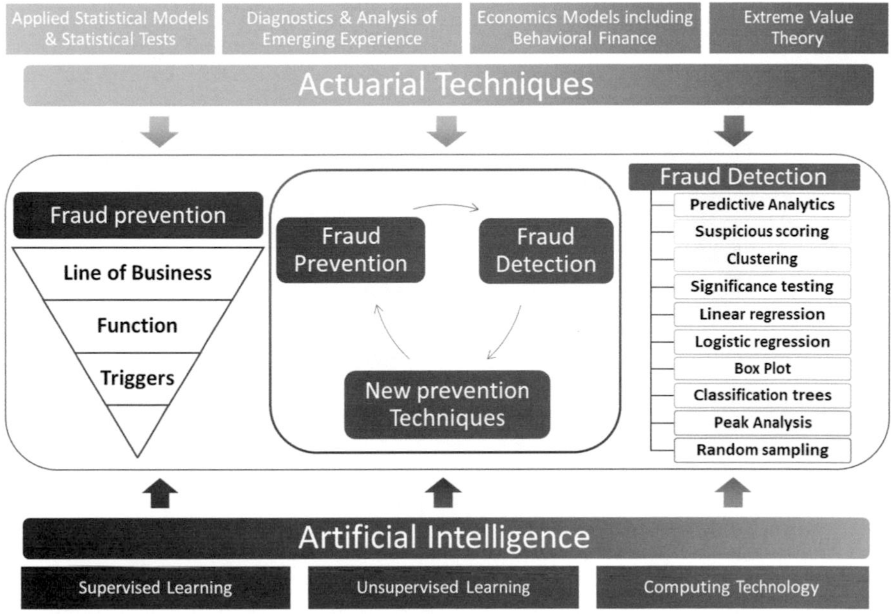

FIGURE 14.5 Framework.

Figure 14.6 represents the technical view of the framework. At the very first level data provided would come from various databases that the organization has, e.g., HQ, MySQL, CSV, Postgres, OracleDB, etc. It is from these databases that we get various data like sales data, policy data, claims data, reporting data, underwriting data, etc. Once the data is selected, a data driven rules are generated using a rule engine. This is dependent on the line of business. Rules could be a combination of multiple triggers chosen, which could also be n in number. Depending on the rules generated, an appropriate model is created, using which some of the potential fraud cases are prevented. Remaining passes through the next stage where the data is passed through the API's (application interface) which has their libraries and are created using various technology, actuarial techniques and methodologies. At this stage, we may further detect some more fraud cases. The results obtained are analyzed further to improve the existing model. With every run of the model, the existing model improves and provides a better solution than the existing model.

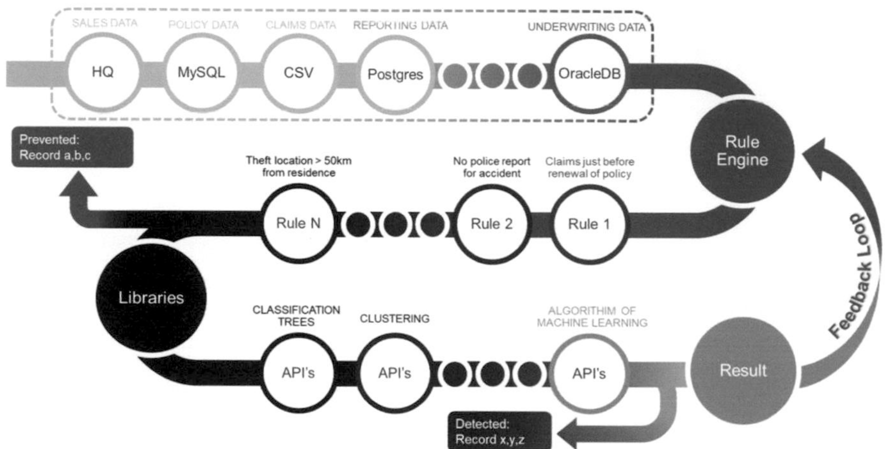

FIGURE 14.6 Technical view of the framework.

14.4 APPLICATIONS-CART-BASED FRAUD DETECTION

Boosting approach is a weak learning process, one of the most efficient ways of learning for an algorithm. In the GBM model, a decision tree is fit on the residual and not on the outcome **y** [28]. Thereafter a new decision tree is added into the fitted function to update the residuals. The trees can be of any size, but a smaller tree is preferred. This approach helps to fit the model better into the area where it does not perform well. To slow down the learning rate further learning shrinkage parameter (learning rate) is set. This allows different shaped trees to attack the residuals. It is found that statistical learning models that have a very low learning rate tend to perform better than other models [12]. In boosting, the trees constructed has a very strong dependence on the trees that have already been grown.

In the boosting method, during the learning phase, each of the prediction is given weights to it. The combination of many weak rules combines to make a model with great predictive capability. A single rule may be very weak, an appropriate combination of these "weak" rules can result in building a very accurate model.

Given a collection of N instances (the training dataset) of known values, the goal is to create a model which recognizes the pattern hidden in the field, which makes the claim instance as fraudulent or not. Once this model is created, it should be able to identify the nature of the claims instance given only the fields. This is a supervised learning method.

A gradient boosting model was used to produce a prediction model with Bernoulli loss function. In the model 100 decision trees were used. The parameters were set such that the maximum depth of any decision tree chosen would be 5. The prediction of each of the model was given a weight of 0.03.

14.4.1 DATA

The dataset used for creating the Fraud Detection Model is a synthetic dataset. It has been constructed using specific rules in discussion with the industry experts and has been validated by actuaries that it represents the real-world scenario. This consists of Motor insurance claims. The dataset includes 147,567 claim instances. Each of the observation in the dataset has 27 attributes including the target variable in it (Fraud Status). "Fraud_Status" attribute is the target/response variable; which will be predicted. It was built as:

0: not investigated or investigated and not fraudulent.
1: investigated and declared as fraud.

Of the 147,567 claim instances, there were only 3,150 fraudulent instances. This amounts to approximately 2.13% of fraudulent cases in our database.

After dividing the database into train and test it is important to check the proportion of fraud in each of the datasets. Ideally, it should have the same fraud rate in each of the datasets. To perform a spot check, please find below Tables 14.1 and 14.2 depicting the proportions of the Fraud and legit data before and after performing the SMOTE (handling imbalance nature of data).

TABLE 14.1 Proportions for Unbalanced Dataset

Data (Percentage of the Total Original Data)		**Train (Percentage of the Total Train Data)**		**Test (Percentage of the Total Test Data)**	
Not-fraud	Fraud	Not-fraud	Fraud	Not-fraud	Fraud
97.87	2.13	97.88	2.12	97.81	2.19

TABLE 14.2 Proportions for Balanced Dataset

Data (Percentage of the Total Original Data)		Train (Percentage of the Total Train Data)		Test (Percentage of the Total Test Data)	
Not-fraud	Fraud	Not-fraud	Fraud	Not-fraud	Fraud
95.82	4.18	95.86	4.14	95.67	4.33

The train and test considered for this work was about 80–20 split following the above discussion. Feature engineering is an important preprocessing step where we need to innovate or identify different features that are correlated so that the model learns efficiently. We also need to modify the features and obtain new features in such a way that the model can be generic. As an example, characters, and continuous variables have been dealt with by making it as factors. However, spot checks have been performed to identify the features that should be converted into factors since the categorical values that were in numbers would not be considered as factors. Default functionality of R takes it as a numerical value [25].

As part of pre-processing, it is important to identify the type of data present in the features too. Some of the features that were created from the available data features are What day of the week did the claim occur, What month did the claim occur, Difference between the claim occurrence and its declaration, Policyholder age, Age of the car (in years), Car age under 2 years, Car age under 10 years.

ROC curve (receiver operating characteristics)—a performance metric used in this chapter to understand the performance of the model. In this curve, TPR (true positive rate) is on the y-axis and FPR (false positive rate) is on the x-axis.

AUC (area under the curve) of the ROC curve is another measurement of the classification problem. AUC represents the degree or measure of separability. Higher the AUC value, the better the model at predicting fraudulent cases as fraudulent and legit cases as legit.

The confusion matrix is built, which is used to derive various metrics that helps arrive at the performance of the model. This is used to arrive at the optimal threshold value for the predictive model. Finally, to aid with more understanding, we included other plots such as specificity vs. sensitivity and rate of positive predictions vs. lift value.

14.5 RESULTS

The accuracy of the model was found to be 99.68%, with sensitivity being 98.39% and specificity being 99.74%. F1-score is about 96.39%.

This matrix was created using the probability threshold as 0.099. For this threshold, we observe that 28,761 of 28,836 non-fraudulent, 1,283 out of 1,304 fraudulent cases were identified. Table 14.3 shows the confusion matrix for the model when test data was used and Table 14.4 shows the results obtained.

The high accuracy of the model indicates that the model identifies 99.68% of the classification made by the model was correct. A sensitivity of 98.39% indicated that of the total number of legit cases (28,836 records), 98.39% of the cases were correctly classified as legit, which amount to 28,761 records. A specificity of 99.74% indicates that of the total number of fraudulent cases (1,304 records), 99.74% of the fraudulent cases were identified correctly, which amount to 1,283 records. The F1 score is the harmonic average of precision and recall. The F1 score reaches its best value at 1. The model created has the F1 score of 96.39%, which is a very good score.

TABLE 14.3 Confusion Matrix for Test Dataset

		Actual	
		Non-Fraud	**Fraud**
Predicted	Non-Fraud	28,761	21
	Fraud	75	1,283

TABLE 14.4 Results

Sensitivity	98.39%
Specificity	99.74%
Precision	94.48%
Accuracy	99.68%
F1-Score	96.39%

Figure 14.7 displays the 12 fields which had non-zero influence in determining the final output of the model. We see that "Type_Claim" is the most influential with 74.66% relative influence. Of all the 12 fields there are only 4 fields which had significant influence with the relative influence of 74.66%, 17.15%, 5.99%, and 1.51%, respectively. The rest of the fields, though non-zero, influenced less than 1%.

The results comply with the business point of view. In this case, the fraud cases are a less frequent event having high severity in some cases [19, 25, 29].

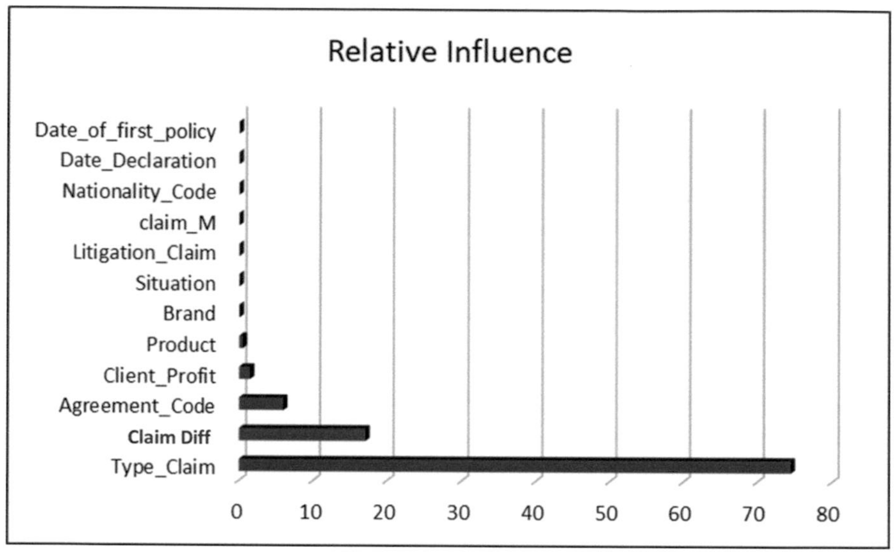

FIGURE 14.7 Relative influence.

14.6 CONCLUSION

Efforts by various organizations are being made towards developing an anti-fraud model and various innovative approaches are being used. Various Actuarial and AI tools and techniques that can be used to detect and prevent fraud has been identified. A fraud detection and prevention framework was proposed, and various data-related challenges were discussed.

A proof of concept was done on an automobile insurance dataset. An innovative data-driven CART-based model for fraud detection and prevention was proposed. F1-Score and accuracy of 96.39 and 99.68 were achieved.

ACKNOWLEDGMENT

We dedicate this work to the Revered Founder Chancellor of Sri Sathya Sai Institute of Higher Learning (SSSIHL), Bhagwan Sri Sathya Sai Baba and express our deep sense of gratitude to SSSIHL-for providing all the facilities to carry out our research work.

APPENDIX

Triggers for Fraud in Automobile Insurance
Misc. Indicators
Automobile fire in a very remote rural area with no witness
Insured is willing to accept a small settlement
The vehicle has an unusual amount of add-ons, e.g., high-end stereo system, wheels, etc.
Claims just a few days before the end of the policy term
Question about recent claims is unanswered
Unusually high parts cost
Very high settlements for a certain court or lawyer
Auto Theft Indicators
Insured has become recently unemployed
Vehicle was stolen from an unusual location
Insured recently had coverage changes (increased coverage)
Late notice about the theft to the police or the insurance company
Insured reports theft and is calm
Theft in the area where there are no CCTVs
Accidents Indicators
No eye-witnesses to the accident
Witness for the accident deliberately tries to hide from the investigator
Vehicle not available for inspection
Delayed reporting of claims
Staged accidents to collect accidents
Produces handwritten receipt for repairs and purchases
During an accident, the damage done to the car and the injury suffered is suspiciously miraculous, e.g., car shattered but only a few scratches
Alcohol/drug involved
Late night/early morning accident
Does the witness have conflicting versions of the same accident?
Repair shop indicated is not equipped with to make repairs
Vehicle repaired before the loss is reported

KEYWORDS

- **actuarial control cycle**
- **application interface**
- **area under the curve**
- **customer relationship management**
- **false-positive rate**
- **receiver operating characteristics**
- **social network analysis**

REFERENCES

1. Barua, S., Md, M. I., Xin, Y., & Kazuyuki, M., (2014). MWMOTE-majority weighted minority oversampling technique for imbalanced data set learning. *IEEE Transactions on Knowledge and Data Engineering, 26*(2), 405–425. https://doi.org/10.1109/TKDE.2012.232.
2. Chawla, N. V., Kevin, W. B., Lawrence, O. H., & Philip, K. W., (2002). SMOTE: Synthetic minority over-sampling technique. *Journal of Artificial Intelligence Research, 16*, 321–357. https://doi.org/10.1613/jair.953.
3. Coles, S., (2001). *Classical Extreme Value Theory and Models* (pp. 45–73). https://doi.org/10.1007/978-1-4471-3675-0-3.
4. Dikaiakos, M. D., Dimitrios, K., Pankaj, M., George, P., & Athena, V., (2009). Cloud computing: Distributed internet computing for IT and scientific research. *IEEE Internet Computing*. https://doi.org/10.1109/MIC.2009.103.
5. Fernanda, M., & Osorio, M., (2017). *Comparing the Performance of Oversampling Techniques for Imbalanced Learning in Insurance Fraud Detection.*
6. Guelman, L., (2012). Gradient boosting trees for auto insurance loss cost modeling and prediction. *Expert Systems with Applications, 39*(3), 3659–3667. https://doi.org/10.1016/j.eswa.2011.09.058.
7. Gumbel, E. J., (1958). *Statistics of Extremes.* Columbia University Press.
8. Haibo, H., Yang, B., Edwardo, A. G., & Shutao, L., (2008). ADASYN: Adaptive synthetic sampling approach for imbalanced learning. In: *2008 IEEE International Joint Conference on Neural Networks (IEEE World Congress on Computational Intelligence)* (pp. 1322–1328). IEEE. https://doi.org/10.1109/IJCNN.2008.4633969.
9. Hormozi, H., Elham, H., Mohammad, K. A., & Morteza, S. J., (2013). Credit cards fraud detection by negative selection algorithm on Hadoop. In: *IKT 2013–2013 5th Conference on Information and Knowledge Technology* (pp. 40–43). https://doi.org/10.1109/IKT.2013.6620035.
10. Insurance Fraud-FBI, (n.d.). Accessed at: https://www.fbi.gov/stats-services/publications/insurance-fraud (accessed on 22 February 2021).

11. Japkowicz, N., & Shaju, S., (2002). The class imbalance problem: A systematic study. *Intelligent Data Analysis, 6*(5), 429–449. https://doi.org/10.3233/IDA-2002-6504.
12. Lemaître, G., Fernando, N., & Christos, K. A., (2017). Imbalanced-learn: A python toolbox to tackle the curse of imbalanced datasets in machine learning. *Journal of Machine Learning Research, 18*. http://jmlr.org/papers/v18/16-365.html (accessed on 22 February 2021).
13. Fen-May, L., Ying-Chan, T., & Jean-Yi, C., (2008). Detecting hospital fraud and claim abuse through diabetic outpatient services. *Health Care Management Science, 11*(4), 353–358. https://doi.org/10.1007/s10729-008-9054-y.
14. Maciejewski, T., & Jerzy, S., (2011). Local neighborhood extension of SMOTE for mining imbalanced data. In: *2011 IEEE Symposium on Computational Intelligence and Data Mining (CIDM)*, 104–111. IEEE. https://doi.org/10.1109/CIDM.2011.5949434.
15. Marie, N., (2015). Sensitivities via rough paths. *ESAIM: Probability and Statistics, 19*, 515–543. https://doi.org/10.1051/ps/2015001.
16. Mcneil, A. J., (1999). *Extreme Value Theory for Risk Managers. Departement Mathematik ETH Zentrum 12*(5), 217–327.
17. Mosley, R. C., & Nick, K., (2014). *The Use of Analytics for Claim Fraud Detection Roose*, 1–15.
18. Pérez, J. M., Javier, M., Olatz, A., Ibai, G., & José, I. M., (2005). Consolidated tree classifier learning in a car insurance fraud detection domain with class imbalance. In: *Lecture Notes in Computer Science* (Vol. 3686, pp. 381–389). https://doi.org/10.1007/11551188-41.
19. Roy, R., & Thomas, G. K., (2017). Detecting insurance claims fraud using machine learning techniques. In: *Proceedings of IEEE International Conference on Circuit, Power and Computing Technologies, ICCPCT 2017*. Institute of Electrical and Electronics Engineers Inc. https://doi.org/10.1109/ICCPCT.2017.8074258.
20. Sheshasaayee, A., & Surya, S. T., (2019). *Usage of R Programming in Data Analytics with Implications on Insurance Fraud Detection* (pp. 416–421). https://doi.org/10.1007/978-3-030-03146-6-46.
21. Subudhi, S., & Suvasini, P., (2018). Effect of class imbalances in detecting automobile insurance fraud. In: *2018 2nd International Conference on Data Science and Business Analytics (ICDSBA)* (pp. 528–531). IEEE. https://doi.org/10.1109/ICDSBA.2018.00104.
22. Sundarkumar, G. G., Vadlamani, R., & Siddeshwar, V., (2015). One-class support vector machine-based under-sampling: Application to churn prediction and insurance fraud detection. In: *2015 IEEE International Conference on Computational Intelligence and Computing Research (ICCIC)* (pp. 1–7). IEEE. https://doi.org/10.1109/ICCIC.2015.7435726.
23. Tenders, (n.d). https://www.irdai.gov.in/ADMINCMS/cms/frmGeneral_List.aspx?DF=irda-tndr&mid=21 (accessed on 22 February 2021).
24. SAS, (n.d.). *The State of Insurance Fraud Technology*. https://www.sas.com/en_in/insights/articles/risk-fraud/the-state-of-insurance-fraud-technology.html (accessed on 22 February 2021).
25. Verma, A., Anu, T., & Anuja, A., (2017). Fraud detection and frequent pattern matching in insurance claims using data mining techniques. In: *2017 Tenth International Conference on Contemporary Computing (IC3)*. IEEE. https://doi.org/10.1109/IC3.2017.8284299.
26. Wu, J., Runtong, Z., Xiaopu, S., & Fuzhi, C., (2017). Medical insurance fraud recognition based on improved outlier detection algorithm. *DEStech Transactions on Computer Science and Engineering*. https://doi.org/10.12783/dtcse/aiea2017/15009.

27. Wan-Shiou, Y., & San-Yih, H., (2006). A process-mining framework for the detection of healthcare fraud and abuse. *Expert Systems with Applications, 31*(1), 56–68. https://doi.org/10.1016/j.eswa.2005.09.003.
28. Zhao, Y., Zain, N., & Zheng, L., (2019). PyOD: A python toolbox for scalable outlier detection. *Journal of Machine Learning Research. 20*. https://pyod.readthedocs.io (accessed on 22 February 2021).
29. Zhengbing, H., Sergiy, G., Oksana, K., Viktor, G., & Serhii, B., (2017). Anomaly detection system in secure cloud computing environment. *International Journal of Computer Network and Information Security, 9*(4), 10–21. https://doi.org/10.5815/ijcnis.2017.04.02.

CHAPTER 15

APPLICATION OF NEURAL NETWORKS FOR ASSESSING THE PERFORMANCE OF INSURANCE BUSINESS

S. R. PRANAV SAI,[1] SATYA SAI MUDIGONDA,[2] PHANI KRISHNA KANDALA,[3] and PALLAV KUMAR BARUAH[4]

[1]*Doctoral Research Scholar in Actuarial Science, Department of Mathematics and Computer Science, Sri Sathya Sai Institute of Higher Learning, Puttaparthi, Andhra Pradesh, India, E-mail: srpranavsai@sssihl.edu.in*

[2]*Honorary Professor in Actuarial Science, Department of Mathematics and Computer Science, Sri Sathya Sai Institute of Higher Learning, Puttaparthi, Andhra Pradesh, India*

[3]*Visiting Faculty in Actuarial Science, Department of Mathematics and Computer Science, Sri Sathya Sai Institute of Higher Learning, Puttaparthi, Andhra Pradesh, India*

[4]*Associate Professor, Department of Mathematics and Computer Science, Sri Sathya Sai Institute of Higher Learning, Puttaparthi, Andhra Pradesh, India*

ABSTRACT

Sustainability of a company is driven by its operational efficiency. The operational efficiency plays a significant role in a company's growth and profitability. Thus, it forms the foundation for the metrics of performance known as the Key Performance Indicators (KPIs). The KPIs establishes a connection between the concept of performance and the means to gauge the same. These KPIs are calculated from the data fields from the data disclosed publicly by the insurance company. In this work, we establish the correlations between the factors which affect the performance of a company and those which measure the performance of the company. This analysis links the underlying operations and the performance of the company quantitatively. Thus, it aids in the increase of the operational efficiency of the insurance company. We then use a neural network with two fully connected layers for predicting the factors. These are used to calculate the KPIs of the company. In this work as a proof of concept, five different non- life insurers in India were considered. The data obtained is the publicly disclosed data by the insurance company. Thus, this model gives the status of a company's performance in an accelerated timeframe. Thus, it enables the company to oversee and monitor its operations for a sustainable future.

15.1 INTRODUCTION

15.1.1 DECISION MAKING WHICH IS DATA-DRIVEN

Decision-making driven by data is a methodology that involves acquiring data based on goals which are measurable of an organization, analyzing patterns, acquiring insights, and utilizing them to come up with strategies and activities that give a lot of benefits to the underlying business in several ways. Fundamentally, it means progressing towards achieving the goals driven from the data rather than going with the intuitions of select individuals. Data-driven decision-making is a four-step process (Figure 15.1).

The importance of data-driven decision-making lies in the underlying consistency. It uses the vast data generated by the companies to create new business opportunities, to generate more revenue, to increase the efficiency in the operations, to predict future trends, and to produce more actionable insights. Thus resulting in a stable and steady growth to an organization over time and making the organization adaptable to the external environment.

15.1.2 ARTIFICIAL INTELLIGENCE (AI) AND NEURAL NETWORKS

The simulations of a working of a human brain in computer systems is what is called artificial intelligence (AI). This simulation has three significant steps, learning, reasoning, and self-correction. Learning is the process of assimilating information and rules based on the information provided to the system. The reasoning is coming up with reasonable and approximate conclusions by using the rules assimilated in the process of learning. Self-correction is an automatic feedback mechanism that enables the system to implement corrective measures based on the rules acquired in the process of learning and reasoning. Machine learning (ML) is an application of AI which primarily focuses on the acquisition of knowledge and skill by a machine. The main objective of ML is to increase the accuracy of the results given out by the machine as close to the underlying real-world experience. ML is broadly classified into two types, supervised learning and unsupervised learning. A supervised learning algorithm learns from labeled training data, and this learning process helps to predict the outcomes of the data not foreseen. The algorithm is said to be supervised if the desired output is already known and the model is trained over this data. In unsupervised learning, the desired output is not known, and the model is allowed to work on the data and discover the information on its own. In other words, to obtain the characteristics of the given information (Figure 15.2).

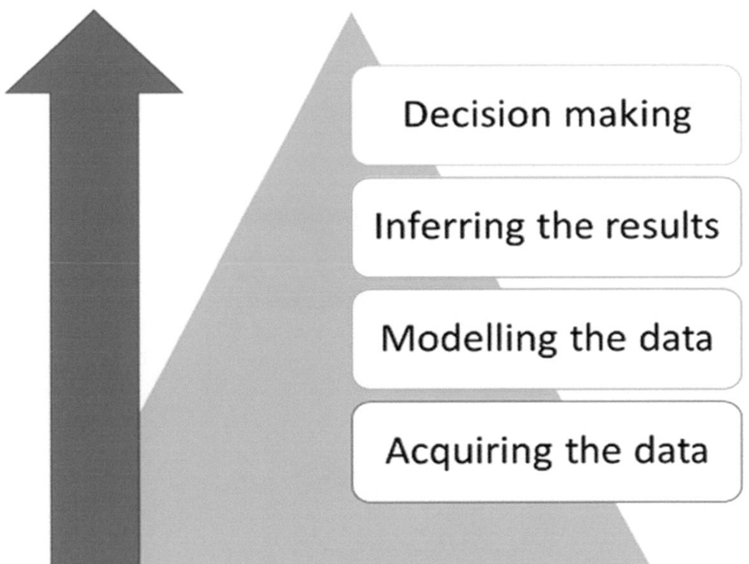

FIGURE 15.1 Decision-making which is data-driven.

Artificial neural network is a supervised ML technique that enables the system's learning from the data. A neural network works like that of the neurons present in a human brain. A neuron in this neural network is a mathematical function that forms the building block to neural network

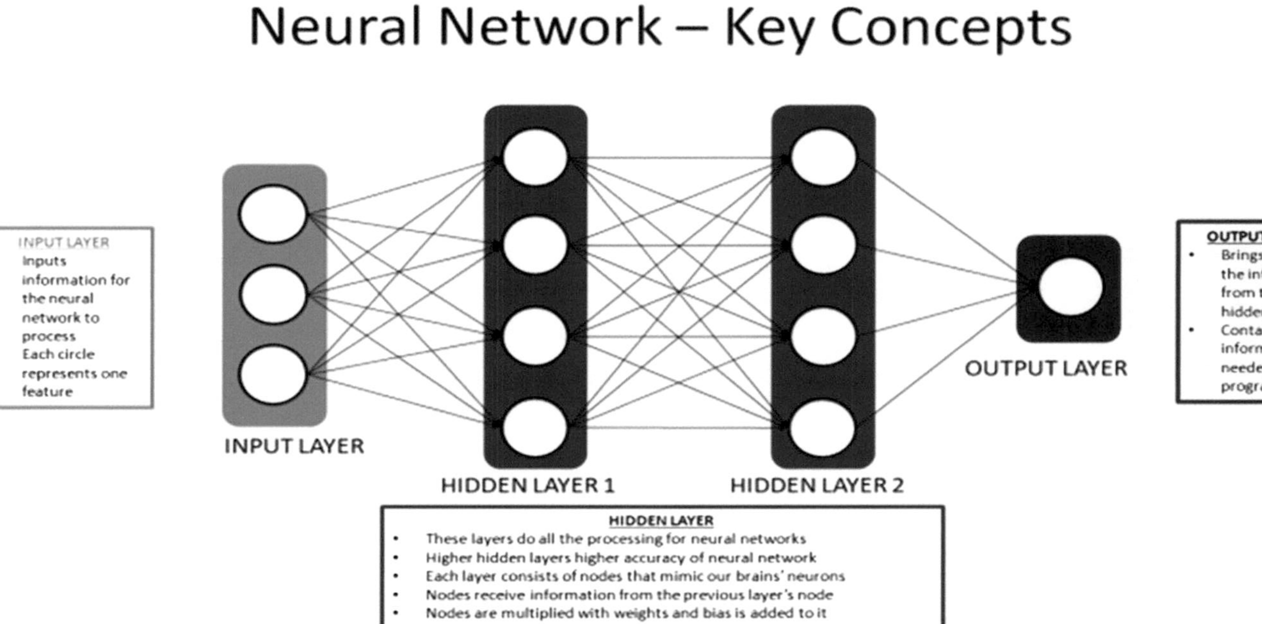

FIGURE 15.2 Artificial neural network framework.

architecture. This neuron classifies the collected information specific to the underlying architecture. The artificial neural network bears a strong resemblance to statistical methods like regression analysis and curve fitting. We used artificial neural networks in order to assess the performance and sustainability of the insurance business.

15.1.3 THE DATA-DRIVEN MODEL

In this work, a data-driven model is proposed for the general insurance companies. This model would help a general insurance company to enhance operational efficiency and to assess its sustainability in the future based on its operations in the present. The basis of this work is driven by the metrics called key performance indicators or KPIs. These establish a connection between the concept of performance with the means to measure them quantitatively. These KPIs are calculated from the data fields from the data disclosed publicly by the insurance company. In this work, we establish the correlations between the factors which affect the performance of a company and those which measure the performance of the company. This analysis links the underlying operations and the performance of the company quantitatively, thus aiding in the increase of the operational efficiency of the insurance company.

We then use a neural network to predict and analyze the factors which are used to calculate the KPIs of the company. In other words, the KPIs are calculated for these predicted factors from the data and analysis is done on these KPIs. In this work, the KPIs are obtained from the public disclosure data of the companies. This analysis gives the status of a company's performance in an accelerated time frame, thus enabling the company and the regulator to oversee and monitor the company's operation for a sustainable future.

The KPIs of insurance companies are affected by several internal and external factors. The internal factors can be the company's risk appetite, line of business, types of policies sold to name a few. The external factors include legislation, regulation, economic environment, accounting standards to name a few. In this work, 17 KPIs are used to assess the company's operations. In specific, the operations of a non-life insurance company. These are categorized into two groups, the dependent KPIs and the independent KPIs. The independent KPIs are those which affect the performance of the company's operations at various levels. Some examples of the independent KPIs are the reinsurance dependence, leverage, stability of the asset structure to name a few. There are 14 independent KPIs considered in this work. The dependent KPIs are those which indicate the performance of the company's operations. The dependent KPIs considered here are the percentage change in shareholders' funds, return on shareholders' funds, and investment yield.

This chapter is divided into eight different sections. The first section would have given an overview of this chapter. The second section gives the motivation behind this work. Section 15.3 talks about the KPIs. Section 15.4 talks about the framework to assess the operational efficiency of the data. This gives a detailed explanation of the KPIs considered. Section 15.5 presents the results of how these KPIs affect each other.

Section 15.6 gives the framework for assessing the sustainability of the insurer. Here, the data obtained is projected for the future using an artificial neural network. It also explains the methodology used for obtaining the KPIs for the future from the given data. Section 15.7 shows the results of these future KPIs. Section 15.8 talks about the conclusions derived from the above frameworks. The last section acknowledges the contribution of people both from academia and the industry.

15.2 MOTIVATION

Capturing unseen patterns from the underlying data, Neural Networks are efficient systems and represent a fast and efficient method of analyzing certain features from our data. Upon analysis, we expand our data set by projecting into the future. Specifically, we shall delineate its importance in projecting KPIs for an insurance company. Padding up the risk of the entire economy, the insurance industry is pivotal and must be governed effectively in a streamlined manner. For developed countries, the insurance industry has approximately an 8% GDP penetration which can be seen from the reports of Ref. [16]. In particular, the Indian Insurance Industry represents 59 companies subdivided into 24 life insurance firms and 36 non-life firms. Incorporating both private and open division companies, India represents a growing economy with premiums sizing up 3.69% of the country's GDP. From a GDP penetration of 2.71% in the year 2001 up to the above-mentioned 3.69% in 2017, India has witnessed a steady, enduring growth in its Insurance Market. India is slated to achieve a market size of 25 lakh crores in INR by the close of 2020. Our interest lies in exploring and achieving a highly efficient and productive method of working in furthering and achieving the targets set out for the Indian Insurance Industry.

15.2.1 BENEFITS OF INSURANCE

Every insurance company has five major goals set. They are:

- Make profit;
- Customer satisfaction;
- Legal compliance;
- Diversify risk; and
- Societal benefits.

But to achieve these goals, a lot of constraints are faced by the insurance company. The internal constraints faced are efficiency, expertise, size, financial resources, and risk appetite to name a few. There are a lot of external constraints faced by the insurance company than its internal, some of them are regulation, rating agencies, accounting standards, legislation, tax, public opinion, and economic conditions.

Thus, this model will help the insurance company to take into account the external constraints to overcome the internal constraints, especially that of operational efficiency. Thus, helping the insurance company to achieve its goals set. This forms the rationale behind this work.

15.3 KEY PERFORMANCE INDICATORS (KPIS)

15.3.1 WHAT ARE KPIS?

KPIs are essential elements in every report in the process of data-driven decision-making. They monitor various operations of the company and quantitatively measure the performance of the underlying operation being monitored. These form the basis for measuring the performance of a company and also projecting the trends in an accelerated time frame. They are significantly affected by the external environment such as legislation, regulation, tax, etc. Some of the important features affecting the KPIs internally are the line of business, area of expertise and so on. We monitor a company's performance on different fronts to improve the operational efficiency of the company.

15.3.2 THE STEPS TO DERIVE THE KPIS

- List the various operations of the company at all levels.
- For each of the operations, get to know all the steps and processes involved.
  - It is ideal to deal with downside risks since we are talking about performance improvements.
- List various risks under each of the operations.
- Formulate the various parameters that measure each of the underlying risks.
- Only the quantifiable risks can be analyzed by the models.
  - It is important to find out how to derive these parameters from the available data factors.
- Once the parameters are in place, they are grouped to form the KPIs for that process (Figure 15.3).

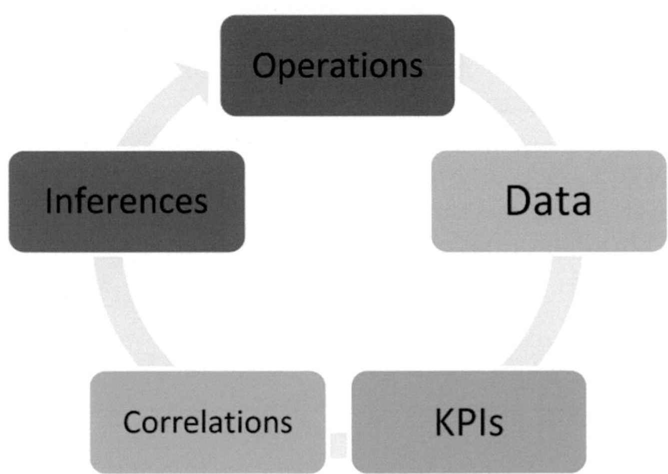

FIGURE 15.3 The steps to obtain the KPIs.

15.4 THE FRAMEWORK TO ASSESS OPERATIONAL EFFICIENCY

This section centers on coming up with a comprehensive framework for sensitivity analysis of the performance of the company with regard to every KPI. We will see this in detail in the following subsections. In this work, as a pilot study, we considered three non-life insurance companies in India. This framework can be extended to other companies in various lines of business as well (Figure 15.4).

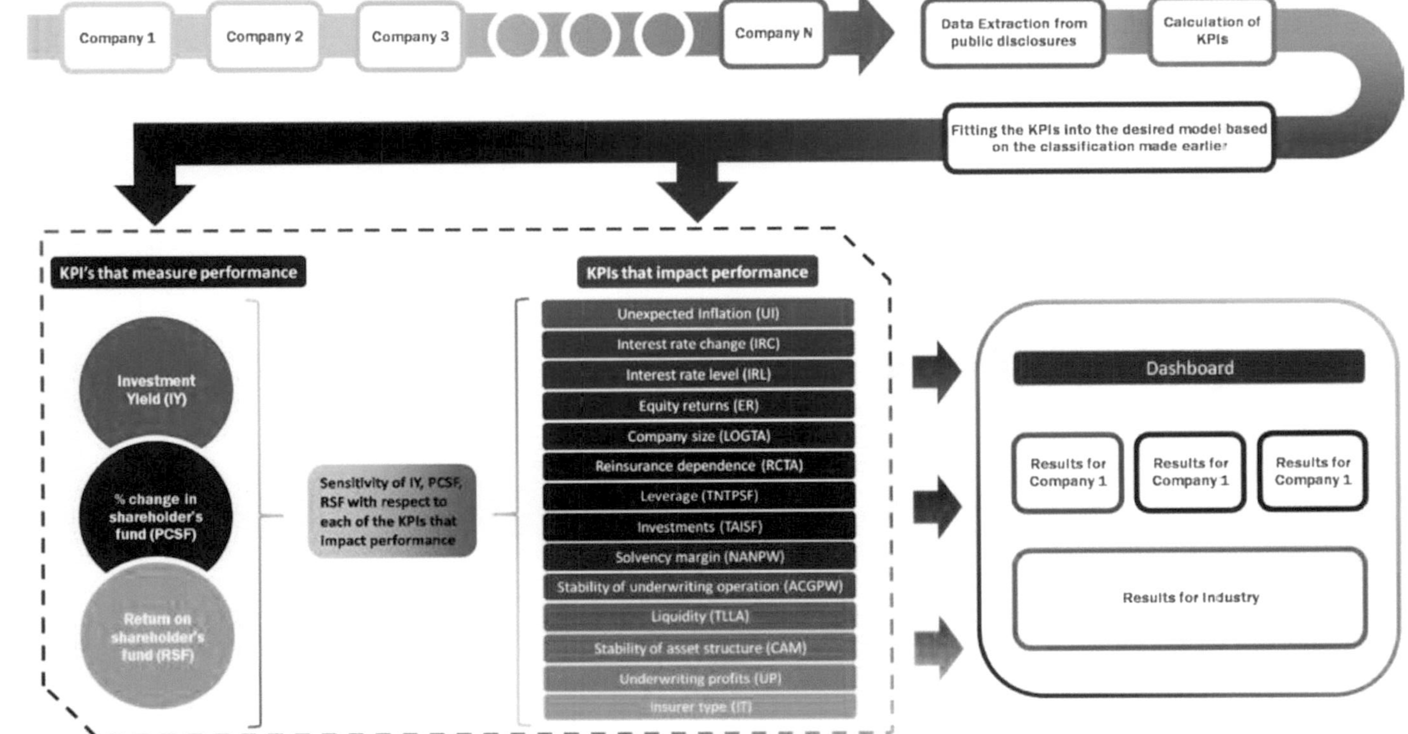

FIGURE 15.4 The framework to assess the sensitivity of the performance of a company using the KPIs.

These KPIs in this work are categorized into two: independent and dependent KPIs. The independent KPIs are those which affect the performance of the company at various levels, the dependent KPIs are those which measure or indicate the performance of the company all in all.

15.4.1 THE INDEPENDENT KPIS

These affect the performance of the company at various levels. Here, we try to establish how each of them is linked to the performance of the company. Table 15.1 lists the variables, and how they affect an organization's overall performance.

TABLE 15.1 The Determinants of an Organization's Performance

SL. No.	Determinants of Performance	What Stand Affected	Relation with Performance
1.	Unexpected inflation	Claims Expenses Provisions	Negative
2.	Interest rate change	Assets Liabilities Claim costs	Duration dependent
3.	Level of interest	Investment income	Positive
4.	Return of equity	Investment income	Positive
5.	The size of the company	Costs	
6.	Dependence on a reinsurer	Profits	Negative
7.	Leverage	Equity Debt	Positive and negative depending on the capital structure.
8.	Affiliated investments	Insolvency risk increases	Negative
9.	Solvency margin	Reserves	Positive
10.	Underwriting operation's stability	Premium rates	No prior expectation
11.	Liquidity	Investments/assets	Positive
12.	Stability of the underlying structure of asset	Assets	Positive
13.	Profits from underwriting	Positive	
14.	Type of insurer	Type of business	Indeterminate

The definitions of all the above-mentioned variables are discussed in the following subsections.

15.4.1.1 UNEXPECTED INFLATION (UI)

Unexpected inflation (UI) is the unaccounted part of the inflation rates being considered. This has a significant impact on the performance of an organization. The formula to calculate UI is given below:

$$\text{UI} = \text{Inflation rate-Interbank rate} \tag{1}$$

15.4.1.2 INTEREST RATE CHANGE (IRC)

Changes in interest rates have a significant impact on the value of a firm's assets and liabilities. Actuarial theory aids us in determining whether the net impact on a company is positive or negative. Reddington's conditions consider such effects and evaluate the potential risks with respect to both length and convexity. Thus, this variable has a direct link to a company's performance as it carries the potential to alter a firm's profitability.

$$\text{IRC} = \text{Difference in the rates of the 91 Indian treasury bill's yield for the year and the year before} \tag{2}$$

15.4.1.3 INTEREST RATE LEVEL (IRL)

The IRL refers to the cost of taking a loan and is specifically set out by the monetary policy of a country. For India, the Reserve Bank of India handles the responsibility of setting the interest rate. Speculation with regard to the interest rate can drive returns for a company positively or negatively.

$$\text{IRL} = \text{Indian government 10-year bond yield} \tag{3}$$

15.4.1.4 RETURNS IN EQUITY (ER)

Equities are regarded as a form of investment with the potential to provide significant gains while allowing for a higher degree of risk. Due to the inherent uncertainty, the performance of an equity is relatively difficult to forecast. With a robust investment strategy, a company can pad itself within a risk range and dilute the hazard. Here, an increase in returns or a rise in stock value carries a positive impact.

$$\text{ER} = \text{Index of equity returns} \tag{4}$$

15.4.1.5 SIZE OF THE COMPANY (LOGTA)

The total assets of a company play a significant role in the overall performance of the organization. The sources of income increase with a company's size. The profits increase as the sources of income increase. Thus, the size of a company plays an important role in analyzing the overall efficiency of the organization.

$$\text{LOGTA} = \text{TA} \tag{5}$$

where; TA = total assets.

15.4.1.6 REINSURANCE DEPENDENCE (RCTA)

Often, an insurer wishes to share or limit one's exposure to risk. With reinsurance, an insurer shares either a proportion of the risk or agrees on an excess of loss coverage form. Further, there can be additional layers to the treaty dependent upon the needs of the insurer. While an insurer covers a degree of risk, reinsurance results in a degree of potential profit eroded. Hence, the greater the reinsurance dependence for an insurer, it negatively impacts potential profits while also decreasing potential losses.

This measure is captured as:

$$\text{RCTA} = \frac{\text{RC}}{\text{TA}} \tag{6}$$

where; RC = reinsurance ceded.

15.4.1.7 LEVERAGE (TNTPSF)

Generally, insurance companies maintain a reserve fund as a precautionary measure for potential payments and unforeseen circumstances in the future. Known as reserving, the insurance company maintains possession of these funds. Typically, policyholders are to be accommodated into different structures due to caps or a limit on premiums. A known case study would be that of that the No Claims Discount Policy in which the company sets out to enhance its capital structure along with its monetary influence in which it optimizes the proportion of the company's obligation to value. Till the optimal point of an ideal capital structure, the company's influence will maintain a positive relationship with its performance.

$$\text{TNTPSF} = \frac{\text{TNTP}}{\text{SF}} \tag{7}$$

where; TNTP = total net technical provisions; SF = Shareholders' funds.

15.4.1.8 INVESTMENTS (TAISF)

This variable defines an umbrella covering various financial instruments such as debentures, bonds, and government securities. A key distinction is to be made between an investment and an affiliated investment which refers to an investment made along with fiduciary acting in an advisory capacity. Thus, the performance of a company is impacted differently dependent on whether the investment is affiliated or not.

$$\text{TAISF} = \frac{\text{TAI}}{\text{SF}} \tag{8}$$

where; TAI = total affiliated investments.

15.4.1.9 SOLVENCY MARGIN (NANPW)

Defined as the difference between a company's assets and liabilities, the solvency margin represents the ability of a company to pay its long-term expenses. With a wider margin, a company is well placed to meet liabilities in the long run as well as indicating that a company is financially healthy. Thus, the variable has a positive impact on an organization's profitability and long-term wellbeing.

$$\text{NANPW} = \frac{\text{NA}}{\text{NPW}} \tag{9}$$

where; NA = net assets; NPW = net premiums written.

15.4.1.10 STABILITY OF UNDERWRITING OPERATION (ACGPW)

Regarded as a core operation for any insurance agency, underwriting often impacts the ability of a firm to advance and improve. Interestingly, a related activity which carries a significant impact on the company's operations is the underwriting cycle. When viewed as delicate, a company prepares a backup solution to accommodate additional business for the firm, and this results in a lower premium. Conversely, in the case of a difficult underwriting cycle, the inclusion provided by insurers is understood to be lesser to the present as exposed to market risk. This results in a hike in premium prices. In conclusion, there is not a definite, binding relationship between performance and ACGPW, with the impact dependent on the given scenario.

$$\mathrm{ACGPW} = \frac{\mathrm{NPW_t} - \mathrm{NPW_{t-1}}}{\mathrm{NPW_t}} \tag{10}$$

15.4.1.11 LIQUIDITY (TLLA)

In contrast to the long-term concept of solvency, liquidity refers to a company's ability to pay immediate liabilities. It can also be understood as to how quickly a company can shift over its assets into money. Liquid assets include cash, short-term investments, and stocks which can be readily turned into cash with minimal expense. The liquidity of a company has a direct impact on a company's capability to meet everyday challenges. Consequently, there exists a positive relationship between liquidity and company's performance.

$$\mathrm{TLLA} = \frac{\mathrm{TL}}{\mathrm{LA}} \tag{11}$$

where; TL = total liabilities; LA = liquid assets.

15.4.1.12 STABILITY OF THE UNDERLYING ASSET STRUCTURE (CAM)

An organization's asset structure refers to how the company's assets are distributed among different asset categories with the intent of maximizing returns from the asset base. Stability in this division inspires reliability with regard to the company's budgetary position. Hence, the variable is directly linked to a company's performance.

$$\mathrm{CAM} = \frac{\sum_{k=1}^{n} \mathrm{P_k}}{\mathrm{n}} \tag{12}$$

$$\mathrm{P_k} = 100\frac{\mathrm{A_t^k} - \mathrm{A_{t-1}^k}}{\mathrm{A_{t-1}^k}} \tag{13}$$

where; A_t^k = value of asset k at time t.

15.4.1.13 UNDERWRITING PROFITS (UP)

Profits arising from core activities such as premium collections and claims payments are referred to as underwriting profits (UP) as they financially map a company's center business movement. Essentially, it amounts to a net figure quantifying the difference between revenue and payments. With a high degree of guarantee, a company can handle its risks in an efficient manner. Therefore, a positive link is drawn up between a company's UP and its performance.

$$UP = NPE - NCI - NOE + AD - CTP - IPUR + OTI \qquad (14)$$

where; OTI = other technical income; NPE = Net premiums earned; CTP = changes in technical provisions; NOE = net operating expenses; AD = adjustment for discounting; NCI = net claims incurred; IPUR = increased in provisions for unexpired risks.

15.4.1.14 INSURER TYPE (IT)

The first insurer type (IT) to discuss would be that of an expert general insurer who provides insurance dispersed for non-life risks such as auto insurance, house protection, among others. Other forms include property and casualty insurance. Also, we have multi-line insurers who aggregate risks and offer a product catering to personalized needs which may arise. This form of insurance is attractive with its bundled nature and lower cost. A composite insurer refers to a company dealing in both life and non-life markets. This can be strategically sound for a company who can sell a general protection good to a consumer who has already purchases a life insurance product. As mentioned above, a reinsurer insures an insurance company itself. This variable is informative in the sense it ascribes a certain quality to the organization with potential strategic benefits rather than a direct impact on a company's performance.

- IT1-multiline general insurer.
- IT2-the composite insurer.
- IT3-reinsurer.

15.4.2 THE DEPENDENT VARIABLES

In the previous section, we have delved into the intricacies of each independent variable while going over the nature of its relationship with the company's performance, regardless of whether it is positive or negative. In the above classification and discussion of how each variable impacts the company, we have quantified the means to assess a company. In this section, we aim to distinguish and understand three factors which screen track execution.

15.4.2.1 INVESTMENT YIELD

Let us start with a situation.

- **Situation 1:** Measurement of the investment yield is essential to understanding the effectiveness of an investment and its profitability. This is better understood with the aid of an example. Consider an initial investment of 1000 units as a security which grows to 1100 units after a period of 1 year. The increase of 100 units is known as the yield, which can be viewed as a 10% increase upon the initial investment. The Investment Yield measures the return on the initial investment after a defined time period. Upon being connected to a series of speculations, we obtain a venture yield. Often, insurance companies distribute their salaries into various classes of benefits. This distribution of benefits can be viewed to understand screen the organization. For this purpose, we aim to quantify the venture yield with the below formula.

$$IY = 100\frac{NII}{0.5(TA_t + TA_{t-1})} \tag{15}$$

where; NII = net investment income; TAt = total asset at time t.

15.4.2.2 SHAREHOLDER'S FUNDS' PERCENTAGE CHANGE

A share or equity price is the standard-bearer with regard to assessing a company's performance and position in the market. A rise in share price is reflective of growing investor confidence and a positive sign for a firm. Analyzing a company's stock prices provides insights into investor perception of the company and its ease of operations. The change in share prices depends upon the demand and supply for the company stock in the market. For further analysis, a company can study the assets of the company. This is directly linked with the company's performance.

$$PCSF = \frac{SF_t - SF_{t-1}}{SF_{t-1}} \quad (16)$$

where; SF = Shareholders' funds at time t.

15.4.2.3 RETURN ON SHAREHOLDER'S FUNDS

Measurement of the investment yield is essential to understanding the effectiveness of an investment and its profitability. This is better understood with the aid of an example. Consider an initial investment of 1000 units as a security which grows to 1100 units after a period of 1 year. The increase of 100 units is known as the yield, which can be viewed as a 10% increase upon the initial investment. The Investment Yield measures the return on the initial investment after a defined time period. Upon being connected to a series of speculations, we obtain a venture yield. Often, insurance companies distribute their salaries into various classes of benefits. This distribution of benefits can be viewed to understand screen the organization. For this purpose, we aim to quantify the venture yield with the below formula.

$$RSF = 100\frac{PBTD}{0.5(SF_t + SF_{t-1})} \quad (17)$$

where; PBTD = profits before tax and dividend.

15.5 RESULTS

We now present the results of the analysis. Table 15.2 gives out the KPI analysis value for three non-life insurance companies operating in India.

15.5.1 LIMITATIONS OF THIS FRAMEWORK

The limitations to the above model are as follows:

- We do not get the perspective of the entire insurance industry. For this to happen, the company analysis should be done for all the 34 non-life insurance organizations operating in India.
- The period of study has to be enhanced since it is small for an effective economic variable change.
- The above-mentioned KPIs are arrived for the UK insurance industry [2]. A new set of KPIs for the Indian industry is necessary.

TABLE 15.2 Results for Insurer A, B, C

	Insurer A			Insurer B			Insurer C		
	IY	**PCSF**	**RSF**	**IY**	**PCSF**	**RSF**	**IY**	**PCSF**	**RSF**
UI	0.0301	–1.2848	2.4892	–0.2509	0.4461	–0.6887	0.0227	–0.0233	–15.1521
IRC	0.1442	–0.8574	–4.3439	0.7859	–0.8558	–2.555	0.0005	0.0128	–0.7298
IRL	0.0838	0.9764	–3.8957	–0.4253	0.3546	–5.6918	0.0226	–0.1611	–12.5288
ER	1.21E-05	–0.0008	0.0016	–0.0007	–0.0004	–0.0014	1.08E-05	0.0048	–0.0088
LOGTA	–1.9535	16.3843	–137.678	18.2309	36.8283	93.3598	0.0187	–0.1092	–11.1913
RCTA	3.5502	52.9458	–167.189	–7.4625	12.8552	–8.6073	3.07E-05	0.0006	–0.0409
TNTPSF	0.5581	0.6916	–10.5075	0.8566	–2.5746	–1.4067	–0.0049	0.6359	–16.6164
TAISF	–0.5118	3.2542	10.0706	–0.0161	–0.1848	–0.4876	–0.0017	–1.0731	7.0058
NANPW	0.0732	6.7283	–2.7245	8.2641	2.3265	16.6563	–0.001	–0.0292	1.5069
ACGPW	0.05	1.0913	10.9136	7.5737	–3.4302	15.317	2.32E-17	–4.85E-16	1.56E-14
TLLA	–0.1801	2.5796	–14.635	–0.0573	–0.0114	–0.0295	0.0127	–0.2305	–3.5835
CAM	–0.0073	0.3427	–0.3851	–0.0007	–0.0059	–0.0027	0.0003	–0.0066	0.0326
UP	2.43E–08	–1.40E-06	7.69E-06	1.39E-06	–4.80E-07	2.49E-06	9.77E-09	8.71E-09	1.64E-06

15.6 THE FRAMEWORK TO ASSESS SUSTAINABILITY

For projecting the data into the future using neural networks, the following four steps were performed:

- Bootstrapping to increase the data size;
- Using ANN framework for projection;
- Calculations of the KPIs; and
- Tabulating the correlations matrix.

15.6.1 BOOTSTRAPPING TO INCREASE THE DATA SIZE

The available data points were bootstrapped in order to increase the data size for a better prediction using the neural network.

15.6.2 USING ANN FRAMEWORK FOR PROJECTION

The data was fed into a neural network framework.

- ➢ ANN specifications include:
  - Number of hidden layers: 2;
  - Activation: ReLU;
  - Optimizer: Adam;
  - Epochs: 1500;
  - MSE on test data: 5.35%.

  This was used to protect the data points for the next five quarters.

- ➢ System specifications:
  - GPU: NVIDIA Tesla K40;
  - Cores: 2880 CUDA cores;
  - Threads: 1024/block;
  - Utilization: 100%.

15.6.3 CALCULATIONS OF THE KPIS

From the projected data, the above-mentioned KPIs were obtained.

15.6.4 TABULATING THE CORRELATIONS MATRIX

Once the KPIs are obtained, the correlations among them were calculated and tabulated in the following section.

15.7 RESULTS FOR PROJECTED VALUES

The following graphs show the trend of the select factors for both the past and the present data. The X-axis has quarters over time. The Y-axis is scaled according to INR.

Thus, with the help of these graphs, we can see the trend with time (Figures 15.5–15.9).

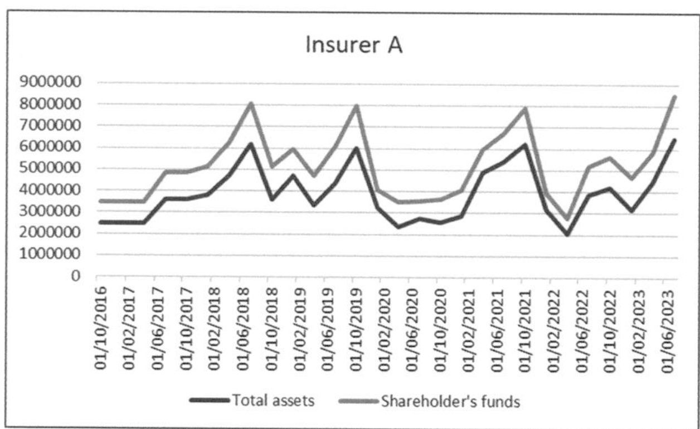

FIGURE 15.5 Insurer A.

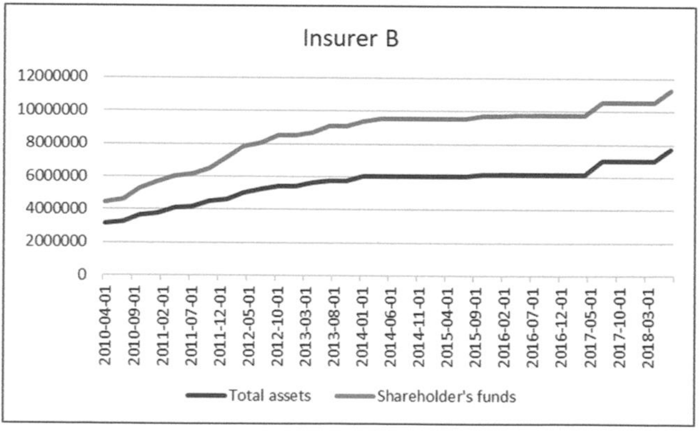

FIGURE 15.6 Insurer B.

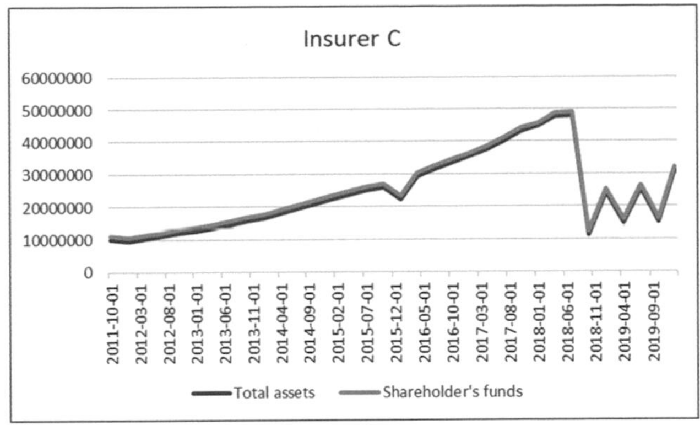

FIGURE 15.7 Insurer C.

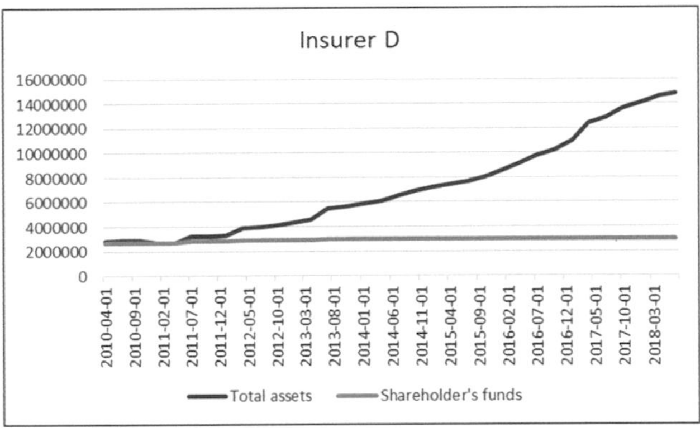

FIGURE 15.8 Insurer D.

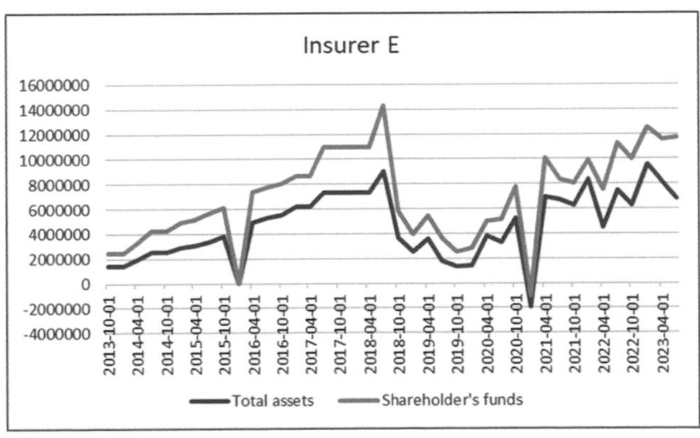

FIGURE 15.9 Insurer E.

The correlations matrix showing the KPI dependencies are given in Tables 15.3–15.5.

TABLE 15.3 Results for Insurer A and Insurer B

Insurer A	IY	PCSF	RSF	Insurer B	IY	PCSF	RSF
LOGTA	–0.56	0.2015	–0.270	LOGTA	–0.462	–0.085	–0.093
RCTA	0.4055	–0.276	0.0863	RCTA	0.104	0.4718	0.11
TNTPCF	0.2939	0.0726	–0.366	TNTPCF	–0.409	–0.214	–0.108
TAISF	–0.022	–0.519	0.1415	TAISF	–0.509	–0.374	0.0630
NANPW	–0.128	–0.273	–0.194	NANPW	0.0005	0.3326	–0.263
TLLA	–0.215	–0.174	–0.026	TLLA	–0.451	–0.214	–0.474
UP	0.1346	0.0807	0.0700	UP	0.2561	–0.036	0.3844
ACGPW	–0.229	0.2042	–0.024	ACGPW	0.3314	0.0121	0.4035
CAM	0.047	0.4859	–0.496	CAM	–0.026	–0.229	–0.228
IY	1	0.2575	–0.084	IY	1	–0.025	0.1200
PCSF	0.2575	1	–0.190	PCSF	–0.025	1	–0.096
RSF	–0.084	–0.190	1	RSF	0.1200	–0.096	1
UI	–0.168	–0.103	–0.038	UI	0.6781	0.0155	0.0870
IRC	–0.168	–0.103	–0.038	IRC	0.6781	0.0155	0.0870
IRL	–2E-17	5E-17	1.20E-16	IRL	1E-16	0	0
ER	0	5E-17	1.59E-16	ER	8E-17	1E-17	–1E-17

15.8 CONCLUSIONS

Thus, in this work, we established a quantitative relationship between the operations and the performance of a non-life insurance company. This can aid the insurance company to better monitor its operations and enhance operational efficiency. Enhancing the operational efficiency can aid the insurance company to outperform the competition present, have a better relationship with the customers and other stakeholders. This analysis would give the regulators a better perspective about the performance and the operations of the insurance companies regulated. Projecting the factors using advanced ML algorithms helps the insurance companies and the regulators a better insight about the operations and the sustainability of the insurance company, thus creating a stable environment in the insurance sector of the country.

TABLE 15.4 Results for Insurer D and Insurer E

Insurer D	IY	PCSF	RSF	Insurer E	IY	PCSF	RSF
LOGTA	–0.202	0.0208	0.2328	LOGTA	–0.74	0.1933	0.432
RCTA	0.2707	0.0552	0.1757	RCTA	–0.460	0.2758	0.20
TNTPCF	–0.065	–0.090	0.1938	TNTPCF	–0.228	–0.137	0.1346
TAISF	0.0079	–0.248	–0.259	TAISF	0.0322	–0.019	–0.281
NANPW	0.0650	0.1073	–0.087	NANPW	0.0047	–0.079	–0.057
TLLA	–0.383	–0.077	0.1244	TLLA	0.1232	0.4568	–0.314
UP	0.1847	–0.155	–0.208	UP	0.2216	–0.673	0.1225
ACGPW	–0.053	–0.219	–0.11	ACGPW	0.0924	–0.51	0.4662
CAM	–0.172	0.3603	–0.164	CAM	–0.099	–0.676	0.2363
IY	1	0.2806	0.6371	IY	1	0.0740	–0.546
PCSF	0.2806	1	0.0255	PCSF	0.0740	1	–0.416
RSF	0.6371	0.0255	1	RSF	–0.546	–0.416	1
UI	0.0569	–0.063	–0.236	UI	0.4299	–0.05	–0.447
IRC	0.0569	–0.063	–0.236	IRC	0.4299	–0.05	–0.447
IRL	8E-17	2E-17	–5E-17	IRL	–5E-17	–1E-17	3E-16
ER	9E-17	3E-17	–6E-17	ER	–8E-17	–1E-17	3E-16

TABLE 15.5 Results for Insurer C

Insurer C	IY	RSF
LOGTA	–0.43	0.4984
RCTA	–0.177	0.5312
TNTPCF	–0.414	0.5458
TAISF	0.1109	0.0456
NANPW	–0.024	–0.244
TLLA	–0.340	0.5238
UP	–0.271	0.408
ACGPW	0.1512	–0.026
CAM	0.0284	–0.322
IY	1	–0.461
RSF	–0.461	1
UI	0.3853	–0.574
IRC	0.3853	–0.574
IRL	–4E-17	–1E-16
ER	–4E-17	–8E-17

KEYWORDS

- **insurer type**
- **interest rate change**
- **interest rate level**
- **key performance indicators**
- **returns in equity**
- **underwriting profits**
- **unexpected inflation**

REFERENCES

1. Pradyumna, M., & Pranav, S. S. R., (2019). A framework for assessing performance sensitivity of select KPIs for general insurance companies in India using risk management dashboard approach. *IJSER, 10*(3).
2. Shiu, Y., (2004). Determinants of United Kingdom general insurance company performance. *British Actuarial Journal,* 10. 10.1017/S1357321700002968.
3. https://www.ibef.org. (n.d.). Retrieved from: https://www.ibef.org/industry/insurance-sector-india.aspx (accessed on 22 February 2021).
4. www.irdai.gov.in. (n.d.). Retrieved from: https://www.irdai.gov.in/ADMINCMS/cms/NormalData_Layout.aspx?page=PageNo765&mid=31.2 (accessed on 22 February 2021).
5. Badi, H. B., (2013). *Econometric Analysis of Panel Data* (5th edn.). ISBN: 978-1-118-67232-7, John Wiley &. Sons, Ltd Copyright © 2005 John Wiley & Sons Ltd, The Atrium, Southern Gate, Chichester, West Sussex P019 8SQ, England.
6. Booth, P., Chadburn, R., Cooper, D., Haberman, S., & James, D., (2004). *Modern Actuarial Theory and Practice* (2nd edn.). ISBN-13: 978-1584883685, Chapman & Hall, U.K. McGraw-Hill, U.K.
7. Browne, M. J., & Robert, E. H., (1995). Economic and market predictors of insolvencies in the property-liability insurance industry. *The Journal of Risk and Insurance, 62*(2), 309–327. JSTOR, www.jstor.org/stable/253794 (accessed on 22 February 2021).
8. Canadian Institute of Actuaries, (1998). *Standard of Practice on Dynamic Capital Adequacy Testing (in effect 1 January, 1999).* This document is available at: https://www.google.com/url?sa=t&rct=j&q=&esrc=s&source=web&cd=&ved=2ahUKEwj46PHzjsTvAhVZT30KHXXpC2sQFjAAegQIBBAD&url=https%3A%2F%2Fwww.cia-ica.ca%2Fdocs%2Fdefault-source%2F2013%2F213077e.pdf&usg=AOvVaw3-El8x4pNop1pPqcFh1JJz (accessed on 22 February 2021).
9. Blum, P., & Michel, D., (2014). *DFA-Dynamic Financial Analysis*. Wiley Stats Ref: Statistics Reference Online.
10. Enz, R., & Karl, K., (2001). The profitability of the non-life insurance industry: It is back-to-basics time. *Swiss Re. Sigma, 5*, 1–37.

11. Greene, W. H., (2003). *Econometric Analysis.* ISBN-13: 9780130132970. Pearson Education India.
12. Gujarati, D. N., (1995). *Basic Econometrics* (3rd edn.). ISBN: 0-07-025214-9, New York: McGraw-Hill.
13. Neter, J., Wasserman, W., & Kutner, M. H., (1989). *Applied Linear Regression Models* (2nd edn.). Richard D. Irwin, Inc., Homewood.
14. Pesaran, H., Smith, R., & Im, K., (1996). Dynamic linear models for heterogeneous panels. In: Ma¨tya¨s, L., & Sevestre, P., (eds.), *The Econometrics of Panel Data* (second revised edition). Kluwer Academic Publishers, The Netherlands.
15. https://www.irdai.gov.in/ADMINCMS/cms/NormalData_Layout.aspx?page=PageNo129&mid=3.1.9 (accessed on 22 February 2021).
16. Gonzalez, R., (2018). *A Work in Progress* (pp. 23–25). The Actuary, The magazine of the Institute and Faculty of Actuaries.
17. https://www.irdai.gov.in/ADMINCMS/cms/NormalData_Layout.aspx?page=PageNo264&mid=3.2.10 (accessed on 22 February 2021).
18. Schmidhuber, J., (2015). Deep learning in neural networks: An overview. *Neural Networks, 61*, 85–117.
19. Glorot, X., & Yoshua, B., (2010). Understanding the difficulty of training deep feedforward neural networks. *Proceedings of the Thirteenth International Conference on Artificial Intelligence and Statistics.*
20. Ilya, S., Oriol, V., & Quoc, V. L., (2014). *Sequence to Sequence Learning with Neural Networks* (Submitted on 10 September 2014 (v1), last revised 14 December 2014 (this version, v3)).
21. Bergstra, J., et al., (2011). *Theano: Deep Learning on GPUs with Python* (Vol. 3). NIPS 2011, big learning workshop, Granada, Spain. Microtome Publishing.
22. Keckler, S. W., Dally, W., Khailany, B., Garland, M., & Glasco, D., (2011). GPUs and the future of parallel computing. *Micro IEEE, 31*, 7–17. 10.1109/MM.2011.89.
23. Warburton, K., (2003). Deep learning and education for sustainability. *International Journal of Sustainability in Higher Education, 4*(1), 44–56.
24. Seiya, T., Kenta, O., Shohei, H., & Justin, C., (2015). Chainer: A next-generation open-source framework for deep learning. In: *Workshop on Machine Learning Systems at Neural Information Processing Systems (NIPS)*.
25. Alec R., Luke, M. I., & Soumith, C. *Unsupervised Representation Learning with Deep Convolutional Generative Adversarial Networks*.
26. Ade Ibiwoye, Olawale O. E. Ajibola, & Ashim B. Sogunro (2012). Artificial neural network model for predicting insurance insolvency. *International Journal of Management and Business Research*, 59–68.
27. Akhter, M. R., Arun Agarwal, & Sastry, V. N. (2015). Recurrent neural network and a hybrid model for prediction of stock returns. *Expert Systems with Applications, 42*(6), 3234–3241.
28. Alev Dilek Aydin & Seyma Caliskan Cavdar (2015). *Prediction of Financial Crisis with Artificial Neural Network: An Empirical Analysis on Turkey*. DOI: https://doi.org/10.5430/ijfr.v6n4p36
29. Chakraborty, S., (2007). Prediction of corporate financial health by an artificial neural network. *International Journal of Electronic Finance*.
30. Constantin, D., (2016). *A New Model for Estimating the Risk of Bankruptcy of the Insurance Companies-Based on the Artificial Neural Networks*. Romania, International Multidisciplinary Scientific Geo Conference.

31. Gulsun, Isseveroglu & Gucenme Umit (2010). "Early warning model with statistical analysis procedures in Turkish insurance companies." *African Journal of Business Management 4*, 623–630.
32. Brockett, Patrick L., et al. (2006). "A Comparison of Neural Network, Statistical Methods, and Variable Choice for Life Insurers' Financial Distress Prediction." *The Journal of Risk and Insurance*, vol. *73*(3), 397–419. *JSTOR*, www.jstor.org/stable/3841001 (accessed 22 March 2021).
33. Salcedo-Sanz, S., (2005). Genetic programming for the prediction of insolvency in non-life insurance companies. In: *Computers and Operations Research*. s.l.:s.n., (pp. 749–765).
34. Peter, D. E., & Richard, J. V., (2002). Stochastic claims reserving in general insurance. *British Actuarial Journal, 8*(3), 443–518.
35. Segovia-Vargas, M. J., (2004). Prediction of insolvency in non-life insurance companies using support vector machines, genetic algorithms, and simulated annealing. *Fuzzy Economic Review*, 79–94.
36. Tadaaki, H., (2019). Bankruptcy prediction using imaged financial ratios and convolutional neural networks. *Expert Systems with Applications, 117*, 287–299.

PART IV

Intelligent Network System and Application

CHAPTER 16

A NEW APPROACH TO EVALUATE COMPUTER NETWORK SECURITY UNDER INTUITIONISTIC TRAPEZOIDAL FUZZY INFORMATION

SAPNA GAHLOT and RAM NARESH SARASWAT

Department of Mathematics and Statistics, Manipal University Jaipur, Jaipur, Rajasthan–303007, India,
E-mail: saraswatramn@gmail.com (R. N. Saraswat)

ABSTRACT

In this chapter, we proposed the MADM problems for evaluating the computer network security with TrIFN. We use the TrIFWA (intuitionistic trapezoidal fuzzy weighted average) operator to aggregate the TrIF, and using this, we will solve the network problem and its solution by proposed information divergence measure for network security.

16.1 INTRODUCTION

With science and innovation advancement, PC innovation improves continually and increasingly more programming and equipment of instruction industry have showed up [9]. Uses in instructing the calling, particularly the product and the equipment seem in a steady progression, have brought a great deal of accommodation for the school teaching management, and at the same time have additionally provided many advantageous conditions for educator's an understudy's day by day life. The use of these high-tech in the school helpful for the instructive circles too gave the instructive circles an inquiry regarding the wellbeing of the data the executives; the system security question has become another inquiry to instructive circles [13, 34]. Because of a one-card appearance, the school has applied this innovation in the first run-through. It gives accommodation for the two instructors and understudies. In the interim, the school likewise should think about the security of the card. The upgrade of system and the server security is the most significant thing for schools.

The rise of one-card likewise as the instruction division advancement has assumed a job and altogether improved the administration of schools in different fields. The presence of the card has tackled a great deal of niggling issues and makes the grounds utilizations progressively helpful. A card can be elusive in school, and it additionally encourages schools in riches the board. The improvement of the instruction area is influenced by the specialized ramifications and furthermore compelled by financial issues. They endeavor to fabricate a cutting-edge grounds and, in this manner, will not forsake trend-setting innovation to serve schools. Nonetheless, because of deficiency of assets, schools are frequently simply setting off to the application however did not think about the quality and future issues. In the delicate, as long as the low cost of whom, let somebody to do the development, this is not right. For present day grounds, improving the innovation is correct, however it is additionally expected to think about the topic of wellbeing and quality, particularly one-card; security is an especially significant issue which cannot be overlooked. The creator took an interest in a one-card instance of a college and is answerable for the development of an equipment and server delicate determination and buying additionally the support work later.

In the past few decades, there has been a spectacular development in the field of information technology. The use of internet is increasing day by day. It has opened a new horizon of communications in various forms. The surprising growth of network information is bound to continue in future as well. We also need to make this network information system more secure and robust. This will in return, help to identify the potential threats that the system will be exposed to network information risk assessment is one of the key factors of the network security field. In the field of network security. In order to ensure normal operations of network hidden troubles in networks identified and analyzed proper measures adopted to decrease the risk with science and technological development, computer technology has improved, and more and more software and hardware industries have come up in educating people and proving convenient methods to them. In modern era, improving the technology is right, but we need to consider the question of safety and quality. If any problem occurs, we will not be able to estimate the consequence. This computer network has played important role in various field of work politics, economy military and social life. Now-a-days, we see the cyber-attack on computers in the world-wise. This has also attracted attention towards the risks of these attacks. Proper measures are needed to decrease it.

Be that as it may, because of the issue of school reserves, this makes some excellent organizations ineffective and the midrange be chosen. The creator likewise went to a review of many organizations and made an examination about the activity of the grounds card, what is more, the collaborations of those colleges. All the establishments the creator picked are able; they just consider the quality, not the cost. To make the card progressively secure for our school, the creator got the school's mystery directions and completed false assaults so as to distinguish the one-card server foundation security issues.

In spite of the fact that we went through less cash, to require security starts things out. Just some schools taking initiatives the instant organizations feel about this movement. About that IP and screenshots are not allowed and not genuine; they are fundamentally the same. This errand is to be conceivable to control the entirety of the servers, so we can expect designers to do the update or troubleshooting, ensure the security of the school organize server, and make future work be solid and steady [2]. This school contains grounds arrange, one-card administration, postal reserve funds, and other money-related frameworks. These four frameworks are in one system, so security is the most significant thing. The data on the system is genuine cash; if any issue happens, the result will be not able to be assessed. With the quick improvement of Internet innovations as of late, PC systems have assumed an undeniably significant job in the fields of governmental issues, economy, military, and public activity. Despite the fact that organize advances realize interminable accommodation for individuals' life and work, the receptiveness, and interconnection of systems make organized assaults become progressively all inclusive, and system security issues have pulled in wide consideration. Hazard consistently exists in the genuine system condition. So as to guarantee typical activity of systems, shrouded inconveniences in systems must be distinguished and broke down, and legitimate estimates must be received to diminish the hazard as indicated by examination results. In this manner, how to precisely assess the security of a system turns into a significant issue, and it has been one of the examination centers in the field of system security [8].

Hao and Li proposed another arranging strategy which utilized the conceivable degree framework to take care of the arranging issue of intuitionistic trapezoidal fuzzy (ITF) numbers. Wang [20] assessed the momentum inquire about on the multicriteria phonetic dynamic strategies and fuzzy multicriteria decision-making strategies dependent on fuzzy number, intuitionistic fuzzy set, and ambiguous set and afterward proposed ITF numbers and interval ITF number. Saraswat and Umar [10]; Saraswat and Khatod [11], and Umar and Saraswat [14, 15] discussed new fuzzy divergence measure and their application in multi-criteria decision making and pattern recognition.

Wang and Zhang [22] proposed a multicriteria dynamic methodology for multicriteria dynamic issues in which weight data was not totally known and the rules esteem were intuitionistic trapezoidal fluffy numbers. Wan and Dong [19] considered the multi-attribute cooperative choice creation technique dependent on intuitionistic trapezoidal fluffy numbers. Right off the bat, the desires also, the normal score of ITF number were characterized dependent on the capacity of the gravity focal point of the picture. Besides the IT-OWA and ITHA operators were proposed. In the opinion of operators' theory, the multi-attribute joint choice, which is dependent on ITFN which was presented. Wang et al. [23] developed the ITF geometric total divergence measures. At that point the multicriteria decision-making strategy dependent on the total operators was proposed. Wu and Liu [26] proposed the interval-valued intuitionistic trapezoidal fuzzy weighted geometric (IVITFWG) operator. Wu and Cao [24]; and Wei et al. [24] established IITFWG operator, IITFOWG administrator, and IITFHG operator.

Firstly, Zadeh [32] developed the concept of FSs. Atanassov invented the AIFs based on the ideas of FSs. Gargov developed the concept of IVIFSs. One of the important concept of fuzzy sets is fuzzy number. IFN [24, 28] is a special case of IFS [33]. Shu et al. [12] introduced the concept of a TIFN. Li [5] developed the TIFN and present a method of ranking by using a ratio of index and ambiguity index. Dong and Wan [20] introduced a new method and applied to MAGDM by TIFNs. Wan and Li introduced a possibility mean and variance-based method for MADM by using TIFNs. Wang [28] developed the trapezoidal IFN (TrIFN) and interval-valued trapezoidal IFN (IVTrIFN) in similar way to TIFNs. Wang and Zhang [21] explore the WAGO (weighted arithmetic averaging operator) which is based on TrIFNs. It can be used directly in MADM problems. Wu and Liu [26] developed some IVTIF geometric aggregation operators and applied to MAGDM by using IVTrIFNs.

TIFN, TrIFN, and IVTrIFN extend IFS from the discrete set to the continuous set. Compared with the IFS, both TrIFN and IVTrIFN are discussed by TFN expressing their membership and non-membership functions. So, TrIFN and IVTrIFN may give better result of decision problems compare to IFS. Here, we present the MADM problem to computer network security with TrIFN information.

16.2 PRELIMINARIES

Here, we will present some important laws related to TrIFN.

- **Definition 16.1:** Let A TrIFN and its membership and non-membership function are given below [4, 5]:

$$\mu_A(x)=\begin{cases}\frac{x-\overline{a}}{\overline{b}-\overline{a}}\mu_A, \overline{a}\le x<\overline{b};\\ \mu_A, \overline{b}\le x\le\overline{c};\\ \frac{\overline{d}-x}{\overline{d}-\overline{c}}, \overline{c}<x\le\overline{d};\\ 0; others\end{cases} \quad (1)$$

$$\upsilon_A(x)=\begin{cases}\frac{\overline{b}-x+\upsilon_A(x-\overline{a})}{\overline{b}-\overline{a}}\upsilon_A, \overline{a}\le x<\overline{b};\\ \upsilon_A, \overline{b}\le x\le\overline{c};\\ \frac{x-\overline{c}+\upsilon_A(\overline{d}-x)}{\overline{d}-\overline{c}}\upsilon_A, \overline{c}<x\le\overline{d};\\ 0; others\end{cases} \quad (2)$$

where; $0\le\mu_A\le 1; 0\le\upsilon_A\le 1$ and $0\le\mu_A+\upsilon_A\le 1; \overline{a},\overline{b},\overline{c},\overline{d}\in R$

- **Definition 16.2:** Let $\overline{\overline{a}}_j=\left\langle(\overline{a}_j,\overline{b}_j,\overline{a}_j,\overline{a}_j)\mu_{\overline{\overline{a}}_j},\upsilon_{\overline{\overline{a}}_j}\right\rangle$ (j = 1, 2,…, n) be a set of TrIFN, and let TrIFWA $k^n\to k$ TrIFWA $A_w(\overline{\overline{a}}_1,\overline{\overline{a}}_2,...,\overline{\overline{a}}_n)=$ $\left\langle\left[\sum_{j=1}^{n}w_j\overline{a}_j,\sum_{i=1}^{n}w_j\overline{b}_j,\sum_{i=1}^{n}w_j\overline{c}_j,\sum_{i=1}^{n}w_j\overline{d}_j\right];1-\prod_{j=1}^{n}(1-\mu_{\overline{\overline{a}}_j})^{w_j},\prod_{j=1}^{n}(\nu_{\overline{\overline{a}}_j})^{w_j},\right\rangle$

  where; $w=(w_1,w_1,...,w_1)^T$ is weight vector space to $\overline{\overline{a}}_j(j=1,2,...,n)$ and $w_j\ge 0,\sum_{j=1}^{n}w_j=1$;

- **Definition 16.3:** For a normalized TrIF decision-making matrix $\overline{\overline{k}}=(k_{ij})_{m.n}=((\overline{a}_{ij},\overline{b}_{ij},\overline{a}_{ij},\overline{a}_{ij})\mu_{ij},\upsilon_{ij})_{m.n}$ Where, $0\le\overline{a}_{ij}\le\overline{b}_{ij}\le\overline{c}_{ij}\le\overline{d}_{ij}\le 1,0$ $\le\mu_{ij},\upsilon_{ij}\le 1,0\le\mu_{ij}+\upsilon_{ij}\le 1$ the TrIFPIS are given below:

$$r^{+} = \left\langle (\overline{a}^{+}, \overline{a}^{+}, \overline{a}^{+}, \overline{a}^{+}); \mu^{+}, \nu^{+} \right\rangle = \langle (1,1,1,1,)1,0 \rangle$$

- **Definition 16.4:** Let $\overline{\overline{a_1}} = \left\langle (\overline{a_1}, \overline{b_1}, \overline{c_1}, \overline{d_1}) \mu_{\overline{\overline{a_1}}}, \upsilon_{\overline{\overline{a_1}}} \right\rangle$ and $\overline{\overline{a_2}} = \left\langle (\overline{a_2}, \overline{b_2}, \overline{c_2}, \overline{d_2}) \mu_{\overline{\overline{a_2}}}, \upsilon_{\overline{\overline{a_2}}} \right\rangle$ be two TrIFN; then the normalized Euclidean distance between $\overline{\overline{a_1}}$ and $\overline{\overline{a_2}}$ are given below:

$$d(\overline{\overline{a_1}}, \overline{\overline{a_2}}) =$$

$$\frac{1}{8}\left[\begin{array}{l} \left((1+\mu_{\overline{\overline{a_1}}}+\upsilon_{\overline{\overline{a_1}}})\overline{a_1}-(1+\mu_{\overline{\overline{a_2}}}+\upsilon_{\overline{\overline{a_2}}})\overline{a_2}\right)^2+\left((1+\mu_{\overline{\overline{a_1}}}+\upsilon_{\overline{\overline{a_1}}})\overline{b_1}-(1+\mu_{\overline{\overline{a_2}}}+\upsilon_{\overline{\overline{a_2}}})\overline{b_2}\right)^2+ \\ \left((1+\mu_{\overline{\overline{a_1}}}+\upsilon_{\overline{\overline{a_1}}})\overline{c_1}-(1+\mu_{\overline{\overline{a_2}}}+\upsilon_{\overline{\overline{a_2}}})\overline{c_2}\right)^2+\left((1+\mu_{\overline{\overline{a_1}}}+\upsilon_{\overline{\overline{a_1}}})\overline{d_1}-(1+\mu_{\overline{\overline{a_2}}}+\upsilon_{\overline{\overline{a_2}}})\overline{d_2}\right)^2 \end{array}\right] \quad (3)$$

16.3 APPLICATION

Here, we apply the information measure presented above to the network problem with intuitionistic fuzzy information. Network security covers a variety of network, both private and public human life day-by-day like jobs, telecommunications between businesses and government. Agencies and individuals network security involves protecting and overseeing orations to be done. Taking so many networks factors into consideration, this network security assessment technology will be a great help to administrations in identifying all possible threats to their systems.

Now, we define the computer network security with uncertain linguistic information. There are +ve possible computer network systems k_i $i = 1, 2, 3, 4, 5$ for four attributes D_j $(j = 1, 2, 3, 4)$. The four attributes include the tactics (D1), technology, and economy (D2), logistics (D3), and strategy (D4), respectively. The positive possibility of network systems, $i = 1, 2, 3, 4, 5$ are to be described by TrIF information by the decision taker using four properties $w = (0.3, 0.2, 0.1, 0.4)^T$ weighting vector are given below:

- **Step 1:** By using the weight vector $w = (0.3, 0.2, 0.1, 0.4)^T$, and by Eqn. (3), the values k_i of network systems are k_i (i = 1, 2, 3, 4, 5):

  k_1 = ([0.37, 0.46, 0.65, 0.71]; 0.2435, 0.6127)
  k_2 = ([0.46, 0.52, 0.66, 0.84]; 0.4780, 0.4011)
  k_3 = ([0.30, 0.43, 0.61, 0.72]; 0.4203, 0.4521)
  k_4 = ([0.22, 0.43, 0.51, 0.67]; 0.3055, 0.4322)
  k_5 = ([0.23, 0.35, 0.42, 0.51]; 0.4954, 0.3247)

➤ **Step 2:** Measure the distances between overall values $k_i = \langle (\overline{a}_i, \overline{b}_i, \overline{c}_i, \overline{d}_i)\mu_i, \upsilon_i \rangle$ and $r^+ = \langle (\overline{a}^+, \overline{a}^+, \overline{a}^+, \overline{a}^+); \mu^+, \nu^+ \rangle$:

$d(k_1, k^+) = 1.37267$
$d(k_2, k^+) = .89995$
$d(k_3, k^+) = 1.13930$
$d(k_4, k^+) = 1.29078$
$d(k_5, k^+) = 1.22095$

➤ **Step 3:** Rank all the alternatives k_i (i = 1, 2, 3, 4, 5) as per with the distances $d(k_1, k^+)$ between overall values $k_i = \langle (\overline{a}_i, \overline{b}_i, \overline{c}_i, \overline{d}_i)\mu_i, \upsilon_i \rangle$ and TrIFPIS.

$$k_2 > k_3 > k_5 > k_4 > k_1$$

Hence, Greatest system is k_2.

16.4 CONCLUSION

Taking so many network factors into consideration, this network security assessment technology will give great help to administrations in identifying all possible threats to their systems which may be useful in the area of network system. In this chapter, We have used the (TrIFWA) operator to aggregate the TrIF corresponding to each substitute and get the overall value of the substitutes using that, to select the most necessary one(s) according to given ideas. Finally, we used the proposed information measure to network security.

KEYWORDS

- **intuitionistic fuzzy set**
- **intuitionistic trapezoidal fuzzy number**
- **intuitionistic trapezoidal fuzzy weighted average**
- **network security**
- **trapezoidal IFN**
- **weighted arithmetic averaging operator**

REFERENCES

1. Atanassov, K. T., (1986). Intuitionistic fuzzy sets. *Fuzzy Sets Syst., 20*(1), 87–96.
2. Dong, J., (2012). An approach to evaluating the computer network security with hesitant fuzzy information. *International Journal of Digital Content Technology and its Applications, 6*(20), 633–639.
3. Dubois, D., & Prade, H., (1978). Operations on fuzzy numbers. *International Journal of Systems Science, 9,* 626–631.
4. Gong, Z. W., Li, L. S., Zhou, F. X., & Yao, T. X., (2009). Goal programming approaches to obtain the priority vectors from the intuitionistic fuzzy preference relations. *Computers and Industrial Engineering, 57*, 1187–1193.
5. Li, D. F., (2010). A ratio ranking method of triangular intuitionistic fuzzy numbers and its application to MADM problems. *Computers and Mathematics with Applications, 60*, 1557–1570.
6. Li, D. F., (2008). A note on using intuitionistic fuzzy sets for fault-tree analysis on printed circuit board assembly. *Microelectronics Reliability, 48*(10), 1741.
7. Liu, P. D., & Jin, F., (2012). A multi-attribute group decision-making method based on weighted geometric aggregation operators of interval-valued trapezoidal fuzzy numbers. *Applied Mathematical Modeling, 36*, 2498–2509.
8. Li, Y., Shan, X., & Wu, G., (2011). Comprehensive evaluation model for computer network security with linguistic information. *Advances in Information Sciences and Service Sciences, 3*(9), 126–131.
9. Mo, X., (2013). Research on the computer network security evaluation based on the ULCGM operator with uncertain linguistic information. *Journal of Convergence Information Technology, 8*(3), 160–166.
10. Saraswat, R. N., & Adeeba, U., (2020). New fuzzy divergence measure and its applications in multi criteria decision making using new tool. *Springer Proceedings in Mathematics and Statistics, 307*, 191–206. doi.org/10.1007/978-981-15-1157-8-17.
11. Saraswat, R. N., & Khatod, N., (2020). New fuzzy divergence measures, series, its bounds and applications in strategic decision-making. *Lecture Notes in Electrical Engineering (Springer), 607*, 641–653. doi.org/10.1007/978–981-15-0214-9-67.
12. Shu, M. H., Cheng, C. H., & Chang, J. R., (2006). Using intuitionistic fuzzy sets for fault tree analysis on printed circuit board assembly. *Microelectronics Reliability, 46*(12), 2139–2148.
13. Song, G., (2013). Computer network security and precaution evaluation based on incremental relevance vector machine algorithm and ACO. *International Journal on Advances in Information Sciences and Service Sciences, 5*(1), 120–127.
14. Umar, A., & Saraswat, R. N., (2020). New generalized intuitionistic fuzzy divergence measure with applications to multi-attribute decision making and pattern recognition. *Recent Patents on Computer Science, 13*(1).
15. Umar, A., & Saraswat, R. N., (2020). Novel divergence measure under neutrosophic environment and its utility in various problems of decision making. *International Journal of Fuzzy System Applications, 9*(4).
16. Wan, S. P., (2011). Multi-attribute decision making method based on interval intuitionistic trapezoidal fuzzy number. *Control and Decision, 26*(6), 857–861.
17. Wan, S. P., (2012). Method based on fractional programming for interval-valued intuitionistic trapezoidal fuzzy number multi-attribute decision making. *Control and Decision, 27*(3), 455–458.

18. Wan, S. P., (2013). Power average operators of trapezoidal intuitionistic fuzzy numbers and application to multi-attribute group decision making. *Applied Mathematical Modeling, 37*(6), 4112–4126.
19. Wan, S. P., & Dong, J. Y., (2010). Method of the intuitionistic trapezoidal fuzzy number for multi-attribute group decision. *Control and Decision, 25*(5), 773–776.
20. Wang, J. Q., (2008). Overview on fuzzy multi-criteria decision-making approach. *Control and Decision, 23*(6), 601–607.
21. Wang, J. Q., & Zhang, Z., (2009). Aggregation operators on intuitionistic trapezoidal fuzzy number and its application to multi-criteria decision-making problems. *Journal of Systems Engineering and Electronics, 20*(2), 321–326.
22. Wang, J. Q., & Zhang, Z., (2009). Multi-criteria decision-making method with incomplete certain information based on intuitionistic fuzzy numbers. *Control and Decision, 24*(2), 226–230.
23. Wang, Y., Zhang, S. F., & Xie, S. Q., (2012). Intuitionistic trapezoidal fuzzy geometric aggregation operators and their application to group decision making. *Value Engineering, 27*, 159–161.
24. Wei, G. W., Zhao, X. F., & Wang, H. J., (2012). An approach to multiple attribute group decision making with interval intuitionistic trapezoidal fuzzy information. *Technological and Economic Development of Economy, 18*(2), 311–324.
25. Wei, G. W., (2010). Some arithmetic aggregation operators with intuitionistic trapezoidal fuzzy numbers and their application to group decision making. *Journal of Computer, 5*(3), 345–351.
26. Wu, J., & Liu, Y. J., (2013). An approach for multiple attribute group decision making problems with interval-valued intuitionistic trapezoidal fuzzy numbers. *Computers and Industrial Engineering, 66*, 311–324.
27. Wu, J., & Cao, Q., (2013). Same families of geometric aggregation operators with intuitionistic trapezoidal fuzzy numbers. *Applied Mathematical Modeling, 37*(1/2), 318–327.
28. Xu, J., Wan, S. P., & Dong, J. Y., (2016). Aggregating decision information into Atanassov's intuitionistic fuzzy numbers for heterogeneous multi-attribute group decision making. *Applied Soft Computing, 41*, 331–351.
29. Xu, Z. S., & Chen, J., (2007). An approach to group decision making based on interval-valued intuitionistic judgment matrices. *System Engineer Theory and Practice, 27*, 126–133.
30. Xu, Y. J., Wang, H. M., & Merigfo, J. M., (2014). Intuitionistic Einstein fuzzy Choquet integral operators for multiple attribute decision making. *Technological and Economic Development of Economy, 20*(2), 227–253.
31. Yu, D. J., Merigfo, J. M., & Zhou, L. G., (2013). Inter valued multiplicative intuitionistic fuzzy preference relations. *International Journal of Fuzzy Systems, 15*(4), 412–422.
32. Zadeh, L. A., (1965). Fuzzy sets, *Inf. Control, 8*(3), 338–356.
33. Zeng, S. Z., Wang, Q. F., Merigfo, J. M., & Pan, T. J., (2014). Induced intuitionistic fuzzy ordered weighted averaging-weighted average operator and its application to business decision-making. *Computer Science and Information Systems, 11*(2), 839–857.
34. Zhang, G., Li, H., Chen, R., et al., (2013). Research and design on vulnerability testing in computer network security system. *Advances in Information Sciences and Service Sciences*, *5*(7), 1–10.

CHAPTER 17

OPTIMIZATION OF CAMPUS-WIDE FIBER NETWORKS: LINGO-BASED DERIVATIVE OF SHORTEST PATH PROBLEMS AND SOLUTION

MOHD. RIZWANULLAH

Associate Professor, Department of Mathematics and Statistics, Manipal University Jaipur, Jaipur, Rajasthan, India, E-mail: rizwansal@yahoo.co.in

ABSTRACT

This chapter presents optimization of a network problem. Using LINGO software, we have to solve a campus-wide optical fiber network problem based on a spanning tree. The generated spanning tree for the network gives the shortest path to led down the optical fiber cable in the campus. This work is based on real data. Data is presented in distance square matrix. Optimization in networks plays a wider role in daily life problems like rail/road networks, different communication systems. Most suitable algorithms have been used to solve this problem.

17.1 INTRODUCTION

Combinatorial theory or analysis is concerned with problems of enumeration and structure of mathematical objects. It is a common practice to refer to the subject matter of combinatorial theory as combinatorics. No other mathematical programming subcategory is more tantalizing than network optimization. Highway, train, electric, communications, and other physical networks can pervade our everyday lives. Consequently, only non-specialists accept the functional significance and wide-ranging network applicability.

In fact, since the functional features of the networks are (e.g., flows on arcs and mass balance at nodes) have natural mathematical representations, practitioners and non-specialists can readily understand the mathematical descriptions of network optimization problems and the basic nature of techniques used to solve these problems.

A spanning tree (N, A) is a collection of arcs, defining a tree and a partial graph. Thus, a spanning tree is a tree that contains a path between each pair of nodes in the graph and is, in a sense, 'minimal' in that it needs every arc. Removal of any one arc forms a spanning tree means that the graph is no longer 'spanned' in the sense that all pairs have a path. Adding an arc to a spanning tree results in a graph that is not a tree, and that has loops that provide alternate paths between certain node pairs. One spanning tree of especial interest is the minimal spanning tree; this is the spanning tree whose length is least, for a given network. The typical application occurs in the creations of a network of paved roads, power/telephone supply cables or gas pipeline, etc.

17.1.1 NETWORK OPTIMIZATION

The network problems in which we analyze certain values for the dimensions of the links and/or flows on the links that maximize the objective function (maximization or minimization), i.e., the methodology that relates to the network problems in order to optimize the objective function in the situations in question.

For the solution of different situation/problems such as minimum cost, length, max. flow, profit, etc., in networks and other like, the following family of network optimization techniques can be used:

1. Minimal spanning tree;
2. Shortest route/path algorithm;
3. Maximum flow algorithm;
4. Minimum cost network flow algorithm;
5. Critical path algorithm (CPM);
6. Assignment, transportation, etc.

17.1.2 CONSTRUCTION OF MINIMAL SPANNING TREE

Construction of a *minimal spanning tree* is a straight-forward. It is evident that the arcs in such a tree will be taken from the shortest arcs in the network, in order that a minimal total to be achieved.

There are two algorithms to construct a minimal spanning tree:

i. Kruskal's algorithm; and
ii. Prim's algorithm.

17.1.3 SHORTEST PATH PROBLEMS (SPP)

The most fundamental and most frequently cited problems in the study of transport and communication networks are shortest path problems (SPP). In trying to decide the fastest, easiest, or most secure route between one or more node pairs in a network, the shortest path issue emerges. More specifically, algorithms for a broad variety of combinatorial optimization concerns such as vehicle routing and network architecture also ask for the solution of a vast number of SPP such as subroutines. The creation and development of effective algorithms for the shortest path problem has also become a significant field of study in network optimization. Researchers have studied many different types of shortest paths: (i) finding shortest paths from one node to all other nodes where arc lengths are non-negative; (ii) finding shortest paths from one node to all other nodes for specific arc length networks; (iii) finding shortest paths from one node to each other node; and (iv) finding various types of constrained shortest paths between nodes (e.g., shortest paths with turn penalties, shortest paths visiting specified nodes, the k-th shortest path).

17.1.4 THE MATHEMATICAL FORMULATION OF SPP

Suppose we are given a network G with m nodes and n arcs and a cost C_{ij} associated with each arc (i, j) in G. The network is such that we wish to send a single unit of flow from node 1 to node m at minimal cost. Thus, $b_1 = 1$, $b_m = -1$, and $b_i = 0$ for $i \neq 1$ or m. Then, the mathematical formulation is as:

$$\text{Minimize} \sum_{i=1}^{m} \sum_{j=1}^{m} C_{ij} X_{ij}$$

$$\text{Subjectto} \sum_{j=1}^{m} X_{ij} - \sum_{k=1}^{m} X_{ki} = \begin{cases} 1 \ if \ i = 1 \\ 0 \ if \ i \neq 1 \ or \ m \\ -1 \ if \ i = m \end{cases}$$

$$X_{ij} = 0 \ or \ 1, \qquad i, j = 1, 2, \dots\dots\dots\dots m.$$

where; the sums and the 0–1 requirements are taken over existing arcs in g. The constraints x_{ij}=0 or 1 indicate that each arc is either in the path or not.

If we replace $x_{ij} = 0$ or 1 by $x_{ij} \geq 0$, and if an optimal solution exists, then the simplex method would obtain an optimal integer solution.

There are several methods which have been produced for dealing with this SPP:

i. Dijkstra's algorithm;
ii. Ford's algorithm;
iii. Floyd's algorithm;
iv. Pollack's algorithm.

17.2 PROBLEM UNDER STUDY

As Aligarh Muslim University (AMU) campus (Figure 17.2) is built over 476.6 hectares of land. It comprises 88 divisions that are put together to create faculties. There is a Central Computing facility known as the "Computer Center" with the intention of connecting to each and every department for dial-up facilities through VSAT for Internet access, but in the first step, it is planned to link the first 23 departments. The dial-up service is combined with hunting system via 16 telephone lines. An Optical Fiber network (Problem I) is set up to provide links to the server (for computing) and to connect directly to the internet service (Figures 17.1 and 17.2).

University has also very good road network which touches each departments/faculties. Among these departments, 12 are connected with Computer Center. On the basis of this network, a problem of maintenance arises, so a Maintenance Engineer will be available at Computer Center. A shortest path problem is formulated for this network through which a maintenance engineer can visit at every node so that he/she can save his/her time. Lingo software helped to approach this result obtaining the optimum route (Problem II).

A LINGO base model (computer program) for spanning tree is used to solve it as an integer program, which gives the optimal route to lay down the optical fiber network. But similar problem is solved by a traveling salesperson problem (or postman problem) to minimize the total distance (shortest path) so that a postman can travel each and every department to delivered letters/notices.

The aim of this chapter is to compare the LINGO-based optimization technique to find the minimal spanning tree and extend to find the optimal postman tour. We concentrate on to find the optimal route of network problem and highlight a number of recent theoretical and algorithmic advances.

The distance among the various departments are given in Tables 17.1 and 17.2.

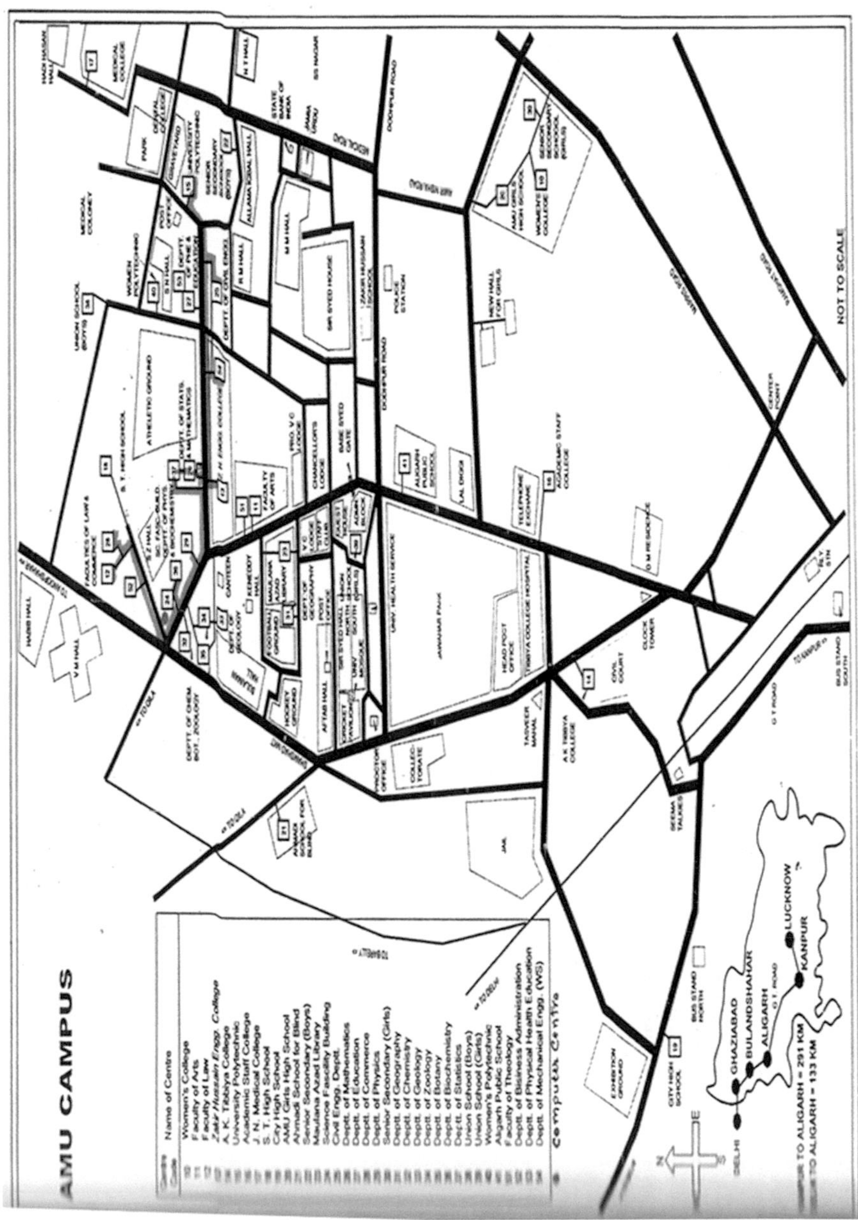

FIGURE 17.1 Spanning Tree-I.

(i) AMU NETWORKS

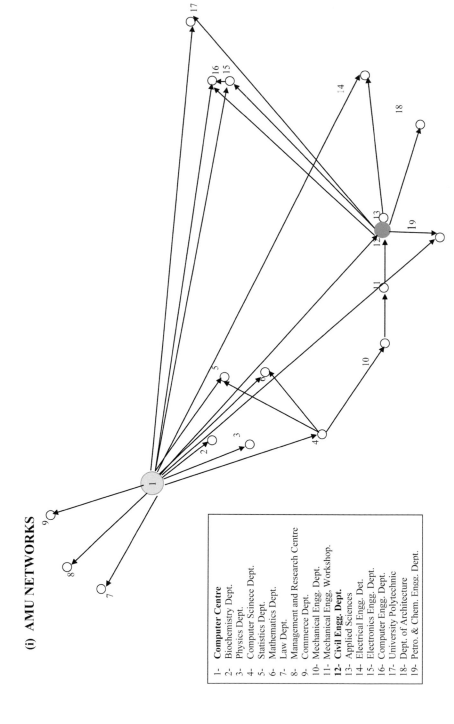

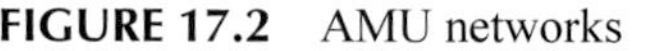

FIGURE 17.2 AMU networks

TABLE 17.1 Distance **Matrix-I**

CITY =	CC	BIOCH	PHY	CS	STATS	MATHS	LAW	MBA	COMM	MED	MEDW	
DIST =	0	46	207	206	442	391	435	390	490	412	528	FROM CC
	46	0	50	251	571	521	481	435	536	541	671	FROM BIOCH
	208	50	0	50	370	319	642	597	997	350	456	FROM PHY
	206	251	50	0	320	269	641	596	696	290	406	FROM CS
	442	571	370	320	0	30	877	832	932	610	726	FROM STATS
	391	521	319	269	30	0	826	781	881	559	675	FROM MATHS
	435	481	642	641	961	826	0	110	30	847	963	FROM LAW
	390	436	597	596	916	781	110	0	80	802	918	FROM MBA
	490	536	697	696	932	881	30	80	0	902	1018	FROM COMM
	412	541	340	290	610	559	847	802	902	0	130	FROM MED
	528	671	456	406	726	675	963	918	1018	130	0	FROM MEDW

TABLE 17.2 Distance Matrix-II

CITY =	CED	AS	ELCAL	ELNIC	COMP	UPOLY	BARCH	CHE_PAT	
DIST =	0	0	76.2	131.1	137.2	297.2	137.2	164.6	FROM CED
	0	0	76.2	131.1	137.2	297.2	137.2	164.6	FROM AS
	76.2	76.2	0	50	56.1	216.1	213.4	240.8	FROM ELCAL
	131.1	131.1	50	0	6.1	166.1	268.3	295.7	FROM ELNIC
	137.2	137.2	56.1	6.1	0	160	274.4	301.8	FROM COMP
	297.2	297.2	216.1	166.1	160	0	434.4	461.8	FROM UPOLY
	137.2	137.2	213.4	268.3	274.4	434.4	0	60	FROM BARCH
	164.6	164.6	240.8	295.7	301.8	461.8	60	0.0;	FROM CHE_PAT

17.2.1 DISCUSSION FOR THE SOLUTION OF THE PROBLEM

17.2.1.1 PROBLEM I

The problem under study is to find a minimal spanning tree for the optical fiber network of campus-wide networking phase-I. Given a set of nodes (Department) to be connected, we want to find a minimum cost network, so every node is connected to the network.

In fact, formulation of the minimum spanning tree problem as Linear Programming problem is a bit tedious, so, the LINGO Model of Spanning Tree is used to solve it as an integer program. The Corresponding values of X in the solution of the spanning tree are given in Appendix A. The value of X = 1 in the solution allows the tree to form a spanning tree.

The first part of the spanning tree of a network is (Figure 17.3):

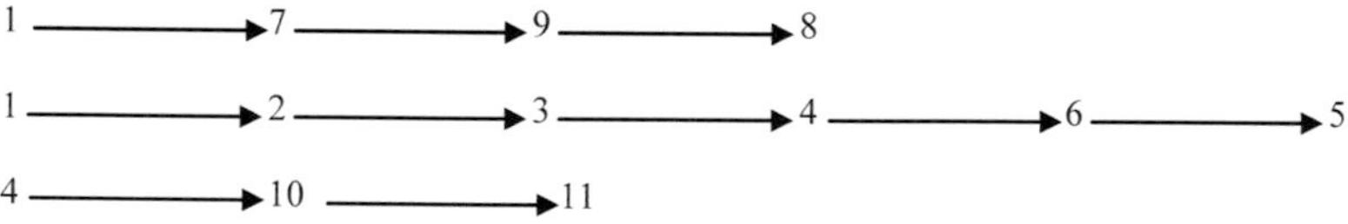

The second part of the spanning tree of a network is given in Figure 17.4.

12 → 13 → 14 → 15 → 16 → 17
13 → 18 → 19

The data set is given in Table 17.3.

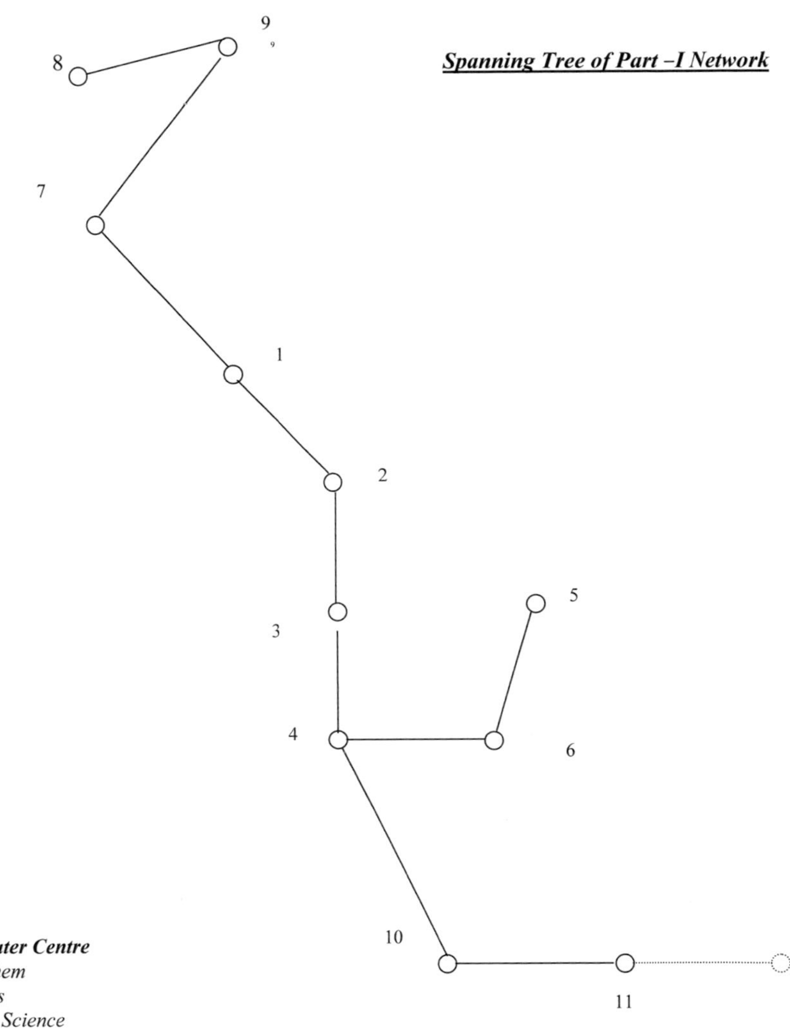

FIGURE 17.3 Spanning tree of part-I network.

Total distance:

390.0+110+30+45.7+
50+50 +269.1+ ....
Tabulated Value = 1364.00
Calculated Value = 1364.00
Cost of 1 meter cable = Rs. 80/-
Total Cost of 1364 meter cable = Rs. 1,09,120/-

Spanning Tree of Part -II

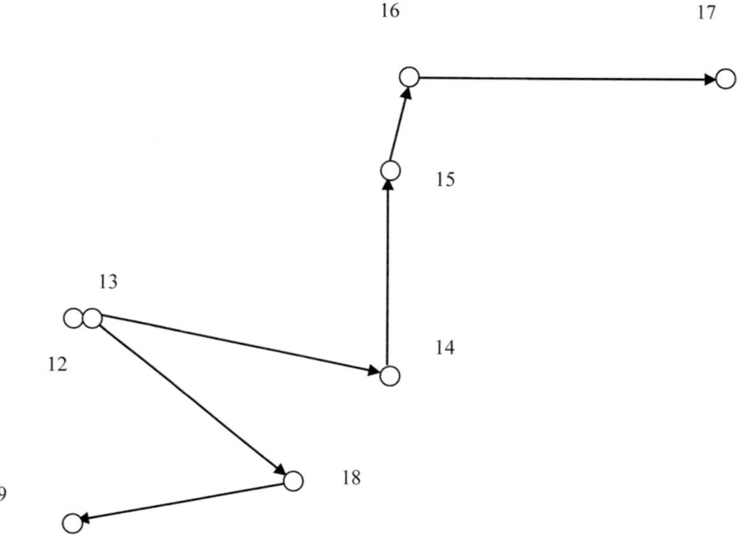

12 – Civil Engg. Deptt.
13 – Applied Science
14 –Electrical Engg. Deptt.
15 –Electronic Engg. Deptt.
16 – Computer Engg. Deptt.
17 –Univ. Polytechnic
18 – Deptt. of Architecture
19 – Deptt. of Chemical/Petroleum Engg.

Total distance
Calculated value = 489.500
Tabulated value = 489.500
Cost of Cable per meter = Rs. 80/-
Total Cost = Rs. 39,160/-

Grand Total:- Cost of Network of Part-I + Cost Network of Part – II

= Rs. 1,09200 + Rs. 39,160

= Rs. 1,48,360/-

FIGURE 17.4 Spanning tree of part-II Network.

TABLE 17.3 Spanning Tree-II.
Distance Matrix (In meters)

		1	2	3	4	5	6	7	8	9	10	11	12	13	14	15	16	17	18	19
	D TO D	**CC**	**BIOCH**	**PHY**	**CS**	**STATS**	**MATHS**	**LAW**	**MBA**	**COMM**	**MED**	**MEOW**	**CED**	**AS**	**ELCAL**	**ELNIC**	**COMP**	**UPOLY**	**BARCH**	**CHE/PAT**
1	**CC**	0.0	45.7	207.3	205.7	442.0	391.1	435.0	390.0	490.0	411.5	527.9	640.1	640.1	716.3	771.2	771.2	876.3	883.9	713.2
2	**BIOCH**	45.7	0.0	50.0	251.4	571.4	520.5	480.7	435.2	535.7	541.0	670.6	792.5	792.5	868.7	923.6	929.7	1089.7	929.7	957.1
3	**PHY**	207.7	50.0	0.0	50.0	370.0	319.1	642.3	597.3	997.3	349.6	456.0	597.9	577.9	654.1	709.0	715.1	875.1	715.1	742.5
4	**CS**	205.7	251.4	50.0	0.0	320.0	269.1	640.7	595.7	695.7	289.6	406.0	518.2	518.2	594.2	649.3	655.4	815.4	655.4	682.8
5	**STATS**	442.0	571.4	370.0	320.0	0.0	30.0	877.0	832.0	932.0	609.6	726.0	847.9	847.9	924.1	979.0	985.1	1145.1	985.1	10·12.5
6	**MATHS**	391.1	520.5	319.1	269.1	30.0	0.0	826.1	781.1	881.1	558.7	675.1	797.0	797.0	873.2	928.1	934.2	1094.2	934.2	961.6
7	**LAW**	435.0	480.7	642.3	640.7	960.7	826.1	0.0	110.0	30.0	846.5	962.9	1075.1	1075.1	1151.3	1206.2	1206.2	1311.3	1318.9	1148.2
8	**MBA**	390.0	435.7	597.3	595.7	915.7	781.1	110.0	0.0	80.0	801.5	917.9	1030.1	1030.1	1106.3	1161.2	1161.2	1266.3	1273.9	1103.2
9	**COMM**	490.0	535.7	697.3	695.7	932.0	881.1	30.0	80.0	0.0	901.5	1017.9	1130.1	1130.1	1206.3	1261.2	1261.2	1366.3	1373.9	1203.2
10	**MED**	411.5	541.0	339.6	289.6	609.6	558.7	846.5	801.5	901.5	0.0	129.6	251.5	251.5	327.7	382.6	388.7	548.7	388.7	416.1
11	**MEOW**	527.9	670.6	456.0	406.0	726.0	675.1	962.9	917.5	1017.9	129.6	0.0	121.9	121.9	198.1	253.0	259.1	419.1	259.1	286.5
12	**CED**	640.1	792.5	577.9	518.2	847.9	797.0	1075.1	1030.1	1130.1	251.5	121.9	0.0	0.0	76.2	131.1	137.2	297.2	137.2	164.6
13	**AS**	640.1	792.5	577.9	518.2	847.9	797.0	1075.1	1030.1	1130.1	251.5	121.9	0.0	0.0	76.2	131.1	137.2	297.2	137.2	164.6
14	**ELCAL**	716.3	868.7	654.1	594.4	924.1	873.2	1151.3	1106.3	1206.3	327.2	198.1	76.2	76.2	0.0	50.0	56.1	216.1	213.4	240.8
15	**ELNIC**	771.2	923.6	709.0	649.3	979.0	928.1	1206.2	1161.2	1261.2	382.6	253.0	131.1	131.1	50.0	0.0	6.1	165.1	268.3	295.7
16	**COMP**	771.2	929.7	715.1	655.4	985.1	934.2	1206.2	1161.2	1261.2	388.7	259.1	137.2	137.2	56.1	6.1	0.0	160.0	274.4	301.8
17	**UPOLY**	876.3	1089.7	875.1	815.4	1145.1	1094.2	1311.3	1266.3	1366.3	548.7	419.1	297.2	297.2	216.1	166.1	160.0	0.0	434.4	461.8
18	**BARCH**	883.9	929.7	715.1	655.4	985.1	934.2	1318.9	1273.3	1373.9	388.7	259.1	137.2	137.2	213.4	268.3	274.4	434.4	0.0	60.0
19	**CHE/PAT**	713.2	957.1	742.5	682.8	1012.5	961.6	1148.2	1103.2	1203.2	416.1	286.5	164.6	164.6	240.8	295.7	301.8	451.8	60.0	0.0

17.2.1.2 PROBLEM II

The problem under review is to have a tour visiting each node, which reduces the total distance traveled. A traveling salesperson problem (TSP) addresses this problem, we have a network of road-connected units. This is because it seems that the approach to large models requires subtours. One may apply constraints to split the subtour, but as the number of nodes increases, the amount of constraints needed dramatically increases.

The above problem has been solved in two parts; Part-I contained node 1 to 11 while Part-II contained node 12 to 19. The Corresponding values of X in the solution of the Traveling salesperson problem are given in Appendix B. The value of X =1 in the solution allows the shortest path.

Optimum distance of Part I = 2647 meters.

Part II = 951.3 meters.

Total optimum distance = 2647 + 951.3 = 3598.3 meters = 3.598 km.

Shortest route from computer center (Network Part-I) is:

1 → 10 → 11 → 5 → 6 → 4 → 3 → 2 → 8 → 9 → 7 → 1

Shortest route from computer center (Network Part-II) is:

12 → 18 → 19 → 13 14→ 15 → 16 → 17 → 12 →

17.2.2 CONCLUSION

Both the method can be used to find the optimum route for the network which has wide application in practical life. LINGO is one of the strong software that can be used to solve such problems at large scale (Figures 17.5 and 17.6).

LINGO software-based network flow optimization allows it easy to find the best route in linear form on a spanning tree. This essentially tends to reduce the time or expense and distance will aid with other real-life problems. With this Lingo-based Optimization approach, the broad network problem can be solved in a fraction of time.

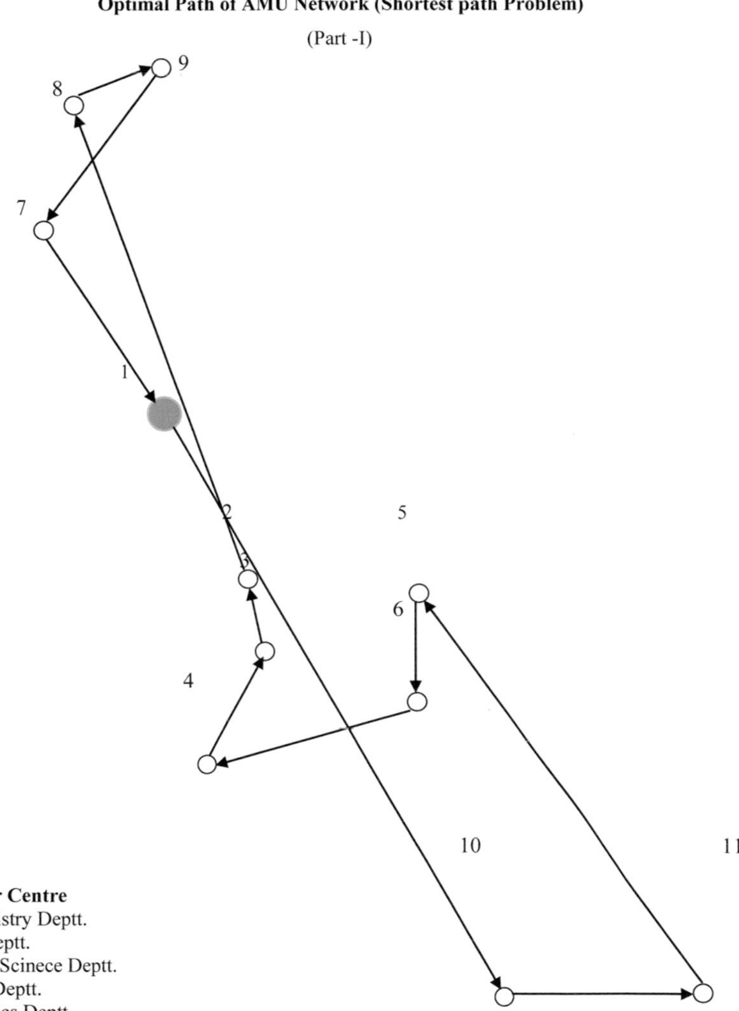

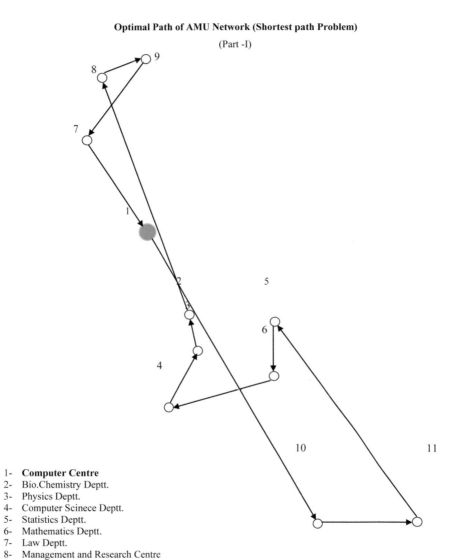

1- **Computer Centre**
2- Bio.Chemistry Deptt.
3- Physics Deptt.
4- Computer Scinece Deptt.
5- Statistics Deptt.
6- Mathematics Deptt.
7- Law Deptt.
8- Management and Research Centre
9- Commerce Deptt.
10- Mechanical Engg. Deptt.
11- Mechanical Engg, Workshop.

FIGURE 17.5 Optimal path of AMU network (shortest path network) (Part I)

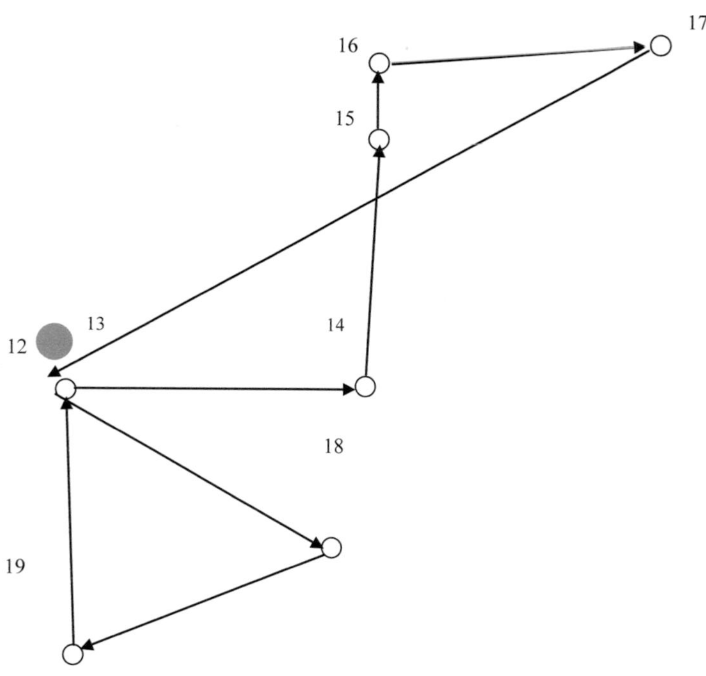

12- Civil Engg. Dept.
13- Applied Sciences
14- Electrical Engg. Dept.
15- Electronic Engg. Dept.
16- Computer Engg. Dept.
17- University Polytechnic
18- Dept. of Architecture

FIGURE 17.6 Optimal path of AMU network (shortest path network) (Part II)

17.2.3 LINGO-BASED COMPUTER PROGRAMS

1. By Spanning Tree Algorithm:

Article II. PART-1

```
SETS:
    CITY: LVL;
    !LVL(I)=LEVEL OF CITY I IN TREE, LVL(1)=0;
    LINK(CITY,CITY):
    DIST, !THE DISTANCE MATRIX;
    X; !X(I,J)=1 IF WE USE LINK I,J;
ENDSETS
DATA:
```

CITY =	CC	BIOCH	PHY	CS	STATS	MATHS	LAW	MBA	COMM	MED	MEDW	!CITY 1 IS BASED;
DIST =	0	46	207	206	442	391	435	390	490	412	528	CC;
	46	0	50	251	571	521	481	435	536	541	671	!FROM BIOCH;
	208	50	0	50	370	319	642	597	997	350	456	!FROM PHY;
	206	251	50	0	320	269	641	596	696	290	406	!FROM CS;
	442	571	370	320	0	30	877	832	932	610	726	!FROM STATS;
	391	521	319	269	30	0	826	781	881	559	675	!FROM MATHS;
	435	481	642	641	961	826	0	110	30	847	963	!FROM LAW;
	390	436	597	596	916	781	110	0	80	802	918	!FROM MBA;
	490	536	697	696	932	881	30	80	0	902	1018	!FROM COMM;
	412	541	340	290	610	559	847	802	902	0	130	!FROM MED;
	528	671	456	406	726	675	963	918	1018	130	0;	!FROM MEDW;

ENDDATA

```
! THE MODEL SIZE N>=8;
    N=@SIZE(CITY);
    MIN=@SUM(LINK:DIST*X);
    @FOR(CITY(K)| K#GT#1:
    @SUM(CITY(I)| I#NE#K: X(I,K))=1;
    @FOR (CITY(J)| J#NE#K:
    LVL(K)>=LVL(J)+X(J,K)
        -(N-2)*(1-X(J,K))
        +(N-3)*X(K,J););};
LVL(1)=0; !CITY 1 HAS LEVEL 0;
    @SUM(CITY(J)| J#GT#1:X(1,J))>=1;
    @FOR(LINK:@BIN(X););
    @FOR(CITY(K)| K#GT#1:
    @BND(1, LVL(K), 9999999);
    LVL(K)<=N-1-(N-2)*X(1,K););
END
Section 2. PART-2
SETS:
    CITY: LVL;
    !LVL(I)=LEVEL OF CITY I IN TREE, LVL(1)=0;
    LINK(CITY,CITY):
    DIST, !THE DISTANCE MATRIX;
    X; !X(I,J)=1 IF WE USE LINK I,J;
ENDSETS
DATA:
```

CITY =	CED	AS	ELCAL	ELNIC	COMP	UPOLY	BARCH	CHE_ PAT;	!CITY 1 IS BASED;
DIST =	0	0	76.2	131.1	137.2	297.2	137.2	164.6	!FROM CED;
	0	0	76.2	131.1	137.2	297.2	137.2	164.6	!FROM AS;
	76.2	76.2	0	50	56.1	216.1	213.4	240.8	!FROM ELCAL;
	131.1	131.1	50	0	6.1	166.1	268.3	295.7	!FROM ELNIC;
	137.2	137.2	56.1	6.1	0	160	274.4	301.8	!FROM COMP;
	297.2	297.2	216.1	166.1	160	0	434.4	461.8	!FROM UPOLY;
	137.2	137.2	213.4	268.3	274.4	434.4	0	60	!FROM BARCH;
	164.6	164.6	240.8	295.7	301.8	461.8	60	0.0;	!FROM CHE_PAT;

```
        ENDDATA
! THE MODEL SIZE N>=8;
    N=@SIZE(CITY);
    MIN=@SUM(LINK:DIST*X);
    @FOR(CITY(K)| K#GT#1:
    @SUM(CITY(I)| I#NE#K: X(I,K))=1;
    @FOR (CITY(J)| J#NE#K:
    LVL(K)>=LVL(J)+X(J,K)
        -(N-2)*(1-X(J,K))
        +(N-3)*X(K,J););Math);
LVL(1)=0; !CITY 1 HAS LEVEL 0;
    @SUM(CITY(J)| J#GT#1:X(1,J))>=1;
    @FOR(LINK:@BIN(X););
    @FOR(CITY(K)| K#GT#1:
    @BND(1, LVL(K), 9999999);
    LVL(K)<=N-1-(N-2)*X(1,K););
END
```

2. By Traveling Salesman Algorithm (A Shortest Path Problem)

! Shortest Path Problem for the COMPUTER CNETRE: PART - I;

SETS:

CITY / 1..11/: U; ! U(I) = sequence no. of city;

LINK(CITY, CITY):

DIST,! The distance matrix;

X;! X(I, J) = 1 if we use link I, J;

ENDSETS

DATA: !Distance matrix, it need not be symmetric;

!CITY =	CC	BIOCH	PHY	CS	STATS	MATHS	LAW	MBA	COMM	MED	MEDW;	!CITY 1 IS BASED;
DIST =	0	46	207	206	442	391	435	390	490	412	528	!FROM CC;
	46	0	50	251	571	521	481	435	536	541	671	!FROM BIOCH;
	208	50	0	50	370	319	642	597	997	350	456	!FROM PHY;
	206	251	50	0	320	269	641	596	696	290	406	!FROM CS;
	442	571	370	320	0	30	877	832	932	610	726	!FROM STATS;
	391	521	319	269	30	0	826	781	881	559	675	!FROM MATHS;
	435	481	642	641	961	826	0	110	30	847	963	!FROM LAW;
	390	436	597	596	916	781	110	0	80	802	918	!FROM MBA;
	490	536	697	696	932	881	30	80	0	902	1018	!FROM COMM;
	412	541	340	290	610	559	847	802	902	0	130	!FROM MED;
	528	671	456	406	726	675	963	918	1018	130	0;	!FROM MEDW;

ENDDATA

```
N = @SIZE(CITY);
MIN = @SUM(LINK: DIST * X);
@FOR(CITY(K):
! It must be entered;
@SUM(CITY(I)| I #NE# K: X(I, K)) = 1;
! It must be departed;
@SUM(CITY(J)| J #NE# K: X(K, J)) = 1;
! Weak form of the subtour breaking constraints;
! These are not very powerful for large problems;
@FOR(CITY(J)| J #GT# 1 #AND# J #NE# K:
    U(J) >= U(K) + X (K, J) -
    (N - 2) * (1 - X(K, J)) +
    (N - 3) * X(J, K));
);
! Make the X's 0/1;
@FOR(LINK: @BIN(X));
! For the first and last stop we know...;
@FOR(CITY(K)| K #GT# 1:
U(K) <= N - 1 - (N - 2) * X(1, K);
U(K) >= 1 + (N - 2) * X(K, 1)
);
END
```

!Shortest Path Problem for the COMPUTER CNETRE PART - II;

```
SETS:
CITY / 1..8/: U; ! U(I) = sequence no. of city;
LINK(CITY, CITY):
DIST, ! The distance matrix;
X; ! X(I, J) = 1 if we use link I, J;
ENDSETS
DATA:
!Distance matrix, it need not be symmetric;
```

CITY=	CED	AS	ELCAL	ELNIC	COMP	UPOLY	BARCH	CHE_ PAT;	!CITY 1 IS BASED;
DIST=	0.0	0.0	76.2	131.1	137.2	297.2	137.2	164.6	!FROM CED;
	0.0	0.0	76.2	131.1	137.2	297.2	137.2	164.6	!FROM AS;
	76.2	76.2	0.0	50.0	56.1	216.1	213.4	240.8	!FROM ELCAL;
	131.1	131.1	50.0	0.0	6.1	166.1	268.3	295.7	!FROM ELNIC;
	137.2	137.2	56.1	6.1	0.0	160.0	274.4	301.8	!FROM COMP;
	297.2	297.2	216.1	166.1	160.0	0.0	434.4	461.8	!FROM UPOLY;
	137.2	137.2	213.4	268.3	274.4	434.4	0.0	60.0	!FROM BARCH;
	164.6	164.6	240.8	295.7	301.8	461.8	60.0	0.0;	!FROM CHE_PAT;

```
ENDDATA
N = @SIZE(CITY);
MIN = @SUM(LINK: DIST * X);
@FOR(CITY(K):
! It must be entered;
@SUM(CITY(I)| I #NE# K: X(I, K)) = 1;
! It must be departed;
@SUM(CITY(J)| J #NE# K: X(K, J)) = 1;
! Weak form of the subtour breaking constraints;
! These are not very powerful for large problems;
@FOR(CITY(J)| J #GT# 1 #AND# J #NE# K:
    U(J) >= U(K) + X (K, J) -
    (N - 2) * (1 - X(K, J)) +
    (N - 3) * X(J, K));
);
! Make the X's 0/1;
@FOR(LINK: @BIN(X));
! For the first and last stop we know...;
@FOR(CITY(K)| K #GT# 1:
U(K) <= N - 1 - (N - 2) * X(1, K);
U(K) >= 1 + (N - 2) * X(K, 1)
);
END
```

Article I. Results:

(Minimal Spanning Tree) Network - I

Global optimal solution found at step: 288

Objective value: 1365.000

Branch count: 17

Variable	Value	Reduced Cost
N	11.00000	0.0000000
LVL (CC)	0.0000000	0.0000000
LVL (BIOCH)	1.000000	0.0000000
LVL (PHY)	2.000000	0.0000000
LVL (CS)	3.000000	0.0000000
LVL (STATS)	5.000000	0.0000000
LVL (MATHS)	4.000000	0.0000000
LVL (LAW)	3.000000	0.0000000
LVL (MBA)	1.000000	0.0000000
LVL (COMM)	2.000000	0.0000000
LVL (MED)	4.000000	0.0000000
LVL (MEDW)	5.000000	0.0000000
DIST (CC, CC)	0.0000000	0.0000000
DIST (CC, BIOCH)	46.00000	0.0000000
DIST (CC, PHY)	207.0000	0.0000000
DIST (CC, CS)	206.0000	0.0000000
DIST (CC, STATS)	442.0000	0.0000000
DIST (CC, MATHS)	391.0000	0.0000000
DIST (CC, LAW)	435.0000	0.0000000
DIST (CC, MBA)	390.0000	0.0000000
DIST (CC, COMM)	490.0000	0.0000000
DIST (CC, MED)	412.0000	0.0000000
DIST (CC, MEDW)	528.0000	0.0000000
DIST (BIOCH, CC)	46.00000	0.0000000
DIST (BIOCH, BIOCH)	0.0000000	0.0000000
DIST (BIOCH, PHY)	50.00000	0.0000000
DIST (BIOCH, CS)	251.0000	0.0000000
DIST (BIOCH, STATS)	571.0000	0.0000000
DIST (BIOCH, MATHS)	521.0000	0.0000000
DIST (BIOCH, LAW)	481.0000	0.0000000
DIST (BIOCH, MBA)	435.0000	0.0000000
DIST (BIOCH, COMM)	536.0000	0.0000000

Row	Slack or Surplus	Dual Price
1	0.0000000	0.0000000
2	1365.000	-1.000000
3	0.0000000	0.0000000
4	0.0000000	0.0000000
5	0.0000000	0.0000000
6	7.000000	0.0000000
7	5.000000	0.0000000
8	6.000000	0.0000000
9	7.000000	0.0000000
10	9.000000	0.0000000
11	8.000000	0.0000000
12	6.000000	0.0000000
13	5.000000	0.0000000
14	0.0000000	0.0000000
15	11.00000	0.0000000
16	0.0000000	0.0000000
17	0.0000000	0.0000000
18	6.000000	0.0000000
19	7.000000	0.0000000
20	8.000000	0.0000000
21	10.00000	0.0000000
22	9.000000	0.0000000
23	7.000000	0.0000000
24	6.000000	0.0000000
25	0.0000000	0.0000000
26	12.00000	0.0000000
27	11.00000	0.0000000
28	0.0000000	0.0000000
29	7.000000	0.0000000
30	0.0000000	0.0000000
31	9.000000	0.0000000

RESULT:

(Minimal Spanning Tree) Network -II

Global optimal solution found at step: 300

Objective value: 489.5000

Branch count: 23

Variable	Value	Reduced Cost
N	8.000000	0.0000000
LVL(CED)	0.0000000	0.0000000
LVL(AS)	1.000000	0.0000000
LVL(ELCAL)	1.000000	0.0000000
LVL(ELNIC)	2.000000	0.0000000
LVL(COMP)	3.000000	0.0000000
LVL(UPOLY)	4.000000	0.0000000
LVL(BARCH)	1.000000	0.0000000
LVL(CHE_PAT)	2.000000	0.0000000
DIST(CED, CED)	0.0000000	0.0000000
DIST(CED, AS)	0.0000000	0.0000000
DIST(CED, ELCAL)	76.20000	0.0000000
DIST(CED, ELNIC)	131.1000	0.0000000
DIST(CED, COMP)	137.2000	0.0000000
DIST(CED, UPOLY)	297.2000	0.0000000
DIST(CED, BARCH)	137.2000	0.0000000
DIST(CED, CHE_PAT)	164.6000	0.0000000
DIST(AS, CED)	0.0000000	0.0000000
DIST(AS, AS)	0.0000000	0.0000000
DIST(AS, ELCAL)	76.20000	0.0000000
DIST(AS, ELNIC)	131.1000	0.0000000
DIST(AS, COMP)	137.2000	0.0000000
DIST(AS, UPOLY)	297.2000	0.0000000
DIST(AS, BARCH)	137.2000	0.0000000
DIST(AS, CHE_PAT)	164.6000	0.0000000
DIST(ELCAL, CED)	76.20000	0.0000000
DIST(ELCAL, AS)	76.20000	0.0000000
DIST(ELCAL, ELCAL)	0.0000000	0.0000000
DIST(ELCAL, ELNIC)	50.00000	0.0000000
DIST(ELCAL, COMP)	56.10000	0.0000000

Row	Slack or Surplus	Dual Price
1	0.0000000	0.0000000
2	489.5000	-1.000000
3	0.0000000	0.0000000
4	0.0000000	0.0000000
5	6.000000	0.0000000
6	5.000000	0.0000000
7	4.000000	0.0000000
8	3.000000	0.0000000
9	6.000000	0.0000000
10	5.000000	0.0000000
11	0.0000000	0.0000000
12	0.0000000	0.0000000
13	6.000000	0.0000000
14	0.0000000	0.0000000
15	4.000000	0.0000000
16	3.000000	0.0000000
17	6.000000	0.0000000
18	5.000000	0.0000000
19	0.0000000	0.0000000
20	8.000000	0.0000000
21	7.000000	0.0000000
22	0.0000000	0.0000000
23	0.0000000	0.0000000
24	4.000000	0.0000000
25	7.000000	0.0000000
26	6.000000	0.0000000
27	0.0000000	0.0000000
28	9.000000	0.0000000
29	8.000000	0.0000000
30	8.000000	0.0000000
31	0.0000000	0.0000000
32	0.0000000	0.0000000
33	8.000000	0.0000000

APPENDIX: B

Result of the Shortest Path Problem for the COMPUTER CNETRE

PART - I

Global optimal solution found at step: 6256

Objective value: 2647.000

Branch count: 180

Variable	Value	Reduced Cost
N	11.00000	0.0000000
U(1)	0.0000000	0.0000000
U(2)	7.000000	0.0000000
U(3)	6.000000	0.0000000
U(4)	5.000000	0.0000000
U(5)	3.000000	0.0000000
U(6)	4.000000	0.0000000
U(7)	10.00000	0.0000000
U(8)	8.000000	0.0000000
U(9)	9.000000	0.0000000
U(10)	1.000000	0.0000000
U(11)	2.000000	0.0000000
DIST(1, 1)	0.0000000	0.0000000
DIST(1, 2)	46.00000	0.0000000
DIST(1, 3)	207.0000	0.0000000
DIST(1, 4)	206.0000	0.0000000
DIST(1, 5)	442.0000	0.0000000
DIST(1, 6)	391.0000	0.0000000
DIST(1, 7)	435.0000	0.0000000
DIST(1, 8)	390.0000	0.0000000
DIST(1, 9)	490.0000	0.0000000
DIST(1, 10)	412.0000	0.0000000
DIST(1, 11)	528.0000	0.0000000
DIST(2, 1)	46.00000	0.0000000
DIST(2, 2)	0.0000000	0.0000000
DIST(2, 3)	50.00000	0.0000000
DIST(2, 4)	251.0000	0.0000000
DIST(2, 5)	571.0000	0.0000000
DIST(2, 6)	521.0000	0.0000000
DIST(2, 7)	481.0000	0.0000000

Row	Slack or Surplus	Dual Price
1	0.0000000	0.0000000
2	2647.000	-1.000000
3	0.0000000	0.0000000
4	0.0000000	0.0000000
5	16.00000	0.0000000
6	15.00000	0.0000000
7	14.00000	0.0000000
8	12.00000	0.0000000
9	13.00000	0.0000000
10	11.00000	0.0000000
11	17.00000	0.0000000
12	18.00000	0.0000000
13	0.0000000	0.0000000
14	11.00000	0.0000000
15	0.0000000	0.0000000
16	0.0000000	0.0000000
17	0.0000000	0.0000000
18	7.000000	0.0000000
19	5.000000	0.0000000
20	6.000000	0.0000000
21	12.00000	0.0000000
22	0.0000000	0.0000000
23	11.00000	0.0000000
24	3.000000	0.0000000
25	4.000000	0.0000000
26	0.0000000	0.0000000
27	0.0000000	0.0000000
28	0.0000000	0.0000000
29	0.0000000	0.0000000
30	6.000000	0.0000000
31	7.000000	0.0000000
32	13.00000	0.0000000
33	11.00000	0.0000000
34	12.00000	0.0000000
35	4.000000	0.0000000

Result of the Shortest Path Problem for the COMPUTER CNETRE

PART - II

Global optimal solution found at step: 2594

Objective value: 951.3000

Branch count: 169

Variable	Value	Reduced Cost
N	8.000000	0.0000000
U(1)	0.0000000	0.0000000
U(2)	3.000000	0.0000000
U(3)	4.000000	0.0000000
U(4)	5.000000	0.0000000
U(5)	6.000000	0.0000000
U(6)	7.000000	0.0000000
U(7)	1.000000	0.0000000
U(8)	2.000000	0.0000000
DIST(1, 1)	0.0000000	0.0000000
DIST(1, 2)	0.0000000	0.0000000
DIST(1, 3)	76.20000	0.0000000
DIST(1, 4)	131.1000	0.0000000
DIST(1, 5)	137.2000	0.0000000
DIST(1, 6)	297.2000	0.0000000
DIST(1, 7)	137.2000	0.0000000
DIST(1, 8)	164.6000	0.0000000
DIST(2, 1)	0.0000000	0.0000000
DIST(2, 2)	0.0000000	0.0000000
DIST(2, 3)	76.20000	0.0000000
DIST(2, 4)	131.1000	0.0000000
DIST(2, 5)	137.2000	0.0000000
DIST(2, 6)	297.2000	0.0000000
DIST(2, 7)	137.2000	0.0000000
DIST(2, 8)	164.6000	0.0000000
DIST(3, 1)	76.20000	0.0000000
DIST(3, 2)	76.20000	0.0000000
DIST(3, 3)	0.0000000	0.0000000
DIST(3, 4)	50.00000	0.0000000
DIST(3, 5)	56.10000	0.0000000

Row	Slack or Surplus	Dual Price
1	0.0000000	0.0000000
2	951.3000	-1.000000
3	0.0000000	0.0000000
4	0.0000000	0.0000000
5	9.000000	0.0000000
6	10.00000	0.0000000
7	11.00000	0.0000000
8	12.00000	0.0000000
9	8.000000	0.0000000
10	0.0000000	0.0000000
11	8.000000	0.0000000
12	0.0000000	0.0000000
13	0.0000000	0.0000000
14	0.0000000	0.0000000
15	8.000000	0.0000000
16	9.000000	0.0000000
17	10.00000	0.0000000
18	4.000000	0.0000000
19	0.0000000	0.0000000
20	0.0000000	0.0000000
21	0.0000000	0.0000000
22	0.0000000	0.0000000
23	0.0000000	0.0000000
24	8.000000	0.0000000
25	9.000000	0.0000000
26	3.000000	0.0000000
27	4.000000	0.0000000
28	0.0000000	0.0000000
29	0.0000000	0.0000000
30	4.000000	0.0000000
31	0.0000000	0.0000000
32	0.0000000	0.0000000
33	8.000000	0.0000000
34	2.000000	0.0000000
35	3.000000	0.0000000

KEYWORDS

- **distance matrix LINGO**
- **network**
- **optimization**
- **shortest path**
- **spanning-tree**
- **traveling salesperson problem**

REFERENCES

1. Abdelfattah, I., et al., (2017). A new time-dependent shortest path algorithm for multimodal transportation network. *Procedia Computer Science, 109C*, 692–697.
2. Ahuja, R. K., Orlin, J. B., Pallottino, S., & Scutella, M. G., (2002). Minimum time and minimum cost path problems in street networks with traffic lights. *Transportation Science, 36*, 326–336.
3. Ahuja, R. K., Magnanti, T. L., & Orlin, J. B., (1993). *Network Flows: Theory Algorithms and Applications.* Prentice-Hall, Englewood Cliffs.
4. Mukherjee, B., (1997). *Optical Communication Networks.* New York: McGraw-Hill.
5. Mukherjee, B., (2000). WDM optical communication networks: Progress and challenges. *IEEE J. Selected Areas Commun., 18*, 1810–1824.
6. Bentley, J. L., (1990). Experiments on traveling salesperson heuristics. *Proceedings of the First Annual ACM-SIAM Symposium on Discrete Algorithms* (pp. 91–99). San Francisco, CA.
7. Ahn, C. W., Ramakrishna, R. S., Kang, C. G., & Choi, I. C., (2001). Shortest path routing algorithm using Hopfield neural network. *IEEE Electronic Letters, 37*(19), 1176–1178.
8. Dantzig, G. B., (1967). All shortest routes in a graph. In: Rosenthiel, P., (ed.), *Theory of Graphs* (pp. 91, 92). Gordon and Breach, NY.
9. Fredrick, S. H., & Lieberman, G. J., (1991). *Introduction to Mathematical Programming.* McGraw- Hill Pub. Company, New Delhi.
10. Goldfarb, D., & Hao, J., (1991). On strongly polynomial variants of the network simplex algorithm for the maximum flow problem. *Operations Research Letters, 10*, 383–387.
11. Gupta, S. H., & Lieberman, G. J., (1991). *Introduction to Mathematical Programming.* McGraw-Hill Company, New Delhi.
12. Peter, A. S., (1978). *Optimization of Transport Networks*. John Wiley & Sons, London.
13. Bentley, J. L., (1990a). Experiments on traveling salesperson heuristics. In: *Proc. 1st Ann. ACM-SIAM Symp. on Discrete Algorithms* (pp. 91–99). SIAM, Philadelphia, PA.
14. Ford, L. R., & Fulkerson, Jr. D. R., (1962). *Flows in Networks*. Princeton University Press, Princeton, New Jersey.

15. Nilofer, M., & Rizwanullah, M., (2018). Shortest path in single commodity flow problem in dynamic networks using modified algorithm. In: *International Journal of Applied Engineering Research* (Vol. 13, No. 8, pp. 1–4).
16. Pallottino, S., & Scutella, M. G., (2003). A new algorithm for re-optimizing shortest paths when the arc costs change. *Operations Research Letters, 31*, 149–160.
17. Peter, A. S., (1973). *Optimization of Transport Networks.* John Wiley and Sons, London.
18. Peng, (Will) C., & Yu, (Marco) N., (2013). Bicriterion shortest path problem with a general nonadditive cost. *Procedia-Social and Behavioral Sciences, 80*, 553–575.
19. Oyama, T., (2000). Weight of shortest path analyses for the optimal location problem. *Journal of the Operations Research Society of Japan, 43*, 176–196.

CHAPTER 18

A NOVEL APPROACH TO SENSORS USING AN INTENSIVE SURVEY

R. RAMESH,[1] E. UDAYAKUMAR,[2] K. SRIHARI,[3] and SUNIL PATHAK[4]

[1]*Department of ECE, Kalaignarkarunanidhi Institute of Technology (KIT), Coimbatore, Tamil Nadu, India, E-mail: vmramesh1993@gmail.com*

[2]*Assistant Professor, Department of ECE, Kalaignarkarunanidhi Institute of Technology (KIT), Coimbatore, Tamil Nadu, India*

[3]*Associate Professor, Department of CSE, SNS College of Technology, Coimbatore, Tamil Nadu, India*

[4]*Associate Professor, Department of CSE, Amity School of Engineering and Technology, Jaipur, Rajasthan, India*

ABSTRACT

A vehicular ad-hoc network (VANET) is a system of vehicles conveying between one another and to the sent side of the road units. They share data with respect to traffic wellbeing and infotainment. The correspondence among hubs in the system could be improved by gathering the vehicles into bunches. The plan of a bunch considering group size and land length has a significant effect on the nature of the correspondence. This chapter centers around the study of different elements that effects grouping configuration so as to give better rules to VANET structure and the board in down to earth applications. A VANET vehicular exceptionally delegated framework is a kind of framework offer vehicle to roadside and vehicle to vehicle correspondence through remote affiliation. Plus, we process the noteworthy possibilities and troubles in flexibility past typically used execution estimations. The reliable vehicles may causes setbacks, finding a leaving more in another city and streets moved parking garages are moving in the direction of the troublesome issues put a highlight of progression of

VANET. Vehicular off-the-cuff frameworks (VANETs) are the specific class of mobile uncommonly selected frameworks (MANETs). Since vehicles will, when all is said in done, move in a quick, the framework topology is immediately changed. VANET is frameworks which confer each other to the sent roadside units and offer information as for traffic and infotainment. The essential purpose of this review chapter is to give a chart of the vehicular exceptionally designated frameworks, its standards, applications, security issues and the current VANET coordinating shows.

18.1 INTRODUCTION

Vehicular transportation is a significant method of transportation which represents about 60% of generally speaking transportation modes. Progressions in innovation prompted the advancement of mechanized vehicles and expanded security-related applications. It can aid path-evolving exercises, impact shirking, giving web get to and to sending crisis notice frameworks. VANET is rising as a field of expanded research exercises. The vehicles in the thruway can be assembled into groups to improve better correspondence.

VANET experiences fast topology changes because of rapid versatility of vehicles. This prompts shaky correspondence and high overhead for refreshing new topology data at each example. The negative effects of these elements on the execution of VANET could be decreased by gathering the close-by vehicles moving same way into groups. The correspondence in bunches is helped by group heads (CH). Handover is the way toward moving the control of specific. Bunching diminishes the multifaceted nature of handover in quick moving vehicular condition by congregating the handover demand. Thus just a single solicitation message is started between the group and side of the road unit. The plan of group is influenced by the MAC activities, PHY layer remote channel condition and versatility of vehicles [24]. Right now, make an overview on different techniques embraced in plan of bunch by dissecting the impacts of MAC tasks, PHY layer remote channel condition and rapid portability of vehicles.

The speedy headway in remote advances, the value as well. By and by a day's VANET used in vehicle makers and media interchanges adventures in various information development benefits in vehicles and besides improve the prosperity out on the town and traffic efficiency. The latest couple of years, VANETs have expanded a huge amount of research.

At this moment that does not rely upon any central association for giving correspondence onboard units (OBUs) near to vehicles. Roadside units (RSU) technique is called, commonly basic in VANET to ensure open and transportation prosperity. IEEE 802.11 is where the correspondence advancement relies upon remote LAN. A repeat go in the 5.9 GHz scattered on coordinated reason in Europe and equivalently task in take a shot at DSRC band and its plan also portrays for the security of message exchange [31, 32].

18.1.1 IEEE 802.11 STANDARD

IEEE 802.11 gauges wireless access in vehicular environment (WAVE). The institutionalization process is gotten from the conveyance of the DSRC range band from the United States and the push to decide the innovation for use in the DSRC band [31, 32]. IEEE 802.11p standard or WAVE is extraordinarily evolved to modification the VANETs necessities and bolster ITS. It has been intended to address the necessities of interfacing remote gadgets in a quickly changing systems administration condition and in situations when in a shorter measure of time, the information exchanges ought to be finished.

18.1.2 CLUSTER DESIGN

Cluster formation involves the grouping of a certain number of nodes into a group and assigning a CH to that particular cluster. The selection of an efficient node to act as a CH, considering various parameters such as its position in cluster and mobility constraints, is a tedious process. In Ref. [1], the authors propose CH selection algorithm and cluster switching algorithm. The CH choice calculation thinks about hub degree, asset accessible with the applicant CH and the speed contrast between the CH and other group individuals. In any purpose of time, the vehicular hub may leave the current group and become an individual from another bunch under the help of some other CH. The cluster switching algorithm renders handover from one cluster to another by taking into account quality of service (QoS) requirements and various utility functions.

The links established between two nodes in wireless environment suffer from fading, shadowing [2] propose a method to utilize the information on vehicle's moment and map information to calculate link duration. It provides stable link by preventing link-breakage before it happens. The impact of Mac operation and its impact on cluster design. In Section 18.4, we discuss impacts of PHY layer wireless channel conditions on cluster design. In Section 18.5, we review the effects of mobility of vehicular nodes in cluster design.

18.2 RELATED WORK

To give the safe of VANET, scientists had presented the arrangement in various point to take care of the security issues. Isaac et al. [46] survey the significant security assaults and cryptographic arrangements. Analysts in Refs. [43–46] directing conventions and it gives powerful arrangements correspondence between the hubs and less blockage of system traffic. Yong Hao et al. [51] proposed a represented answer for RSU, which results simple to repudiation of malignant vehicle, its improved area security assurance and keep up the framework adaptable.

Chowdhury et al. [55] proposed a blend methodology says about the upside of both hilter-kilter and symmetric cryptographic plans. It uses that organizes both lopsided and for prosperity illuminating.

Azogue et al. [57] investigate security measurements for VANET. It can help manual for a plan for security components against sticking, i.e., Denial of Service assaults. For that, specialists propose a new class against sticking defensive instruments: hideaway methodology; it succeeds examine through the reenactments. They execute a reenactment bundle for incorporating VANET modules and assault/security alongside. It is about the hideaway methodology that accomplishes consistent proficiency advantage over conventional enemy of sticking plans.

Prabhakar et al. [58] proposed a fundamental supplements to the latent instruments of encryption. The information sources are safety efforts of VANET; the protective instrument embraces game-theoretic methodologies are of three phases were to advance the known recognize and obscure challengers.

He Li, Mianxiong Dong [59] present the information on SDN in VANETs and it is a sort of remote systems, work is talk about on remote southbound interchanges. Mendonca, proposed a center association between the impromptu system and framework based to apply SDN in heterogeneous (blended) organize. SDN brings about the ability of naturally reconfigure for middle-person correspondence. For southbound correspondence open networking foundation (ONF) is proposed and is utilized to usage of controller-switch and in southbound correspondence gives to help to scrambled transport layer security correspondence.

Shaikhul et al. [60] analyze the exhibitions of receptive directing conventions in VANET by utilizing NS-2. After reenactment, Shaikhul et al. shows that DSR has better PDF it has lesser steering over-burden and AOMDV has better execution in start to finish delay.

Hua-Wen [61] proposed a totaling information spread and disclosure of calculation in vehicular impromptu system by utilizing NS2. After recreation, Hua-Wen inferred that ADD calculation could diminish accumulation and scattering cost in correspondence. At the point when a client needs the information, it can transmit rapidly.

Sun et al. [62] considered the utilization test framework. Later, the reenactment maker assumed that responsive coordinating shows progressively fitting for VANET.

18.3 NECESSITY OF ROUTING PROTOCOLS IN VANET

VANET is a difficult directing convention however it is unique in relation to customary specially appointed systems. Right now, move quick and the system topology changes quickly by discontinuous connection availability. The work depends on the continuous procedure where the street vehicle thickness and it is recognizable to the dynamic vehicular so as to give quick and solid correspondences. VANET varies from MANET on account of its high unique topology. The dynamic idea of the portable hubs in the system is a trying for finding and keeping up the courses. Steering in VANETs is absolutely founded on specially appointed designs it has been considered, and various conventions were proposed. It might characterize into two primary classifications they are topology-based and geographic-based conventions (Figure 18.1).

Topology is a sort of directing is considered for sending the data among sender and collector. It very well may be partitioned into proactive (table-driven), responsive (on-request) and half and half conventions.

Proactive protocol is steering convention can be occasionally kept up the present rundown of goals [33] sharing the directing tables and it is an intermittent premise regardless of whether any connection transforms it does not happen.

FSR is like to LSR (link-state routing convention). Right now is kept up by topology table base and cutting-edge got data from the neighboring hubs. Steering table is utilized to trade and decrease [34].

OLSR is a connection state convention for portable impromptu systems. Multipoint transfers (MPR) will choose the neighbor hubs to retransmits the parcels, when the hubs are not in MPR. It is perused just and decreases the quantity of retransmissions in a communicate system [35].

TBRPF is a connection state steering convention and intended for specially appointed systems. By utilizing the topology table every hub will

structure to the hub. Intermittently the hubs will be refreshed for the past and current system state by utilizing HELLO messages [36].

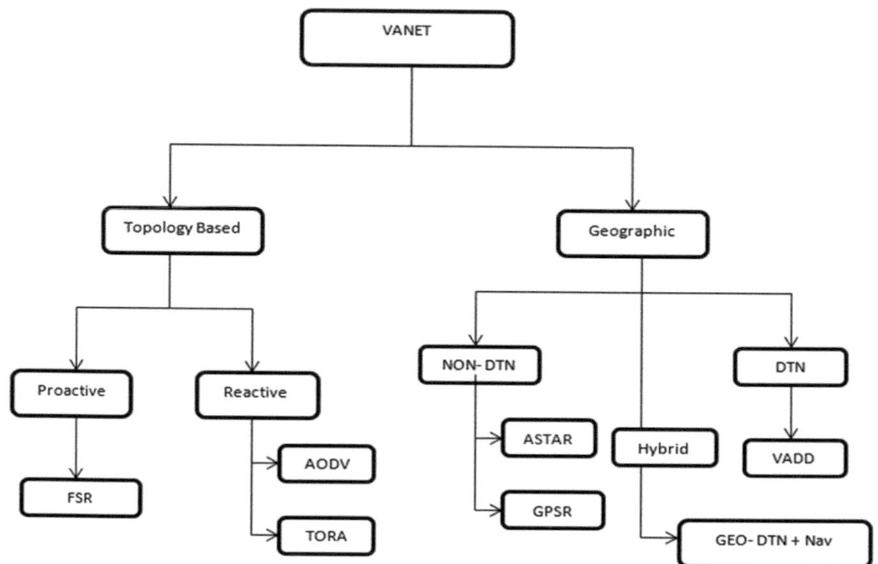

FIGURE 18.1 Block of VANET routing protocols.

18.3.1 REACTIVE ROUTING PROTOCOL (ON-DEMAND)

Responsive steering is utilized to discover the course just when it is vital for route request packets (RRP) the courses are presently utilized, and it decreases the data transfer capacity utilization issue as on account of proactive directing.

HRP is the blend of both proactive and reactive steering calculation. The control overhead is to be diminished in proactive steering conventions, and it diminishes the underlying course disclosure delay in receptive directing conventions.

18.4 SECURITY ISSUES IN VANET

VANET was moving the issue of scientists to digital dangers and the message passing may be hack in the framework execution [41, 42]. Security challenges, security necessities and different assaults in the VANET are to be concentrated right now.

18.4.1 SECURITY CHALLENGES IN VANET

While plan a VANET engineering the security challenges is to be considered. Security conventions, cryptographic calculation are to be broke down. Real time evasion, and mishap cautioning data are to be exacting in the conveyance of messages.

18.4.2 DATA CONSISTENCY LIABILITY

Even in authenticate hub dynamic can causes mishaps or upset the system, so instrument ought to be intended to evade.

18.4.3 LOCATION AWARENESS

In the event that any blunder happens, the area-based instruments may influence.

18.4.4 LOW RESILIENCE FOR MISTAKE

Based on probability, a couple of shows are to be arranged, and in a brief time span, VANET perform future fundamental information.

18.4.5 EXCHANGE OFF AMONG VALIDATION AND PROTECTION

For affirmation of the cannot as most purchasers will not enjoy others to consider their own distinctive confirmation. Right now needs to come in balance and a tradeoff must be kept up between the affirmation and security of the centers.

18.5 SAFETY REQUIREMENTS IN VANET

The necessities of VANET related to security are discussed in subsections.

18.5.1 ASSAILANTS ON VANETS

To ensure the approved people from sort out however untouchables are the interlopers and therefore confined capacity to ambush. Noxious and rational:

has no near and dear favorable position to ambush; they just hurt the handiness of the framework. Perceiving attackers have the individual advantage subsequently they are obvious.

18.5.2 DYNAMIC AND PASSIVE

Active attackers make the signs or bundle; however, the separated aggressors simply sense the framework.

18.6 ATTACK ON IDENTIFICATION AND AUTHENTICATION

18.6.1 SYBIL

A noxious vehicle proclaims to be at various zones with various characters right now a fantasy of traffic blockage. The malignant center point can even destroy the most ideal working of the framework by injecting fake information (Figure 18.2).

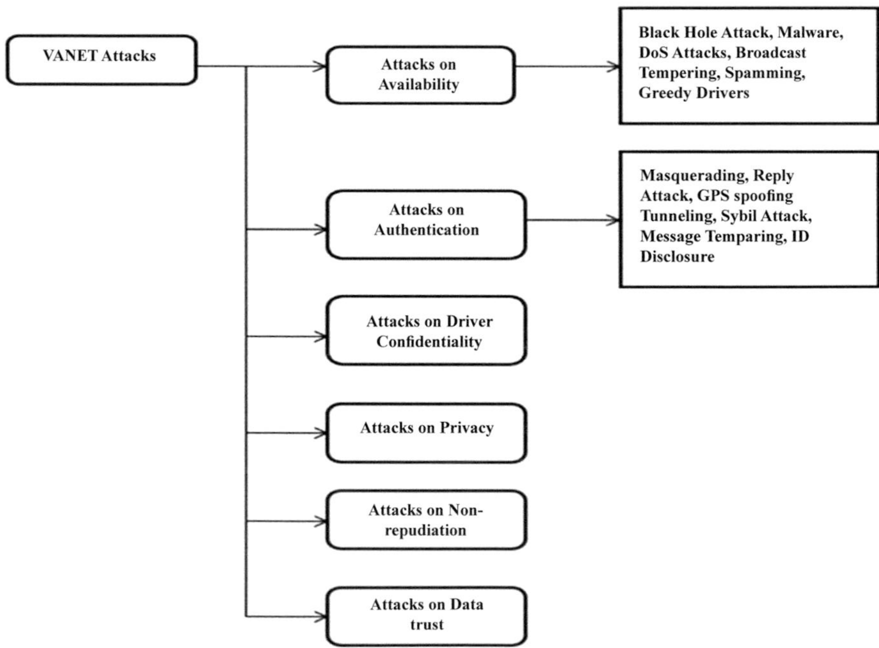

FIGURE 18.2 VANET attacks.

18.6.2 CIRCULATED DOS ASSAULT

Multiple assailants assault the casualty hub and keep it authentic.

18.6.3 SYN FLOODING

A tremendous number of the loss center, mocking the dispatcher address. Loss center sends back the area, yet center point does not get any ACK group be subsequently.

18.6.4 ROUTING ASSAULT

The package or agitates the guiding technique of the framework. The most generally perceived guiding ambushes in VANET [45, 46].

18.6.5 DARK HOLE ASSAULT

Malicious center points imagine a perfect course for the objective center and it shows that package should flow through this center consequent.

18.6.6 DIM HOLE ASSAULT

The malicious center acts like a dim opening attack anyway it drops the package explicitly. It can be acted in three distinct manners (i) threatening center may drop moving toward groups while license a couple of groups to pass (ii) malignant center point may carry on a run of the mill for a long-predefined center points for a long time and later on it carries on as a common center.

18.6.7 DANIEL OF SERVICE (DOS) ASSAULT

It should be conceivable framework the direct in the wake of transmitting hoax messages and it stops the framework affiliation. A pariah attacker can dispatch a DoS ambush by more than once spreading disregard messages with invalid imprints to eat up the information move limit or various resources of a concentrated-on vehicle.

18.6.8 REVOCATION

The essential peril in denial is the test that the center point related with correspondence. At this moment or more noteworthy component has ordinary character from now on it is definitely not hard to get unclear and subsequently they can be denied.

18.7 MAC OPERATION

The MAC method utilized unmistakably in IEEE802.11p standard is enhanced disseminated channel get to (EDCA), which is a propelled form of dispersed coordination function (DCF). DCF with a paired exponential back off, which deals with the retransmission of impacted bundles in the system [3]. DCF transmits bundle into the system just in the event that it detects the channel to be inactive for certain span called distributed entomb outline space (DIFS). On the off chance that channel is occupied, it would start a back off clock. DCF utilizes two methods for parcel transmission, for example, two-way handshaking procedure and four-way handshaking strategy. The fundamental access component is two-way handshaking method, which is described by transmission of quick positive affirmation (ACK) by the goal hub on fruitful gathering.

In four-manner handshaking system, which is otherwise called solicitation instrument, the hub would hold the channel by sending RTS short casing. The goal would react with CTS outline after with the genuine transmission of information happens. Bianchi proposed the presentation of DCF is assessed utilizing a Markov display where each station is demonstrated by a couple of whole numbers I, begins at 0 and expanded by 1 for each transmission that outcomes in crash up to the most extreme estimation of m. The counter k is picked to be in the scope of relies upon contention window (CW) least worth (CW_{min}) parameter of 802.11. On contrasting the consequences of two access instruments, the RTS/CTS is better in execution and proficient than adapt to concealed terminals. Since the genuine traffic situation does not have perfect station condition with a limited number of vehicles, the model dependent on immersed traffic suspicion could not be pertinent for pragmatic applications in the certifiable situation.

David et al. [4] stretched out crafted by Bianchi to be material for non-immersed condition. The web applications, for example, internet browser and e-mail produces bursty information while voice data cannot. This differing scope of information rate requires a neon-soaked activity. The immersed information stream may diminish the data transfer capacity accessible for low-rate voice over IP (VoIP). The 2-dimensional Markov model (i,k) utilized is a limited cushion model and changed to be working in present back off conversely on that in Ref. [3]. The utilization of 2-D Markov chain model does not give the quality of administration (QoS) execution and lining conduct.

Liu et al. [5] proposed a that coordinates the lining procedure and dispute goals into one model. This is a limited support model and is able to do precisely estimating the significant QoS measures, throughput, and line length. The 3-D Markov chain models the station utilizing a 3-tuple rather than the 2-D model which utilizes just (I, k). The list h in 3-D model models the line inhabitance and it is in the scope of where L is the most extreme line length. It does not consider blemished remote channel conditions, which has a significant effect on organize execution in pragmatic application.

Zheng et al. [6] proposed a logical to assess the exhibition of DCF in defective remote channel conditions. The different factors, for example, twofold exponential back off component in DCF, different traffic load given to the system, and lining framework at the MAC layer and flawed remote channels, has sway on the general system execution.

Communicate informing mode is unmistakable in VANETs explicitly in open wellbeing applications. The vehicular hubs need to refresh its situation in the system to all its close by hubs occasionally, and this is normally done in communicated mode. Routine data, for example, increasing speed, speed, and position of vehicular hub or basic data, for example, mishap, unexpected brake or changes in moving example, for example, change of path and surpassing a vehicle are done in communicate. These typically do not have ACK as sending an ACK for each message got would bring about flooding of messages in the system at once. There is no RTS/CTS handshake component in communicate which gives the purpose behind more event of impact in communicate contrasted and the unicast mode. Yang et al. [7] proposed a model for investigation of intermittent communicate messages in VANET. They have considered just a one-dimensional Markov model since there is no bundle retransmission in communicating mode. The presumption of having unsaturated traffic and there is no bundle sitting tight for transmission in the cushion of the hub. These suppositions make it hard to actualize progressively situation. It does not stretch out for powerfully changing CW sizes.

The data with respect to the vehicular hubs position, speed, and quickening are in fact known as cooperative mindfulness message (CAM). These messages are constantly communicated in the control channel and are known as "heartbeat" messages. The effectives of such communication transmission are generally estimated by two measurements, for example, proficiency, and unwavering quality. The productivity of the communication transmission is characterized as the normal rate with which a source can convey its transmitted parcels to its neighboring hubs. Unwavering quality in communication transmission is characterized as the normal number of hubs that can get a particular transmitted parcel effectively.

EDCA is intended for conflict-based QoS support. The working of EDCA is like that of DCF however, with some extra characteristics. The EDCA component characterizes four access classes that give information traffic four distinct needs. Each entrance classification is identical to a DCF station with its own EDCA parameters. Rather than DIFS as in DCF, EDCA utilizes assertion between outline space (AIFS). Each entrance class had distinctive AIFS, CW_{min}, and CW_{max} esteem. Han et al. [8] proposed a logical model that is reasonable for both the fundamental access mode and RTS/CTS mode so that it is material every one of the four access classifications of IEEE 802.11p. In light of the examination they have inferred that the IEEE 802.11p standard offers a viable support separation system. Thought of soaked traffic situation makes diagnostic model dreary to actualize in non-immersed genuine situation. It could not bolster data transfer capacity devouring enormous applications as it requires a difficult degree of asset allotment which cannot here.

Kim et al. [9] proposed a multi-channel MAC convention dependent on grouping process. The accessible channel is partitioned into two as control channel and information channel. Control channel is utilized by the bunch header to send channel utilization list (CUL) to its group individuals occasionally. The information channel is used by the group individuals to transmit information bundle all the while. As the proposed model has numerous channels, it permits more than one hub to send parcel at same time, which thus diminished clog and bundle crash in the system. As it depends on bunching process the choice of group head and making a decent group configuration has significant effect on the system execution.

Wu et al. [10] proposed an expository model for dissecting DCF based reasonable channel get to. In VANET, there are conditions when more than one vehicular hub gets to a solitary passageway. During which the hub moving at higher speed does not have same open door as vehicle moving with lower speed to speak with the street side passageway. The way toward changing the transmission likelihood by changing conflict window size is called reasonable channel impact. They have done the examination in non-soaked condition.

18.8 PHYSICAL LAYER

The smaller channel width is progressively vigorous to blurring in vehicular situations. It gives information trade among vehicles (V2V) and among vehicles and side of the road unit (V2U) inside the scope of 1 km with information pace of 3 Mbps to 27 Mbps. Abdeldime et al. [11] portrayed the details and different difficulties looked in the PHY layer. The impacts of Doppler move and different multipath impacts, for example, Rayleigh blurring, defer spread and recurrence specific blurring are the primary factors that have impacts on PHY layer activity.

Chandrasekhara Menon et al. [12] proposed a model for investigating availability properties considering different blurring models. Remote channel predominantly experiences two sorts of blurring to be specific enormous scope blurring (slow blurring) and little scope blurring (quick blurring). Complex condition with snags as a rule show huge scope blurring because of diffraction, which could be described by the lognormal shadow blurring model. Interestingly, of sign outcomes in little scope blurring. Blurring models, for example, Rayleigh, Rician, and Weibull are utilized dependent on condition. Rayleigh blurring is utilized for the situation where the model has multi-way blurring with no immediate view (LOS) way. This depends on the way that in V2V correspondence as the separation between two vehicles expands there would be misfortune in LOS way. In situations like clogged city streets, multi-way segment is more noticeable than LOS way where Rayleigh blurring can be utilized viably. Rician blurring is favored for situations like country interstates, where the proliferation way ought to have one in number LOS and numerous arbitrary more vulnerable parts. Weibull circulation is utilized in serious blurring conditions. It is reasonable for non-LOS V2V channel estimations. The model gave availability investigation in various blurring channels however it does not give any answer for diminish effects of blurring impacts.

Ye et al. [13] communicate transmission on-premise of measurements, for example, productivity and unwavering quality for Rayleigh blurring channels. It depends on the presumption of immersed connect with bundles transmitted by hubs are of equivalent length, which cannot valid if there should arise an occurrence of ongoing situation.

Chen et al. [14] proposed an ideal numerous measurements passage determination instrument for VANET. The portable entryways are utilized to diminish the traffic load when the hubs are associated with 3G arrange legitimately. They are chosen by considering measurements like system delay, Doppler move and relative speed in blurring channels. So as to suit the constant situation where the quick blurring and slow blurring wonders coincide, the channel model is viewed as a superposed model of both quick blurring and slow blurring. The model of Rayleigh blurring with superimposed log typical shadowing is considered for investigation.

Because of rapid portability of vehicles the bearer recurrence of sign endures Doppler move. So as to keep up network between vehicles for a longer span, street-side frameworks can be utilized as transfer focuses through which the information transmission would happen. For such hand-off correspondence physical-layer network coding (PNC) is utilized to improve the general transmission throughput inside the constrained contact length. Wang-Hei Ho et al. [15] have a model to test the physical-layer plausibility for applying PNC. In IEEE802.11p, the orthogonal frequency division multiplexing (OFDM) subcarriers may endure transporter recurrence counterbalance because of Doppler move which thusly results in between bearer obstruction between subcarriers. Some balance methods can be utilized to smother bearer recurrence counterbalance so as to improve the start to finish bit blunder rate.

Guo et al. [16] for control of vehicles in VANET with constrained fading channels. The fading channel usually varies with time, environment, and radiofrequency aspects. Block channel fading model can be used to characterize fading channel, where channel fading gain is invariant within the block but may vary from one block to another. The multiple access protocol considered in this model allows it to be utilized in groups and reduces collision. It may not be suitable for channel-wise random-access protocol like ALOHA where collision is inevitable.

The vehicles in VANET usually exhibit broadcast transmission, and this may lead to overcrowded communication channels. In order to sustain in-network, vehicles should be capable of switching from one radio frequency band to another using spectrum-agile wireless environment. Rawat et al. [17] proposed a model. The transmission range/power transmitted by each vehicle can be adjusted. The adaptation of vehicles to available frequency bands and varying environment has improved the performance of VANET in fading environment.

In order to overcome the spectrum scarcity, the method of utilizing unused spectrum or vacant portions of digital television band for VANET is introduced. This technology is known as cognitive radio networks. This would enable the secondary unlicensed band user to have access over primary user's licensed band unused frequencies without any negative effects. Souid et al. [18] proposed a model for sensing the available vacant spectrum over

Nakagami-m fading channels for cognitive VANETs. It is also prominent that the narrow band allocated for VANET usually follows nakagami distribution. Blind Eigen value-based sensing method is used for analysis.

18.8.1 MOBILITY OF VEHICULAR NODES

Regardless of the profoundly powerful nature of vehicular hubs, it is vital to keep up a stable group for better correspondence.

Luan et al. [19] thinking about high hub versatility and examinations the effect of portability on resultant throughput. The moving example/course and vehicle speed are contemplated. They have added to upgrade of MAC convention thinking about effects of hub portability. The model does not give any insight concerning much of the time changing driving examples of vehicle. It does not think about steadiness of group for execution assessment.

Shea et al. [20] planned a model for versatility-based grouping in VANET using the liking engendering calculation. The hubs are arranged dependent on the speed into a few gatherings called bunch with an effective hub going about as group head. The previous models dependent on versatility neglected to think about the strength of the group. Steadiness is normally characterized by longer bunch head term, longer group part length and low pace of progress in bunch head. The proposed fondness spread calculation frames a bunch considering both the base separation and least relative speed between-group head and part. Subsequently, by thinking about run of the mill vehicular portability, the model creates a superior group with high strength.

Yousefi et al. [21] projected a model to contemplate the availability properties in VANET. The model depends on barely any presumptions that the conveyance of separation between two vehicles can be displayed by Laplace change. The assessment gives the effects of speed appropriation and traffic stream on the network. The model depends on certain suspicions with respect to traffic stream, which make it a less noteworthy continuously situation.

Nagel et al. [22] anticipated a to break down the effect of vehicular traffic and portability on vehicular interchanges. Nagel et al. has thought about three conditions of traffic, for example, free stream, synchronized stream, and wide jam. The aftereffects of the model demonstrate that an arbitrary course versatility model cannot allow for the recreation of vehicular systems. It likewise gives a geometry-based model that renders calculation of the conveyance of association term as indicated by separation and speed disseminations. This does not consider information from continuous traffic situations, which makes it for all intents and purposes less effective.

Akhtar et al. [23] proposed a minute portability model to create practical traffic streams. They have incorporated true street topology and constant information extricated from the turnpike execution estimation framework database. It examines different framework measurements, for example, hub degree, neighbor bunch span, and connection length and their effects. As the model depends on ongoing traffic information, it is increasingly reasonable for down-to-earth applications.

18.9 VANET APPLICATIONS

Correspondence between the vehicles has prompted the improvement of various applications and gives a wide scope of data to drivers and explorers. This has expanded the street wellbeing and solace of the travelers. Applications can be characterized into safety and non-safety oriented applications.

18.9.1 NON-SAFETY ORIENTED

It incorporates business and comfort applications which give amusement and administrations to drivers and furthermore manage traffic the executives to improve traffic proficiency.

18.10 CONCLUSION

We have examined the effects of MAC layer, PHY layer remote channel situations, and versatility of vehicles on group structure. The itemized examination of different chapters gives the unmistakable thought on group plan improvement. Different models are concentrated altogether to show signs of improvement thought on impacts they make. This work would enjoy musings about further upgrades that could be made on existing conventions. Controlling expects a fundamental activity in vehicle-to-vehicle (V2V) and infrastructure-to-vehicle (I2V) correspondence. Vehicles are transforming into a principal bit of the overall framework. At this moment, it is mainly researched considering the way that various new sorts of ambushes are being made. Later on work, we hope to propose new game plans and show the survey of VANET.

KEYWORDS

- **channel utilization list**
- **cooperative mindfulness message**
- **digital information**
- **sensors**
- **sequential analysis**
- **system design**
- **vehicular ad-hoc network**

REFERENCES

1. Chai, R., Yang, B., Li, L., Sun, L., & Chen, Q., (2013). Clustering-based data transmission algorithms for VANET. In: *Wireless Comm. and Signal Proc. (WCSP), 2013 International Conf.* (pp. 1–6).
2. Lee, J., & Sang-Sun, L., (2014). A study on maintaining links in urban VANET using handover method. In: *Net Infrastructure and Digital Content (IC-NIDC) 4th IEEE Int. Conf.* (pp. 32–35).
3. Bianchi, G., (2000). Performance analysis of IEEE 802.11 distributed coordination functions. *IEEE J. Sel. Areas Commun.*, 535–547.
4. Malone, D., Duffy, K., & Leith, D., (2007). Modeling the 802.11 distributed coordination function in non-saturated heterogeneous conditions. *IEEE/ACM Trans. Network,* 159–172.
5. Liu, R. P., Sutton, G. J., & Collings, I. B., (2010). A new queueing model for QoS analysis of IEEE 802.11 DCF with finite buffer and load. *IEEE Trans. Wireless Commun.*, 2664–2675.
6. Zheng, Y., Lu, K., Wu, D., & Fang, Y., (2006). Performance analysis of IEEE 802.11 DCF in imperfect channels. *IEEE Trans. Veh. Technol.,* 1648–1656.
7. Yang, Q., Zheng, J., & Shen, L., (2011). Modeling and performance analysis of periodic broadcast in vehicular ad hoc networks. In: *Proc. IEEE GLOBE-COM* (pp. 1–5). Houston, TX, USA.
8. Han, C., Dianati, M., Tafazolli, R., Kernchen, R., & Shen, X. S., (2012). Analytical study of the IEEE 802.11p MAC sublayer in vehicular networks. *IEEE Trans. Intell. Transp. Syst., 13*, 873–886.
9. Kim, T., Jung, S., & Lee, S., (2009). CMMP: Clustering-based multi-channel MAC protocol in VANET in computer and electrical engineering. *ICCEE '09. Second International Conf., 1*, 380–383.
10. Wu, Q., & Zheng, J., (2014). Performance modeling of IEEE 802.11 DCF based fair channel access for vehicular-to-roadside communication in a non-saturated state in communications (ICC). *IEEE International Conference*, 2575–2580.

11. Abdeldime, A. M. S., & Lenan, W., (2014). The physical layer of the IEEE 802.11p WAVE communication standard: The specification and challenges. *Proceedings of the World Congress on Engineering and Computer Science, WCECS*, 22–24.
12. Chandrasekhara, M. N. P., & Anchare, B., (2012). Connectivity analysis of one-dimensional vehicular ad hoc networks in fading channels. *EURASIP J. Wireless Commun. Netw.*
13. Ye, F., Yim, R., Roy, S., & Zhang, J., (2011). Efficiency and reliability of one-hop broadcasting in vehicular ad hoc networks. *IEEE J. Sel. Areas Commun., 29*, 151–160.
14. Chen, K., Chen, L., & Ju, K., (2013). A gateway selection mechanism based on stability of vehicular ad hoc networks in fading channels. In: *TENCON 2013 IEEE Region Conference*, 22–25.
15. Wang-Hei, H. I., Chang, L. S., & Lu, L., (2014). Feasibility study of physical-layer network coding in 802.11p VANETs. In *Information Theory (ISIT), 2014 IEEE International Symposium*, 646–650.
16. Guo, G., & Wang, L., (2015). Control over medium-constrained vehicular networks with fading channels and random-access protocol: A networked systems approach. In: *Vehicular Technology, IEEE Trans.* (Vol. 64, No. 8, pp. 3347–3358).
17. Rawat, D. B., & Shetty, S., (2014). Enhancing connectivity for spectrum-agile vehicular ad hoc networks in fading channels. In: *Intelligent Vehicles Symposium Proceedings, IEEE*, (pp. 957–962).
18. Souid, I., Ben, C. H., & Attia, R., (2014). Blind spectrum sensing in cognitive vehicular ad hoc networks over Nakagami-m fading channels. In: *Electrical Sciences and Technologies in Maghreb (CISTEM), International Conference* (pp. 1–5).
19. Luan, T. H., Ling, X., & Shen, X., (2012). MAC in motion: Impact of mobility on the MAC of drive-thru internet. In: *Mobile Computing, IEEE Trans.* (pp. 305–319).
20. Shea, C., Hassanabadi, B., & Valaee, S., (2009). Mobility-based clustering in VANETs using affinity propagation. In: *Global Telecommunications Conference, GLOBECOM* (pp. 1–6).
21. Yousefi, S., Altman, E., El-Azouzi, R., & Fathy, M., (2008). Analytical model for connectivity in vehicular ad hoc networks. In: *Vehicular Technology, IEEE Trans.* (Vol. 57, No. 6, pp. 3341–3356).
22. Nagel, R., (2010). The effect of vehicular distance distributions and mobility on VANET communications. In: *Intelligent Vehicles Symposium (IV)* (pp. 1190–1194). IEEE.
23. Akhtar, N., Ergen, S. C., & Ozkasap, O., (2015). Vehicle mobility and communication channel models for realistic and efficient highway VANET simulation. In: *Vehicular Technology, IEEE Trans.* (Vol. 64, No. 1, pp. 248–262).
24. Wang, H., Liu, R. P., Ni, W., Chen, W., & Collings, I. B., (2014). A new analytical model for highway inter-vehicle communication systems. *Communications (ICC), IEEE International Conference*, 2581–2586.
25. Wang, H., Liu, R. P., Ni, W., Chen, W., & Collings, I. B., (2015). VANET modeling and clustering design under practical traffic, channel and mobility conditions. *IEEE Transactions on Communications, 63*(3), 870–881.
26. Santhi, S., (2019). SoS emergency ad-hoc wireless network. Computational intelligence and sustainable systems (CISS). *EAI/Springer Innovations in Communications and Computing* (pp. 227–234). Springer, Chapter 15.
27. Santhi, S., (2019). Design and implementation of area and delay efficient FXLMS filter for active noise cancellation. *Computational Intelligence and Sustainable Systems*

(CISS), EAI/Springer Innovations in Communications and Computing (pp. 115–129). Springer, Chapter 9.

28. Vetrivelan, P., (2019). A neural network based automatic crop monitoring robot for agriculture. *The IoT and the Next Revolutions Automating the World,* 203–212. IGI Global.
29. Kanagaraj, T., (2020). Control of home appliances and projector by smart application using SEAP protocol. *Intelligence in Big Data Technologies-Beyond the Hype, Advances in Intelligent Systems and Computing (AISC) Series, 1119*(1), 603–610. Springer Nature.
30. Vetrivelan, P., (2015). Design of smart surveillance security system based on wireless sensor network. *International Journal of Research Studies in Science, Engineering and Technology, 4*, 23–26. Sryahwa Publications.
31. Kumar, B. S., & Mohan, K. P., (2013). Vehicular comm: A survey. *The Institution of Engg. and Tech., 3*(3), 204–217.
32. Raya, M., & Papadimitratos, P., & Hubaux, J. P., (2006). Securing vehicular communications. *IEEE Wireless Communications*, *13*(5), 8–13.
33. Bijan, P., (2011). VANET routing protocols: Pros and cons. Dept. of Computer Science and Engineering, Shahjalal University of Science and Technology, Sylhet, Bangladesh. *International Journal of Computer Applications, 20*(3).
34. Gerla, M., Hong, X., & Pei, G., (2002). *Fisheye State Routing Protocol (FSR).* IETF internet-draft, Work in Progress. Draft-ietfmanet- fsr-03.
35. Clausen, T., et al., (2003). *Optimized Link State Routing Protocol (OLSR).* RFC 3626, Network Working Group.
36. Ogier, R., et al., (2004). *Topology Dissemination-Based on Reverse-Path Forwarding (TBRPF).* RFC 3684, Network Working Group.
37. Johnson, D., Maltz, B. A. D., & Hu, Y. C., (2004). *The Dynamic Source Routing Protocol for Mobile Ad Hoc Networks (DSR).* Draft-ietf-manet-dsr-10.
38. Perkins, C., Belding-Royer, E., & Das, S., (2003). *Ad Hoc On-Demand Distance Vector (AODV) Routing.* RFC 3561, Network Working Group.
39. Park, V., & Corson, S., (2001). *Temporally-Ordered Routing Algorithm (TORA) Version 1 Functional Specification.* IETF Internet draft, work in progress, draft-ietf-manct-toraspec-04.txt.
40. Haas, Z. J., (1997). *The Zone Routing Protocol (ZRP) for Ad Hoc Networks*. Internet draft.
41. Johnson, D., & Hu, Y. C., (2004). *The Dynamic Source Routing Protocol for Mobile Ad Hoc Nextjs (DSR).* Draft-ietf-manet-dsr-10.txt.
42. Perkins, C., Belding-Royer, E., & Das, S., (2003). *Ad Hoc on-Demand Distance Vector (AODV) Routing.* RFC 3561, Network Working Group.
43. Park, V., & Corson, S., (2001). *Temporally-Ordered Routing Algorithm (TORA) Version 1 Functional Specification.* IETF Internet draft, work in progress, draft-ietf-manet-toraspec, 04.
44. Haas, Z. J., (1997). *The Zone Routing Protocol (ZRP) for Ad Hoc Networks.* Internet draft.
45. (2009). Survey of routing protocols for mobile ad-hoc network‖ Humayun Bakht Taitec college Manchester, United Kingdom. *IEEE Transactions on Vehicular Technology, 58*(7), 3609.
46. Isaac, J. T., Zeadally, S., & Camara, S. J., (2010). Security attacks and solutions for vehicular ad hoc networks. *Communications IET, 4*(7), 894, 903.

47. Hui, F., (2005). A survey on the characterization of vehicular ad hoc networks routing solutions. *ECS 257 Winter*, 1–15.
48. Yin, J., Batt, E. T., Yeung, G., & Ryu, B., (2004). Perform evaluation of safety appl over DSRC vehicular ad hoc net. *Proc. of Int. Workp on Vehicular Ad. Hoc. Net.*
49. Wang, S. Y., (2004). Preceding the lifetime of repairable unicast ring paths in-vehicle-for mobile ad hoc net on higys. In: *15th IEEE Int. Symposium on Personal, Indoor and Mobile Radio Comm, (PIMRC)* (Vol. 4, pp. 2815–2829).
50. Briesemeister, L., (2000). Role-based multicast in highly mobile but sparsely conn ad hoc net. *First Annual Work on Mob and Ad. Hoc. Net and Comp. (MobiHOC)*, 45–50.
51. Hao, Y., Cheng, Y., & Ren, K., (2008). Distributed key management with protection against RSU compromise in group signature based VANETs. *IEEE Globecom.*, 4951–4955.
52. Wang, J., & Yan, W., (2009). RBM: A role-based mobility model for VANET. *Proc. Int. Conf. Communications and Mobile Computing, 2*, 437–443.
53. Liu, B., Khorashadi, B., Du, H., Ghosal, D., Chuah, C. Z., & Zhang, M., (2009). VGSim: An integrated networking and microscopic vehicular mobility simulation platform. *IEEE Communication Magazine Automotive Networking Series, 47*(5), 134–141.
54. Sun, J., Zhang, C., Zhang, Y., & Fang, Y., (2010). An identity-based security system for user privacy in vehicular ad hoc networks. *IEEE Transactions on, Parallel and Distributed Systems, 21*(9).
55. Chowdhury, P., Tornatore, M., Sarkar, S., Mukherjee, B., Wagan, A. A., Mughal, B. M., & Hasbullah, H., (2010). VANET security framework for trusted grouping using TPM hardware. *Second International Conference on Communication Software and Networks, (ICCSN '10)*, 309–312.
56. Samara, G., & Al-Salihy, W., (2012). A new security mechanism for vehicular communication networks. *Proceeding of the International Conference on Cyber Security. Cyber Warfare and Digital Forensic (CyberSec)*, 18–22.
57. Azogu, I. K., Ferreira, M. T., Larcom, J. A., & Liu, H., (2013). A new antijamming strategy for VANET metrics directed security defense. *IEEE Globecom Workshops (GC Wkshps)*, 1344–1349.
58. Prabhakar, M., Singh, J. N., & Mahadevan, G., (2013). Defensive mechanism for VANET security in game-theoretic approach using heuristic-based ant colony optimization. *IEEE International Conference on Computer Communication and Informatics (ICCCI)*, 1–7.
59. He, L., Mianxiong, D., & Kaoru, O., (2016). Control plane optimization in software defined vehicular ad-hoc networks. *IEEE Transactions on Vehicular Technology*, 0018–9545.
60. Shaikhul, I. C., Won-Il, L., Youn-Sang, C., Guen-Young, K., & Jae-Young, P., (2011). Performance evaluation of reactive routing protocols in VANET. In: *17th Asia-Pacific Conference on Communications (APCC).*
61. Hua-Wen, T., (2012). Aggregating data dissemination and discovery in vehicular Ad Hoc networks. *Telecommun. Syst., 50*, 285–295.
62. Sun, X., & Xia-Miao, L., (2008). *Study of the Feasibility of VANET and its Routing Protocols.* IEEE.
63. Josiane, N., Neeraj, R., Guiling, (Grace) W., & Cristian, B., (2009). VANET routing on city roads using real-time vehicular traffic information. *IEEE Transactions on Vehicular Technology, 58*(7).
64. Azogu, I. K., Ferreira, M. T., & Liu, H., (2012). A security metric for VANET content delivery. *Global Communications Conference (GLOBECOM), 37*, 991, 996.

65. Tamilselvan, S., (2020). A smart industrial pollution detection and monitoring using the internet of things (IoT). *Futuristic Trends in Network and Communication Technologies, Communication in Computer and Information Science (CCIS) Series, 1206*(1), 233–242 Springer Nature.
66. Tamilselvan, S., (2020). An enhanced face and iris recognition based new generation security system. *Computing, Communications, and Cyber-Security, Lecture Notes in Networks and Systems (LNNS) Series, 121*(1), 845–855. Springer Nature.
67. Srihari, K., (2020). Implementation of Alexa based intelligent voice response system for smart campus. *Innovations in Electrical and Electronics Engineering, Lecture Notes in Electrical Engineering (LNEE) Series, 626*(1), 849–855. Springer Nature.

CHAPTER 19

ROBOTIC PROCESS AUTOMATION: AN APPLICATION

SONIYA SONI,[1] GIREESH KUMAR,[1] and RICHA SHARMA[2]

[1]*Department of Computer Science Engineering, JK Lakshmipat University, Jaipur, Rajasthan, India*

[2]*Department of Mathematics, JK Lakshmipat University, Jaipur, Rajasthan, India, E-mails: richasharma@jklu.edu.in; aligarh.richa@gmail.com*

ABSTRACT

In this study, we explore the process automation in order to find the best journal for publication with respect to our study. Process automation plays an efficient role to find out the best journal suited for manuscript publication. Robotic process automation (RPA) is slowly taking the place of human manual work in computer software's which are based on repetitive tasks, now a robot will do the work on behalf of human in the same manner. A robot can capture and interpret existing applications for manipulating data, processing transactions, communicating with other digital systems and triggering responses. Moreover, we use UiPath tools (UiPath Studio and UiPath Orchestrator) to build process automation for exploring best journals for manuscript publication. This process requires few minutes for providing a list of best suitable journals for your research publication on the basis of standard journal database.

19.1 INTRODUCTION

Robotic process automation (RPA) is an automation technology based on software tools that could imitate human behavior for repetitive and on-value-added tasks such as tipping, copying, pasting, extracting, merging, and moving data from one system to another system. The main features of RPA are cost reduction, increasing process speed, error reduction and productivity improvement. It works very well in every field of business process and is an emerging technology which can help humans to minimize the repeated software tasks as a result they can give their precious time to other tasks which needs more attention like customer interaction and other development lifecycle processes [1, 2]. RPA is used to configure software robots that capture existing applications for automating transactions, etc. According to the institution for RPA and artificial intelligence (AI), this technology can be used for processing software, data manipulation, and other software systems to communicate with.

RPA uses software package and methodologies that can work with most recent technologies like AI, machine learning (ML), voice recognition, and linguistic communication process to require automation for future level. Also, it becomes a basic requirement for corporations of all industries that wish to convey their business right along the digital transformation journey. Technologies like AI and ML can also be used to make the results better and error-free [3]. RPA is easy to configure, and no programming skills are needed to develop a robot. RPA software is non-invasive. RPA software accesses the computer system the way a human does. It accesses other systems through presentation layer. RPA is a robust platform and designed to meet the security, scalability, audibility, and change management of an enterprise [4]. The industrialization process has led to progressive task automation, which aim at economic efficiencies and better product quality. Firms started to mix advanced automation technologies with analytics and cognitive technologies [5].

Process automation is broadly categorized into two parts, namely hard automation and soft automation. Hard automation or fixed automation refers to a robot which is designed to perform a specific yet repetitive task. Soft automation or flexible automation refers to the programming of different tasks as per the need of the product. RPA is a part of soft automation [6]. Organizations now started with a proof of concept (POC) for validating the concept used in building a robot. After some time, organizations realized to set up a team for handling the robots as well as to do additional process required for the advancement of the robots [7]. Changes in workplace can take place when organizations opt RPA as a tool which replaces human with robots. This can create a fear in individuals about their jobs because employees are frightened and hard to learn about new technologies. On the other side almost, every job will be reworked not replaced [8]. RPA can also be used for creating intelligent systems in data extracted from real time system, considering time as an object for data abstraction [9]. The front office jobs like support, selling, requirement handling and back-office jobs like finance and human resource can be converted into RPA tasks. Back office processes like travel, billing, expenses, accounts payable, accounts receivable are best suited for the RPA processes, which results in cost and error reduction [10]. To make robots intelligent, AI plays a major role. Robots challenge AI to deal with real objects in the real world. A robot is a combination of sensors, mechanical effectors and computers and AI is applicable in all the mentioned components. Robotics and AI should be move simultaneously [11].

In the world of extreme competition, writing a manuscript involves understanding the topic in a better way by exploring, synthesizing, and evaluating it. Every individual wants to showcase their hard work for a unique idea having research in their field of interest and because writing a research chapter and then to search the suitable journals is not an easy task. In this chapter, we cite an application of RPA using which one can explore the best journals for manuscript publication in their research area. The present robot comprises a quick result for the best journals according to the Scopus indexed list of 2019 with ranking according to 2017 source normalized impact per paper (SNIP) using UiPath tool. Moreover, a workflow has been designed in the UiPath Studio which contains activities where a set of keywords as an input is taken from the user. Using Google Scholar, the published research chapter names are extracted with its URL and the description of authors and journal name mention under the title. The workflow works by scraping the data from Google Scholar, putting it in an excel sheet and then by matching the journal names found from data scraping with the source title of journals present in the Scopus indexed file. After matching the journal names, an output excel file shows the best-matched journals for the keywords given by the user in descending order of 2017 SNIP ranking.

The output for the same is mailed to the user containing the best top-ranking journals name for manuscript publication in excel sheet. The rest of the chapter is structured as follows. Step by step analysis of methodology is given in Section 19.2. In Section 19.3, the outcome of the study has provided as results. Finally, conclusions are given in Section 19.4.

19.2 ANALYSIS

UiPath tool plays an important role in finding the best-suited journals for manuscript publication. UiPath tool [12] has the following platforms which are given below:

1. **UiPath Studio:** This software is used to design the workflows and debug it by run file option to check for errors.
2. **UiPath Orchestrator:** It is a cloud platform provided by UiPath academy to run the workflow on the cloud by publishing the workflow as a package and running it on the cloud as a robot.
3. **UiPath Robot:** It is used to connect the local machine to the cloud (UiPath Orchestrator).

19.2.1 STEP BY STEP DESCRIPTION OF THE WORK

- **Step 1:** In UiPath studio a new project is set by clicking "Process" and filling the asked credentials like project name and project file location in the new generated box.
- **Step 2:** By clicking on "New" in the studio, a flowchart is created and then the activities are added using drag and drop functionality from the activity section.

The invention is described by flowchart as shown in Figure 19.1 which also describes the activities used in UiPath Studio:

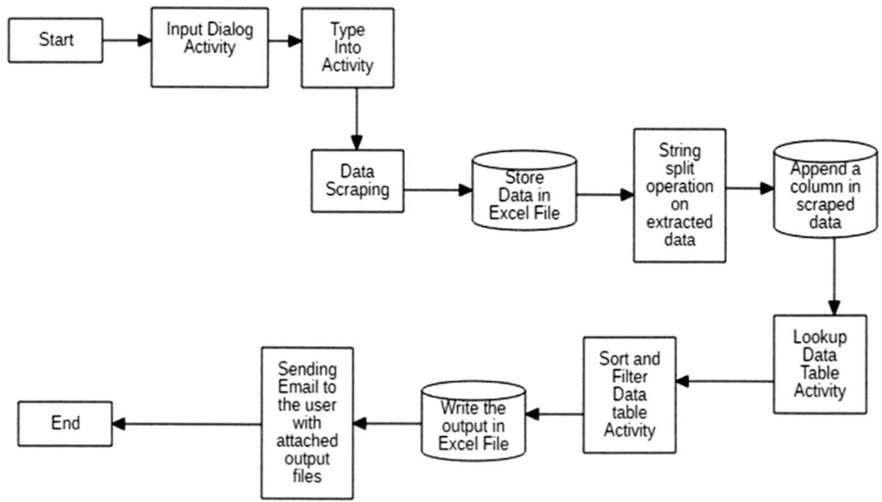

FIGURE 19.1 Flowchart of invention.

- **Step 3:** The flowchart diagram of workflow in UiPath which is divided into three parts: enter input into web browser followed by data scraping and generating output file followed by e-mail automation which automatically sends the output file to the user as shown in Figure 19.2.

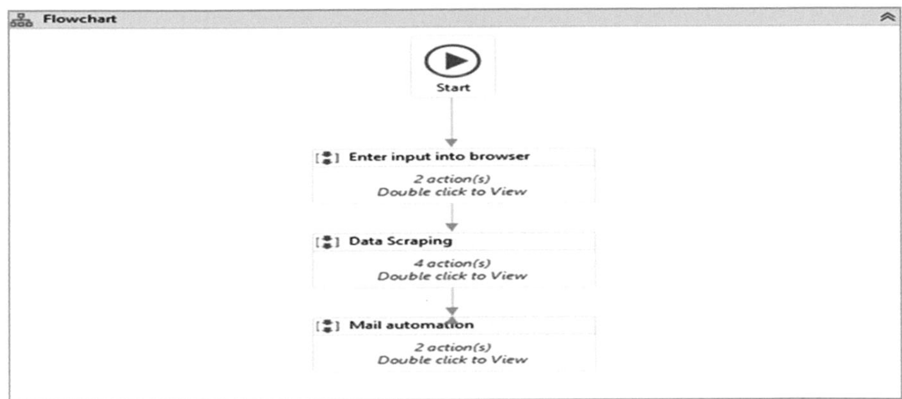

FIGURE 19.2 Flowchart activity.

- **Step 4:** In flowchart activity insert sequence activity in it. Join the sequence activity with start node. In sequence, the input dialog activity is used to take the keywords as an input from the user and type into activity to enter the credentials into a web browser ("Journal of " +Keywords+ "[k(enter)]"). Here "[k(enter)]" is a hotkey similar as press enter key from the keyboard as shown in Figure 19.3.

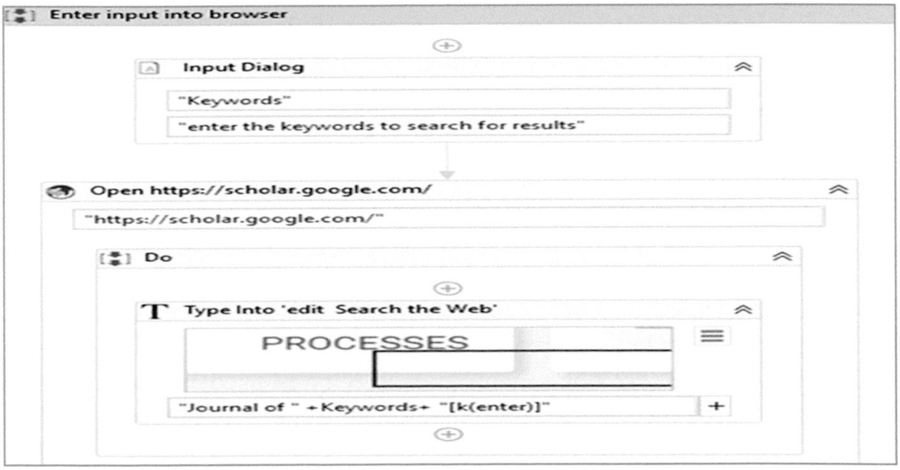

Enter input into browser
Input Dialog
"Keywords"
"enter the keywords to search for results"
Open https://scholar.google.com/
"https://scholar.google.com/"
Do
Type Into 'edit Search the Web'
PROCESSES
"Journal of " +Keywords+ "[k(enter)]"

FIGURE 19.3 Input dialog and type into activity.

➢ **Step 5:** The Scopus indexed file of 2019 is added as Sheet2 in AllData.xlsx file where column B1 was replaced as 'Source Title' and a last column in excel sheet is added as 'URL' (uniform resource locator) as shown in Figure 19.4.

B1 | Source Title

	A	B	C	D	E	F	G	H	I	J	K	L	
1	Sourcerecord id	Source Title	Print-ISSN	E-ISSN	Active or Inactive	Coverage	Article languag	2015 CiteScor	2015 SJR	2015 SNIP	2016 CiteScor	2016 SJR	20 SN
2	1.9E+10	21st Century Music	15343219		Inactive	2002-2011	ENG						
3	2.1E+10	2D Materials		20531583	Active	2014-ongc	ENG	5.89	4.602	1.009	4.26	2.314	0.9
4	2.1E+10	3 Biotech	2190572X	21905738	Active	2015-ongc	ENG		0.145	0.119	2.15	0.462	1.1
5	2.1E+10	3D Printing and Additive Manufacturing	23297662	23297670	Active	2014-ongc	ENG		0.388	2.100	0.80	0.547	1.3
6	21100854	3D Printing in Medicine		23656271	Active	2017-ongc	ENG						0.0
7	2.1E+10	3D Research		20926731	Active	2010-ongc	ENG	0.80	0.211	0.599	0.62	0.166	0.3
8	2E+10	3L: Language, Linguistics, Literature	01285157		Active	2008-ongc	ENG	0.38	0.521	0.758	0.38	0.298	0.9
9	145295	4OR	16194500	16142411	Active	2003-ongc	ENG	1.19	0.974	1.022	1.83	1.463	1.5
10	2.1E+10	A & A case reports	23257237		Active	2015-ongc	ENG				0.53	0.239	
11	1.6E+10	A + U-Architecture and Urbanism	03899160		Active	2002-ongc	JPN, ENG	0.00	0.100	0.000	0.01	0.101	0.0
12	5.7E+09	A Contrario	16607880		Active	2009-ongc	FRE, ENG	0.00	0.101	0.269	0.00	0.101	0.0
13	2E+10	A.M.A. American Journal of Diseases of Children	00968994		Inactive	1945-1955							
14	1.9E+10	A.M.A. archives of dermatology	00965359		Inactive	1955-1959							
15	2E+10	A.M.A. Archives of Dermatology and Syphilology	00965979		Inactive	1950-1954							
16	1.9E+10	A.M.A. archives of industrial health	05673933		Inactive	1954-1960							
17	2E+10	A.M.A. Archives of Industrial Hygiene and Occupational Medicir	00966703		Inactive	1950-1954							
18	1.9E+10	A.M.A. archives of internal medicine	08882479		Inactive	1950-1959							

Sheet1 | Sheet2

FIGURE 19.4 Sheet2 in AllData.xlsx file.

➢ **Step 6:** Now, data scraping as shown in Figure 19.5 is done where the title name, title URL and title index containing details is extracted and filled in a data table (by write range activity as shown in Figure 19.6) containing the above mentioned three elements as columns in excel file in Sheet1 as shown in Figure 19.7. The 'Name' column is generated by taking only column 'journal' into the data table using filter data table activity. Build data table activity is used to build a data table of column 'Name.' In for each activity as shown in Figure 19.8 which is a row by row loop the data table is converted into a string and then the journal name is fetched from it using assign activity and split operation on the string and using add data row activity the column is appended in the excel file as "D1" as shown in Figure 19.9.

➢ **Step 7:** To match the 'Name' column of Sheet1 with the 'Source Title' of Sheet2 column lookup activity is used where for each row in the data table a loop is made and the if condition says that if cell does not matches then assign "No match found" in URL column and increase row index by 1, else assign the URL in the

URL column is match found and increase row index by 1 as shown in Figure 19.10.

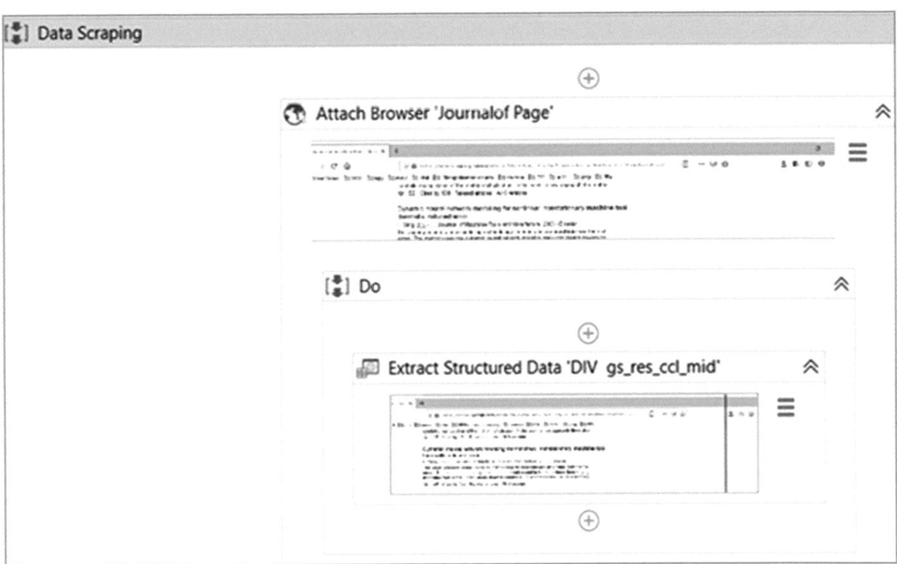

FIGURE 19.5 Data scraping activity.

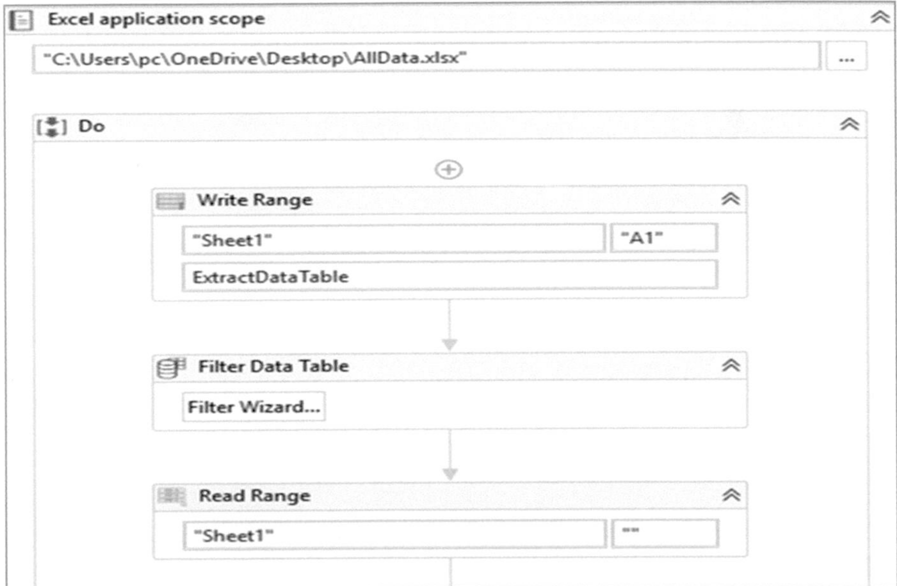

FIGURE 19.6 Write range activity.

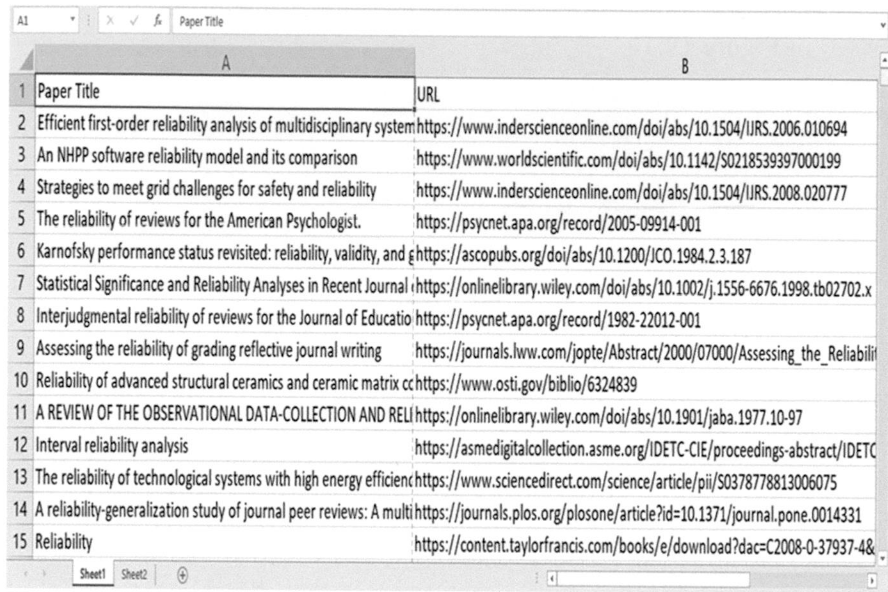

	A	B
1	Paper Title	URL
2	Efficient first-order reliability analysis of multidisciplinary system	https://www.inderscienceonline.com/doi/abs/10.1504/IJRS.2006.010694
3	An NHPP software reliability model and its comparison	https://www.worldscientific.com/doi/abs/10.1142/S0218539397000199
4	Strategies to meet grid challenges for safety and reliability	https://www.inderscienceonline.com/doi/abs/10.1504/IJRS.2008.020777
5	The reliability of reviews for the American Psychologist.	https://psycnet.apa.org/record/2005-09914-001
6	Karnofsky performance status revisited: reliability, validity, and g	https://ascopubs.org/doi/abs/10.1200/JCO.1984.2.3.187
7	Statistical Significance and Reliability Analyses in Recent Journal	https://onlinelibrary.wiley.com/doi/abs/10.1002/j.1556-6676.1998.tb02702.x
8	Interjudgmental reliability of reviews for the Journal of Educatio	https://psycnet.apa.org/record/1982-22012-001
9	Assessing the reliability of grading reflective journal writing	https://journals.lww.com/jopte/Abstract/2000/07000/Assessing_the_Reliabili
10	Reliability of advanced structural ceramics and ceramic matrix cc	https://www.osti.gov/biblio/6324839
11	A REVIEW OF THE OBSERVATIONAL DATA-COLLECTION AND RELI	https://onlinelibrary.wiley.com/doi/abs/10.1901/jaba.1977.10-97
12	Interval reliability analysis	https://asmedigitalcollection.asme.org/IDETC-CIE/proceedings-abstract/IDETC
13	The reliability of technological systems with high energy efficienc	https://www.sciencedirect.com/science/article/pii/S0378778813006075
14	A reliability-generalization study of journal peer reviews: A multi	https://journals.plos.org/plosone/article?id=10.1371/journal.pone.0014331
15	Reliability	https://content.taylorfrancis.com/books/e/download?dac=C2008-0-37937-4&

FIGURE 19.7 Sheet1 in AllData.xlsx file where scrapped data is stored.

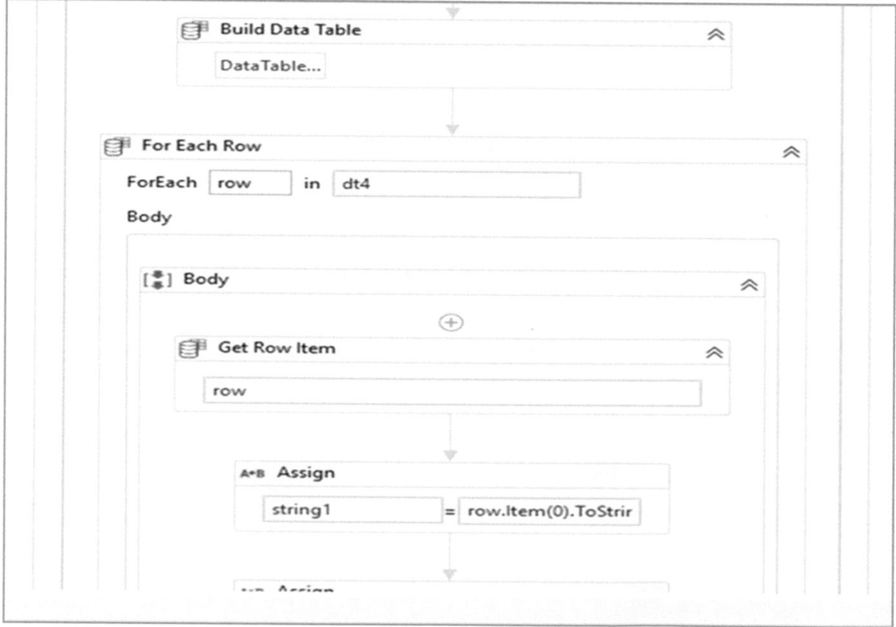

FIGURE 19.8 Build data table and for each activity.

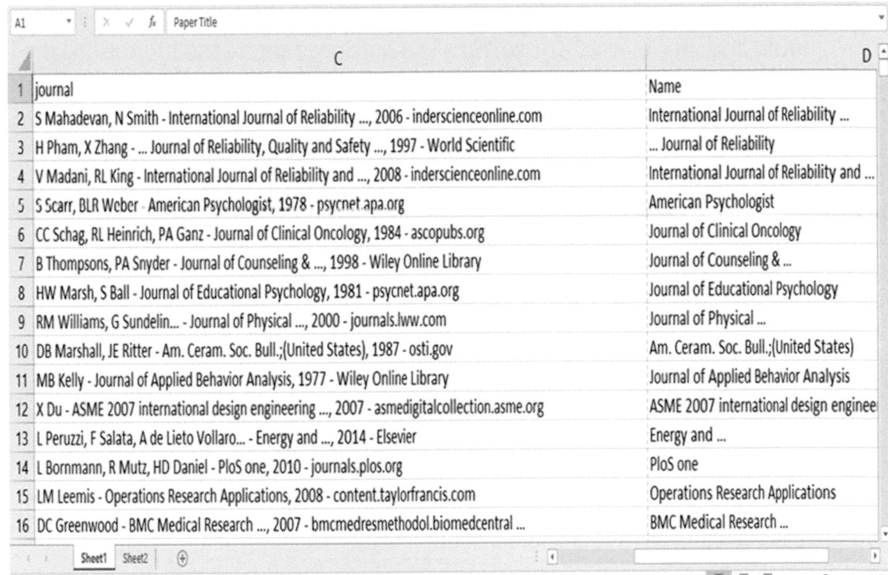

	C	D
1	journal	Name
2	S Mahadevan, N Smith - International Journal of Reliability ..., 2006 - inderscienceonline.com	International Journal of Reliability ...
3	H Pham, X Zhang - ... Journal of Reliability, Quality and Safety ..., 1997 - World Scientific	... Journal of Reliability
4	V Madani, RL King - International Journal of Reliability and ..., 2008 - inderscienceonline.com	International Journal of Reliability and ...
5	S Scarr, BLR Weber - American Psychologist, 1978 - psycnet.apa.org	American Psychologist
6	CC Schag, RL Heinrich, PA Ganz - Journal of Clinical Oncology, 1984 - ascopubs.org	Journal of Clinical Oncology
7	B Thompsons, PA Snyder - Journal of Counseling & ..., 1998 - Wiley Online Library	Journal of Counseling & ...
8	HW Marsh, S Ball - Journal of Educational Psychology, 1981 - psycnet.apa.org	Journal of Educational Psychology
9	RM Williams, G Sundelin... - Journal of Physical ..., 2000 - journals.lww.com	Journal of Physical ...
10	DB Marshall, JE Ritter - Am. Ceram. Soc. Bull.;(United States), 1987 - osti.gov	Am. Ceram. Soc. Bull.;(United States)
11	MB Kelly - Journal of Applied Behavior Analysis, 1977 - Wiley Online Library	Journal of Applied Behavior Analysis
12	X Du - ASME 2007 international design engineering ..., 2007 - asmedigitalcollection.asme.org	ASME 2007 international design enginee
13	L Peruzzi, F Salata, A de Lieto Vollaro... - Energy and ..., 2014 - Elsevier	Energy and ...
14	L Bornmann, R Mutz, HD Daniel - PloS one, 2010 - journals.plos.org	PloS one
15	LM Leemis - Operations Research Applications, 2008 - content.taylorfrancis.com	Operations Research Applications
16	DC Greenwood - BMC Medical Research ..., 2007 - bmcmedresmethodol.biomedcentral ...	BMC Medical Research ...

FIGURE 19.9 Filtered 'Name' column.

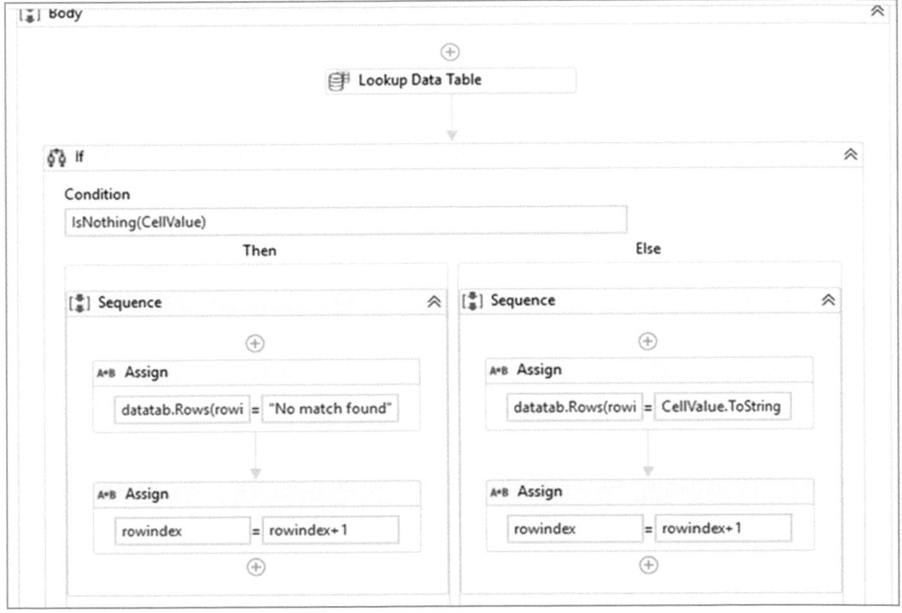

FIGURE 19.10 Lookup activity.

- **Step 8:** As the data will be stored in a data table variable sort data table activity is used for sorting the outcome into descending order of 2017 SNIP followed by filter data table which remove the "No match found rows" from the data table followed by write range activity as shown in Figure 19.11.

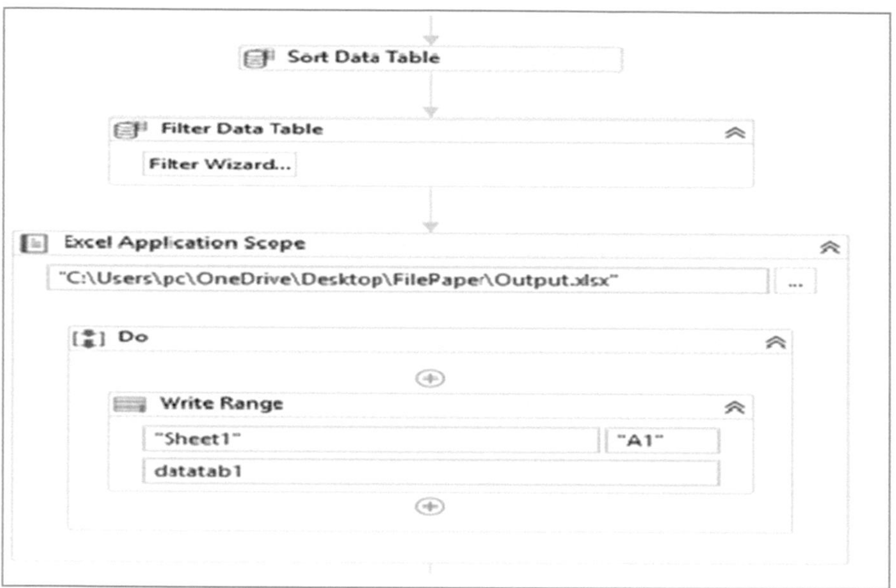

FIGURE 19.11 Sort data table, filter data table, write range activity.

19.3 RESULTS

In this section, we provide the outcome of searched keyword as results following steps 1–8 in the previous section. The output will be written in Output.xlsx excel file as shown in Figure 19.12.

To make the output available to the user an e-mail activity (such as Outlook, Gmail, etc.), is used which attaches the scrapped data excel file and the output excel file to send the user where user mail id is mentioned as an input in the mail automation activity as shown in Figure 19.13.

The whole workflow is published on the UiPath Orchestrator as shown in Figure 19.14 and run on the machine with UiPath Robot as shown in Figure 19.15.

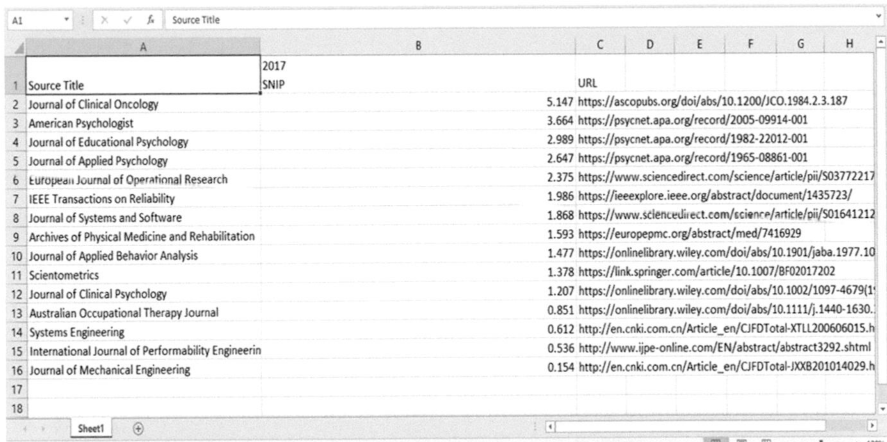

	A	B	C
1	Source Title	2017 SNIP	URL
2	Journal of Clinical Oncology	5.147	https://ascopubs.org/doi/abs/10.1200/JCO.1984.2.3.187
3	American Psychologist	3.664	https://psycnet.apa.org/record/2005-09914-001
4	Journal of Educational Psychology	2.989	https://psycnet.apa.org/record/1982-22012-001
5	Journal of Applied Psychology	2.647	https://psycnet.apa.org/record/1965-08861-001
6	European Journal of Operational Research	2.375	https://www.sciencedirect.com/science/article/pii/S03772217
7	IEEE Transactions on Reliability	1.986	https://ieeexplore.ieee.org/abstract/document/1435723/
8	Journal of Systems and Software	1.868	https://www.sciencedirect.com/science/article/pii/S01641212
9	Archives of Physical Medicine and Rehabilitation	1.593	https://europepmc.org/abstract/med/7416929
10	Journal of Applied Behavior Analysis	1.477	https://onlinelibrary.wiley.com/doi/abs/10.1901/jaba.1977.10
11	Scientometrics	1.378	https://link.springer.com/article/10.1007/BF02017202
12	Journal of Clinical Psychology	1.207	https://onlinelibrary.wiley.com/doi/abs/10.1002/1097-4679(1
13	Australian Occupational Therapy Journal	0.851	https://onlinelibrary.wiley.com/doi/abs/10.1111/j.1440-1630.
14	Systems Engineering	0.612	http://en.cnki.com.cn/Article_en/CJFDTotal-XTLL200606015.h
15	International Journal of Performability Engineerin	0.536	http://www.ijpe-online.com/EN/abstract/abstract3292.shtml
16	Journal of Mechanical Engineering	0.154	http://en.cnki.com.cn/Article_en/CJFDTotal-JXXB201014029.h

FIGURE 19.12 Output.xlsx file (final result).

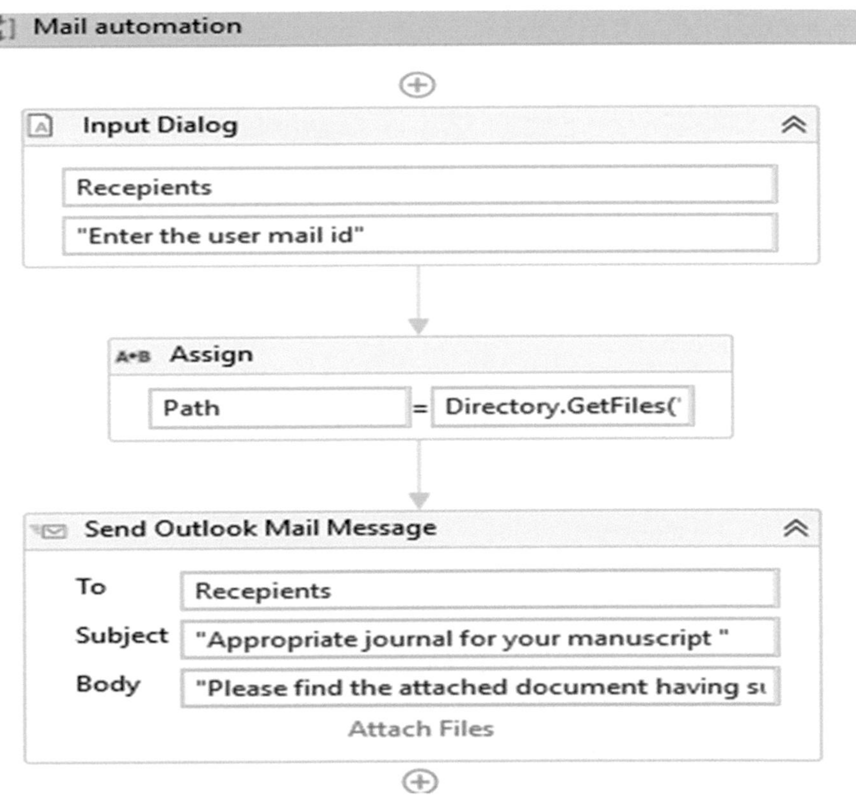

FIGURE 19.13 Mail automation.

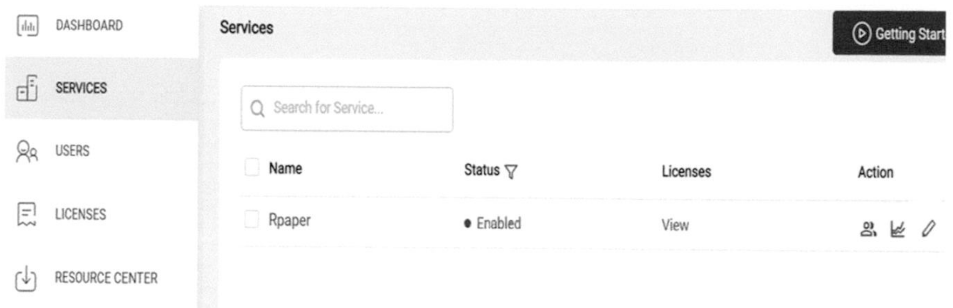

FIGURE 19.14 UiPath orchestrator cloud platform.

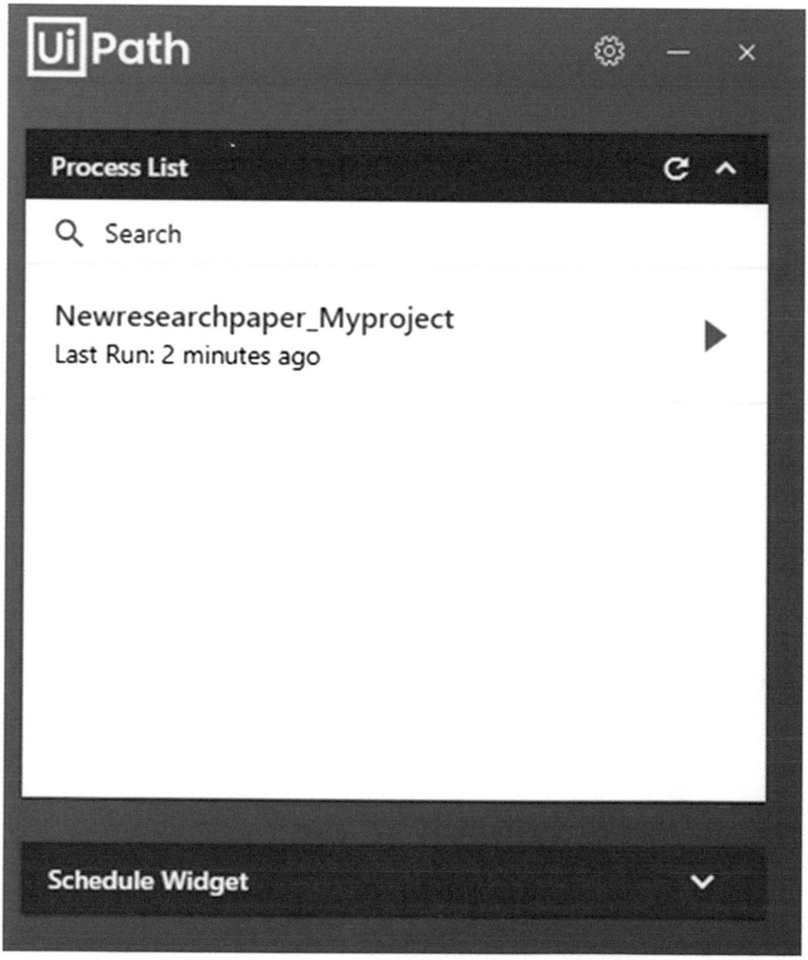

FIGURE 19.15 UiPath robot.

After running the robot on UiPath Orchestrator, the robot will send the generated "Output.xlsx" file on the provided e-mail id, which was entered by the user when robot asked to input the e-mail id. The output file includes "Source Title," i.e., name of the journals, "2017 SNIP," i.e., indexing done in decreasing order according to 2017 SNIP indexing and "URL," i.e., URL of the journals.

19.4 CONCLUSION

The invention can help the researchers to find the best (top-rated) journals name in their research area for publication. The user can easily find the results just by providing the related keywords and e-mail id to the robot in just 3 minutes which is very less as compared to manual search. The robot can be made available for everyone by providing an online platform to it like: .exe application or public cloud platform as it is now working on the orchestrator which has admin privileges only. The robot is using Scopus indexed file 2019 for finding the best journals, which can be further extended to other indexed files also.

KEYWORDS

- **journals**
- **mail automation**
- **robotic process automation (RPA)**
- **UiPath**

REFERENCES

1. Reddy, K. P. N., Harichandana, U., Alekhya, T., & Rajesh, M., (2019). A study of robotic process automation among artificial intelligence. *International Journal of Scientific and Research Publication, 9*, 392–397.
2. Madakam, S., Holmukhe, R. M., & Jaiswal, D. K., (2019). The future digital workforce: Robotic process automation (RPA). *JISTEM-Journal of Information Systems and Technology Management-US, 16*, 1–17.
3. Willcocks, L., & Lacity, M., (2018). Robotic process automation in the real world: How 3 companies are innovating with RPA. *Institute of Robotic Process Automation and Artificial Intelligence, 7*, 1–35.

4. Ansari, W. A., Diya, P., & Patil, S., (2019). A review on robotic process automation-the future of business organizations. *2nd International Conference on Advances in Science and Technology (ICAST)*. http://dx.doi.org/10.2139/ssrn.3372171.
5. Moffitt, K. C., Rozario, A. M., & Vasarhelyi, M. A., (2018). Robotic process automation for auditing. *Journal of Emerging Technologies in Accounting, 15*, 1–10.
6. Isaac, R., Muni, R., & Desai, K., (2018). Delineated analysis of robotic process automation tools. *Second International Conference on Advances in Electronics, Computer and Communications (ICAECC-2018), 9.*
7. Anagnoste, S., (2013). Setting up a robotic process automation center of excellence. *Management Dynamics in the Knowledge Economy, 6*, 307–322.
8. Fernandez, D., & Aman, A., (2018). Impacts of robotic process automation on global accounting services. *Asian Journal of Accounting and Governance, 9*, 127–140.
9. Rybina, G. V., & Danyakin, I. D., (2017). Combined method of automated temporal information acquisition for development of knowledge bases of intelligent systems. In: *2nd International Conference on Knowledge Engineering and Applications (ICKEA)* (pp. 123–127).
10. Aguirre, S., & Rodriguez, A., (2017). Automation of a business process using robotic process automation (RPA): A case study. In: Figueroa-García, J., López-Santana, E., Villa-Ramírez, J., & Ferro-Escobar, R., (eds.), *Applied Computer Sciences in Engineering: Communications in Computer and Information Science* (p. 742). Springer, Cham.
11. Brady, M., (1985). Artificial intelligence and robotics. *Artificial Intelligence, 26*, 79–121.
12. https://www.uipath.com (accessed on 22 February 2021).

PART V

Inequalities and Process Control Systems: Application and Methods

CHAPTER 20

(λ_{IR}, μ_{IR}) FUZZY IDEALS IN Γ-NEAR-RINGS

NEHA GAHLOT and NAGARAJU DASARI

Department of Mathematics and Statistics, Manipal University Jaipur, Rajasthan, India, E-mail: gahlotneha1995@gmail.com (N. Gahlot)

ABSTRACT

In this chapter, we study about an new idea (λ_{IR}, μ_{IR})-fuzzy ideals in Γ-near rings. Also we will study some different topics (λ_{IR}, μ_{IR})-cut set, on direct product (λ_{IR}, μ_{IR})-fuzzy ideals.

20.1 INTRODUCTION

In 1965, fuzzy sets were introduced by Zadeh [6]. Since then, many researchers applying this concept both in applied and pure fields of Mathematics. The notion of fuzzy groups was introduced by Rosenfeld [11]; Fuzzy subgroups and anti-fuzzy subgroups were studied by Biswas [4]; Dixit, Kumar, and Ajmal [16] introduced level subgroups and studied some results; Bhakat and Das [19] introduced $(\in, \in \vee q)$-fuzzy subgroups and studied some elementary properties; Ray [15] has studied product of fuzzy subgroups; (λ, μ) fuzzy normal subgroups was introduced by Yao [9] and continued his study on quotient structure.

Mukherjee and Sen [12] introduced fuzzy ideals of rings. Later, Dutta and Chanda [13] started studying fuzzy ideal structure in Γ-rings. Yao [14] studied (λ, μ)-fuzzy subrings and (λ, μ)-fuzzy ideals, which was the extension of his study on (λ, μ) fuzzy normal subgroups; Ali [19] studied the direct product of fuzzy subrings; Selvaraj and Sivakumar [10] studied direct product of (λ, μ) fuzzy subrings. Feng and Corsini [2] extended the study in (λ, μ)-fuzzy version of ideals, interior ideals, quasi-ideals, and bi-ideals; Anita and Sivakumar [1] introduced (λ, μ)-Anti fuzzy subrings and established the study through some results.

Zaid [7] introduced fuzzy sub-near-rings and ideals. Latter, Kim and Kim [5] studied few results in fuzzy ideals of near-rings; Hong, Jun, and Kim [3] extended this study. Narayana and Manikantan [21] introduced (∈, ∈ ∨ q)-fuzzy subnear-rings and (∈, ∈ ∨ q)-fuzzy ideals in near-rings. Chandrasekhara Rao and Swaminathan [17] studied anti homomorphism in near rings; Anitha and Aruna [20] recently started their study in T-fuzzy TL-ideal of G-near rings.

An algebraic structure Γ-near rings was introduced by Satyanarayana [8], which is a generalization of near-rings and Γ-rings. Many researchers have been studying fuzzy structure in Γ-near-rings because of his generalized structures. In this chapter, we have introduced (λ_R, μ_R) fuzzy ideals in Γ-near-rings and derived few basic results.

The structure of this chapter is as follows: After the introduction, in next Section 202, we give the definition of (λ_{IR}, μ_{IR})-fuzzy ideals in Γ-near ring, example, and verify few properties. In Section 20.3, we study (λ_{IR}, μ_{IR})-cut sets in Γ-near-rings and in last Section 20.4, we study some results in direct product of (λ_{IR}, μ_{IR})-fuzzy Γ-near rings.

For the sake of completeness, we present below a few definitions and results from the existing literature.

A non-empty set *N* together with two binary operations (+) and (.) is called a near-ring if it satisfy following conditions:

1. (N, +) is a (not necessarily abelian) group;
2. (N.) is a semigroup;
3. (u + v).w = u.w + v.w for all u, v, w ∈ N.

It is also called a right near-ring because the multiplication is distributive over the addition from the right-hand side. We simply use the word near-ring instead of right near-ring. We use xy in place of x.y.

➢ **Definition 20.1:** [11] A Fuzzy subset *A* defined on a Γ-near-ring *N* is said to be a fuzzy ideal of a *N* if:

i. $A(u - v) \geq \min\{A(u), A(v)\}$ for all u, v ∈ *N*
ii. $A(u + v - u) \geq A(v)$, for u, v, w ∈ *N*
iii. $A(u\alpha(v + w) - u\alpha w) \geq A(v)$, for u, v, w *N* and $\alpha \in \Gamma$.
iv. $A(u\alpha v) \geq A(u)$, for u, v ∈ *N* and $\alpha \in \Gamma$.

A fuzzy subset with (i), (ii) and (iv) is called a fuzzy right ideal of *N* whereas a fuzzy subset with (i), (ii) and (iii) is called a fuzzy left ideal of *N*.

From the above definition it follows that $A(0) \geq A(u)$ for all elements u of N.

For a fuzzy subset A of a set X and $t \in [0, 1]$, the level set of A is defined as $A_t = \{u \in X \mid A(u) \geq t\}$.

A fuzzy point u_t is said to belong to (resp. be quasi-coincident with) a fuzzy subset A, written as $u_t \in A$ (resp. $u_t qA$), if $A(u) \geq t$ (resp. $A(u) + t > 1$), $u_t \in A$ or $u_t qA$ will be denoted by $u_t \in \vee q\Lambda$.

Let N and M be two Γ-near rings with identity 0 and 0^1, respectively, then product $N \times M$ is also a Γ-near ring with the identity $(0, 0^1)$ if we define $(u_1, v_1)(u_2, v_2) = (u_1u_2, v_1v_2)$ for all $(u_1, v_1), (u_2, v_2) \in N \times M$. Moreover, the inverse element of any $(u, v) \in N \times M$ is (x, y) $N \times M$ if and only if x is the inverse of u in N and y is the inverse element of v in M.

- **Definition 20.2:** [18] we mean a fuzzy subset by function from X into [0,1]. The set of all fuzzy subsets of X is called fuzzy power set of X and is denoted by $I^X = [0, 1]^X$.

20.2 (λ_{IR}, μ_{IR}) FUZZY IDEAL OF Γ-NEAR-RINGS

A fuzzy subset A of N is said to be a (λ_{IR}, μ_{IR}) fuzzy ideal of Γ-Near-ring N if:

i. $A(u - v) \vee \lambda_{IR} \geq \min\{A(u), A(v)\} \wedge \mu_{IR}$, for $u, v \in N$;
ii. $A(v + u - v) \vee \lambda_{IR} \geq A(u) \wedge \mu_{IR}$, for $u, v \in N$;
iii. $A(u\alpha(v + w) - u\alpha w) \vee \lambda_{IR} \geq A(v) \wedge \mu_{IR}$, for $u, v, w \in N$ and $\alpha \in \Gamma$;
iv. $A(u\alpha v) \vee \lambda_{IR} \geq A(u) \wedge \mu_{IR}$, for $u, v \in N$ and $\alpha \in \Gamma$.

A fuzzy subset satisfies (i), (ii) and (iv) it is (λ_{IR}, μ_{IR}) fuzzy right ideal of N whereas a fuzzy subset satisfies (i), (ii) and (iii) it is (λ_{IR}, μ_{IR}) fuzzy left ideal of N.

Here λ_{IR}, μ_{IR} are two real numbers lying between 0 and 1 with $\lambda_{IR} < \mu_{IR}$ and also min(m, n) and max(m, n) is represented by $(m \wedge n)$ and $(m \vee n)$ respectively.

Obviously, an $(\in, \in Vq)$-fuzzy Γ-near ring (fuzzy ideal) of N is a (λ_{IR}, μ_{IR})-fuzzy Γ-near ring (fuzzy ideal) of N with $\lambda_{IR} = 0$ and $\mu_{IR} = 0.5$.

- **Example 20.1:** Let consider integers modulo 4, $Z_4 = \{0, 1, 2, 3\}$ be a near ring and let Γ = {set of integers} be a set of operations defined as follow:

$$A(u) = \begin{cases} 0.6, & if\ u \in Z_4 \\ 0, & if\ u \notin Z_4 \end{cases}$$

Clearly, Z_4 is a near-ring. Now, if $\lambda_{IR} = 0.5$ and $\mu_{IR} = 0.9$, then A is a (λ_{IR}, μ_{IR}) fuzzy ideal of Γ-near-ring Z_4.

➤ **Example 20.2:** Let N = {p, q, r, s} be a set and Γ be a set of operation defined as follows:

+	p	q	r	s
p	p	q	r	s
q	q	p	r	s
r	s	r	q	p
s	r	s	p	q

α	p	q	r	s
p	p	p	p	p
q	p	p	p	p
r	p	p	p	p
s	p	q	r	s

Clearly, N is a Γ-near-ring. By defining A(q) = A(s) < A(q) < A(p) clearly if $\lambda_{IR} \leq A(p)$ and $\mu_{IR} > A(p)$, then A is a (λ_{IR}, μ_{IR}) fuzzy ideal of M.

➤ **Lemma 20.1:** Let A be a (λ_{IR}, μ_{IR}) fuzzy ideal of a Γ-near-ring N. Then $A(0) \vee \lambda_{IR} \geq A(u) \wedge \mu_{IR}$, for every $u \in N$ where 0 is the additive identity of N.

➤ **Theorem 20.1:** If A is a fuzzy subset of a Γ-Near-ring N, then the following are equivalent:

i. A is a (λ_{IR}, μ_{IR}) fuzzy ideal of N.
ii. A_t is an ideal of N for any $t \in (\lambda_{IR}, \mu_{IR}]$.

➤ **Proof 20.1:** (i) ⇒ (ii)

For any $t \in (\lambda_{IR}, \mu_{IR}]$, since A is a fuzzy ideal of N clearly $A_t \neq \varphi$. Now we want to show that A_t is an ideal of N:

i. for every $u, v \in A_t$, $A(u - v) \vee \lambda_{IR} \geq \min(A(u), A(v)) \Lambda\, \mu_{IR} = (t, t)\, \Lambda\, \mu_{IR} = t$. Thus $u - v \in A_t$;
ii. let for every $u \in A_t$, $v \in N$, $A(v + u - v) \vee \lambda_{IR} \geq A(u) \vee \mu_{IR} = (t, t)\, \Lambda\, \mu_{IR} = t$. So, $v + u - v \in A_t$.
iii. let for every $v \in A_t$, $u, w \in N$ and $\alpha \in \Gamma$, $A(u\alpha(v + w) - v\alpha w) \vee \lambda_{IR} \geq A(v)\, \Lambda\, \mu_{IR} = (t, t)\, \Lambda\, \mu_{IR} = t$. Thus, $u\alpha(v + w) - v\alpha w\, A_t$. Hence A_t is an ideal of N.

(ii) ⇒ (i)

Suppose that A_t is an ideal of N and $t \in (\lambda_{IR}, \mu_{IR}]$. Now we have to prove that A is an (λ_{IR}, μ_{IR}) fuzzy ideal of Γ-near ring N.

i. Let for any $u, v \in A_t$ if $A(u - v) \vee \lambda_{IR} < (A(u) \wedge A(v))\, \Lambda\, \mu_{IR} = t$ thus $A(u - v) \vee \lambda_{IR} < t$ (since $t \in (\lambda_{IR}, \mu_{IR}]$) so, $u - v \notin A_t$ which is contradiction therefore $A(u - v) \vee \lambda_{IR} \geq (A(u) \wedge A(v))\, \Lambda\, \mu_{IR}$.

Similarly we can prove all conditions to prove A is (λ_{IR}, μ_{IR}) fuzzy ideal of Γ-near ring N.

- **Theorem 20.2:** Let P be any non-empty subset of an Γ-near ring N and A_P be an (λ_{IR}, μ_{IR}) fuzzy set in N defined by $A_P(u) = \begin{cases} t, & if\ u \in P \\ s, & if\ u \notin P \end{cases}$ For all u ∈ M and s, t ⊂ (λ_{IR}, μ_{IR}] with t < s. Then A_P is (λ_{IR}, μ_{IR}) fuzzy ideal of Γ-near ring N if and only if P is an ideal of Γ-near ring N. Also $N_A p = P$.
- **Proof 20.2:** It is straight forward.
- **Corollary 20.1:** Let R be a non-empty subset of a Γ-near ring N. Then it is ideal of N iff δ_R is a (λ_{IR}, μ_{IR}) fuzzy ideal of Γ-near ring N (where δ_R is a characteristic function of R).
- **Theorem 20.3:** Let A, B be (λ_{IR}, μ_{IR}) fuzzy left ideals (right ideals) of Γ-near ring N. Then A + B is also a (λ_{IR}, μ_{IR}) fuzzy left ideal (right ideal) of N, where $(A + B)(u) = \sup\{A(u_1) \wedge B(u_2) \mid u = u_1 + u_2\}$, for all u ∈ N.
- **Proof 20.3:** For all u, v ∈ N and $\alpha \in \Gamma$, we have:
  i. $(A + B)(u - v) \vee \lambda_{IR} = \sup\{A(u_1 - u_2) \wedge B(v_1 - v_2) \mid u = u_1 + v_1, v = u_2 + v_2\} \vee \lambda_{IR} \geq \sup\{A(u_1) \wedge A(u_2) \wedge B(v_1) \wedge B(v_2) \wedge \mu_{IR} \mid u = u_1 + v_1, v = u_2 + v_2\} = \sup\{A(u_1) \wedge B(v_1) \mid u = u_1 + v_1\} = \sup\{A(u_2) \wedge B(v_2) \mid v = u_2 + v_2\} \wedge \mu_{IR} = (A + B)(u) \wedge (A + B)(v) \wedge \mu_{IR}$.
  ii. $(A + B)(v + u - v) \vee \lambda_{IR} = \sup\{A(v + u_1 - v) \wedge B(v + u_2 - v) \mid u = u_1 + u_2\} \vee \lambda_{IR} \geq \sup\{A(u_1) \wedge B(u_2) \wedge \mu_{IR} \mid u = u_1 + u_2\} = \sup\{A(u_1) \wedge B(u_2) \mid u = u_1 + u_2\} \wedge \mu_{IR} = (A + B)(u) \wedge \mu_{IR}$.
  iii. $(A + B)(u\alpha(v + w) - u\alpha w) \vee \lambda_{IR} = \sup A(u\alpha(v_1 + w) - u\alpha w) \wedge B(u\alpha(v_1 + w) - u\alpha w) \mid v = v_1 + v_2\} \vee \lambda_{IR} \geq \sup\{A(v_1) \wedge B(v_2) \vee \mu_{IR} \mid v = v_1 + v_2\} = \sup\{A(v_1) \wedge B(v_2) \mid v = v_1 + v_2\} \wedge \mu_{IR} = (A + B)(v) \wedge \mu_{IR}$. So, A + B is a ($\lambda_{IR}$, μ_{IR}) fuzzy left ideals of N.
- **Definition 20.3:** [17]: Let N and M be Γ-Near-rings. A mapping $\eta: N \to M$ is called a homomorphism if $\eta(u + v) = \eta(u) + \eta(v)$ and $\eta(u\alpha v) = \eta(u)\alpha\eta(v)$ for all u, v ∈ N and $\alpha \in \Gamma$.
- **Theorem 20.4:** Let η: N → M be a homomorphism and A be (λ_{IR}, μ_{IR})-fuzzy ideal of Γ-Near-ring N. Then η(A) is also an (λ_{IR}, μ_{IR}) fuzzy ideal of a Γ-Near-ring M. Where; $\eta(A)(v) = \inf_{u \in N} \{A(u) \mid \eta(u) = v\}$ for all v ∈ M.
- **Proof 20.4:** Let A be an (λ_{IR}, μ_{IR}) fuzzy ideal of Γ-Near Ring N. Now we want to show that η(A) is a (λ_{IR}, μ_{IR}) fuzzy ideal of Γ-Near Ring M.

i. For any $u_1, u_2 \in N$ and $v_1, v_2 \in M$ we have $\eta(A)(v_1 - v_2) \vee \lambda_{IR} = \inf_{u1, u2 \in N} \{A(u_1 - u_2) \mid \eta(u_1 - u_2) = v_1 - v_2\} \vee \lambda_{IR} = \inf_{u1, u2 \in N} \{A(u_1 - u_2) \vee \lambda_{IR} \mid \eta(u_1 - u_2) = v_1 - v_2\} \geq \inf_{u1, u2 \in N} \{(A(u_1) \wedge A(u_2)) \wedge \mu_{IR} \mid \eta(u_1) = v_1, \eta(u_2) = v_2\} = \inf_{u1 \in N} \{(A(u_1)) \wedge \mu_{IR} \mid \eta(u_1) = v_1\} \wedge \inf_{u2 \in N} \{(A(u_2)) \wedge \mu_{IR} \mid \eta(u_2) = v_2\} = \eta(A)(v_1) \wedge \eta(A)(v_2) \wedge \mu_{IR}$.

ii. For any $u_1, u_2 \in N$ and $v_1, v_2 \in M$ we have $\eta(A)(v_2 + v_1 - v_2) \vee \lambda_{IR} = \inf_{u1}, u_2 \in N \{A(u_2 + u_1 - u_2) \mid \eta(u_2 + u_1 - u_2) = v_2 + v_1 - v_2\} \vee \lambda_{IR} = \inf_{u1, u2 \in N}\{A(u_2 + u_1 - u_2) \vee \lambda_{IR} \mid f(u_2 + u_1 - u_2) = v_2 + v_1 - v_2\} \geq \inf_{u1 \in N} \{(A(u_1)) \wedge \mu_{IR} \mid \eta(u_1) = v_1)\} = \inf_{u1 \in N} \{(A(u_1)) \wedge \mu_{IR} \mid f(u_1) = v_1\} \wedge \mu_{IR} = A(v_1) \wedge \mu_{IR}$.

iii. For any $v, u_1, u_2 \in N$ and $v', w_1, w_2 \in M$ and $\alpha \in \Gamma$ then we have then we have $\eta(A)(w_1\alpha(v' + w_2) - w_1\alpha w_2) \vee \lambda_{IR} = \inf_{v, u1, u2 \in N} \{A(u_1\alpha(v + u_2) - u_1\alpha u_2) \mid \eta(u_1\alpha(v + u_2) - u_1\alpha u_2) = w_1\alpha(v' + w_2) - w_1\alpha w_2\} \vee \lambda_{IR} = \inf_{v, u1, u2 \in N} \{A(u_1\alpha(v + u_2) - u_1\alpha u_2) \vee \lambda_{IR} \mid \eta(u_1\alpha(v + u_2) - u_1\alpha u_2) = w_1\alpha(v' + w_2) - w_1\alpha w_2\} \geq \inf_{v \in N} \{A(v) \wedge \mu_{IR} \mid \eta(v) = v')\} = A(v') \wedge \mu_{IR}$.

iv. Let $u_1, u_2 \in N$ and $v_1, v_2 \in M$, then we have $\eta(A)(v_1\alpha v_2) \vee \lambda_{IR} = \inf_{v, u1, u2 \in N} \{A(u_1\alpha u_2) \mid \eta(u_1\alpha u_2) = v_1\alpha v_2\} \vee \lambda_{IR} = \inf_{v, u1, u2 \in N}\{A(u_1 u_2) \vee \lambda_{IR} \mid \eta(u_1\alpha u_2) = v_1\alpha v_2\} \geq \inf_{u \in N} \{(A(u_1)) \wedge \mu_{IR} \mid \eta(u_1) = v_1\} = \inf_{u1 \in N} \{(A(u_1)) \Lambda\mu_{IR} \mid \eta(u_1) = v_1\} = \mu_{IR} = A(v_1) \wedge \mu_{IR}$.

Hence $\eta(A)$ is also an (λ_{IR}, μ_{IR}) fuzzy ideal of a Γ-Near-ring M.

- **Theorem 20.5:** Let $\eta: N \rightarrow M$ is called a homomorphism and D be an (λ_{IR}, μ_{IR}) fuzzy ideal of a Γ-Near ring M, then $\eta^{-1}(D)$ is also an (λ_{IR}, μ_{IR}) fuzzy ideal of a Γ-Near ring N. Where $\eta^{-1}(D)(x) = D(\eta(x))$

- **Proof 20.5:**

i. For any $u, v \in N$ then we have $\eta^{-1}(D)(u - v) \vee \lambda_{IR} = D(\eta(u - v)) \vee \lambda_{IR}$.
$= D(\eta(u) - \eta(v)) \vee \lambda_{IR} \geq D(\eta(u)) \wedge D(\eta(v)) \wedge \mu_{IR} = \eta^{-1}(D)(u) \wedge \eta^{-1}(D)(v) \wedge \mu_{IR}$.

ii. For any $u, v \in N$ then we have $\eta^{-1}(D)(v + u - v) \vee \lambda_{IR} = D(\eta(v + u - v)) \vee \lambda_{IR}$.
$= D(\eta(v) + \eta(u) - \eta(v)) \vee \lambda_{IR} \geq D(\eta(u)) \wedge \mu_{IR} = \eta^{-1}(D)(u) \wedge \mu_{IR}$.

iii. For any $u, v, w \in N$ and $\alpha \in \Gamma$, we have $\eta^{-1}(D)(u\alpha(v + w) - u\alpha w) \vee \lambda_{IR}$.
$= D(\eta(u\alpha(v + w) - u\alpha w)) \vee \lambda_{IR} = D(\eta(u)\alpha(\eta(v) + \eta(w)) - \eta(u)\alpha\eta(w)) \vee \lambda_{IR} \geq D(\eta(v)) \wedge \mu_{IR} = \eta^{-1}(D)(v) \wedge \mu_{IR}$.

iv. Let for any $u, v \in N$ and $\alpha \in \Gamma$ then we have $\eta^{-1}(D)(u\alpha v) \vee \lambda_{IR}$.
$= D(\eta(u\alpha v)) \vee \lambda_{IR} = D(\eta(u)\alpha\eta(v)) \vee \lambda_{IR} \geq D(\eta(u)) \wedge \mu_{IR} = \eta^{-1}(D)(u) \wedge \mu_{IR}$. Hence η^{-1}(D) is a (λ_{IR}, μ_{IR}) fuzzy ideal of Γ-Near Ring *N*.

- **Theorem 20.6:** Let I be an ideal of Γ-near ring M and A be a (λ_{IR}, μ_{IR}) fuzzy subset of M. If the fuzzy subset θ of M/I, defined by θ(u + I) = A(u), for all u M, is an (λ_{IR}, μ_{IR}) fuzzy ideal of near ring M/I then A is also (λ_{IR}, μ_{IR}) fuzzy ideal of Γ-near ring M.
- **Proof 20.6:** Let I is an ideal of Γ-near ring M and μ be a (λ_{IR}, μ_{IR}) fuzzy subset of M. Suppose the fuzzy subset θ of M/I, defined by θ(u + I) = A(u), for all u ЄM and α Є Γ, is (λ_{IR}, μ_{IR}) fuzzy ideal of Γ-near ring M/I and for u, v Є M. $A(u - v) \vee \lambda_{IR} = \theta(u - v + I) \vee \lambda_{IR} = \theta(u + I - (u + I)) \vee \lambda_{IR} \geq \min \theta(u + I), \theta(v + I) \wedge \mu_{IR} = \min \{A(u) \wedge \mu_{IR}, A(v) \wedge \mu_{IR}\}$. $A(v + u - v) \vee \lambda_{IR} = \theta(v + u - v + I) \vee \lambda_{IR} = \theta((v + I) + (u + I) - (v + I)) \vee \lambda_{IR} \geq \theta(u + I) \wedge \mu_{IR} = A(u) \wedge \mu_{IR}$. $A(u\alpha(v + w) - u\alpha w) \vee \lambda_{IR} = \theta(u\alpha(v + w) - u\alpha w + I) \vee \lambda_{IR} = \theta((u + I)\alpha((v + I) + (w + I)) - (u + I)\alpha(w + I))) \vee \lambda_{IR} \geq \theta(v + I) \wedge \mu_{IR} = A(v) \wedge \mu_{IR}$ Hence A is an (λ_{IR}, μ_{IR}) fuzzy ideal of Γ-near ring M.
- **Theorem 20.7:** If $\{A_i(u) \mid i \in I\}$ be a family of (λ_{IR}, μ_{IR})fuzzy ideals of Γ-near ring M, then $\bigvee_{i \in I} A_i$ is also (λ_{IR}, μ_{IR}) fuzzy ideal of Γ-near ring M.
- **Proof 20.7:** It is straightforward.
- **Theorem 20.8:** If $\{A_i(u) \mid i \in I\}$ be a family of (λ_{IR}, μ_{IR}) fuzzy ideals of Γ-near ring M, then $\bigwedge_{i \in I} A_i$ is also (λ_{IR}, μ_{IR}) fuzzy ideal of Γ-near ring M.
- **Proof 20.8:** It is straightforward.
- **Theorem 20.9:** Given a (λ_{IR}, μ_{IR}) fuzzy ideal A of an Γ-near ring M, and suppose A^* is a fuzzy set in M defined by $A^*(u) = A(u) + 1 - A(0)$ for all u Є M. Then A^* is also a (λ_{IR}, μ_{IR}) fuzzy ideal of N.
- **Proof 20.9:** *Note that* $A^*(0) = A(0) + 1 - A(0) = 1$ and for $A^*(u - v) \vee \lambda_{IR} = (A(u - v) + 1 - A(0)) \vee \lambda_{IR} \geq \min\{A(u), A(v)\} \vee \lambda_{IR} + (1 \vee \lambda_{IR}) - (A(0) \vee \lambda_{IR}) = \min\{A((u) + 1 - A(0)) \wedge \mu_{IR}, (A((v) + 1 - A(0)) \wedge \mu_{IR}\} = \min\{A^*(u) \wedge \mu_{IR}, A^*(v) \wedge \mu_{IR}\}$. $A^*(v + u - v) \vee \lambda_{IR} = (A(v + u - v) + 1 - A(0)) \vee \lambda_{IR} \geq A(u) \vee \lambda_{IR} + (1 \vee \lambda_{IR}) - (A(0) \vee \lambda_{IR}) = A((u) + 1 - A(0)) \wedge \mu_{IR} = A^*(u) \wedge \mu_{IR}$. $A^*(v\alpha(u + w) - v\alpha w) \vee \lambda_{IR} = (A(v\alpha(u + w) - v\alpha w) + 1 - A(0)) \vee \lambda_{IR} \geq A(u) \vee \lambda_{IR} + (1 \vee \lambda_{IR}) - (A(0) \vee \lambda_{IR}) = A((u) + 1 - A(0)) \wedge \mu_{IR} = A^*(u) \wedge \mu_{IR}$. Hence A^* is a normal (λ_{IR}, μ_{IR}) fuzzy ideal of N. Obviously that $A \subseteq A^*$.
- **Definition 20.4:** By a (λ_{IR}, μ_{IR}) fuzzy subset of a set X, we mean a function from X into [0,1]. The set of all (λ_{IR}, μ_{IR}) fuzzy subsets of X is called (λ_{IR}, μ_{IR}) fuzzy power set of X and is denoted by $I^X_{\lambda IR, \mu IR} = [0,1]^X$.

- **Lemma 20.2:** Let A ∈ $I^{M}_{\lambda IR,\ \mu IR}$. Then A is a ($\lambda_{IR}$, μ_{IR}) fuzzy ideal Γ-near rings of M if and only if the level subset A_t is a Γ-near ring of N for all t ∈ Im(A).
- **Proof 20.10:** It is straightforward.

20.3 (λ_{IR}, μ_{IR})-CUT SET

- **Definition 20.5:** Based on the notion of an (Є, Є vq)-level subset defined in, we introduce the concept of a (λ_{IR}, μ_{IR})-cut set of a fuzzy subset. Let A be a fuzzy subset of a set X and t ∈ [0,1]. Then the subset $A_t^{(\lambda_R, \mu_R)}$ of X defined by:

$$A_t^{(\lambda_R,\mu_R)} = \{x \in X / A(u) \vee \lambda_R \geq t \wedge \mu_R \ or \ A(u) > 2\mu_R - t \vee \lambda_R\}$$

Is said to be a (λ_R, μ_R)-cut set of A. We denote u_t ∈ (λ_R, μ_R)A if u ∈ $A_t^{(\lambda_R, \mu_R)}$

$$A_t^{(\lambda_R,\mu_R)} = \begin{cases} X, & if\ t \leq \lambda_R \\ A_T, & if\ \lambda_R < t \leq \mu_R \\ A_{(2\mu_R - t)\vee\lambda_R}, & if\ t > \mu_R \end{cases}$$

is a (λ_R, μ_R)-cut set of A.

- **Theorem 20.10:** Let A be a (λ_{IR}, μ_{IR})-fuzzy Γ-near ring (fuzzy ideal) of N, for all t ∈ [0,1] if and only if $A_t^{(\lambda_R, \mu_R)}$ is a fuzzy ideals in Γ-near ring N or $A_t^{(\lambda_R, \mu_R)} = \emptyset$.
- **Proof 20.11:** We only prove the case of a (λ_R, μ_R)-fuzzy Γ-near ring (fuzzy ideal) of N. If t ≥ λ_R, then $A_t^{(\lambda_R, \mu_R)}$ = N. If λ_R < t ≤ μ_R, then $A_t^{(\lambda_R, \mu_R)}$ = A_t and A_t is a Γ-near ring (ideal) of N from Theorem 20.2. If t > μ_R, then $A_t^{(\lambda_R, \mu_R)}$ = $A_{(2R\ -\ t)\ \wedge\ \lambda R}$ and (2μ_R – t) ∧ λ_R ∈ [λ_R, μ_R). So, $A_t^{(\lambda_R, \mu_R)}$ is a Γ-near-ring (ideal) of N from Theorem 20.1.

20.4 ON DIRECT PRODUCT OF (λ_{IR}, μ_{IR})-FUZZY Γ-NEAR RING

Let N and M be two Γ-near rings with identity 0 and 0` respectively, then Γ-Near ring N × M is an identity (0, 0`) if we define (u_1, v_1)(u_2, v_2) = (u_1u_2, v_1v_2) for all (u_1, v_1)(u_2, v_2) Є N × M. Moreover, the inverse element of any (u, v) Є N χ M is (x, y) Є N × M if and only if x is the inverse of u in N and y is the inverse element of v in M.

- **Definition 20.6:** [10] Let A and B be two (λ_{IR}, μ_{IR}) fuzzy sub-set of X and Y, respectively. Then the product of A and B, denoted by $(A \times B) \vee \lambda_{IR}$ is a (λ_{IR}, μ_{IR}) fuzzy sub-set of $(X \times Y) \vee \lambda_{IR}$ defined as follows; $((A \times B)(u, v) \vee \lambda_{IR} = ((A(u))\,(B(v)) \wedge \mu_{IR})$. Where sum, multiplication, inverse of (λ_{IR}, μ_{IR}) defined as follow:

$$((q_1, s_1) + (q_2, s_2)) \vee \lambda_{IR} = (q_1 + q_2, s_1 + s_2) \wedge \mu_{IR}$$
$$((q_1, s_1).(q_2, s_2)) \vee \lambda_{IR} = (q_1q_2, s_1s_2) \wedge \mu_{IR}$$
$$-(q, s) \vee \lambda_{IR} = (-q, -s) \wedge \mu_{IR}$$

- **Theorem 20.11:** If A and B be two (λ_{IR}, μ_{IR}) fuzzy ideals of Γ-Near Rings M and N, respectively then A × B is a (λ_{IR}, μ_{IR}) fuzzy ideal of M × N.
- **Proof 20.12:** Let $(u_1, v_1), (u_1, v_2) \vee \lambda_{IR} \in (M \times N) \vee \lambda_{IR}$. Now,
  i. $[(A \times B)((u_1, v_1) - (u_1, v_2))] \vee \lambda_{IR} = [(A \times B)((u_1 - u_2), (v_1 - v_2)) \vee \lambda_{IR}] = \{A(u_1 - u_2) \wedge B(u_1 - v_2)\} \wedge \mu_{IR} \geq \{(A(u_1) \wedge A(u_2)) \wedge \mu_{IR}) \wedge (B(v_1) \wedge B(v_2)) \wedge \mu_{IR}) \wedge \mu_{IR}\} = \{((A(u_1) \wedge B(v_1)) \wedge (A(u_2) \wedge B(v_2)) \wedge \mu_{IR}\} = \{(A{\times}B)(u_1, v_1) \wedge (A \times B)(u_2, v_2)\} \wedge \mu_{IR}$.
  ii. $[(A \times B)((u_2, v_2) + (u_1, v_1) - (u_2, v_2))] \vee \lambda_{IR} = [(A \times B)((u_2 + u_1 - u_2), (v_2 + v_1 - v_2)) \vee \lambda_{IR}] = \{A(u_2 + u_1 - u_2) \wedge B(v_2 + v_1 - v_2)\} \wedge \mu_{IR} \geq \{(A(u_1)) \wedge \mu_{IR}) \wedge (B(v_1)) \wedge \mu_{IR}) \wedge \mu_{IR}\} = \{((A(u_1) \wedge (B(v_1)) \wedge \mu_{IR}\} = \{(A{\times}B)(u_1, v_1)\} \wedge \mu_{IR}$.
  iii. For any $\alpha_1, \alpha_2 \in \Gamma$ then, $[(A \times B)(u_1, w_1)(\alpha_1, \alpha_2)((v_1, v_2) + (u_2, w_2)) - (u_1, w_1)\,(\alpha_1, \alpha_2)(u_2, w_2))] \vee \lambda_{IR} = [(A \times B)(u_1\alpha_1(v_1 + u_2) - u_1\alpha_1\, u_2), w_1\alpha_2(v_2 + w_2) - w_1\alpha_2 w_2) \vee \lambda_{IR}] \geq \{(A(v_1) \wedge \mu_{IR}) \wedge (B(v_2) \wedge \mu_{IR}) \wedge \mu_{IR}\} = \{A(v_1) \wedge B(v_2) \wedge \mu_{IR}\} = \{(A{\times}B)(v_1, v_2)\} \wedge \mu_{IR}$.

Hence A × B is a (λ_{IR}, μ_{IR})-fuzzy ideal of Γ-near ring M × N.

- **Lemma 20.3:** Let A and B be a two fuzzy subset of Γ-near-rings M and N, respectively, if A × B is a (λ_{IR}, μ_{IR}) fuzzy ideal of Near Ring M × N, then:
  i. $(A \times B)(0, 0^1) \vee \lambda_{IR} \geq (A \times B)(u, v) \wedge \mu_{IR}$.
  ii. $(A_1 \times A_2 \ldots \times A_n)(0_1, 0_2, \ldots 0_n) \vee \lambda_{IR} \geq (A_1 \times A_2 \ldots \times A_n)(u_1, u_2, \ldots u_n) \wedge \mu_{IR}$.
- **Theorem 20.12:** Let A and B be a two fuzzy subset of Γ-near ring M and N, respectively. If A × B is a (λ_{IR}, μ_{IR}) fuzzy ideal of Γ-Near Ring M × N, then at least one of the following must be true:
  i. $A(0) \vee \lambda_{IR} \geq B(v) \wedge \mu_{IR}$, for all $v \in N$.
  ii. $B(0^1) \vee \lambda_{IR} \geq A(u) \wedge \mu_{IR}$. For all $u \in M$.

- **Proof 20.13:** Let $A \times B$ is the (λ_{IR}, μ_{IR}) fuzzy ideal of $M \times N$. By contradiction suppose that there exist u $\in M$ and v $\in N$ such that $B(0^1) \vee \lambda_{IR} < A(u) \wedge \mu_{IR}$ and $A(0) \vee \lambda_{IR} < B(v) \wedge \mu_{IR}$. Now $(A \times B)(u, v) \wedge \mu_{IR} = (A(u) \wedge B(v)) \wedge \mu_{IR} = (A(u) \wedge \mu_{IR}) \wedge (B(v) \wedge \mu_{IR}) > (A(0) \vee \lambda_{IR}) \wedge (B(0^1) \vee \lambda_{IR}) = (A(0) \wedge B(0^1)) \vee \lambda_{IR} = (A \times B)(0, 0^0)$ v λ_{IR}. Thus A × B is a (λ_{IR}, μ_{IR})-fuzzy ideals of the $M \times N$ satisfying $(A \times B)(u, v) \Lambda \mu_{IR} > (A \times B)(0, 0^0)$ v λ_{IR} This is a contradict to Lemma 20.3.
- **Theorem 20.13:** Let A and B be a two fuzzy subset of Γ-near ring M and N, respectively if A × B is a (λ_{IR}, μ_{IR}) fuzzy ideal of Γ-Near Ring M × N, then either A is a (λ_{IR}, μ_{IR}) fuzzy ideal M or B is a (λ_{IR}, μ_{IR}) fuzzy ideal N.
- **Proof 20.14:** Suppose $A \times B$ is a (λ_{IR}, μ_{IR}) fuzzy ideal M then by using the property $B(0^1) \vee \lambda_{IR} \geq A(u) \wedge \mu_{IR}$ for all u, v, w $\in M$ and $\alpha \in \Gamma$, then two cases are possible $\lambda_{IR} \geq A(u) \wedge \mu_{IR}$ or $B(0^1) \geq A(u) \wedge \mu_{IR}$.

  Case (i): If $\lambda_{IR} \geq A(u) \wedge \mu_{IR}$ for all u $\in M$ then, $A(u - v)$ v $\lambda_{IR} \geq \lambda_{IR} \geq A(u) \Lambda \mu_{IR} \geq (A(u) \Lambda A(v)) \Lambda \mu_{IR}$. $A(v + u - v)$ v $\lambda_{IR} \geq \lambda_{IR} \geq A(u) \Lambda \mu_{IR}$. $A(u\alpha(v + w) - u\alpha w)$ v $\lambda_{IR} \geq \lambda_{IR} \geq A(v) \Lambda \mu_{IR}$. Hence, in this case A is a (λ_{IR}, μ_{IR}) fuzzy ideal M.

  Case (ii): If $B(0^1) \geq A(u) \wedge \mu_{IR}$ then (i) for u, v, w $\in M$, $A(u - v)$ v $\lambda_{IR} \geq [A(u - v) \Lambda B(0^1)]$ v $\lambda_{IR} = [A(u - v) \Lambda B(0^1 - 0^1)]$ v $\lambda_{IR} = [(A \times B)(u, 0^1) - (v, 0^1))]$ v $\lambda_{IR} \geq [(A \times B)(u, 0^1) \Lambda (A \times B)(v, 0^1)] \Lambda \mu_{IR} = [(A(u) \Lambda B(0^1)) \Lambda (A(v) \Lambda B(0^1))] \Lambda \mu_{IR} = (A(u) \Lambda (A(v)) \Lambda \mu_{IR}$; (ii) $A(v + u - v)$ v $\lambda_{IR} \geq [A(v + u - v) \Lambda B(0^1)]$ v $\lambda_{IR} = [A(u - v) \Lambda B(0^1 + 0^1 - 0^1)]$ v $\lambda_{IR} = [(A \times B) ((v, 0^1) + (u, 0^1) - (v, 0^1))]$ v $\lambda_{IR} \geq (A \times B)(u, 0^1) \Lambda \mu_{IR} = (A(u) \Lambda B(0^1)) = A(u) \Lambda \mu_{IR}$; (iii) For u, v, w $\in M$ and $\alpha \in \Gamma$ then, $A(u\alpha(v + w) - u\alpha z)$ v $\lambda_{IR} \geq [A(u\alpha(v + w) - u\alpha z) \Lambda B(0^1)]$ v $\lambda_{IR} = [A(u - v) \Lambda B(0^1\, 0^1\, (0^1 + 0^1) - 0^1 0^1 0^1)]$ v $\lambda_{IR} = [(A \times B) ((u, 0^1)(\alpha, 0^1)((w, 0^1) + (v, 0^1)) - (u, 0^1)(\alpha, 0^1)(w, 0^1))]$ v $\lambda_{IR} \geq (A \times B)(u, 0^1) \Lambda \mu_{IR} = (A(u) \Lambda B(0^1)) = A(u) \Lambda \mu_{IR}$.

Hence in this case A is a (λ_{IR}, μ_{IR}) fuzzy ideal M. Similarly, we can show that using property $A(0)$ v$\lambda_{IR} \geq B(v) \Lambda \mu_{IR}$, for all v $\in N$, B is a (λ_{IR}, μ_{IR}) fuzzy ideal N.

- **Corollary 20.2:** Let $A_1, A_2 \ldots$An be a (λ_{IR}, μ_{IR}) fuzzy subset of Γ-near rings $N_1, N_2 \ldots N_n$, respectively if $A_1 \times A_2 \times \ldots$An is a (λ_{IR}, μ_{IR}) fuzzy ideal of Γ-Near Ring $N_1 \times N_2 \times \ldots N_n$, then at least for one i:
  $A_i(0_i)$ v $\lambda_{IR} \geq A_k(u) \Lambda \mu_{IR}$ for all u $\in N_k$, for k = 1, 2,…n where 0_i is an identity of N_i.

- **Corollary 20.3:** Let $A_1, A_2 \ldots$An be a (λ_{IR}, μ_{IR}) fuzzy subset of Γ-near rings $N_1, N_2 \ldots N_n$, respectively if $A_1 \times A_2 \times \ldots$An is a ($\lambda_{IR}$, μ_{IR}) fuzzy ideal of Γ-Near Ring $N_1 \times N_2 \times \ldots N_n$, then at least for one i, A_i is fuzzy ideals of N_i.

20.5 CONCLUSION

In this chapter, we have introduced (λ_{IR}, μ_{IR})-fuzzy ideals in Γ-near ring, example, and verify few properties. Further, we studied (λ_{IR}, μ_{IR})-cut sets in Γ-near-rings and some results in direct product of (λ_{IR}, μ_{IR})-fuzzy Γ-near rings.

KEYWORDS

- **(λ_{IR}, μ_{IR})-cut set**
- **(λ_{IR}, μ_{IR})-fuzzy ideals in Γ-near-ring**
- **anti homomorphism**
- **direct product of (λ_{IR}, μ_{IR})-fuzzy Γ-near-ring**
- **fuzzy ideal structure**
- **near ring**

REFERENCES

1. Anitha, B., & Sivakumar, D., (2013). On (λ, μ)-anti-fuzzy subrings. *International Journal of Computer Applications, 75*, 0975–8887.
2. Yuming, F., & Corsini, P., (2012). (λ, μ)- Fuzzy version of ideals, interior ideals, quasi-ideals, and bi-ideals. *Journal of Applied Mathematics, 10*, 0–7.
3. Sung, M. H., Young, B. J., & Hee, S. K., (1998). Fuzzy ideals in near-rings. *Bull. Korean Math. Soc., 35*, 455–464.
4. Biswas, R., (1990). Fuzzy subgroups and anti-fuzzy subgroups. *Fuzzy Sets Systems, 44*, 121–124.
5. Kim, S. D., & Kim, H. S., (1996). On fuzzy ideals of near-rings. *Bull. Korean Math. Soc., 33*, 593–601.
6. Zadeh, L. A., (1965). Fuzzy sets. *Information and Control, 8*, 338–353.
7. Abou-Zaid, S., (1991). On fuzzy subnear-rings and ideals. *Fuzzy Sets and Systems, 44*, 139–146.

8. Satyanarayana, B., (1984). *Contributions to Near-Ring Theory.* Doctoral Thesis, Nagarjuna University, India.
9. Yao, B., (2005). (λ, μ)-fuzzy normal subgroups and (λ, μ)-fuzzy quotients sub- groups. *The Journal of Fuzzy Mathematics, 13*(3), 695–705.
10. Arul, S. X., & Sivakumar, D., (2011). On direct product of (λ, μ)-fuzzy subring. *International Mathematical Form, 6*(41), 2037–2044.
11. Rosenfeld, (1971). Fuzzy groups. *J. Math. Anal. Appl., 35*, 512–517.
12. Mukherjee, T. K., & Sen, M. K., (1987). On fuzzy ideals of a ring. *Fuzzy Set and Systems, 21*, 99–104.
13. Dutta, T. K., & Chanda, T., (2005). Structures of fuzzy ideals in Γ-rings. *Bulletin of the Malaysian Mathematical Science Society, 2*, 9–18.
14. Yao, (2007). (λ, μ)-fuzzy subrings and (λ, μ)- fuzzy ideals. *The Journal of Fuzzy Mathematics, 15*(4), 981–987.
15. Asok, K. R., (1999). On product of fuzzy subgroups. *Fuzzy Sets and Systems, 105*, 181–183.
16. Dixit, V., Rajesh, K., & Naseem, A., (1990). Level subgroups and union of fuzzy subgroups. *Fuzzy Sets and Systems, 37*, 359–371.
17. Chandrasekhara, R. K., & Swaminathan, V., (2008). Anti homomorphism in a near ring. *Jour. of Maths. and Comp. Sciences, 21*, 83–88.
18. Tazid, A., (2009). On direct product of fuzzy subrings. *The Journal of Fuzzy Mathematics, 17*(2), 481–485.
19. Bhakat, S. K., & Das, P., (1996). (Є, Є Vq)-fuzzy subgroup. *Fuzzy Sets and Systems, 80*, 359–393.
20. Anitha, N., & Aruna, J., (2018). T-fuzzy TL-ideal of G-near ring. *An International Journal of Mathematical and Computer Applications, 80*, 359–393.
21. Narayana, A., & Manikantan, T., (2005). (Є, Є Vq)-fuzzy subnear-rings and (Є, Є Vq)-fuzzy ideals of near-rings. *J. Appl. Math. and Computing, 18*, 419–430.

CHAPTER 21

APPROXIMATION FOR CHI-SQUARE F-DIVERGENCE VIA MIDPOINT INEQUALITIES

ANULIKA SHARMA and R. N. SARASWAT

Department of Mathematics and Statistics,
Manipal University Jaipur, Jaipur, Rajasthan–303007, India,
E-mails: anulikasharma022@gmail.com (A. Sharma),
saraswatramn@gmail.com (R. N. Saraswat)

ABSTRACT

Here we are using midpoint inequalities, arising in numerical integration, and derived a continuous function f. The approximation of Chi-Square information and divergence measure for probability distributions and applications are also applied Kullback-Leibler distance, Hellinger discrimination and Renyi -entropy.

21.1 INTRODUCTION

Consider Two probability distributions $p = (p_1 \ldots\ldots\ldots p_n)$ and $q = (q_1, \ldots\ldots\ldots q_2)$ are defined on an alpha-beta $\{a_i \mid 1 \le i \le n\}$, p_i, q_i are the point probabilities associated with event a_i $(i = 1\ldots\ldots\ldots n)$. For example, p, q represents pre and posts probability distributions associated with the alphabet.

Thus, the variational distance and information divergence (Kullback-Leibler divergence) are defined by:

$$V(p; q) := \sum_{i=1}^{n} | p_i - q_i | \tag{1}$$

$$D(p,q) := \sum_{i=1}^{n} p_i ln \frac{p_i}{q_i} \tag{2}$$

Now introduce the triangular discrimination by:

$$(p,q):=\sum_{i=1}^{n}\frac{|p_i-q_i|^2}{p_i+q_i} \tag{3}$$

Then, we get Hellinger divergence measure:

$$h^2(p,q):=\frac{1}{2}\sum_{i=2}^{n}(\sqrt{p_i}-\sqrt{q_i}) \tag{4}$$

The basic relations between *v,* Δ and h^2 are:

$$\frac{1}{2}v^2(p,q)\le\Delta(p,q)\le v(p,q)$$

and,

$$2h^2(p, q)\le\Delta\,(p, q)\le 4h^2(p, q)$$

From these can be deduce that:

$$\frac{1}{8}v^2(p,q)\le h^2(p,q)\le\frac{1}{2}v(p,q)$$

The coefficients in these inequalities are most fitting.

The first half of this result has been improved, shown by:

$$\frac{1}{8}v^2(p,q)\le h^2(p,q)\le\frac{1}{2}v(p,q)$$

the important inequality:

$$\text{D (p, q)}\ge -21\text{n}\,(1-h^2(p, q))$$

It follows from this:

$$D(p; q)\ge h^2(p, q)$$

Again, the coefficient is most fitting.

For a convex function *f:* $[0;1)\to$ R, the *Csisźar f-divergence* between *p* and *q* is defined by:

$$S_f(p,q):=\sum q_i f\left(\frac{p_i+q_i}{2q_i}\right) \tag{5}$$

Thus, the variational divergence measure by $f(u)=|u-1|$, KL information divergence measure by $f(u)=u\ln u$, triangular discrimination by $f(u)=(u-1)^2/(u+1)$ and Hellinger discrimination by:

$$f(u)=\frac{1}{2}(\sqrt{u}-1)^2$$

Some options of *f* satisfy $f(1)=0$, so that $s_f(p, q)$

Convexity then ensures that $s_f(p, q)$ is non-negative. Achieved the applications by convexity. These are related to obtained approximations. For instances, the exact value of *pi* and *qi* are not available, it is capable to give an estimated for $s_f(p; q)$ or to obtained upper bounds of *p* and *q*. For absolutely continuous functions, using approximation theorem of Ostrowski's integral inequality, It may be useful and the chi-square information divergence measure:

$$\aleph^2(p,q) := \frac{1}{4}\sum \frac{(p_i - q_i)^2}{4q_i}$$

Which arises from Eqn. (5) as the particular case $f(u) = (u - 1)^2$

- **Theorem 21.1:** Suppose that there exist real numbers a, A with:

$$0 < a \le \frac{p_i}{q_i} \le A \ < \text{for all } i \in \{1, \ldots\ldots\ldots, n\} \tag{6}$$

Assume that f: [a A] → A is absolutely continuous on [a A] and f' $\in L_\infty$ [a,A] that is, that,

$$\left\|f'\right\| = ess\ Sup_{t\in[a\ A]}\left|f'(t)\right| < \infty$$

Then,

$$s_f(p,q) - \frac{1}{A-a}\int_a^A f(t)\,dt \ |\le \left[\frac{1}{4} + \frac{1}{(A-a)^2}\left\{\aleph^2(p,q) + \left(\frac{A+a}{2} - 1\right)^2\right\}\right]$$

$$(A-a)\,|\,|f'|\,|_\infty \le \frac{1}{2}(A-a)\,|\,|f'|\,|_\infty$$

Suppose that *p* and *q* are related that $\in := A - a$ is less than. Theorem 21.1 indicates an approximation for the Csisźar *f*-divergence of accuracy of order $O(\in)$ with a lenient assumption on *f*'. However, some options of *f* in the literature of all branches of engineering's, here stronger statements are not necessarily limiting. It may be expect that, with appropriate restrictions, approximations to the Csisźar *f*-divergence can be obtained with higher-order accuracy in ($\in$). In this chapter, we obtained the approximations on the order of accuracy $O(\in^2)$ and $O(\in^3)$. Such approximations may be only a limited amount be obtained in line to the aim of utilizing approximants to $s_f(p; q)$ that involve *p*, *q* through *a* and *A* alone.

This can achieve with accuracy order $O(\in^2)$ but not in general with accuracy order $O(\in^3)$. Section 21.2 obtained some starting ideas and tried to prove a general proposition that may be useful in problems of relating approximations. Section 21.3 discusses some basic results and Section 21.4 tries to give some examples on f.

21.2 PRELIMINARIES

According to the introduction, Let f'is absolutely continuous on [a.A] and $f' \in L_{\infty}[a, A]$. Then $t \in [a, A]$ we have:

$$f(t) := f(1) + (t-1) f^{i}(t) + \frac{(t-1)^2}{2} f^{\cdot}(\in_i)$$

for some $\in_x \in [a, A]$. Setting $t = t = \dfrac{q_i + p_i}{2q_i}$ gives for each $i = 1,\ldots\ldots, n$ that,

$$q_i f\left(\frac{p_i + q_i}{2q_i}\right) = q_i f(1) + \frac{(p_i - q_i)}{2} f^{\cdot}(1) + \frac{(p_i - q_i)^2}{8q_i} f^{\cdot}(\in_i)$$

for some $\in_i, \in [a, A]$. Since $\sum_{i=1}^{n} p_i = 1 = \sum_{i=1}^{n} q_i$

Summation over i we have:

$$s_f(p_i, q_i) = q_i f(1) + \frac{1}{8} \frac{(p_i - q_i)^2}{q_i} f^{\cdot}(\in_i)$$

deduce that:

$$| s_f(p, q) - f(1) | \leq \frac{1}{8} \aleph^2(p, q) \, \| f^{\cdot} \|_{\infty}$$

$$\aleph^2(p, q) \leq (A-1)(1-a) \tag{7}$$

Also take $\propto = A-1, \beta = 1-a$ in the elementary inequality:

$$\propto \beta \leq \frac{1}{4} (\propto + \beta)^2$$

give (A–1) (1–a) $\leq \dfrac{(A-a)^2}{4}$, the generalization of Eqn. (7) is:

$$\aleph^2(p, q) \leq (A-1)(1-a) \leq \frac{(A-a)^2}{4} \tag{8}$$

This leads to:

$$| s_f(p, q) - f(1) | \leq \frac{\in^2}{32} \, \| f^{\cdot} \|_{\infty} \tag{9}$$

In which the approximant does not depends on p and q. So function is normalized, i.e., $f(1) = 0$ for some options of f. f' is absolutely continuous on the interval $[a, A]$ the comparable argument uses, and $f' \in L_{\infty}[a, A]$ Paralleling the line of reasoning above leads to:

$$s_f(p,q) = f(1) + \frac{1}{8}\sum_{i=1}^{n}\frac{(p_i - q_i)^2}{q_i} f^{\cdot}(1) + \frac{1}{24}\sum_{i=1}^{n}\frac{(p_i - q_i)^3}{q^2_i} f^{\cdot}(q_i)$$

where each τ_i, whence:

$$| s_f(p,q) - f(1) \left| - \frac{1}{8}\aleph^2(p,q) f^{\cdot}(1) \right| \leq \frac{1}{24}\aleph^3(p,q) \| f^{\cdot} \|_\infty$$

Here,

$$\aleph^3(p,q) = \sum_{i=1}^{n}\frac{| p_i - q_i |^3}{q_i^2}$$

is the chi-cubed discrepancy, which corresponds to $f(u) = (u - 1)^3$. It follows at once from Eqn. (6) and,

$$\sum_{i=1}^{n} p_i = 1 = \sum_{i=1}^{n} q_i \text{ that } \leq i \leq A.$$

Hence,

$$\left| \frac{p_i}{q_i} - 1 \right| \leq Max(1-a, A-1) \leq A - a \; for \; i = 1, \ldots\ldots\ldots, n$$

and from Eqn. (8) we have:

$$\aleph^3(p,q) \leq (A-a)\aleph^2(p,q) \leq (A-a)(A-1)(1-a) \leq \frac{1}{4}(A-a)^3 \tag{4}$$

Therefore,

$$| s_f(p,q) - f(1) - \frac{1}{8}\aleph^2(p,q) f^{\cdot}(1) | \leq \frac{\in^3}{96} \| f^{\cdot} \|_\infty \tag{5}$$

Here, the estimated involves p and q are non-trivially. In this research chapter, obtained some results are parallel to Eqns. (9) and (11) but approximate for $s_f(p, q)$, So can obtain tight error bounds. The aim is bases on absolutely continuous mappings of Ostrowski's integral inequality for.

- **Theorem 21.2:** Assume that g: [b,d] → A is absolutely continuous with $g' \in L_\infty[b, d]$.
  Then,

$$| g(x) - \frac{1}{d-b}\int_b^d g(t)\,dt \left| \leq \left[\frac{1}{4} + \left(\frac{x - \frac{(b+d)}{2}}{d-b} \right)^2 \right] (d-b) \right| \| g^{\cdot} \|_\infty$$

  for all $x \in [b, d]$.

We make the use of a result on generalizes and improvement of Eqn. (10).

Assume the divergence measure:

$$\aleph^{m}(p,q):=\sum_{i=1}^{n}\frac{|p_{i-q_i}|^{m}}{q_i^{m-1}}$$

With $m \geq 1$.

- **Proposition 21.1:** Suppose that Eqn. (6) is satisfied with $a < A$ and that $l \geq 1$. Then,

$$\aleph_{|x|^l}(p,q) \leq \frac{(A-1)(1-a)}{A-a}[((1-a)^{l-1}+(A-1)^{l-1}] \leq (\frac{A-a}{2})$$

In the first inequality, p, and q form a boundary pair with respect to a and A, that is, for each i either $p_i = q_i = a$ or $p_i = q_i = A$. The 2nd relation is an equality iff $A + a = 2$, that is, a, and A are middle from unity.

- **Proof 21.1:** Let us consider the value of $i \in \{1, \ldots\ldots n\}$ for which $\frac{p_i}{q_i} = \alpha$ with:

$a < a < A$ We can put:

$$p_i = a\frac{A-\alpha}{A-a}q_i + A\frac{\alpha-a}{A-a}q_i = p_{i,1} + q_{i,2}$$

Similarly,

$$q_i = \frac{A-\alpha}{A-a}q_i + \frac{\alpha-a}{A-a}q_i = q_{i,1} + q_{i,2}$$

We have:

$$\frac{p_{i,1}}{q_{i,1}} = a \text{ and } \frac{p_{i,2}}{q_{i,2}} = A$$

We may replace the probability n-vector p,q with probability (n + 1)-vectors by putting p_i by pairs $p_{i,1}, p_{i,2}$ and q_i by $q_{i,1}, q_{i,2}$

Then $\aleph_{|x|^l}(p,q)$ from $p_{i,1}$ and, q_i is:

$$\frac{|p_i - q_i|^l}{q^{l-1}{}_i} = q_i\,|1-\alpha|^l$$

After replacement, we get:

$$\frac{A-\alpha}{A-a}q_i(1-a)^m + \frac{\alpha-a}{A-a}(A-1)^l - |1-\alpha|^l$$

Is positive if $a < a < A$

First suppose that $l > 1$. Since,

$$\text{Ø}(\alpha) = -l(l-1)(1-\alpha)^{l-2} \text{ for } a < \alpha < 1$$

Ø is strictly can have on (a,1). Also Ø (a) = 0 and Ø (1) > 0 so that Ø (α) is positive on (a,1].

Similarly, $\varnothing^{\cdot}(\alpha) = -l(l-1)(\alpha-1)^{l-2} \; for\, 1 < \alpha < A$

So Ø is strictly concave on (1, A), since Ø (1) > 0 and Ø (A) = 0, Ø is positive on [1,A) thus Ø (α) > 0 on (a,A).

Now suppose $l = 1$, we have:

$$\varnothing^{\cdot}(\alpha) = -2\frac{A-1}{A-a} > 0 \; for\, a < \alpha < 1$$

With Ø (a) = 0, *so* Ø *is positive on* (a, 1], *thus we have again that* Ø (α) > 0 *on (a, A)*

In any case, demonstrated the stated increase in the information and divergence measure. Normally we see the upper bound of $\aleph_{|x|^m}(p,q)$, then generality to limiting pairs p, q. We get:

$$\frac{p_i}{q_i} = a \; for\, i = 1\ldots\ldots\ldots k$$

$$\frac{p_i}{q_i} = A \; for\, i = k+1,\ldots\ldots.n$$

Then,

$$1 = \sum_{i=1}^{n} p_i = a\sum_{i=1}^{n} q_i + A\sum_{i=k+1}^{n} q_i = a\sum_{i=1}^{k} q_i + A[1 - \sum_{i=1}^{k} q_i$$

And we have $\sum_{i=1}^{k} q_i = \frac{A-1}{A-a}, \sum_{i=k+1}^{n} q_i = \frac{1-a}{A-a}$

For the pairs p and q,

$$\aleph_{|x|^l}(p,q) = \sum_{i=1}^{k} \frac{(q_i - p_i)^l}{q_i^{l-1}} + \sum_{i=k+1}^{n} \frac{(p_i - q_i)^l}{q_i^{l-1}}$$

$$= (1-a)^l \sum_{i=1}^{k} q_i + (A-1)^l \sum_{i=k=1}^{n} q_i$$

$$= \frac{A-1}{A-a}(1-a)^l + \frac{1-a}{A-a}(A-1)^l$$

Now we have that $x \geq 0$, $y \geq 0$ with $x + y = 2c$, a constant the function $yx^m + xy^m$ takes its maximum value $2c^{l+1}$ when $x = y = c$. Applying this with $x = 1 - a$, $y = A - 1$.

Gives that:

$$\frac{A-1}{A-a}(1-a)^l + \frac{1-a}{A-a}(A-1)^l \leq \frac{(A-1)^l}{2}$$

With equality occurring when $A - 1 = 1 - a$

The case $l = 2$ this is the main part of the result. The result for $l = 3$ enables us to strengthen Eqn. (11) to:

$$| s_f(p,q) - f(1) - \frac{1}{8}\aleph_{|x|^2}(p,q) f^{\cdot}(1) | \leq \frac{\epsilon^3}{96} ||f^{\cdot}||_\infty$$

We shall, look for a much closer approximation for $s_f(p,q)$

21.3 BASIC RESULT

We assume in what follows that there exits real number a, A satisfying Eqn. (6) and $a \leq 1 \leq A$.

For f satisfying the conditions of Theorem 21.1, we define f: $[a, A] \rightarrow$ by:

$$f^*(t) := f(1) + (t-1) f^{\cdot}\left(\frac{1+t}{2}\right)$$

This gives $f^*(1) = f(1)$

- **Theorem 21.3:** Assume that f: $[0, \infty] \rightarrow A$ is such that f: $[a, A] \rightarrow A$ is absolutely on $[a, A]$ and $f' \in L_\infty[a, A]$. Then,

$$\left|s_f(p,q) - s_{f^*}(p,q)\right| \leq \frac{1}{4}\left\|f^{\cdot}\right\|_\infty \aleph_{|x|^2}(p,q)$$

$$\leq \frac{1}{4}\left\|f^{\cdot}\right\|_\infty (A-1)(1-a)$$

$$\leq \frac{1}{16} ||f^{\cdot}||_\infty (A-a)^2 \tag{7}$$

- **Proof 21.2:** Taking $x = \dfrac{(a+b)}{2}$ in Theorem 21.2 yield the midpoint inequality:

$$| g\left(\frac{a+b}{2}\right)(b-a) - \int_a^b g(t)\,dt | \leq \frac{1}{4}(b-a)^2 ||g^{\cdot}||_\infty$$

Now $g = f', a = 1 \, and \, b = x \in [a, A]$ provide:

$$| f(x) - f(1) - (x-1) f'\left(\frac{1+x}{2}\right) | \leq \frac{1}{4}(x-1)^2 \, || f' ||_\infty$$

For all $x \in [a, A]$

Putting $x = \frac{p_i + q_i}{2q_i} \in [a, A] \, gives$

$$| q_i f\left(\frac{p_i + q_i}{2q_i}\right) - q_i f(1) - \left(\frac{p_i - q_i}{2q_i}\right) f'\left(\frac{p_i + 3q_i}{4q_i}\right) | \leq \frac{1}{4}\left(\frac{p_i - q_i}{2q_i}\right)^2 q_i \, || f' ||_\infty$$

for $i \in \{1 \ldots\ldots n]$

Taking summation over I and with the help of generalized triangle inequality, we get:

$$| s_f(p,q) - f(1) - \sum_{i=1}^{n} \frac{(p_i - q_i)}{2} f'\left(\frac{p_i + q_i}{2q_i}\right) | \leq \frac{1}{16} || f' ||_\infty \sum_{i=1}^{n} \frac{(p_i - q_i)^2}{4q_i}$$

Whence we have the first relation in Eqn. (12).

the 2nd and 3rd inequalities of Eqn. (8)

- **Corollary 21.1:** Assuming Theorem 21.3. Let $\in > 0$ and $0 \leq A - a \leq 4\sqrt{\in / || f' ||_\infty}$

  Then $| s_f(p,q) - s_{f^*}(p,q) | \leq \in$

  A 2nd corollary accentuates the calculation feature of probability distributions p, q are close.

- **Corollary 21.2:** let: $[0,2] \rightarrow A$ and the differentiation f' :$[0,2] \rightarrow A$ is absolutely continuous and $f' \in L_\infty[0,2]$. If $\mu \in (0,1)$ and p (μ), q (μ), we get:

$$\left| \frac{p_i(\mu)}{q_i(\mu)} - 1 \right| \leq \mu \, for \, all \, i \in \{1 \ldots\ldots\ldots n\} \tag{8}$$

Then,

$$\left| S_f(p,q) - S_{f^*}(p,q) \right| \leq \frac{1}{24} \left\| f' \right\|_\infty \aleph_{x^2}(p,q)$$

And remainder $A_f(p, q, \mu)$ satisfies the estimate:

$$A_f(p,q,\mu) \leq \frac{1}{4} || f' ||_\infty \aleph_{|x|^2}(p(\mu), q(\mu)) \leq \frac{1}{4} || f' ||_\infty \mu^2$$

- **Proof 21.3:** set A = 1 + μ and $a = 1 - \mu$
- **Theorem 21.4:** If f: [b, d] $\rightarrow A$ is such that f'is absolutely continuous and $f' \in L_\infty$ [a, A]. Then,

$$\left|S_f(p,q) - S_{f^*}(p,q)\right| \leq \frac{1}{24}\left\|f^{\cdot}\right\|_\infty \aleph_{x^2}(p,q)$$

$$\leq \frac{1}{24}\left|\left|f^{\cdot}\right|\right|_\infty \frac{(A-1)(1-a)}{A-a}\left[(A-1)^2 + (1-a)^2\right]$$

$$\leq \frac{1}{192}\left|\left|f^{\cdot}\right|\right|_\infty (A-a)^3$$

The constant is best possible:

- **Proof 21.4:** For g: [b, d] $\rightarrow A$ such that g' is absolutely continuous on [b, d] and $g' \in L_\infty$[a, A], we get middle inequality.

$$|g\left(\frac{(b+d)}{2}\right)(d-b) - \int_b^d g(t)\,dt = \frac{1}{24}(d-b)^3 \left|\left|g^{\cdot}\right|\right|_\infty$$

Arising in numerical integration. Setting $g = f'$, $b = 1$ *and* $d = x \in$ [a, A]varies:

$$\left|f(x) - f(1) - (x-1)f^{\cdot}\left(\frac{1+x}{2}\right)\right| = \frac{1}{24}|x-1|^3\left|\left|f^{\cdot}\right|\right|_\infty$$

For all $x \in$ [a, A], we can proceed as in the proof of Theorem 21.3 to deduce the first inequality in Eqn. (3.7) for m = 3 provides the other. To complete the proof if suffices to prove that the constant 1/24 in the first inequality is best possible.

Now take $f(t) = (t-1)^3$ so that $S_f(p,q) = \aleph_{|x|^2}(p,q)$ then:

$$f^*(t) = \frac{3}{4}(t-1)^3 = \frac{3}{4}f(t)$$

So that $\left|S_f(p,q) - S_{f^*}(p,q)\right| = \frac{1}{4}\aleph_{|x|^3}(p,q)$

As $\left|\left|f^{\cdot}\right|\right|_\infty = 24,$ the first inequality in Eqn. (3.7) for this choice of f.

- **Corollary 21.3:** Assume that f be the function as in Theorem 21.4. Let $\in > 0$ and,

$$0 \leq A - a \leq 4.\sqrt[3]{3\in \big/ \left|\left|f^{\cdot}\right|\right|_\infty}$$

Then $|S_f(p,q) - S_{f^*}(p,q)| \leq \in$

Also, the following approximation result holds.

- **Corollary 21.4:** Let f: [0,2] $\rightarrow A$ be so that $f' \in L_{\infty}$ [0, 2]. If $\mu \in (0,1)$ *and* p (μ), q (μ) satisfy Eqn. (13) then we get from Eqn. (3.7) and the remainder $A_f(p, q, \mu)$ satisfies the estimate:

$$|A_f(p,q,\mu)| \le \frac{1}{24} ||f^{\cdot}||_{\infty} \mu^3$$

Proof the result follows from Theorem 21.4 with $a = 1 - \mu$ *and* $A = 1 + \mu$

21.4 APPLICATION TO SOME COMMON DIVERGENCE MEASURES

When f: $(0, \infty) \rightarrow A$ is the convex map $f(t) = tlnt$, $S_f(p, q)$ becomes the Kullback-Leibler distance D(p,q). We denote $S_f(p, q)$ by $\aleph^*(p,q)$ and adopt a similar notation for other specific divergence. We have:

$$\aleph^*(p,q) = \sum_{i=1}^{n}(p_i - q_i)\left[ln\left(\frac{p_i + q_i}{2q_i}\right) + 1\right]$$

$$= \sum_{i=1}^{n}(p_i - q_i)ln\left(\frac{p_i + q_i}{2q_i}\right)$$

As $f^{\cdot}(t) = {}^{1}\!/_{t}$, we have:

$$||f^{\cdot}||_{\infty} = Sup_{t\in[a,A]}|f^{\cdot}| = {}^{1}\!/_{a}$$

And the conclusion of Theorem 21.3 becomes:

$$\left|\aleph(p,q) - \aleph^*(p,q)\right| \le \frac{1}{4a}\aleph_{x^2}(p,q) \le \frac{(A-1)(1-a)}{4a} \le \frac{(A-a)^2}{16a}$$

An example of a concave f: $(0, \infty) \rightarrow A$ *with* $f(1) = 0$ is f(t)=lnt.

We have $s_f(p,q) = \sum_{i=1}^{n} p_i ln\left(\frac{p_i + q_i}{2q_i}\right) = -\aleph(p,q)$

And-$\aleph^*(p,q) = \sum_{i=1}^{n}(p_i - q_i)\frac{2q_i}{p_i + q_i} = 2\sum_{i=1}^{n} q_i \frac{p_i - q_i}{p_i + q_i}$

As $f^{\cdot}(t) = -\frac{1}{t^2}$, *we have* $\left\|f^{\cdot}\right\|_{\infty} = \frac{1}{a^2}$

Consequently Eqn. (12) reads:

$$|\aleph(p,q)-s^{*}(p,q)|\leq\frac{1}{4a^{2}}\aleph_{|x|^{2}}(p,q)\leq\frac{(A-1)(a-1)}{4a^{2}}\leq\frac{1}{16}\left(\frac{A}{a}-1\right)^{2}$$

For f: $(0,\infty)\to A$ given by $(u)=\frac{1}{2}\left(\sqrt{t}-1\right)$, the f-divergence. $S_f(p,q)$ becomes the Hellinger discriminate and,

$$h^{2*}(p,q)=\frac{1}{2}\sum_{i=1}^{n}(p_i-q_i)\frac{\sqrt{p_i+q_i}\left(\sqrt{p_i+q_i}-\sqrt{2q_i}\right)}{p_i+q_i}$$

As $f^{"}(t)=\frac{1}{4t^{2/3}}$ for $t\in(0,\infty)$

$$\left\|f^{\cdot}\right\|_{\infty}=Sup_{t\in[a,A]}|f^{\cdot}(t)|=\frac{1}{4a^{2/3}}$$

By Theorem 21.3 we have:

$$|h^{2}(p,q)-h^{2*}(p,q)|\leq\frac{1}{16a^{2/3}}\aleph^{2}_{|x|^{2}}(p,q)$$
$$\leq\frac{(A-1)(1-a)}{16a^{2/3}}\leq\frac{1}{64a^{2/3}}(A-a)^{2}$$

The range θ – order distance $A_\theta(p,q):=\sum_{i=1}^{n}p^{\theta}{}_{i}q^{1-\theta}{}_{i}$ is given by f: $(0,\infty)\to A$ with $f(t)=t^{\theta}(\theta>1)$. This provides an example in which f may not be convex and $f(1)\neq 0$

We have:

$$A^{*}_{\theta}(p,q)=\frac{1+\theta}{2^{\theta-1}}\sum_{i=1}^{n}p_i-q_i\left(\frac{p_i+q_i}{q_i}\right)^{\theta-1}$$

KEYWORDS

- **Chi-square divergence**
- **Hellinger discrimination**
- **Kullback-Leibler distance**
- **numerical integration**
- **Ostrowski's integral inequality**
- **Renyi entropy**

REFERENCES

1. Csiszar, I., (1967). On topological properties of f-divergence. *Studia. Sci. Math. Hung., 2*, 329–339.
2. Csiszar, I., & Korner, J., (1981). *Information Theory: Coding Theorem for Discrete Memory Less Systems*. Academic Press, New York.
3. Dragomir, S. S., (1999). Ostrowski's inequality for monotonous mappings and applications. *J. KSIAM, 3*(1), 127–135.
4. Dragomir, S. S., (1999). The Ostrowski integral inequality for Lipschitzian mappings and applications. *Comp. Math. Appl., 38*, 33–37.
5. Dragomir, S. S., (1999). The Ostrowski integral inequality for mappings of bounded variation. *Bull. Austral. Soc., 60*(1), 495–508.
6. Dragomir, S. S., (1999/2000). A converse result for Jensen's inequality via gruss in-equality and application in information theory. *An. Univ. Oradea Fasc. Mat., 7*, 178–189.
7. Hooda, D. S., & Bhaker, U. S., (1995). On a weighted entropy generating function. *Research Bulletin of Punjab University, 45*, 181–189.
8. Hooda, D. S., & Ram, A., (2002). On useful relative information and J divergence measures. *Tamkang Journal of Mathematics, 33*, 146–160.
9. Jain, K. C., & Saraswat, R. N., (2013). Some bounds of information divergence measures in terms of relative-arithmetic divergence measure. *International Journal of Applied Mathematics and Statistics, 32*(2), 48–58.
10. Jain, K. C., & Saraswat, R. N., (2012). A new information inequality and its application in establishing relation among various f-divergence measures. *Journal of Applied Mathematics, Statistics, and Informatics, 8*(1), 17–32.
11. Saraswat, R. N., & Ajay, T., (2019). New f-divergence and Jensen-Ostrowski's type inequalities. *Tamkang Journal of Mathematics, 50*(1), 111–118.
12. Saraswat, R. N., & Ajay, T., (2018). Ostrowski inequality and applications in information theory. *Jordan Journal of Mathematics and Statistics, 11*(4), 309–323.
13. Taneja, I. J., (1995). New developments in generalized information measures. Chapter In: Hawkes, P. W., (ed.), *Advances in Imaging and Electron Physics* (Vol. 91, pp. 37–135).
14. Taneja, I. J., (2012). *Inequalities Having Seven Means and Proportionality Relations.* Available online: http://arxiv.org/abs/1203.2288/ (accessed on 22 February 2021).
15. Taneja, I. J., (2004). *Generalized Symmetric Divergence Measures and Inequalities: RGMIA Research Report Collection, 7*(4), Article 9. https://rgmia.org/monographs.php. Available on-line at: arXiv:math.ST/0501301 v1 19 Jan 2005.

CHAPTER 22

NEW CODING INFORMATION INEQUALITIES

RAM NARESH SARASWAT and ADEEBA UMAR

Department of Mathematics and Statistics, Manipal University Jaipur, Jaipur, Rajasthan–303007, India, E-mails: saraswatramn@gmail.com (R. N. Saraswat); adeeba1506@gmail.com (A. Umar)

ABSTRACT

Inequalities are greatly useful for new results to information theory and widely used in Information divergence measures and coding. There are many bounds which are discussed earlier like Kraft inequalities, Hamming bounds, etc., in coding theory which exist in the literature of information and coding theory. In this chapter, some new coding bounds are established using well-known inequalities, and the results are proved through numerical illustrations, which will interest information and coding theory.

22.1 INTRODUCTION

To communicate information from one place to another is an activity that is as pristine as humanity. The mathematical theory of the main principles is not so ancient. In 1948, Shannon introduced a description of communication system and also suggested a beautiful theory about the concept of information, which includes a measure for the amount of information in a message. Shannon [20] gave two fundamental concepts of information in the context of communication. If we can determine a piece of information without any certainty, then that information has no value because it is already known.

Shannon [20] gave bounds for the average codeword length, for uniquely decodable codes, in terms of his own entropy. By applying Kraft's inequality [10], Campbell [3] presented his own average codeword length and in terms of Renyi's [16] entropy, he gave bonds for his average codeword length. Longo [13] developed noiseless coding theorems of weighted entropy which was given by Belis and Guiasu [1] for useful mean codeword length. Gurdial [6]; Guiasu and Picard [5], developed the noiseless coding theorem for advantageous mean codeword length of α. Many generalized coding theorems were also introduced by many authors like Taneja et al. [21]; Jain and Tuteja [8]; Bhat and Baig [2]. Shannon also introduced two important theorems. The first theorem is known as source coding theorem, which states that entropy is the fundamental measure of information. The second theorem is known as the channel coding theorem, which introduces communication through a noisy channel.

According to Shannon's Source coding theorem, when we consider an information source whose symbols s_i are emitted from the source, then the source output is given to the encoder, and the output of the source encoder is the information which is coded. If l_i is the codeword length for i^{th} symbol and p_i be the corresponding probability, then average codeword length is given by $L=\sum p_i l_i$. The source encoder's efficiency is given by $\eta'=L_{min}/L$. The source conveys the average information as its entropy. Symbols which are emitted from the source are represented with an equal or greater number of bits than that of its entropy. Hence, $L \geq H(S)$ then $L_{min} = H(X)$. For lossless communication, we need at least H(X) number of bits to represent any of the symbols emitted by the source. So, $\eta'=H(X)/L$. The source redundancy is given by $R_{nD} = 1 - \eta'$. $H(X)/L \leq R_{nD}$ or $\eta' \leq R_{nD}$.

In a digital communication system, the information symbols are represented in terms of a bit sequence, which is called a codeword. If we take a binary encoder, the codeword will take the symbols (0, 1); for a ternary code, it will take (0, 1, 2), for quaternary, it will take (0, 1, 2, 3) and so on. According to Kraft-McMillan Inequality, the following property is satisfied by all prefix codes: $\sum D^{-ni} \leq 1$, where D is the number of symbols in code alphabet, i.e., D = 2, for binary, 3 for ternary, 4 for quaternary and so on and n_i is the codeword length of the ith symbol.

22.2 SOME WELL-KNOWN INEQUALITIES

Inequalities are useful and perform a vital role in information and coding theory, statistics, and different branches of engineering. Mutual information and entropy are represented in the form of inequalities. The entropy, whether single, joint or conditional and the mutual information involving conditional and including multiple random variables are the information measures.

Though, it is possible to find a non-linear expression including these measures. The inequalities which are well known in the literature of pure and applied mathematics are given as:

$$\frac{x}{1+x} \leq \log(1+x) \leq x, \;\; x > 0 \tag{1}$$

$$x - \frac{x^2}{2} \leq \log(1+x) \leq x - \frac{x^2}{2(1+x)}, \;\; x > 0 \tag{2}$$

22.3 NEW CODING BOUNDS USING INEQUALITIES

Some bounds of well-known information divergence measures using inequalities Eqns. (1) and (2) are discussed in this section.

- **Proposition 22.1:** Let $P, Q \in \Gamma_n$ be two probability distributions, then we have the following inequalities:

For $\eta = \frac{1}{\eta'} = \frac{\bar{L}}{H(X)}$

$$\frac{\bar{L}}{H(X)} \leq R_{nD} \;\; or \;\; \eta \leq R_{nD} \tag{3}$$

- **Proof 22.1:** Using the inequality Eqn. (1):

$$\frac{x}{1=x} \leq \log\,(1+x), x > 0$$

Taking $x = \frac{D^{-n_i}}{\sum_{i=1}^{n} D^{-n_i}}$ then we get:

$$\frac{\frac{D^{-n_i}}{\sum_{i=1}^{n} D^{-n_i}}}{1+\frac{D^{-n_i}}{\sum_{i=1}^{n} D^{-n_i}}} \leq \log\,(1+\frac{D^{-n_i}}{\sum_{i=1}^{n} D^{-n_i}}) \tag{4}$$

$$\frac{D^{-n_i}}{\sum_{i=1}^{n} D^{-n_i} + D^{-n_i}} \leq \log\left(\frac{D^{-n_i}}{\sum_{i=1}^{n} D^{-n_i}}\right), \ x > 0$$

$$\frac{D^{-n_i}}{\sum_{i=1}^{n} D^{-n_i} + D^{-n_i}} \leq \log\,(D^{-n_i}) - \log\sum_{i=1}^{n} D^{-n_i}, \ x > 0$$

$$\frac{D^{-n_i}}{\sum_{i=1}^{n} D^{-n_i} + D^{-n_i}} \leq \log\,(D^{-n_i}), \ x > 0 \ \because \log\sum_{i=1}^{n} D^{-n_i} = 0$$

$$\frac{D^{-n_i}}{\sum_{i=1}^{n} D^{-n_i} + D^{-n_i}} \leq -n_i \log(D)$$

$$\frac{D^{-n_i}}{1 + D^{-n_i}} \leq -n_i \log(D) \leq D^{-n_i}, \ if \sum_{i=1}^{n} D^{-n_i} = 1 \ x > 0$$

$$\sum_{i=1}^{n} D^{-n_i} \leq -\sum_{i=1}^{n} n_i (1 + D^{-n_i}) \log\,(D)$$

$$\sum_{i=1}^{n} D^{-n_i} \leq -\sum_{i=1}^{n} n_i (1 + D^{-n_i})\left(\frac{H(X)}{\bar{L}}\right),$$

$$-\sum_{i=1}^{n} D^{-n_i} \geq -1 \geq \sum_{i=1}^{n} n_i (1 + D^{-n_i})\left(\frac{H(X)}{\bar{L}}\right),$$

$$-1 \geq \sum_{i=1}^{n} n_i (1 + D^{-n_i})\left(\frac{H(X)}{\bar{L}}\right),$$

$$\eta = \frac{\bar{L}}{H(X)} \leq -\sum_{i=1}^{n} n_i (1 + D^{-n_i})$$

$$\eta = \frac{\bar{L}}{H(X)} \leq -\sum_{i=1}^{n} n_i (1 + D^{-n_i})$$

$$\text{Let} - \sum_{i=1}^{n} n_i (1 + D^{-n_i}) = R_{nD}$$

$$\eta = \frac{\bar{L}}{H(X)} \leq R_{nD}$$

$$D^{-n_i} \leq -n_i (1 + D^{-n_i}) \log\,(D)$$

$$-n_i \log(D) \le D^{-n_i}$$

Hence proved of the result.

- **Proposition 22.2:** Let $P, Q \in \Gamma_n$ be two probability distributions then the following inequalities are:

$$\eta(D) - \xi(D) \le D^{-n_i} \tag{5}$$

- **Proof 22.2:** Using the first and second relation of inequality Eqn. (2):

$$\log(1 + x) \le x$$

Put:

$$x = \frac{D^{-n_i}}{\sum_{i=1}^{n} D^{-n_i}}$$

$$\log\left(1 + \frac{D^{-n_i}}{\sum_{i=1}^{n} D^{-n_i}}\right) \le \frac{D^{-n_i}}{\sum_{i=1}^{n} D^{-n_i}}$$

$$\sum_{i=1}^{n} D^{-n_i} \log\left(\sum_{i=1}^{n} D^{-n_i} + D^{-n_i}\right) - \sum_{i=1}^{n} D^{-n_i} \log\left(\sum_{i=1}^{n} D^{-n_i}\right) \le D^{-n_i}$$

$$\eta(D) - \xi(\mathrm{D}) \le D^{-n_i}$$

where;

$$\eta(D) = \sum_{i=1}^{n} D^{-n_i} \log\left(\sum_{i=1}^{n} D^{-n_i} + D^{-n_i}\right),\ \xi(D) = \sum_{i=1}^{n} D^{-n_i} \log\left(\sum_{i=1}^{n} D^{-n_i}\right)$$

- **Proposition 22.3:** Let $P, Q \in \Gamma_n$ be two probability distributions then the following inequalities are:

$$if\ \sum_{i=1}^{n} D^{-n_i} = 1$$

$$\frac{\left(D^{-n_i}\right)^4}{4} + \frac{\left(D^{-n_i}\right)^6}{6} + \text{--} \le \frac{\left(D^{-n_i}\right)^3}{3} + \frac{\left(D^{-n_i}\right)^5}{5} + \text{--} \tag{6}$$

$$if\ \sum_{i=1}^{n} D^{-n_i} \ne 1$$

Then,

$$\left|\xi(D) - \eta(D)\right| \ge 1 \tag{7}$$

➤ **Proof 22.3:** Using the first and second relation of inequality Eqn. (2):

$$x - \frac{x^2}{2} \le \log(1+x) \;\; x > 0$$

Now we take $x = \left(\frac{D^{-n_i}}{\sum_{i=1}^{n} D^{-n_i}} \right)$ and taking summation of both side:

$$1 - \frac{x}{2} \le \frac{\log(1+x)}{x}, \;\; x > 0$$

$$1 - \frac{\left(\frac{D^{-n_i}}{\sum_{i=1}^{n} D^{-n_i}} \right)}{2} \le \frac{\log\left(1 + \frac{D^{-n_i}}{\sum_{i=1}^{n} D^{-n_i}} \right)}{\left(\frac{D^{-n_i}}{\sum_{i=1}^{n} D^{-n_i}} \right)},$$

$$2 - \left(\frac{D^{-n_i}}{\sum_{i=1}^{n} D^{-n_i}} \right) \le \frac{2\log\left(1 + \frac{D^{-n_i}}{\sum_{i=1}^{n} D^{-n_i}} \right)}{\left(\frac{D^{-n_i}}{\sum_{i=1}^{n} D^{-n_i}} \right)},$$

$$\left[2\left(\frac{D^{-n_i}}{\sum_{i=1}^{n} D^{-n_i}} \right) - \left(\frac{D^{-n_i}}{\sum_{i=1}^{n} D^{-n_i}} \right)^2 - 1 + 1 \right] \le 2\log\left(1 + \frac{D^{-n_i}}{\sum_{i=1}^{n} D^{-n_i}} \right),$$

$$\left[1 - \left(1 - \frac{D^{-n_i}}{\sum_{i=1}^{n} D^{-n_i}} \right)^2 \right] \le 2\log\left(1 + \frac{D^{-n_i}}{\sum_{i=1}^{n} D^{-n_i}} \right),$$

$$\left[1-\left(1-D^{-n_i}\right)^2\right]\le 2\log\left(1+D^{-n_i}\right), \qquad \left[if\sum_{i=1}^{n} D^{-n_i}=1\right]$$

$$\left[1-\left(1+\left(D^{-n_i}\right)^2-2D^{-n_i}\right)\right]\le 2\left[D^{-n_i}-\frac{\left(D^{-n_i}\right)^2}{2}+\frac{\left(D^{-n_i}\right)^3}{3}-\frac{\left(D^{-n_i}\right)^4}{4}-----\right],$$

$$\left[2D^{-n_i}-\left(D^{-n_i}\right)^2\right]\le 2D^{-n_i}-\left(D^{-n_i}\right)^2+\frac{2\left(D^{-n_i}\right)^3}{3}-\frac{2\left(D^{-n_i}\right)^4}{4}-----$$

$$0\le\frac{2\left(D^{-n_i}\right)^3}{3}-\frac{2\left(D^{-n_i}\right)^4}{4}-----$$

$$\frac{\left(D^{-n_i}\right)^4}{4}+\frac{\left(D^{-n_i}\right)^6}{6}+---+\textit{for all even terms}$$
$$\le\frac{\left(D^{-n_i}\right)^3}{3}+\frac{\left(D^{-n_i}\right)^5}{5}+---+\textit{for all odd terms}$$

Also,

$$\left[1-\left(1-D^{-n_i}\right)^2\right]\le 2\log\left(1+D^{-n_i}\right), \qquad \left[if\sum_{i=1}^{n} D^{-n_i}\ne 1\right]$$

$$\left(\frac{D^{-n_i}}{\sum_{i=1}^{n}D^{-n_i}}\right)\left[2-\left(\frac{D^{-n_i}}{\sum_{i=1}^{n}D^{-n_i}}\right)\right]\le 2\log\left(1+\frac{D^{-n_i}}{\sum_{i=1}^{n}D^{-n_i}}\right),$$

$$\left(\frac{D^{-n_i}}{\sum_{i=1}^{n}D^{-n_i}}\right)\left[2-\left(\frac{D^{-n_i}}{\sum_{i=1}^{n}D^{-n_i}}\right)\right]+2\log\left(\sum_{i=1}^{n}D^{-n_i}\right)\le 2\log\left(\sum_{i=1}^{n}D^{-n_i}+D^{-n_i}\right)$$

$$2D^{-n_i}-\frac{\left(D^{-n_i}\right)^2}{\sum_{i=1}^{n}D^{-n_i}}+2\eta(D)\le 2\,\xi(D)$$

$$\left(D^{-n_i}\right)\left[2-\left(\frac{D^{-n_i}}{\sum_{i=1}^{n} D^{-n_i}}\right)\right]+2\sum_{i=1}^{n} D^{-n_i}\log\left(\sum_{i=1}^{n} D^{-n_i}\right)$$

$$\leq 2\sum_{i=1}^{n} D^{-n_i}\log\left(\sum_{i=1}^{n} D^{-n_i}+D^{-n_i}\right)$$

$$D^{-n_i}-\frac{1}{2}\frac{\left(D^{-n_i}\right)^2}{\sum_{i=1}^{n} D^{-n_i}}\leq\left|\xi(D)-\eta(D)\right|$$

but we know that from Kraft inequalities:

$$\sum_{i=1}^{n} D^{-n_i}\leq 1 \text{ or } 1\leq\frac{1}{\sum_{i=1}^{n} D^{-n_i}}$$

We get:

$$D^{-n_i}-\frac{1}{2}\frac{\left(D^{-n_i}\right)^2}{\sum_{i=1}^{n} D^{-n_i}}\leq\sum_{i=1}^{n} D^{-n_i}\leq 1\leq\left|\xi(D)-\eta(D)\right|$$

$$D^{-n_i}\leq\sum_{i=1}^{n} D^{-n_i}\leq 1$$

$$1\leq\left|\xi(D)-\eta(D)\right|$$

which proves the result.

- **Proposition 22.4:** Let $P, Q\in\Gamma_n$ be two probability distributions then the following inequalities are:

$$0\leq\left[1+\frac{D^{-n_i}}{\sum_{i=1}^{n} D^{-n_i}}\right]^{-1}\leq 1 \tag{8}$$

- **Proof 22.4:** Using the first and last relation of inequality Eqn. (2):

$$x-\frac{x^2}{2}\leq x-\frac{x^2}{2(1+x)},\quad x>0 \tag{9}$$

Now we take $x = \dfrac{D^{-n_i}}{\sum_{i=1}^{n} D^{-n_i}}$ then we get:

$$\frac{D^{-n_i}}{\sum_{i=1}^{n} D^{-n_i}} - \frac{\left(\frac{D^{-n_i}}{\sum_{i=1}^{n} D^{-n_i}}\right)^2}{2} \le \left(\frac{D^{-n_i}}{\sum_{i=1}^{n} D^{-n_i}}\right) - \frac{\left(\frac{D^{-n_i}}{\sum_{i=1}^{n} D^{-n_i}}\right)^2}{2\left(1+\frac{D^{-n_i}}{\sum_{i=1}^{n} D^{-n_i}}\right)},$$

$$\frac{D^{-n_i}}{\sum_{i=1}^{n} D^{-n_i}} - \frac{\left(\frac{D^{-n_i}}{\sum_{i=1}^{n} D^{-n_i}}\right)^2}{2} \le \left(\frac{D^{-n_i}}{\sum_{i=1}^{n} D^{-n_i}}\right) - \frac{\left(\frac{D^{-n_i}}{\sum_{i=1}^{n} D^{-n_i}}\right)^2}{2\left(1+\frac{D^{-n_i}}{\sum_{i=1}^{n} D^{-n_i}}\right)} \tag{10}$$

$$\frac{D^{-n_i}}{\sum_{i=1}^{n} D^{-n_i}} - \frac{1}{2}\left(\frac{D^{-n_i}}{\sum_{i=1}^{n} D^{-n_i}}\right)^2 \le \left(\frac{D^{-n_i}}{\sum_{i=1}^{n} D^{-n_i}}\right) - \frac{1}{2}\left(\frac{D^{-n_i}}{\sum_{i=1}^{n} D^{-n_i}}\right)^2\left(1+\frac{D^{-n_i}}{\sum_{i=1}^{n} D^{-n_i}}\right)^{-1}$$

$$-\frac{1}{2}\left(\frac{D^{-n_i}}{\sum_{i=1}^{n} D^{-n_i}}\right)^2 \le -\frac{1}{2}\left(\frac{D^{-n_i}}{\sum_{i=1}^{n} D^{-n_i}}\right)^2\left[1+\frac{D^{-n_i}}{\sum_{i=1}^{n} D^{-n_i}}\right]^{-1}$$

$$-1 \le -\left[1+\frac{D^{-n_i}}{\sum_{i=1}^{n} D^{-n_i}}\right]^{-1}$$

$$-1 \leq -\left(1-\frac{D^{-n_i}}{\sum_{i=1}^{n} D^{-n_i}}+\left(\frac{D^{-n_i}}{\sum_{i=1}^{n} D^{-n_i}}\right)^2-\dots\dots\dots\right)$$

$$\left(1-\frac{D^{-n_i}}{\sum_{i=1}^{n} D^{-n_i}}+\left(\frac{D^{-n_i}}{\sum_{i=1}^{n} D^{-n_i}}\right)^2-\dots\dots\dots\right) \leq 1$$

$$\left[1+\frac{D^{-n_i}}{\sum_{i=1}^{n} D^{-n_i}}\right]^{-1} \leq 1 \tag{11}$$

Again from Eqn. (10):

$$\frac{D^{-n_i}}{\sum_{i=1}^{n} D^{-n_i}}\left[1-\frac{1}{2}\left(\frac{D^{-n_i}}{\sum_{i=1}^{n} D^{-n_i}}\right)\right] \leq \frac{D^{-n_i}}{\sum_{i=1}^{n} D^{-n_i}}\left[1-\frac{1}{2}\frac{D^{-n_i}}{\sum_{i=1}^{n} D^{-n_i}}\left(1+\frac{D^{-n_i}}{\sum_{i=1}^{n} D^{-n_i}}\right)^{-1}\right]$$

$$-\frac{1}{2}\frac{D^{-n_i}}{\sum_{i=1}^{n} D^{-n_i}} \leq -\frac{1}{2}\frac{D^{-n_i}}{\sum_{i=1}^{n} D^{-n_i}}\left\{1-\frac{D^{-n_i}}{\sum_{i=1}^{n} D^{-n_i}}+\left(\frac{D^{-n_i}}{\sum_{i=1}^{n} D^{-n_i}}\right)^2-\dots\dots\dots\dots\right\}$$

$$1-\frac{1}{2}\left(\frac{D^{-n_i}}{\sum_{i=1}^{n} D^{-n_i}}\right) \leq 1-\frac{1}{2}\left(\frac{D^{-n_i}}{\sum_{i=1}^{n} D^{-n_i}}\right)\left(1+\frac{D^{-n_i}}{\sum_{i=1}^{n} D^{-n_i}}\right)^{-1}$$

$$-\frac{1}{2}\frac{D^{-n_i}}{\sum_{i=1}^{n} D^{-n_i}} \leq -\frac{1}{2}\frac{D^{-n_i}}{\sum_{i=1}^{n} D^{-n_i}}+\frac{1}{2}\left(\frac{D^{-n_i}}{\sum_{i=1}^{n} D^{-n_i}}\right)^2-\frac{1}{2}\left(\frac{D^{-n_i}}{\sum_{i=1}^{n} D^{-n_i}}\right)^3+\dots\dots\dots\dots\dots\dots$$

$$0 \leq \frac{1}{2}\frac{D^{-n_i}}{\sum_{i=1}^{n} D^{-n_i}}\left[1-\frac{D^{-n_i}}{\sum_{i=1}^{n} D^{-n_i}}+\left(\frac{D^{-n_i}}{\sum_{i=1}^{n} D^{-n_i}}\right)^2-\dots\dots\dots\dots\right]$$

$$0 \leq \left[1+\frac{D^{-n_i}}{\sum_{i=1}^{n} D^{-n_i}}\right]^{-1} \tag{12}$$

From Eqns. (11) and (12):

$$0 \leq \left[1+\frac{D^{-n_i}}{\sum_{i=1}^{n} D^{-n_i}}\right] \leq 1 \tag{13}$$

which proves the result.

- **Proposition 22.5:** Let $P, Q \in \Gamma_n$ be two probability distributions then the following inequalities are:

$$\sum_{i=1}^{n} \frac{(-1)^n}{n+3}\left(\frac{D^{-n_i}}{\sum_{i=1}^{n} D^{-n_i}}\right)^n \leq \frac{1}{2}\sum_{i=1}^{n}(-1)^n\left(\frac{D^{-n_i}}{\sum_{i=1}^{n} D^{-n_i}}\right)^n, \quad \frac{D^{-n_i}}{\sum_{i=1}^{n} D^{-n_i}} > 0 \tag{14}$$

- **Proof 22.5:** Using the second and last relation of inequality Eqn. (2):

$$x = \frac{D^{-n_i}}{\sum_{i=1}^{n} D^{-n_i}}$$

we get,

$$\log\left(1+\frac{D^{-n_i}}{\sum_{i=1}^{n} D^{-n_i}}\right) \leq \frac{D^{-n_i}}{\sum_{i=1}^{n} D^{-n_i}} - \frac{\left[\frac{D^{-n_i}}{\sum_{i=1}^{n} D^{-n_i}}\right]^2}{2\left[1+\frac{D^{-n_i}}{\sum_{i=1}^{n} D^{-n_i}}\right]}, \quad x > 0$$

$$\log\left(1+\frac{D^{-n_i}}{\sum_{i=1}^{n} D^{-n_i}}\right) \leq \frac{D^{-n_i}}{\sum_{i=1}^{n} D^{-n_i}} - \frac{1}{2}\left[\frac{D^{-n_i}}{\sum_{i=1}^{n} D^{-n_i}}\right]^2\left[1+\frac{D^{-n_i}}{\sum_{i=1}^{n} D^{-n_i}}\right]^{-1}, \quad \frac{D^{-n_i}}{\sum_{i=1}^{n} D^{-n_i}} > 0$$

$$\frac{\sum_{i=1}^{n} D^{-n_i}}{D^{-n_i}} \log\left(1+\frac{D^{-n_i}}{\sum_{i=1}^{n} D^{-n_i}}\right) \leq 1-\frac{1}{2}\left[\frac{D^{-n_i}}{\sum_{i=1}^{n} D^{-n_i}}\right]\left[1+\frac{D^{-n_i}}{\sum_{i=1}^{n} D^{-n_i}}\right]^{-1}, \quad \frac{D^{-n_i}}{\sum_{i=1}^{n} D^{-n_i}} > 0$$

$$\frac{D^{-n_i}}{\sum_{i=1}^{n} D^{-n_i}}\left[\frac{D^{-n_i}}{\sum_{i=1}^{n} D^{-n_i}}-\frac{1}{2}\left(\frac{D^{-n_i}}{\sum_{i=1}^{n} D^{-n_i}}\right)^{2}+\frac{1}{3}\left(\frac{D^{-n_i}}{\sum_{i=1}^{n} D^{-n_i}}\right)^{3}-\ldots\ldots..\right]$$

$$\leq 1-\frac{1}{2}\frac{D^{-n_i}}{\sum_{i=1}^{n} D^{-n_i}}\left[1-\frac{D^{-n_i}}{\sum_{i=1}^{n} D^{-n_i}}+\left(\frac{D^{-n_i}}{\sum_{i=1}^{n} D^{-n_i}}\right)^{2}-\left(\frac{D^{-n_i}}{\sum_{i=1}^{n} D^{-n_i}}\right)^{3}+\ldots\ldots.\right]$$

$$1-\frac{1}{2}\frac{D^{-n_i}}{\sum_{i=1}^{n} D^{-n_i}}+\frac{1}{3}\left(\frac{D^{-n_i}}{\sum_{i=1}^{n} D^{-n_i}}\right)^{2}-\ldots\ldots\ldots\ldots..$$

$$\leq 1-\frac{1}{2}\frac{D^{-n_i}}{\sum_{i=1}^{n} D^{-n_i}}+\frac{1}{2}\left(\frac{D^{-n_i}}{\sum_{i=1}^{n} D^{-n_i}}\right)^{2}-\frac{1}{2}\left(\frac{D^{-n_i}}{\sum_{i=1}^{n} D^{-n_i}}\right)^{3}+\ldots\ldots\ldots\ldots.. \tag{15}$$

$$\frac{1}{3}\left(\frac{D^{-n_i}}{\sum_{i=1}^{n} D^{-n_i}}\right)^{2}-\frac{1}{4}\left(\frac{D^{-n_i}}{\sum_{i=1}^{n} D^{-n_i}}\right)^{3}+\ldots\ldots\ldots..$$

$$\leq \frac{1}{2}\left(\frac{D^{-n_i}}{\sum_{i=1}^{n} D^{-n_i}}\right)^{2}-\frac{1}{2}\left(\frac{D^{-n_i}}{\sum_{i=1}^{n} D^{-n_i}}\right)^{3}+\frac{1}{2}\left(\frac{D^{-n_i}}{\sum_{i=1}^{n} D^{-n_i}}\right)^{4}-\ldots\ldots\ldots.$$

$$\frac{1}{3}-\frac{1}{4}\left(\frac{D^{-n_i}}{\sum_{i=1}^{n} D^{-n_i}}\right)+\frac{1}{5}\left(\frac{D^{-n_i}}{\sum_{i=1}^{n} D^{-n_i}}\right)^2-\ldots\ldots\ldots$$

$$\leq \frac{1}{2}\left[1-\frac{D^{-n_i}}{\sum_{i=1}^{n} D^{-n_i}}+\left(\frac{D^{-n_i}}{\sum_{i=1}^{n} D^{-n_i}}\right)^2-\ldots\ldots\ldots\ldots\right]$$

$$\sum_{i=1}^{n}\frac{(-1)^n}{n+3}\left(\frac{D^{-n_i}}{\sum_{i=1}^{n} D^{-n_i}}\right)^n \leq \frac{1}{2}\sum_{i=1}^{n}(-1)^n\left(\frac{D^{-n_i}}{\sum_{i=1}^{n} D^{-n_i}}\right)^n$$

Again from Eqn. (15):

$$\sum_{i=1}^{n}\frac{(-1)^n}{n+3}\left(\frac{D^{-n_i}}{\sum_{i=1}^{n} D^{-n_i}}\right)^n \leq \frac{1}{2}\left[1+\frac{D^{-n_i}}{\sum_{i=1}^{n} D^{-n_i}}\right]^{-1} \tag{16}$$

$$\log(2)\leq\frac{3}{4},\ \ if\ \frac{D^{-n_i}}{\sum_{i=1}^{n} D^{-n_i}}=1 \tag{17}$$

Hence proved the result.

22.4 SOME NUMERICAL ILLUSTRATIONS

Here, numerical justification of inequalities Eqns. (5), (6), (8) and (14) is discussed. Taking, $n_i = 1, 2, 3$ and $D = 2$ for binary.

- **Example 22.1:** To Prove: $\eta(D)-\xi(D)\leq D^{-n_i}$
  where;

$$\eta(D)=\sum_{i=1}^{n} D^{-n_i}\log\left(\sum_{i=1}^{n} D^{-n_i}+D^{-n_i}\right)\ \text{and}$$

$$\xi(D) = \sum_{i=1}^{n} D^{-n_i} \log\left(\sum_{i=1}^{n} D^{-n_i}\right)$$

➢ **Proof 22.6:** $D^{-n_i} = 0.875$

$$\eta(D) = \sum_{i=1}^{n} D^{-n_i} \log\left(\sum_{i=1}^{n} D^{-n_i} + D^{-n_i}\right) = 0.1210$$

$$\xi(D) = \sum_{i=1}^{n} D^{-n_i} \log\left(\sum_{i=1}^{n} D^{-n_i}\right) = -0.0507$$

$$\text{Now, } \eta(D) - \xi(D) \le D^{-n_i}$$

$$0.1717 \le 0.875$$

Hence proved the result.

➢ **Example 22.2:** To Prove:

$$\frac{\left(D^{-n_i}\right)^4}{4} + \frac{\left(D^{-n_i}\right)^6}{6} + -- \le \frac{\left(D^{-n_i}\right)^3}{3} + \frac{\left(D^{-n_i}\right)^5}{5} + --$$

$$if \ \sum_{i=1}^{n} D^{-n_i} = 1$$

➢ **Proof 22.7:**

$$\frac{\left(D^{-n_i}\right)^4}{4} + \frac{\left(D^{-n_i}\right)^6}{6} \le \frac{\left(D^{-n_i}\right)^3}{3} + \frac{\left(D^{-n_i}\right)^5}{5}$$

$$0.1666 \le 0.3833$$

So,

$$\frac{\left(D^{-n_i}\right)^4}{4} + \frac{\left(D^{-n_i}\right)^6}{6} + -- \le \frac{\left(D^{-n_i}\right)^3}{3} + \frac{\left(D^{-n_i}\right)^5}{5} + --$$

Hence proved the result.

➢ **Example 22.3:** To prove: $0 \le \left[1 + \frac{D^{-n_i}}{\sum_{i=1}^{n} D^{-n_i}}\right] \le 1$

➢ **Proof 22.8:**

$$\left[1+\frac{D^{-n_i}}{\sum_{i=1}^{n} D^{-n_i}}\right] = 0.6363$$

$$0 \leq \left[1+\frac{D^{-n_i}}{\sum_{i=1}^{n} D^{-n_i}}\right] \leq 1$$

which proved the result.

➢ **Example 22.4:** To prove:

$$\sum_{i=1}^{n}\frac{(-1)^n}{n+3}\left(\frac{D^{-n_i}}{\sum_{i=1}^{n} D^{-n_i}}\right)^n \leq \frac{1}{2}\sum_{i=1}^{n}(-1)^n\left(\frac{D^{-n_i}}{\sum_{i=1}^{n} D^{-n_i}}\right)^n$$

➢ **Proof 22.9:**

$$\sum_{i=1}^{n}\frac{(-1)^n}{n+3}\left(\frac{D^{-n_i}}{\sum_{i=1}^{n} D^{-n_i}}\right)^n = 0.2248$$

$$\frac{1}{2}\left[1+\frac{D^{-n_i}}{\sum_{i=1}^{n} D^{-n_i}}\right]^{-1} = 0.3181$$

Hence,

$$\sum_{i=1}^{n}\frac{(-1)^n}{n+3}\left(\frac{D^{-n_i}}{\sum_{i=1}^{n} D^{-n_i}}\right)^n \leq \frac{1}{2}\left[1+\frac{D^{-n_i}}{\sum_{i=1}^{n} D^{-n_i}}\right]^{-1}$$

which proves the result.

22.5 CONCLUSION

In this chapter, new coding bounds are established using well-known inequalities. A major toolchain is formed by these inequalities for proving many outcomes in information theory. Possibilities from impossibilities are isolated by these inequalities of information theory, as for solving key results in information theory. Also, we have verified inequalities through numerical illustrations.

KEYWORDS

- **channel coding**
- **hamming bounds**
- **kraft inequality**
- **Kraft-McMillan inequality**
- **mathematical theory**
- **source coding**

REFERENCES

1. Belis, M., Guiasu, (1968). A quantitative- qualitative measure of information in cybernetic systems. *IEEE Transactions on Information Theory, 14*(4), 593–594.
2. Bhat, A. H., Dar, M. J., & Baig, M. A. K., (2018). Two parametric new generalized average codeword length and its bounds in terms of new generalized inaccuracy measure and their characterization. *Pakistan Journal of Statistics, 32*(2), 147–162.
3. Campbell, L. L., (1965). A coding theorem and Rényi's entropy. *Information and Control, 8,* 423–429.
4. Eswaran, K., & Gastpar, M., (2019). Remote source coding under Gaussian noise: Dueling rules of power and entropy power. *IEEE Transactions on Information Theory, 65*(7), 4486–4498.
5. Guiasu, S. & Picard, C. F. (1971). Lower bound of the length of certain codes, reviews. *Mathematique academie des sciences, Paris, 273*(A), 248–251.
6. Gurdial, P. F., (1977). On useful information of order α. *Journal of Combinatorics Information and System Sciences, 2,* 158–162.
7. Ihara, S., (1974). Coding theory in white Gaussian channel with feedback. *Journal of Multivariate Analysis, 4*, 74–87.
8. Jain, P., & Tuteja, R. K., (1989). On coding theorem connected with useful entropy of order β. *International Journal of Mathematics and Mathematical Sciences, 12*, 193–198.

9. Klapper, A., (1999). Improved lower bounds for multi covering codes. *IEEE Transactions on Information Theory, 45*, 2532–2534.
10. Kraf, L. G., (1949). *A Device for Quantizing, Grouping and Coding Amplitude Modulated Pulses.* Doctoral Dissertation, Massachusetts Institute of Technology, Cambridge.
11. Kulkarni, M., & Shivaprakasha, K. S., (2015). *Information Theory and Coding*. Wiley, New Delhi, India.
12. Li, D., & Chen, W., (1994). New lower bounds for binary covering codes. *IEEE Transactions on Information Theory, 40*, 1122–1129.
13. Longo, G., (1976). A noiseless coding theorem for sources having utilities. *SIAM Journal on Applied Mathematics, 30*(4), 739–748.
14. McEliece, R. J., Rodemich, E. R., Howard, R. J. R., & Welch, L. R., (1977). New upper bounds on the rate of a code via the Delsarte-mac Williams inequalities. *IEEE Transactions on Information Theory, 23*(2), 157–166.
15. Mondal, S. R., (2019). Bounds and inequalities of the modified Lommel functions. *Communications of Korean Mathematical Society, 34*(2), 573–583.
16. Renyi, A., (1961). On measure of entropy and information, *Proceedings Fourth Berkeley Symposium on Mathematical Statistics and Probability* (Vol. 1, pp. 547–561). University of California Press.
17. Saraswat, R. N., & Tak, A., (2019). new f-divergence and Jensen-Ostrowski's type inequalities. *Tamkang Journal of Mathematics, 50*(1), 111–118.
18. Sason, I., & Verdu, S., (2018). Improved bounds on lose less source coding and guessing moments via Renyi measures. *IEEE Transactions on Information Theory, 64*(6), 4323–4346.
19. Schalwijk, J. P. M., (1972). An algorithm for source coding. *IEEE Transactions on Information Theory, 18,* 395.
20. Shannon, C. E., (1948). A mathematical theory of communication. *The Bell System Technical Journal, 27*, 379–423, 623–656.
21. Taneja, H., Hooda, D. S., & Tuteja, R. K., (1985). Coding theorems on a generalized useful information. *Soochow Journal of Mathematics, 11*, 123–131.
22. Wondie, L., & Kumar, S., (2018). Some inequalities in information theory using Tsallis entropy. *International Journal of Mathematics and Mathematical Sciences, 4*.
23. Yang, S., Schoeny, C., & Dolecek, L., (2019). Theoretical bounds and constructions of codes in the generalized Cayley metric. *IEEE Transactions on Information Theory, 65*(8), 4746–4763.

CHAPTER 23

METAHEURISTICS-BASED MULTI-OBJECTIVE DESIGN OF ROBUST PROCESS CONTROL SYSTEMS

NITISH KATAL[1] and SANJAY KUMAR SINGH[2]

[1]*School of Electronics, Indian Institute of Information Technology, Una, Himachal Pradesh, India, E-mail: nitishkatal@iiitu.ac.in*

[2]*Department of EEE, Amity University Jaipur, Jaipur, Rajasthan, India*

ABSTRACT

The process control applications are highly dynamic and it is very crucial for the system to maintain its state, any deviation from the desired state will affect the quality of the products, the energy consumption, wastage of raw material and this will impact the overall operational costs and economy of the industry. So, it becomes crucial for the control systems to maintain their states during the operation even under the influence of uncertainties and unwanted disturbances. This chapter explores one such example of an uncertain pH neutralization process. The work focuses on the multi-objective design of controllers considering the robustness and tracking performance objectives. The controller synthesis problem has been expressed as an optimization problem and multi-objective evolutionary algorithm with decomposition has been used to find the optimal gains and the performance of the obtained controller has also been compared with the controllers designed using classical control methodologies and the results obtained established the superiority of the designed controller.

23.1 INTRODUCTION

In industries, the role of process control is to ensure that the key process must maintain their states throughout the operation of the plant. Any deviation from the desired state will directly affect the quality of the product, the energy consumed by the plant, wastage of raw material, the overall operational costs, and the economy. So, the improved control schemes will aid in improving the quality of the product and will boost the profit. But these industrial processes are subjected to various uncertainties that can be due to unmodeled dynamics, approximations while linearizing the plant, variations in the operational conditions, measurement noise., uncertainties, inherent dead-time, etc., and the plant that has been considered for controller synthesis is just an approximation of the practical system. These factors pose a challenge to assure that the key processes maintain their optimum states throughout the plant operation.

In process control systems, there is a need of maintaining adequate stability margins, so that reliability of the processes can be ensured. Thus to achieve such good stability margins and performance objectives, the robustness of the system to uncertainties and disturbances becomes a crucial element in control system design [4, 11]. So, it becomes crucial to model these uncertainties and other factors itself in the controller synthesis problem formulation and design controllers that are robust to such uncertainties.'

To cope up with such problem, robust control and adaptive control methods aid in designing controllers that an easily handle such uncertainties. Adaptive control varies the control law online by identifying the process variations; while robust control follows the worst-case design approach by incorporating the uncertainties in the controller synthesis problem and aim to maintain adequate performance and stability margins, despite the presence of uncertainty in the dynamics of the plant [8, 9]. There are several classical robust control methods like, H_∞ control, μ synthesis, QFT, etc. But, the controllers obtained by these methods generally have a high order, are not always optimal and are limited by design constraints and objectives. So, there is an immense scope for designing for designing robust control systems [3].

As the design requirements in process control are very strict and adequate stability margins must be maintained, formulating the controller design problem as an optimization problem and solving it using meta-heuristic algorithms will aid in finding globally optimum controllers that satisfy the design objectives and constraints. This also gives complete freedom to the control designer to choose the desired controller structure and formulate the desired objective function based on requirements. As controller synthesis is a multi-objective design problem, so several design objectives can be used to formulate the problem either as a weighted sum of objectives or as based in Pareto based approach.

This chapter investigates the metaheuristics-based multi-objective optimal design of robust controllers for parametrically uncertain pH neutralization process. In this work, the controller design problem has been formulated as a multi-objective optimization problem (MOP) using various time domain and frequency domain performance indices and has been solved using a multi-objective evolutionary algorithm based on decomposition (MOEA/D). To demonstrate the efficacy of the approach, a pH neutralization process system has been considered, and the problem has been formulated by minimizing the objectives of rise time, overshoot percentage and peak gain of the complementary sensitivity function. The results have been compared with the controllers designed using classical control methodologies and the ones already reported in literature. To check the efficacy of the designed controller, a comparison has been made with the uncertain plant with a parametric uncertainty of $\pm$10%, and the results obtained establish the efficacy of the proposed controller.

23.2 pH NEUTRALIZATION PROCESS

In industries such as pharmaceuticals, textile, biotechnological, etc., host several chemical processing units and the discharge of waste through such chemical processing units is rarely neutral. So, to neutralize the acidity of this discharge, wastewater treatment plants are used in such industrial establishments. One of the most crucial components of the wastewater treatment units is the pH neutralization process. The pH is "*the measurement of acidity or alkalinity of a liquid that may contain a proportion of water*." The pH neutralization process deals with the neutralization of the acidity of the wastewater before it is discharged to the rivers or can be reused. The purpose of neutralization of the discharge is to protect the environment, rivers, aquatic life, to prevent soil acidity, and also to make the discharge reusable if being recycled back to the processes. But of the biggest problem in pH neutralization is the strong nonlinearity of the process. Many researchers have focused on the development of improved controlled schemes, so that the pH of the discharge remains consistent irrespective of the varying plant conditions and the non-linearity of the process [1, 2, 5, 6, 16, 17, 19].

There are two primary reactor architectures considered for the neutralization of the pH, continuous, and batch processing. In this study, the continuous stirred tank reactor (CSTR) based architecture has been considered. In CSTR based pH neutralization process, the inflow of the influent liquid is done the bottom of the reactor tank, the whole neutralization process is carried out at a certain set temperature and pressure. To neutralize the pH, the release of acid or base to the tank is regulated by the pH controller, e.g., if the influent liquid is acidic, then the pH sensor will get to know about the increase in the acidity of the liquid, the information is sent to the controller, so to regulate this the controller will release the base based upon error in the acidity (desired acidity minus current acidity), so that the neutralization of the liquid in the tank is achieved. The schematic diagram of the CSTR based pH neutralization process is shown in Figure 23.1.

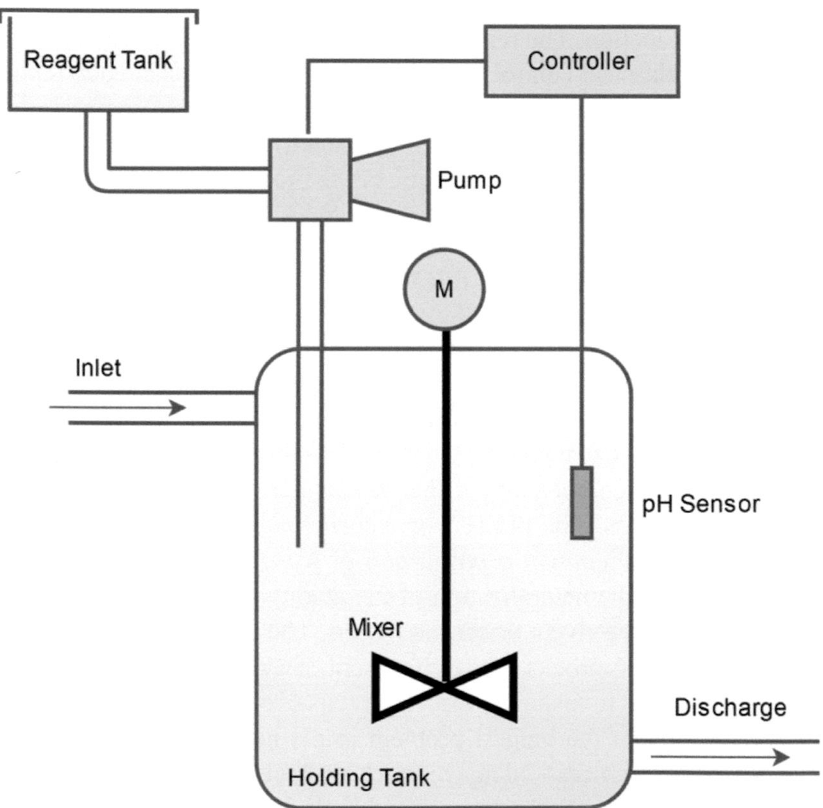

FIGURE 23.1 The schematic representation of CSTR based pH neutralization process.

In this work, the CSTR based pH neutralization process is considered as proposed in Ref. [13]. The process model has been estimated as a first order with a time-delay system, and the transfer function is given by Eqn. (1) as:

$$G(s) = \frac{K}{\tau \cdot s + 1} e^{-\tau_D \cdot s} = \frac{0.276}{3.2s + 1} e^{-5.005s} \quad (1)$$

where; K is the gain, τ is the time constant, τ_D is the time delay and $G(s)$ is the transfer function CSTR based pH neutralization plant.

23.3 MULTI-OBJECTIVE EVOLUTIONARY ALGORITHM-BASED ON DECOMPOSITION (MOEA/D)

In 2007, Zhang and Li proposed a MOEA/D [18]. The algorithm unambiguously decomposes a MOP into subsequent scalar optimization subproblems using Tchebycheff approach, and tries to concurrently solve these sub-objectives, and as the optimization process progresses, the set of solutions are also evolved. At each generation, the set of solutions have the current best solution for each design sub-objective. This decomposition of the MOP to scalar sub-optimization problems accelerates the search and also minimizes the computational requirements. In MOEA/D, the solution to each design sub-objective is governed by the minimization of the sum of distances of the coefficient vectors of the neighboring sub-objectives. Thus the optimal solutions to neighboring sub-objectives will be likely same.

23.4 OPTIMIZATION-BASED DESIGN

In this section, the controller synthesis problem has been formulated as an optimization algorithm. Initially, the classical methods for the PID controller synthesis have been considered, followed by the formulation of controller synthesis problem as an optimization problem and has been solved using GA by minimizing the time domain performances. But, this does not assure robustness to noise, disturbance or parametric variations. To achieve robustness, the controller synthesis problem has been formulated as the MOP, and objectives of both time and frequency domain objectives are used in the controller synthesis. MOEA/D has been used for the controller synthesis.

23.4.1 CONTROLLER SYNTHESIS USING CLASSICAL METHODS

The PID controllers are the simplest and most widely controllers used controllers, and contribute to 90% of the total controllers used in industries [12]. The transfer function of a standard PID controller is given by Eqn. (2) as:

$$K(s) = K_P + \frac{K_I}{s} + K_D s \tag{2}$$

The PID controllers can be easily tuned using classical methods like Ziegler Nichols (ZN) method, but the response offered is not optimal, and very large values of overshoot percentages are observed. Here, the ZN method has been initially used to estimate the controller gains, but it is not possible to directly apply the ZN method to FODT systems. So, to apply the ZN method to tune the PID controller for the pH neutralization process, the transfer function, Eqn. (1), is converted to a 4th order delay-free system using Padé approximation, and is given by Eqn. (3). In Figure 23.2, it can be observed that the open-loop behavior of the estimated delay-free plant mimics the behavior of the original FODT system.

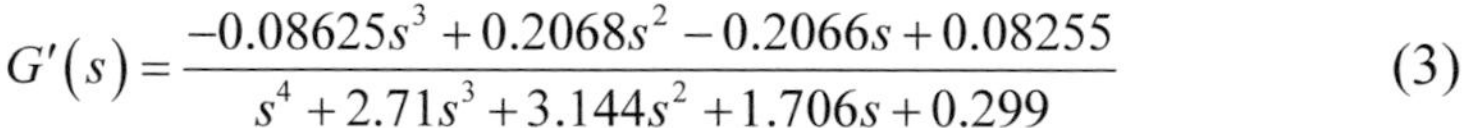

$$G'(s) = \frac{-0.08625s^3 + 0.2068s^2 - 0.2066s + 0.08255}{s^4 + 2.71s^3 + 3.144s^2 + 1.706s + 0.299} \tag{3}$$

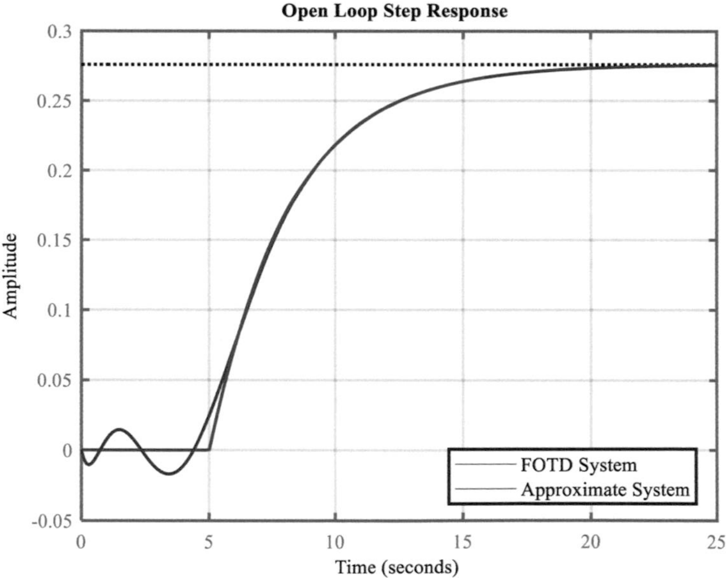

FIGURE 23.2 The open-loop step response of the estimated system compared with the original FOPD system.

The controller gains obtained using the ZN method are given by Eqn. (4) and the closed-loop response can be seen in Figure 23.3, and it can be observed that the PID controller gains are not optimal, as high values of overshoot percentage can be observed. This high vales of overshoot percentages will lead to the increase in the acidity levels of the liquid for a certain time period, and the huge volume of base has to be released to regulate this increase in acidity, leading to the wastage of resources.

$$K_{ZN}(s) = 3.743 + \frac{0.522}{s} + 6.711s \tag{4}$$

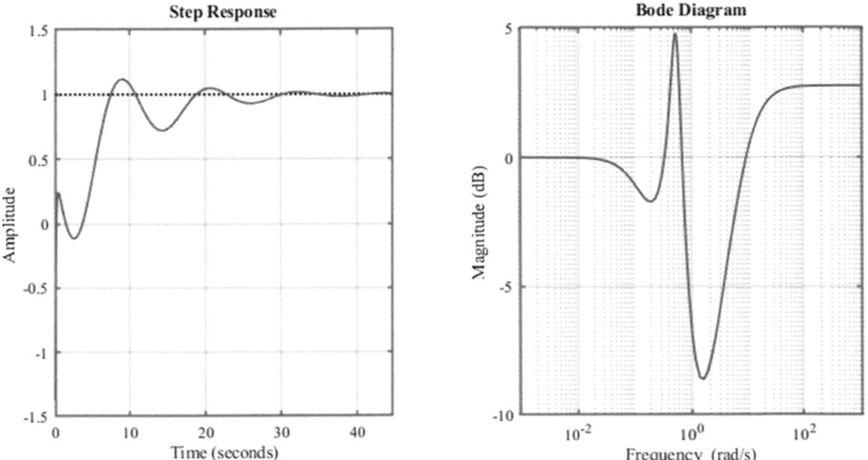

FIGURE 23.3 The closed-loop step response of the closed-loop pH neutralization system with ZN PID controller.

23.4.2 CONTROLLER SYNTHESIS USING TIME DOMAIN PERFORMANCE INDICES

To obtain the optimal gains of the PID controller, the use of GA [7] has been explored for controller synthesis [10, 14, 15]. The use of minimization of integral square of error (ISE) has been considered and is given by equation as:

$$J_{ISE} = \int (e(t))^2 dt \tag{5}$$

The GA aim at finding the optimal values of [K_P, K_1, K_D] that minimizes the ISE. The genetic algorithmic specific parameters used in the optimization are, a population size of 45 and tournament-based selection has been considered. The controller gains obtained after the optimization process are given by Eqn. (6) and the closed-loop time and frequency response is shown in Figure 23.4.

$$K_{GA-ISE}(s) = 1.989 + \frac{0.409}{s} - 2.891s \tag{6}$$

From Figure 23.4, it can be observed that the time response has improved significantly, but the frequency response is not yet optimal, as high magnitude of the peak gain can be observed in Figure 23.4(b).

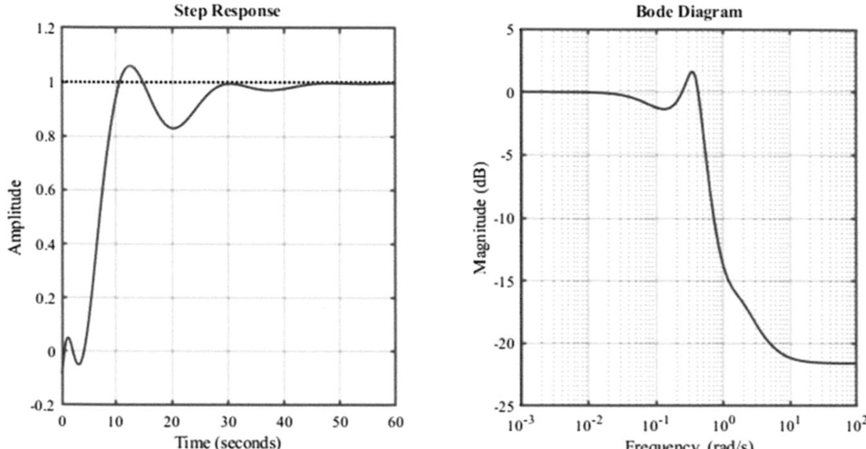

FIGURE 23.4 The closed-loop time and frequency response of the closed-loop pH neutralization system with GA tuned PID controller.

23.4.3 CONTROLLER SYNTHESIS USING TIME DOMAIN PERFORMANCE INDICES

So, in order to improve the overall response of the closed-loop pH neutralization process, both in time and frequency domain, so that the designed control system offers a robust response even in the presence of noise, disturbances, and parameter variations. So, here the objectives of rise time, equation, overshoot percentage, Eqn. (7) and magnitude of the peak gain of the complementary sensitivity function (Eqn. (8)) are used to pose the controller design problem as a MOP as give in Eqn. (10). MOEA/D has been used to find the optimum controller parameters. The use of minimization of rise time, overshoot, and peak gain has been considered.

$$\%overshoot = \frac{M_p}{y_{ss}} \times 100 \tag{7}$$

where; $M_p = y_{max} - y_{ss}$.

$$\text{Max. Peak Gain} = \max\left|\frac{G(j\omega)K(j\omega)}{1+G(j\omega)K(j\omega)}\right| \tag{8}$$

The optimization algorithm, MOEA/D, aim at finding the optimal values of [K_P, K_1, K_D] that minimizes the proposed objective function. A population size of 45 is considered. The optimization problem has been formulated as an aggregate of function given by Eqn. (10).

Find the set of controller and pre-filter parameters x which minimizes $J(x)$.

$$J(x) = \min\left[J_1(x), \quad J_2(x), \quad \cdots \quad J_i(x)\right] \tag{9}$$

Subject to, $\underline{x_i} \le x_i \le \overline{x_i}$

where; $i = 1,\ldots, n$

In this work, the objective function has been formulated as:

$$J(x) = \min\begin{bmatrix} RT \\ OS\% \\ \max\left|\dfrac{G(j\omega)K(j\omega)}{1+G(j\omega)K(j\omega)}\right| \end{bmatrix} \tag{10}$$

The controller chosen is a standard PID controller given by equation and after the optimization process, a set of Pareto optimal solutions (POS) has been obtained. The various controller parameters obtained in the POS are shown in Figure 23.5, and the values of chosen objectives of overshoot percentage, rise time, and magnitude of the maximum peak gain of the complementary sensitivity is shown in Figure 23.6. The Pareto front visualization is shown in Figure 23.7.

Since all the solutions in the POS are Pareto optimal, hence it is not possible to improve one objective while compromising the other. Hence, based on the design requirements, the control designer or decision-maker can choose the desired solution from the POS. Figures 23.8 and 23.9 shows the closed-loop system's time and frequency response with all the controllers obtained in the POS. The chosen controller from the POS is given by Eqn. (11) and the respective time and frequency response is shown in Figure 23.10.

$$K_{MOEA/D}(s) = 1.99 + \frac{0.396}{s} + 0.0121s \tag{11}$$

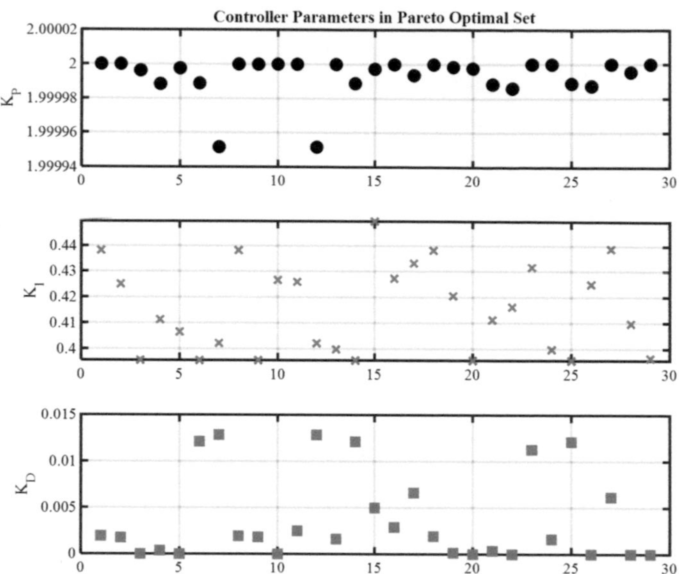

FIGURE 23.5 The plot for all the controller gains obtained in POS using MOEA/D.

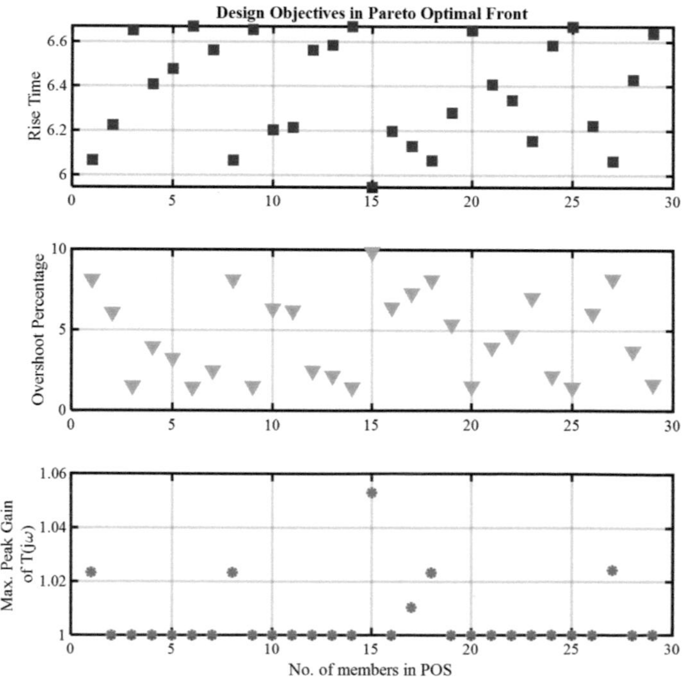

FIGURE 23.6 The plot for all the design objectives obtained in POS using MOEA/D.

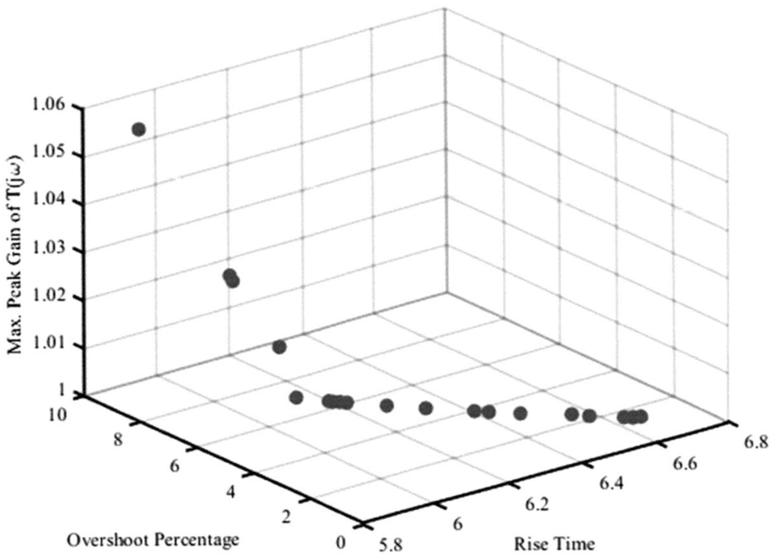

FIGURE 23.7 The Pareto front of the objectives as obtained in POS using MOEA/D.

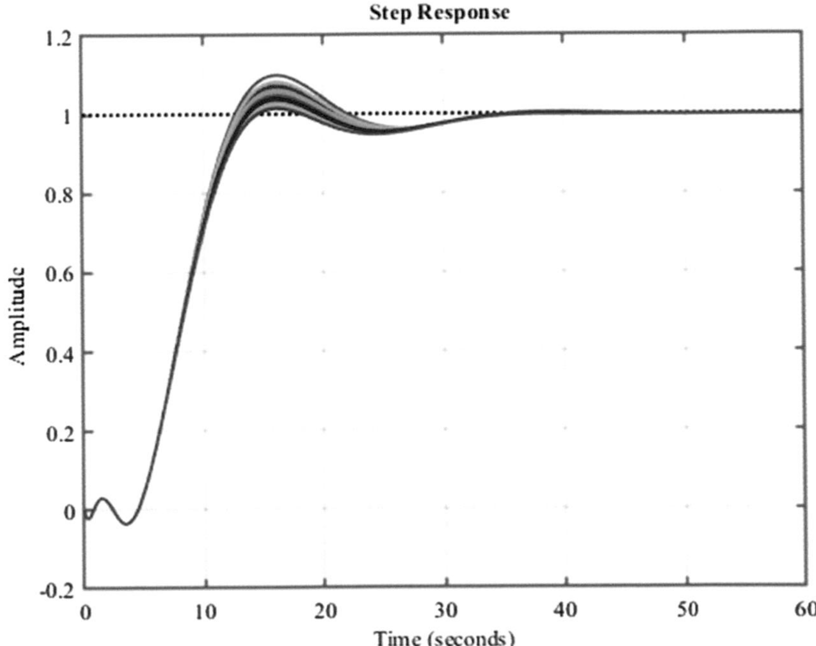

FIGURE 23.8 The closed-loop step response of the closed-loop pH neutralization system with all the PID gains obtained in POS using MOEA/D.

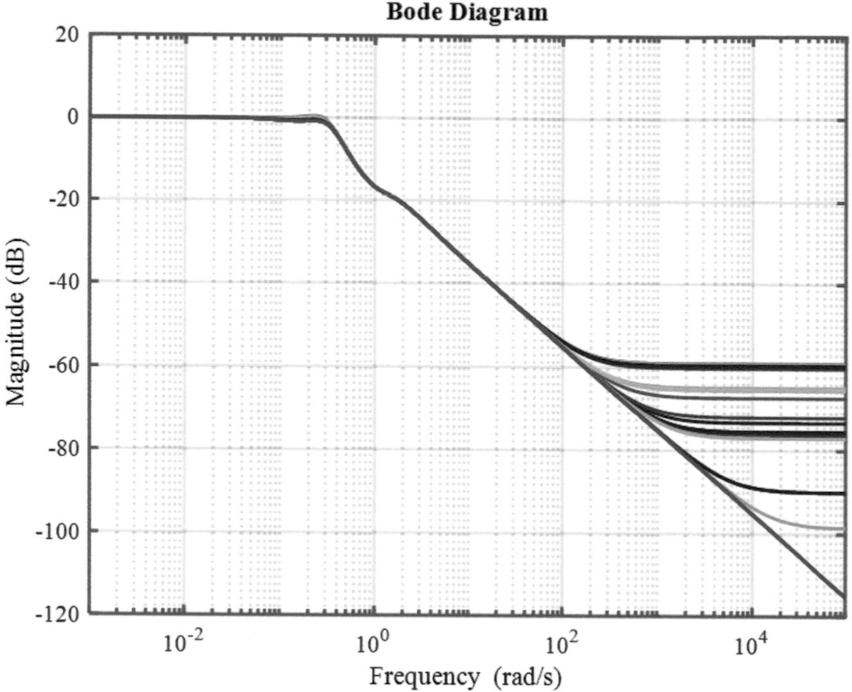

FIGURE 23.9 The frequency response of the closed-loop pH neutralization system with all the PID gains obtained in POS using MOEA/D.

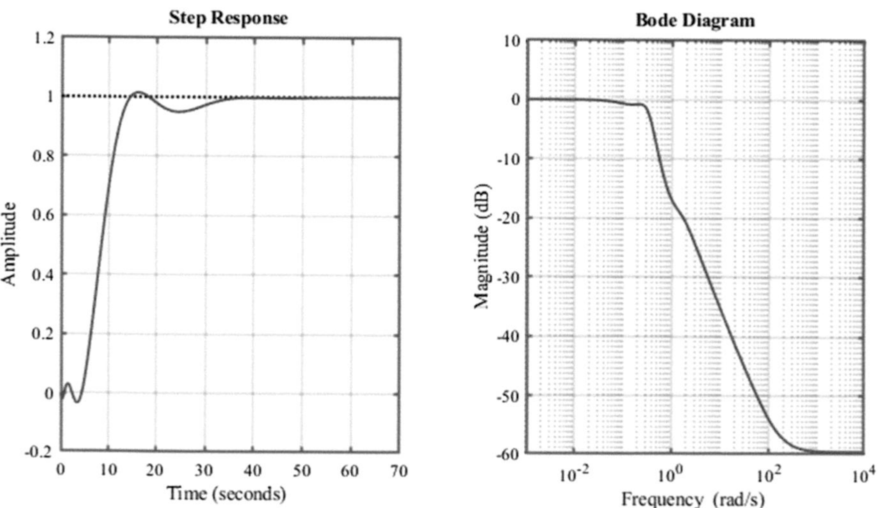

FIGURE 23.10 The time and frequency response of the closed-loop pH neutralization system with all the PID gains chosen in Eqn. (11).

23.5 RESULTS AND DISCUSSION

Since, the classical method for the PID controller did not offered satisfactory time domain response, as large overshoot percentages have been observed. So, then to improve the time response of the closed-loop system, the minimization of the square of error (ISE) has been considered using genetic algorithm, though the designed closed-loop system offers better time-domain response but the frequency response is not optimal. So, finally, to improve the time as well as frequency response of the closed-loop system and also to minimize the impact of any disturbance either due to process's parametric changes or due to heavy influx of liquid, the synthesis of the robust PID controller has been considered using both time and frequency domain objectives and the problem has been formulated as a MOP and has been solved using multi-objective evolutionary algorithm with decomposition.

The results have also been compared with the various controllers proposed in Ref. [13], controller obtained by Marlin et al. $K_{MM}(s)$, Smith et al. and Branica et al. are given by Eqns. (12), (13) and (14). Table 23.1 shows the values of various time and frequency domain performance indices. Figure 23.11 shows the compared step response of the closed-loop system and Figure 23.12 shows the compared frequency domain response of the closed-loop system.

$$K_{MM}(s) = 2.355 + \frac{0.725}{s} + 1.179s \tag{12}$$

$$K_{SM}(s) = 2.316 + \frac{0.723}{s} + 5.707s \tag{13}$$

$$K_{BM}(s) = 2.66 + \frac{0.537}{s} + 2.912s \tag{14}$$

TABLE 23.1 Time and Frequency Domain Performance Indices

Performance Index	Proposed	ZN	GA	MM	SM	BM
Rise Time (secs.)	6.687	6.393	8.944	8.871	7.761	9.07
Settling Time (secs.)	31.006	27.95	40.653	43.793	25.576	15.869
Overshoot Percentage	1.517	11.733	5.957	40.518	17.377	5.064
Under Shoot	3.42	137.43	8.325	11.32	96.94	33.54
Gain Margin	2.413	1.578	1.931	1.804	2.032	2.361
Phase Margin	65.924	74.739	71.185	36.854	48.522	60.811
Peak Gain of $T(j\omega)$	1.000	1.721	1.207	1.852	1.207	1.000

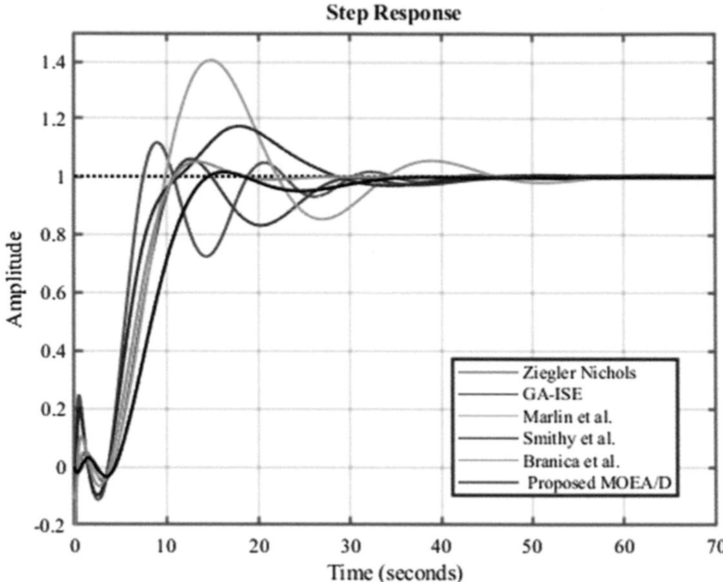

FIGURE 23.11 Compared time-domain response of the closed-loop pH neutralization system.

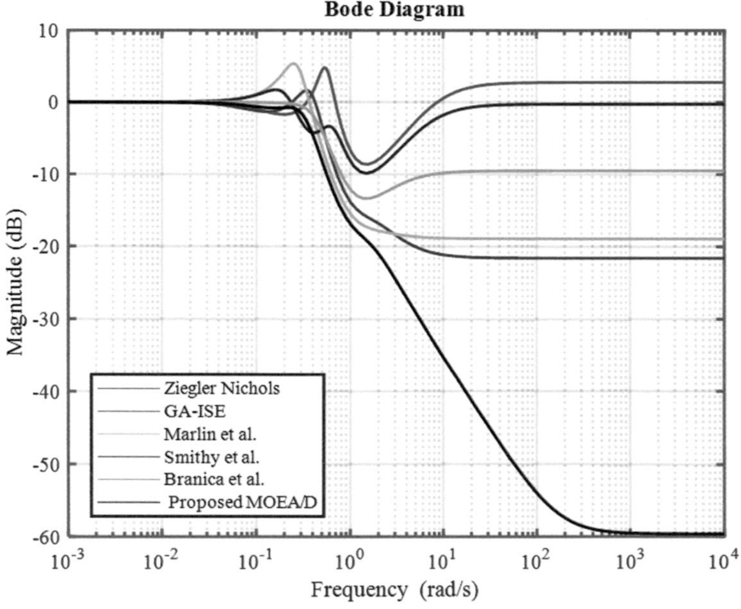

FIGURE 23.12 Compared frequency domain response of the closed-loop pH neutralization system.

To check the robustness of the designed system, a variation of ±10% in the plant parameters has been considered. Figure 23.13 shows the compared step response and Figure 23.14 shows the compared frequency domain response of the closed-loop system with parametrically uncertain system. From the above plots, it can be observed that the proposed controller offers a much better response both in time and frequency domain and efficiently stabilizes the system within a very narrow envelope.

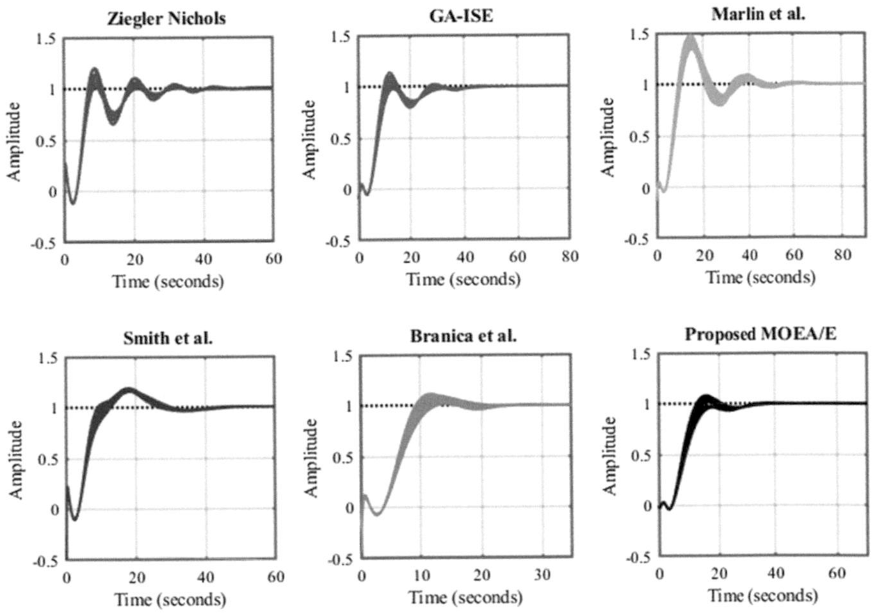

FIGURE 23.13 Compared time-domain response of the closed-loop pH neutralization system with uncertain plant.

23.6 CONCLUSION

The role of process control is to ensure that the key process must maintain their states throughout the operation of the plant. Any deviation from the desired state will directly affect the quality of the product, the energy consumed by the plant, wastage of raw material the overall operational costs and economy. This chapter investigates a metaheuristics-based multi-objective optimal design of robust controllers for a parametrically uncertain pH neutralization process. In this work, the controller design problem has been formulated as a MOP using various time domain and frequency domain performance indices and has been solved using MOEA/D and the efficacy of the approach has been established by compared with the controllers designed using classical control methodologies and the ones already reported in literature. It has been observed that the designed controller offers a better response both in time and frequency domain and efficiently handles the impact of any parametric uncertainty that may occur in the plant.

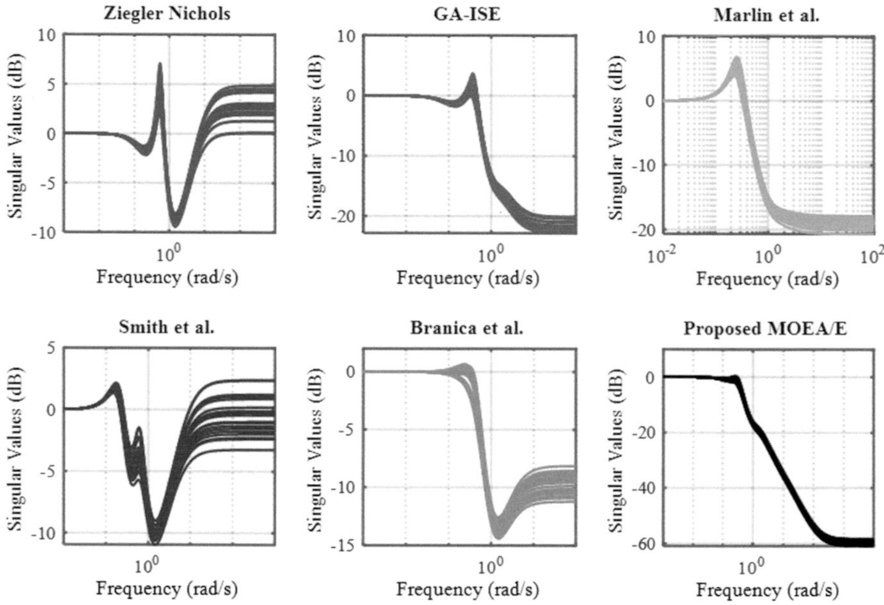

FIGURE 23.14 Compared frequency domain response of the closed-loop pH neutralization system with uncertain plant.

KEYWORDS

- **metaheuristic algorithms**
- **multi-objective evolutionary algorithm**
- **pH neutralization process**
- **process control**
- **robust control**
- **wastewater treatment**

REFERENCES

1. Aguiar, R. A., Franco, I. C., Leonardi, F., & Lima, F., (2018). Fractional PID controller applied to a chemical plant with level and pH control. *Chemical Product and Process Modeling, 13*(4).
2. Akshay, N., & Subbulekshmi, D., (2017). Online auto-selection of tuning methods and auto-tuning PI controller in FOPDT real-time process-pH neutralization. *Energy Procedia, 117*, 1109–1116.
3. Åström, K. J., & Kumar, P. R., (2014). Control: A perspective. *Automatica, 50*(1), 3–43.
4. Bequette, B. W., (2003). *Process Control: Modeling, Design, and Simulation*. Prentice-Hall Professional.
5. Bingi, K., Ibrahim, R., Karsiti, M. N., & Hassan, S. M., (2018). Fractional-order set-point weighted PID controller for pH neutralization process using accelerated PSO algorithm. *Arabian Journal for Science and Engineering, 43*(6), 2687–2701.
6. Böling, J. M., Seborg, D. E., & Hespanha, J. P., (2007). Multi-model adaptive control of a simulated pH neutralization process. *Control Engineering Practice, 15*(6), 663–672.
7. Goldberg, D. E., (1990). *Real-Coded Genetic Algorithms, Virtual Alphabets and Blocking*. University of Illinois at Urbana Champaign.
8. Katal, N., & Narayan, S., (2017). Design of robust fractional order PID controllers for coupled tank systems using multi-objective particle swarm optimization. *International Journal of Systems, Control and Communications, 8*(3), 250–267.
9. Katal, N., & Narayan, S., (2016). Multi-objective optimization-based design of robust fractional-order PI λ D μ controller for coupled tank systems. In: *Proceedings of Fifth International Conference on Soft Computing for Problem Solving* (pp. 27–38). Springer, Singapore.
10. Katal, N., Kumar, P., & Narayan, S., (2014). Optimal PID controller for coupled-tank liquid-level control system using bat algorithm. In: *2014 International Conference on Power, Control and Embedded Systems (ICPCES)* (pp. 1–4). IEEE.
11. Luyben, W. L., (1989). *Process Modeling, Simulation and Control for Chemical Engineers*. McGraw-Hill Higher Education.
12. Nise, N. S., (2007). *Control Systems Engineering*. John Wiley & Sons.
13. Ram, S. S., Kumar, D. D., & Meenakshipriya, B., (2016). Designing of PID controllers for pH neutralization process. *Indian Journal of Science and Technology, 9*(12).
14. Singh, S. K., & Katal, N., (2017). Optimal tuning of PID controller for coupled tank liquid level control system using particle swarm optimization. In: *Proceedings of Sixth International Conference on Soft Computing for Problem Solving* (pp. 68–75). Springer, Singapore.
15. Singh, S. K., Katal, N., & Modani, S. G., (2014). Multi-objective optimization of PID controller for coupled-tank liquid-level control system using genetic algorithm. In: *Proceedings of the Second International Conference on Soft Computing for Problem Solving (SocProS 2012)* (pp. 59–66). Springer, New Delhi.
16. Sreepriya, S., Aparna, K., & Vinila, M. L., (2019). Evolutionary algorithm based robust fixed structure controller for pH in sodium chlorate process. In: *International Conference on Intelligent Computing, Information and Control Systems* (pp. 282–291). Springer, Cham.

17. Tong, L. H., Li, Y. G., Zhu, H. Q., & Li, W. T., (2020). Fractional order PID optimal control in pH neutralization process. In: *IOP Conference Series: Earth and Environmental Science* (Vol. 427, No. 1, p. 012002). IOP Publishing.
18. Zhang, Q., & Li, H., (2007). MOEA/D: A multi objective evolutionary algorithm based on decomposition. *IEEE Transactions on Evolutionary Computation, 11*(6), 712–731.
19. Zhou, H., & Qiao, J., (2019). Multi-objective optimal control for wastewater treatment process using adaptive MOEA/D. *Applied Intelligence*, *49*(3), 1098–1126.

CHAPTER 24

BIANCHI TYPE IX AXIALLY SYMMETRIC COSMOLOGICAL MODEL WITH NEGATIVE DECELERATION PARAMETER IN GENERAL RELATIVITY

SANJAY SHARMA and LAXMI POONIA

Department of Mathematics and Statistics,
Manipal University Jaipur, Jaipur, Rajasthan–303007, India,
E-mail: laxmi.poonia@jaipur.manipal.edu (L. Poonia)

ABSTRACT

We have investigated Bianchi type IX axially symmetric cosmological model with negative deceleration parameter to study inflationary scenario of universe. To obtained inflationary model we considered the flat region in which potential $V(\phi)$ is constant and scalar factor $R \sim e^{nHt}$ where H is Hubble constant and n is fractional constant. We observed the universe is increasing in exponentially way. The behavior of model for different value of n is discussed. The cosmological properties for model are also discussed.

24.1 INTRODUCTION

In modern research, Einstein's theory becomes a subject of interest due to its attainment in explaining the accelerated cosmic expansion of the physical universe. Many cosmological problems like isotropy, homogeneity, monopole, and flatness can be successfully explained by inflationary theory. Bianchi space IX investigated familiar standard models like Robertson-Walker (RW) universe [1], the de-sitter universe [2], and the Taub-nut solution [3]. Bianchi space IX also leads to closed FRW space-time. This model allows not only universe expansion but also shearing, rotation, and anisotropic more generally. The initial idea of inflation in the early universe is proposed by Guth [4] in the context of GUT. Modern cosmological models provide a framework for the investigation of the early evolution of the universe. Standard models indicates universe is purely isotropic and homogeneous which agreed with astronomical facts about early stage of universe, but this model are unstable near cosmological singularities so the choice of antistrophic model for Einstein field equations provides a systemic explanation of physical universe rather than standard model.

Inflation is considered as highly rapid expansion of early cosmos by a factor of 10^{78} in volume drives under effect of false vacuum energy density. Inflationary scenario in different aspects is developed by many cosmologist [5–12]. Vaidya and Patel [13] have developed spatially homogenous Bianchi IX space that provides exact solution of system of field equation for perfect fluid and the pure radiation. Bali and Goyal [14] have resulted in various model to explain inflation under consideration of distribution in perfect fluid by assuming the appropriate condition that shear scalar is proportional to expansion scalar. The effect of the Higgs field together with potential plays a vital role in this discussion. Various aspects of inflationary scenarios and the importance of the scalar field in the study of universe evolution are observed by many researchers [15–22].

Motivated by the situations discussed above, in this work, we have derived an axially symmetrical Bianchi space IX cosmological model in the existence of flat potential under scalar fields, which is purely massless and in which $V(\phi)$ is constant. Also, supplementary condition with scalar factor $R \sim e^{nHt}$ is assumed where H is Hubble parameter and n is constant. We find the proper volume (R^3) increase with cosmic time which represent universe expands in exponentially way, and for different value of n, we have observed deceleration parameter $q < 0$, shear (σ) is zero and expansion (θ) is constant. This model represents an accelerated expansion of the physical universe, and the de-sitter universe is observed. The present work is classified in the following sections: Section 24.2 deals with the metric equation and system of nonlinear differential equations. Section 24.3 is concerned with the solution of field equations by using suitable conditions. Section 24.4 is concerned with the geometrical and structural features of the current model. Section 24.5 provides major conclusions.

24.2 METRIC AND FIELD EQUATIONS

Anisotropic Bianchi type IX metric in homogeneous form can be described by:

$$ds^2 = -dt^2 + a^2dx^2 + b^2dy^2 + (b^2\sin^2 y + a^2\cos^2 y)dz^2 - 2a^2\cos y\,dx\,dz \quad (1)$$

where; *a* and *b* are matric coefficients.

The action of the field of gravitation coupled minimally to a scalar field region with potential v(ϕ) is given by:

$$L = \int\left(R - \frac{1}{2}g^{ij}\phi_{,i}\,\phi_{,j} - V(\phi)\right)\sqrt{-g}\,dx^4 \quad (2)$$

which provides Einstein field equations for the dynamical field is obtained as:

$$R_{ij} - \frac{1}{2}Rg_{ij} = -8\pi T_{ij} \quad (3)$$

(in geometrical unit we have G = C = 1).

The Energy-momentum tensor for this configuration is considered as:

$$T_{ij} = \phi_{,i}\,\phi_{,j} - \left[\frac{1}{2}\phi_{,k}\,\phi^{,k} + v(\phi)\right]g_{ij} \quad (4)$$

$$\text{with: } \frac{1}{\sqrt{-g}}\partial_i(\sqrt{-g}\phi_{,i}) = -\frac{dV}{d\phi} \quad (5)$$

$$\text{where; } \phi_{,i} = \frac{\partial\phi}{\partial x^i}, \phi_{,j} = \frac{\partial\phi}{\partial x^j}, \phi^{,k} = g^{kv}\frac{\partial\phi}{\partial x^v}$$

Now the system of Einstein field Eqn. (3) for metric Eqn. (1) leads to:

$$\frac{2b_{44}}{b} + \frac{(b_4)^2}{b^2} + \frac{1}{b^2} - \frac{3}{4}\frac{a^2}{b^4} = \left[\frac{\phi_4^{\ 2}}{2} - v(\phi)\right] \quad (6)$$

$$\frac{a^2}{4b^4} + \frac{a_4b_4}{ab} + \frac{b_{44}}{b} + \frac{a_{44}}{a} = \left[\frac{\phi_4^{\ 2}}{2} - v(\phi)\right] \quad (7)$$

$$\frac{2a_4b_4}{ab} - \frac{a^2}{4b^4} + \frac{b_4^{\ 2}}{b^2} + \frac{1}{b^2} = -\left[\frac{\phi_4^{\ 2}}{2} - v(\phi)\right] \quad (8)$$

$$\left[\frac{a_{44}}{a} - \frac{b_{44}}{b} + \frac{a^2}{b^4} + \frac{a_4b_4}{ab} - \frac{1}{b^2} - \frac{b_4^{\ 2}}{b^2}\right]\cos y = 0 \quad (9)$$

Using scalar field Eqn. (5), the line element Eqn. (1) leads to:

$$\phi_{44} + \left(\frac{a_4}{a} + \frac{2b_4}{b}\right)\phi_4 = \frac{-dV}{d\phi} \quad (10)$$

Here indices 4 indicate the differentiation with respect to time, and other symbols have the usual meaning.

24.3 SOLUTION OF FIELD EQUATIONS

Here we are interested to find inflationary solution, for this purpose we consider flat regions where potential is constant, i.e.,

$$V(\phi) = \xi \tag{11}$$

Using Eqn. (11) in Eqn. (10) we have:

$$\phi_{44} + \left(\frac{a_4}{a} + \frac{2b_4}{b}\right)\phi_4 = 0 \tag{12}$$

On solving Eqn. (12), we get:

$$\phi_4 = \frac{\mu}{ab^2} \text{ where } \mu \text{ is constant of integration} \tag{13}$$

Since Eqns. (16)–(19) are nonlinear set of differential equations, to find metric coefficients, we required extra condition:

$$R \sim e^{nHt} \qquad \text{i.e. } R^3 = ab^2 = e^{3nHt} \tag{14}$$

where; n is arbitrary constant and H is Hubble constant.

Eqns. (13) and (14) gives:

$$\phi_4 = \frac{\mu}{e^{3nHt}} \tag{15}$$

where; μ is integrating constant.

From Eqn. (14) we have:

$$\frac{a_4}{a} + \frac{2b_4}{b} = 3nH \tag{16}$$

From Eqn. (16) we get:

$$\frac{a_{44}}{a} - \frac{a_4^{\,2}}{a^2} + 2\left[\frac{b_{44}}{b} - \frac{b_4^{\,2}}{b^2}\right] = 0 \tag{17}$$

Using Eqns. (16) and (17) we have:

$$\frac{a_{44}}{a} = -\frac{2b_{44}}{b} + \frac{6b_4^{\,2}}{b^2} + 9n^2H^2 - 12nH\frac{b_4}{b} \tag{18}$$

Now using Eqns. (6), (7) and (8) we get:

$$\frac{4b_{44}}{b} + \frac{2a_{44}}{a} = 2\phi_4^{\,2} - 2V(\phi) \tag{19}$$

Using Eqn. (18) in Eqn. (19) we get:

$$\frac{4b_{44}}{b}+2\left[-\frac{2b_{44}}{b}+\frac{6b_4^{\,2}}{b^2}+9n^2H^2-12nH\frac{b_4}{b}\right]=2\phi_4^{\,2}+2V(\phi) \tag{20}$$

We obtain:

$$\frac{12b_4^{\,2}}{b^2}-24nH\frac{b_4}{b}+18n^2H^2-2\mu^2e^{-6nHt}+2V(\phi)=0 \tag{21}$$

Eqn. (21) is quadratic equation and taking 2V (ϕ) = S

$$\frac{12b_4^{\,2}}{b^2}-24nH\frac{b_4}{b}+18n^2H^2-2\mu^2e^{-6nHt}+S=0 \tag{22}$$

which leads to:

$$\frac{b_4}{b}=\frac{24nH\pm\sqrt{576n^2H^2+48(2\mu^2e^{-6nHt}+18n^2H^2-S)}}{24} \tag{23}$$

for simplicity, we assume:

$$576n^2H^2+48(2\mu^2e^{-6nHt}+18n^2H^2-S)=0 \tag{24}$$

By solving Eqn. (24) we obtain:

$$e^{6nHt}=\frac{2\mu^2}{6n^2H^2+S}=\text{constant} \tag{25}$$

Now Eqn. (23) become:

$$\frac{b_4}{b}=nH \tag{26}$$

which leads to:

$$b=\omega e^{nHt} \tag{27}$$

where; ω is integrating constant.

$$\text{Now } ab^2=e^{3nHt} \tag{28}$$

Eqns. (27) and (28) gives:

$$a=\frac{1}{\omega^2}e^{nHt} \tag{29}$$

Using Eqns. (27) and (29):

$$\frac{a_4}{a}=nH,\ \frac{b_4}{b}=nH \tag{30}$$

Using Eqns. (27), (29) in Eqn. (1):

$$ds^2 = -dt^2 + \frac{e^{2nHt}}{\omega^4}dx^2 + \omega^2 e^{2nHt}dy^2 + (\omega^2 e^{2nHt}$$
$$\sin^2 y + \frac{e^{2nHt}}{\omega^4}\cos^2 y)dz^2 - \frac{2e^{2nHt}}{\omega^4}\cos ydxdz \tag{31}$$

24.4 PHYSICAL AND GEOMETRICAL FEATURES OF MODEL

From Eqn. (15) we have:

$$\phi_4 = \frac{\mu}{e^{3nHt}} \text{ gives}$$

$$\phi = -\frac{\mu}{3nH}e^{-3nHt} + c \tag{32}$$

where; c is the integrating constant.

The expansion scalar (θ) and the shear (σ) for model Eqn. (28) is obtained as:

$$\theta = \frac{a_4}{a} + \frac{2b_4}{b} = nH + 2nH = 3nH \tag{33}$$

$$\sigma = \frac{1}{\sqrt{3}}\left(\frac{a_4}{a} - \frac{b_4}{b}\right) = \frac{1}{\sqrt{3}}(nH - nH) = 0 \tag{34}$$

The proper volume V is given by:

$$R^3 = ab^2 = e^{3nHt} \tag{35}$$

Deceleration Parameter (q) for cosmological axially symmetric Bianchi IX model is given by:

$$q = \frac{R_{44}/R}{(R_4/R)^2} = -1 \tag{36}$$

The negative value of the declaration parameter shows that model Eqn. (31) inflates.

Now for the different fractional values of n, we will discuss the following aspect for the model.

- **Case I:** For $n = \frac{1}{2}$ Eqn. (14) leads to:

$$R^3 = ab^2 = e^{3/2Ht} \tag{37}$$

We get:

$$a = \frac{e^{Ht/2}}{\omega^2} \text{ and } b = \omega e^{Ht/2} \tag{38}$$

also,

$$\frac{a_4}{a} = \frac{H}{2}, \frac{b_4}{b} = \frac{H}{2} \tag{39}$$

Model Eqn. (31) leads to:

$$ds^2 = dt^2 + \frac{e^{Ht}}{\omega^4}dx^2 + \omega^2 e^{Ht}dy^2 + \left[\omega^2 e^{Ht}\sin^2 y + \frac{e^{Ht}}{\omega^4}\cos^2 y\right] dz^2 - \frac{2e^{Ht}}{\omega^4}\cos y dx dz \tag{40}$$

The rate of a scalar field is given by:

$$\phi_4 = \frac{\mu}{ab^2} = \frac{\mu}{e^{3/2Ht}}$$

$$\phi = \mu\frac{e^{-3/2Ht}}{-3/_2 H} + C_1 \tag{41}$$

where; C_1 is integration constant.
Expansion (θ) is given by:

$$\theta = \frac{a_4}{a} + \frac{2b_4}{b} = \frac{H}{2} + 2\frac{H}{2} = \frac{3}{2}H \tag{42}$$

Shear (σ) is given by:

$$\sigma = \frac{1}{\sqrt{3}}\left[\frac{a_4}{a} - \frac{b_4}{b}\right] = 0 \tag{43}$$

Proper volume of universe is given by:

$$R^3 = ab^2 = e^{3/2Ht}$$

The deceleration parameter (q) for model Eqn. (40) is:

$$q = \frac{R_{44}/R}{(R_4/R)^2} = -1$$

- **Case 2:** For $n = \frac{3}{2}$ Eqn. (14) leads to:

$$R^3 = ab^2 = e^{9/2Ht}$$

We get the metric coefficient is given by:

$$a = \frac{e^{3Ht/2}}{\omega^2} \text{ and } b = \omega e^{3Ht/2} \tag{44}$$

Model Eqn. (31) reduces in to:

$$ds^2 = -dt^2 + \frac{e^{3Ht}}{\omega^4}dx^2 + \omega^2 e^{3Ht}dy^2 + (\omega^2 e^{3Ht}\sin^2 y + \frac{e^{3Ht}}{\omega^4}\cos^2 y)$$
$$dz^2 - \frac{2e^{3Ht}}{\omega^4}\cos y dx dz \tag{45}$$

Expansion (θ) and shear (σ) in this case is given by:

$$\theta = \frac{a_4}{a} + \frac{2b_4}{b} = \frac{3H}{2} + 2\frac{3H}{2} = \frac{9}{2}H$$

$$\sigma = \frac{1}{\sqrt{3}}\left[\frac{a_4}{a} - \frac{b_4}{b}\right] = 0$$

Deceleration parameter (q) for model Eqn. (45) is $q = -1$ (de-sitter universe).

24.5 DISCUSSION AND CONCLUSION

In the current work, we have derived a model for a physical inflationary universe under the effect of the scalar field, which is purely massless and with a flat potential. For generalization, we assumed the condition ($R^3 = ab^2 = e^{nHt}$) and observed that the deceleration parameter (q) is negative, also valid for the fractional value of n. This shows that proper volume (R^3) increases exponentially, represents inflationary scenario of the universe in Bianchi type ix axially symmetric cosmological model. The Higgs field (ϕ) decreases at a slow rate, and it approaches to finite value when t approaches to infinity. The expansion factor (θ) is constant but shear (σ) is zero for different value of n. There is uniformly expansion in the universe and the deceleration parameter $q = -1$ is obtained. Hence the model indicated the de-Sitter universe and it represents an accelerated phase of the universe. There exist no initial singularities in model Eqn. (31). Thus the model obeys big-bang at the initial epoch, and accelerated inflationary universe is obtained with some dynamical features.

KEYWORDS

- **Bianchi type IX**
- **cosmological model**
- **deceleration parameter**
- **Einstein theory**
- **flat potential**
- **homogeneity**
- **inflationary theory**
- **metric coefficients**

REFERENCES

1. Robertson, H. P., (1936). Kinematics and world-structure II. *Astrophysical Journal, 83*, 187–201.
2. De Sitter, W., (1917). On Einstein's theory of gravitation, and its astronomical consequences. *Monthly Notices of the Royal Astronomical Society, 78*, 3–28.
3. Taub, A. H., (1951). Empty space-times admitting a three-parameter group of motions. *Annals of Mathematics. Second Series, 53*, 472–490.
4. Guth, A. H., (1981). Inflationary universe: A possible solution to the horizon and flatness problem. *Physical Review B, 91*, 99–102.
5. Linde, A. D., (1982). A new inflationary universe scenario: A possible solution of the horizon, flatness, homogeneity, isotropy and primordial monopole problems. *Physics Letters B, 108*, 389–393.
6. Albrecht, A., & Steinhardt, P. J., (1982). Cosmology for grand unified theories with radiatively induced symmetry breaking. *Physical Review Letters, 48*, 1220–1223.
7. Abbott, L. F., & Wise, M. B., (1984). Constraints on generalized inflationary cosmologies. *Nuclear Physics B, 244*, 541–548.
8. Lucchin, F., & Mataresse, S., (1985). Power-law inflation. *Physical Review D, 32*, 1316–1322.
9. Mijjic, M. B., Marris, M. S., & Suen, W. M., (1936). The R^2 cosmology: Inflation without a phase transition. *Physical Review D, 34*, 2934–2946.
10. La, D., & Steinhardt, P. J., (1989). Extended inflationary cosmology. *Physical Review Letters, 62*, 376–378.
11. Chakraborty, S., (1991). A study on Bianchi-IX cosmological model. *Astrophysics and Space Science, 180*, 293–303.
12. Chakraborty, & Nandy, G. C., (1992). Cosmological studies in Bianchi II, VIII space-time. *Astrophysics and Space Science, 198*, 299–308.

13. Vaidya, P. C., & Patel, L. K., (1986). Gravitational fields with space-times of Bianchi type IX. *Pramana J. Physics, 27*, 63–72.
14. Bali, R., & Goyal, R., (2009). Bianchi type IX inflationary cosmological models for perfect fluid distribution in general relativity. *International Journal of Physical Science, 21*, 181–186.
15. Bali, R., & Yadav, M. K., (2005). Bianchi type-IX viscous fluid cosmological model in general relativity. *Pramana J. Physics, 64*, 187–196.
16. Rahaman, F., Begum, N., Bag, G., & Bhui, B. C., (2005). Cosmological models with negative constant deceleration parameter in lyra geometry. *Astrophysics and Space Science, 299*, 211–218.
17. Reddy, D. R. K., & Naidu, R. L., (2008). A higher dimensional inflationary universe in general relativity. *International Journal of Theoretical Physics, 47*, 2339–2343.
18. Starobinski, A. A., (1980). A new type of cosmological model without singularity. *Physics Letter B, 91*, 99–102.
19. Rothman, T., & Ellis, G. F. R., (1986). Can inflation occur in anisotropic cosmologies. *Physics Letter B, 180*, 19–24.
20. Bali, R., & Jain, V. C., (2002). Bianchi Type I inflationary cosmological model in general relativity. *Pramana J. Physics, 59*, 1–7.
21. Bali, R., & Poonia, L., (2016). Inflationary scenario in spatially homogeneous Bianchi type IX space-time with flat potential. *JUSPS, 28*, 361–366.
22. Bali, R., & Poonia, L., (2013). Bianchi type VI_0 inflationary cosmological model in general relativity. *International Journal of Modern Physics, Conferences Series, 22*, 593–602.

INDEX

E

F

N

O

R

S

T